Advertising, Literature and Print Culture in Ireland, 1891–1922

Also by John Strachan

ADVERTISING AND SATIRICAL CULTURE IN THE ROMANTIC PERIOD

BLACKWOOD'S MAGAZINE, 1817–1825 (*co-edited with Nicholas Mason, 6 vols*)

ESSAYS ON MODERN IRISH LITERATURE (*co-edited with Alison O'Malley-Younger*)

IRELAND AT WAR AND PEACE (*co-edited with Alison O'Malley-Younger*)

IRELAND: REVOLUTION AND EVOLUTION (*co-edited with Alison O'Malley-Younger*)

KEY CONCEPTS IN ROMANTIC LITERATURE (*with Jane Moore*)

POETRY (*with Richard Terry*, 2nd edition)

Also by Claire Nally

ENVISIONING IRELAND: OCCULT NATIONALISM IN THE WORK OF W. B. YEATS

NAKED EXHIBITIONISM: GENDER, PERFORMANCE AND PUBLIC EXPOSURE (*co-edited with Angela Smith*)

W. B. YEATS'S *A VISION*: EXPLICATIONS AND CONTEXTS (*co-edited with Matthew Gibson and Neil Mann*)

Advertising, Literature and Print Culture in Ireland, 1891–1922

John Strachan and Claire Nally
University of Northumbria at Newcastle, UK

palgrave
macmillan

First published 2012 by
PALGRAVE MACMILLAN

Palgrave Macmillan in the UK is an imprint of Macmillan Publishers Limited, registered in England, company number 785998, of Houndmills, Basingstoke, Hampshire RG21 6XS.

Palgrave Macmillan in the US is a division of St Martin's Press LLC, 175 Fifth Avenue, New York, NY 10010.

Palgrave Macmillan is the global academic imprint of the above companies and has companies and representatives throughout the world.

ISBN 978–0–230–29873–6

This book is printed on paper suitable for recycling and made from fully managed and sustained forest sources. Logging, pulping and manufacturing processes are expected to conform to the environmental regulations of the country of origin.

A catalogue record for this book is available from the British Library.

Library of Congress Cataloging-in-Publication Data
Strachan, John (John R.), 1961–
Advertising, literature, and print culture in Ireland, 1891–1922 / John Strachan and Claire Nally.
p. cm.
"This book emerges from "Consumer Culture, Advertising, and Literature in Ireland 1848–1921", a Leverhulme Major Research Project . . . funded by the Trust between 2008 and 2011 . . . a joint venture between the universities of Durham and Sunderland"—P.
ISBN 978–0–230–29873–6
1. Advertising—Ireland—History. 2. Advertising, Magazine—Ireland—History. 3. Popular literature—Ireland—History and criticism. 4. National characteristics in literature. 5. National characteristics, Irish—History. 6. Literature and society—Ireland—History. 7. Consumption (Economics)—Ireland—History. I. Nally, Claire, 1979– II. Title.
HF5813.I73S87 2012
659.13′20941509041—dc23 2012023568

10 9 8 7 6 5 4 3 2 1
21 20 19 18 17 16 15 14 13 12

Printed and bound in the United States of America

Contents

Illustrations

Acknowledgements

This book emerges from 'Consumer Culture, Advertising and Literature in Ireland 1848–1921', a Leverhulme Major Research Project which was funded by the Leverhulme Trust between 2008 and 2011. The Leverhulme's generous assistance to the project, which was a joint venture between the universities of Durham and Sunderland, funded Claire Nally's tenure as Post-Doctoral Research Associate at Sunderland, the project director John Strachan's Research Fellowship in the second year of the project, the PhD studentships held by Lauren Clark and Matthew Hayward at Sunderland and Durham universities, respectively, and a series of public lectures and conferences. The trust also funded our website, www.ccalireland.com, as it did the exhibitions of Irish advertising art and historical advertisements which were shown at the Sunderland City Library and Arts Centre (2009) and at the University of Durham (2010). Our debt to the Leverhulme Trust is immense, and we would like to record our gratitude to it here.

In personal terms, we are very much indebted to the Leverhulme co-directors John Nash and Alison O'Malley-Younger. We would also like to thank the public speakers in the 2008/9 Sunderland 'Consumer Culture and Literature in Ireland' lecture series: Willy Maley, Joseph McBrinn, Helen O'Connell, Alison O'Malley-Younger and Stephanie Rains, and those in the Durham 'James Joyce' public lectures featured at the 'James Joyce in the Nineteenth-Century' conference, organised by John Nash and held at the University of Durham in 2010: Anne Fogarty, Luke Gibbons, Andrew Gibson and Emer Nolan. Willy refereed the Leverhulme project in its initial stages, as did Dinah Birch and Bernard O'Donoghue, and we are grateful to them all for their valuable support, as we are to the anonymous readers who also commented on the project for the Trust. Allan Ingram, Jane Moore, Richard Terry and Patricia Waugh were very helpful in offering detailed advice on the first part of the grant application process, and Andrew Carpenter and Nicholas Daly offered invaluable support in the second. Stephen Regan was a supportive co-applicant.

We are also indebted to the following people who have helped our project in various ways over its duration: Claire Connolly, Ulf Dantanus, Peter Durrans, Terry Eagleton, Luke Gibbons, Lesley Grieves, the late A. C. Hepburn, Gary Holmes, Declan Kiberd, Elena Loukopoulou, Ian Neal, Eliza O'Brien, Francis O'Gorman, Aidan O'Malley, Katy Mullen, Shaun Richards, Flavia Swann, Hilary Weeks and Colin Younger. Special thanks go to David Newton, webmaster to the project and, with Colin, provider of much of the live music at our various events. The 'Consumer Culture, Advertising and Literature in Ireland, 1848–1921' website, which contains all of the images found in this book and many more examples of Irish historical advertising, is to be found at www.ccalireland.com. At the Leverhulme Trust, we are indebted to Sir Richard Brook and his staff, in particular Anne Dean, Matt Dilnutt and Cassandra Hughes. At Palgrave, we are very grateful to Felicity Plester, Catherine Mitchell, Kate Boothby and Devasena Vedamurthi. We also thank Palgrave's anonymous readers for their expert and extremely useful advice on the proposal and final manuscript. Don MacRaild, Willy Maley, Jane Moore and Angela Smith offered valuable criticism on early draft chapters of this book. Patrick Maume read the entire completed manuscript and made invaluable comments upon it.

We would also like to thank the National Library of Ireland, for permission to reproduce several images contained in this volume, and especially Honora Faul, Assistant Keeper of the Ephemera Collection, and Elizabeth Kirwan, Assistant Keeper at the National Photographic Archive. Additionally, we would like to acknowledge Trinity College Dublin, for access to their Evelyn Gleeson archival material; Dublin City Library and Archive, Pearse Street, for access to their Findlater Collection; and the Linen Hall Library, Belfast for access to its collection of anti-Home Rule print ephemera. Colum Kenny offered valuable material related to his grandfather, the renowned Irish advertising man Kevin J. Kenny. Alex Findlater also provided much helpful advice in relation to *The Lady of the House* and his family's business, while Dorothea Findlater offered valuable recollections of the Tea Rooms on Dublin's O'Connell Street in the 1920s and 1930s. Sincere gratitude to Iarfhlaith Watson at University College, Dublin, and Brian Griffin, of Bath Spa University, for their assistance in translating Irish language material, and to Stephen Turner for editing many of the images.

Introduction

Self-Determination is the Question of the Hour.

Ireland demands an *Irish Republic,* and Ireland can only obtain its object by Unity and Strength. John Fallon is ever foremost in the rank to strengthen the Manhood and Womanhood of Ireland by supplying only the very best of Beef and Mutton. Fallon has already united the housekeepers of Galway, and he will now strengthen them to win their Independence. Build yourself up, be on the strong side, and send your orders for Best Home-Killed Beef and Mutton to John Fallon, Victualler, Galway. Prompt delivery in City and Suburbs.

Advertisement for John Fallon, *Connacht Tribune* (1921)

This study addresses the literary and historical resonance of Irish advertising in the late nineteenth and early twentieth centuries. In its detailed accounts of individual advertisements and publicity campaigns, *Advertising, Literature and Print Culture in Ireland, 1891–1922* is the first book in Irish studies to pay close attention to the cultural meanings of advertising during the Revival era. It particularly engages with the concept of 'Irish consciousness'[1] – Declan Kiberd's phrase in his account of the Revival in *Inventing Ireland* (1996) – as it was manifested in Irish consumer culture between the early 1890s and the 1920s. Much of the copy which is discussed in the pages of this book addresses – sometimes obliquely, sometimes not – issues of nationhood. As we will see, advertisers in this period frequently defined themselves and their products in terms of 'Irishness', in brand name, visual image, font and typography, and – sometimes – in overtly nationalistic rhetoric of various political hues. Irish advertisements in the last decade of the nineteenth century and beyond began to be charged with an ideological resonance (sometimes implicit, sometimes explicit) as the national campaign gathered pace. 'The Home Rule movement', declared the *Gentleman's Magazine* in 1888, 'brought Irish goods [...]

Figure I.1 Advertisement for Gleeson and Co., Tailors and Drapers, 11 Upper O'Connell Street, Dublin (1916): 'Irish Xmas Presents – Irish Goods Only'.

to the front',[2] and entrepreneurs began to appeal to national sentiment in their advertising and to use the concept of Irishness to commercial effect (Figure I.1).

This study also closely engages with the manner in which important Irish literary figures reacted to the consumer society which surrounded them, and in so doing places some pressure on conventional distinctions between 'high' and 'low' aspects of Revival-era Irish culture. Sometimes, indeed, the commercial world of the Revival seemed intertwined, with various degrees of proximity, with the most visible of the literary titans of the day. The advertisement reproduced above, for example, issued in 1916 by the enthusiastic 'Irish Ireland' manufacturers Gleeson and Co., both demonstrates the nation-soaked commercial rhetoric so common in this period and glances tangentially towards the man whom Oliver St John Gogarty called the 'arch-poet' of the day in its reference to the calendars and Christmas cards made by the Cuala Press and Dun Emer, co-operatives which had been established by W. B. Yeats's enterprising if less well-known sisters Elizabeth and Lily, and to which the poet acted as literary adviser for some time.

While Yeats's own opinions of middle-class economics are generally thought to be summed up in his *de haut en bas* address in 'September 1913' to those who 'fumble in a greasy till', and though the 'home' and 'cottage' industry ethos of Dun Emer and Cuala might suggest a rejection of modern consumerist values, the archive at the National Library of Ireland of the Cuala Press, which contains a large collection of business cards, Christmas cards and other ephemera, as well as bookplates and book cover designs, suggests a willingness to engage with commercial realities and, indeed, a flair for publicity. Yeats's attitude towards consumer culture was much more complex than a half line of 'September 1913' might suggest.

James Joyce has been the subject of an important and welcome body of recent critical work discussing his attitude to advertising,[3] but our study widens the analysis of Irish literary–mercantile relations in addressing under-researched aspects of literary engagements between advertising and consumer culture in Yeats and in Oscar Wilde, as in our consideration of the complex response to the rise of consumerism in the latter's work: as a writer in *The Picture of Dorian Gray*, with its philosophical espousal of craftsmanship over reproduction, as a lecturer in his American tour, notably in 'The House Beautiful' and 'The Decorative Arts' (through which he might be said to have 'sold' a particular aesthetic), and, finally, as an editor of *The Woman's World* magazine, in which he conducted discussions of fashion, the arts and literature. Irish commodity culture and Irish literary culture were often surprisingly close to one another in the late nineteenth and early twentieth centuries.

I

In 1929, the firm of Arthur Guinness, based at St James's Gate in Dublin, did something new, and something remarkable. Throughout the nineteenth century it had stoutly – so to speak – refused to advertise its product. 'The Messrs. Guinness and Co.', the *Pharmaceutical Journal* noted in 1853, 'will not condescend to puff their stout'.[4] However, after setting its face against advertising for over 150 years since its foundation in 1759, the company brought in advertising agents to promote the famous beer, and the rest, to risk a cliché, is history. Guinness's campaigns, from John Gilroy's famed Toucan birds and pint-swallowing ostriches onwards, are generally seen as among the triumphs of twentieth-century advertising culture, and the company's television commercials have won innumerable awards in recent decades.[5]

The 1920s, the decade in which Guinness first ventured into the waters of commercial advertising, are generally seen as the era in which modern Irish advertising – exemplified in the *success fou* of Guinness – emerged. Indeed, the vacuum evident in the commercial history of Arthur Guinness and Co. might be seen as emblematic of conventional opinion of advertising's role within what one might call the cultural economy of Ireland as a whole. The only book-length history of the subject, Hugh Oram's invaluable study *The Advertising Book: The History of Advertising in Ireland* (1986), begins by suggesting that wide-scale Irish advertising originated with the Free State: 'It was not until the arrival of Fianna Fail at the beginning of the 1930s [that] a consciousness of the benefits of advertising percolated through Irish business on a wide scale, for the first time.'[6] 'Throughout the nineteenth century, the idea of advertising agencies in Ireland scarcely caught on', writes Oram, 'and in many respects, Irish advertising did not come of age until the start of Teilifis Éireann on January 1, 1962.'[7] If the most notable historian of Irish advertising spends so little time in what is, after all, a huge and fascinating book – it runs to nearly 700 pages – addressing the commercial culture of pre-partition days, then perhaps it is unsurprising that there is relatively little academic work on the history of advertising in Ireland in the period in which the country remained within the UK.

To our minds, however, this lack of curiosity has something remarkable about it, given the general historical consensus that Ireland's development as a nation reached into what might seem, on the face of it, to be some fairly arcane areas. Almost every aspect of Irish culture in the three decades from the death of Charles Stewart Parnell in 1891 to the establishment of the Irish Free State in 1922 has been seen as being immersed in national significance. As Declan Kiberd writes of the Revival in *Inventing Ireland: The Literature of the Modern Nation* (1996), 'That enterprise achieved nothing less than a renovation of Irish consciousness and a new understanding of politics, economics, philosophy, sport, language and culture in its widest sense'.[8] Literary scholars and historians before and after Kiberd have shared this point of view, and have demonstrated how Irish poetry, language, dance, the fine arts and sport were all nationally revealing. However, the critical net has not spread widely enough. This book, which closely engages with Kiberd's interface of 'politics', 'economics' and 'culture in its widest sense', argues that the relatively neglected issue of Irish consumer culture is equally significant and that there is much of interest in historical advertising in Ireland before the Free State.

Our study addresses the political significance and nationalistic resonance of Irish advertising literature, if one might call it that, in the late nineteenth and early twentieth centuries. From the 1890s onwards Irish advertising, like a great deal of the wider culture which surrounded it, was preoccupied with a sense of its own 'Irishness'. Early twentieth-century advertisements for 'Irel' coffee, to give but one small example, were emblazoned with the map of the island, and proudly announced that 'This delicious beverage is made in Ireland and the Map of Ireland is on every bottle'. However, this was just the caffeinated tip of an iceberg of large size; time and again, advertisers appealed to the patriotic spirit of the consumer and did their best to exploit it commercially. Such advertising was metaphorically stamped with a symbolic map of Ireland.

We are not claiming here that all of this advertising's engagement with Irishness was intended to promote either Home Rule or 'the separatist idea', to borrow a phrase from Patrick Pearse. Doubtless, money alone was incentive enough for some, and, furthermore, it might also be pointed out that though advanced nationalists and supporters of the Irish Parliamentary Party alike endorsed campaigns for economic renewal, so did many who slept outside those stables. The broad trope of Irishness allowed most to nod in agreement, but not necessarily for identical reasons. We pay some attention here to the manner in which unionist Anglo-Irish philanthropists such as Sir Josslyn Gore-Booth – brother to two more well-known, and nationalist, sisters, Eva Gore-Booth and Constance Markievicz – and the Protestant Gaelic Leaguer Captain Otway Cuffe were enthusiastic advocates of the 'Buy Irish' campaigns of the 1880s onwards and also offered much practical assistance in sponsoring co-operative, home and 'peasant' industries. Nonetheless, we do pay detailed and sustained attention to advanced nationalist print culture, given that much of the most interesting Irish advertising of the period came from the radical nationalist papers. The advertising columns of journals such as *The Shan van Vocht, Sinn Féin* and *Irish Freedom* (*Saoirseacht na hEireann*) are fascinating, if decidedly neglected, places. That said, this book addresses a diverse constituency within Irish advertising: the pages of *An Claidheamh Soluis* under Pearse's editorship, the selling of the Ulster Volunteer Force, the remarkable self-promotions of the indefatigable Eugene Mac Sweeny, industrial chemist and chair of the Cork Publicity Association, the advertising columns of the *Irish Sportsman* and *The Lady of the House*, the use of Irish Party luminaries in First World War recruitment campaigns, the activities of the Irish Industrial Development Association, and the relationship of Murphy's stout with the British military, Sinn Féin and the Irish Free State.

II

The Irish register that was associated with so many Irish companies' self-representations at the turn of the twentieth century was also evident in the country's most renowned brand. Even Arthur Guinness and Co., though refusing to use press columns to advertise its wares, employed specifically 'Irish' fonts and iconography throughout the period under discussion here, notably in the harps which adorned its labels and its widely distributed trade cards and public house mirrors. Indeed, let us return for a moment to this most enduringly famous of all Irish companies. Why did Guinness refuse to advertise for so long? The company archives at St James's Gate in Dublin provide no answer, but let us consider the possibilities. Was this a principled stand, which stemmed from a sense that advertising was vulgar, tawdry or ungentlemanly? Or was it a publicity stunt, like the founder's brilliant manoeuvre of taking of a 9000-year lease on the brewery at the Gate? Perhaps this most notable Irish product was actually promoted by its manufacturer's reluctance to bark its products, this anti-advertising stance actually a subtle form of advertising. Guinness, the beer that needs no introduction. Even when the company did eventually condescend to advertise, its copy was squeamish about direct allusions to its beer's alcoholic potency or winning flavour, employing instead a quasi-medical discourse and marketing the famous stout as a spur to health – 'Guinness is good for you' – rather than as a trip on Bacchus's cart.

All this notwithstanding, there was, perhaps, a certain disingenuousness in the company's stance before the 1929 landmark. Though it never paid for copy in the public prints, Guinness and Co. did have an advertising budget, used on such things as show-cards, small placards and the aforesaid pub mirrors – adorned with the harp of ould Erin – which persist to this day. Throughout the period under discussion in this book, Guinness was also promoted via third party advertisements in both Ireland and England (see Figure I.2 for a splendid English example from Robert Porter, one of Guinness's principal English bottlers, which dates from 1896), and it never exercised itself to prevent such puffery, unlike the brisk manner with which it pursued copyright infringers and those who forged its labels (the company brought several test case prosecutions in England in the 1880s and 1890s to protect its copyright against counterfeits). Indeed, it might be pointed out that as early as 1843, in his entertaining survey of early Victorian 'puffery', 'The Advertisement Literature of the Age', the comic poet and journalist Thomas Hood ranked Guinness as one of the most notable and noisiest of contemporary brands:

> The advertisement writer [...] claims kindred with genius of all sorts, and considers himself entitled to a share of the glory of all undertakings [...] In fact, he is to the [...] shopkeeper what Homer was to Achilles, Tasso to Godfrey [...] or Milton to Cromwell: without him, what would his shops avail a Mechi, his XX a Guinness, his pills a Cockle, his Chesterfields a Doudney, his locks a Chubb, or his envelope a Stocken?[9]

In letting second parties puff its product, Guinness and Co. displaced advertising, and this might be seen as synecdochic of the way in which this particular cultural form has tended to be overlooked in the history of Revival-era Ireland. Advertising was *there*, but we have tended not to look at it. This is despite the fact that, as we will demonstrate, Irish journals of all kinds teemed with advertising of a diverting, suggestive and entertaining nature in the late nineteenth and early twentieth centuries. Jean Baudrillard once wrote perceptively that 'There is no such thing as advertising strictly confined to the supplying of information',[10] and Ireland, decades ago, was suffused by commercial information of a highly symbolic kind.

Certainly the civic landscape of Ireland, at least in its principal cities, was inscribed by the visual language of advertising at the turn of the last century. That capacious portrait of what was then Edwardian Dublin, James Joyce's *Ulysses* (1922), is, as all Joyceans know, immersed in advertising. Its hero, Leopold Bloom, is, of course, an advertising canvasser and his relative lack of success in that trade does not detract from the grandeur of his ambitions. Consider how 'Ithaca' summarises his visions of commercial triumph:

> What were habitually his final meditations?
>
> Of some one sole unique advertisement to cause passers to stop in wonder, a poster novelty, with all extraneous accretions excluded, reduced to its simplest and most efficient terms not exceeding the span of casual vision and congruous with the velocity of modern life.[11]

For Leopold Bloom, advertising, whether on a grand scale such as this or in quieter guises (such as the advertisement for the grocer Alexander Keyes that

Figure I.2 Advertisement for 'Bull Dog Bottled Stout', aka Guinness, for Robert Porter, Pancras Road. From *Hearth and Home* (1896).

preoccupies him rather more in *Ulysses*), was part of 'the velocity of modern life'. And so it was for James Joyce. As Garry M. Leonard has written,

> From the very beginning, according to his brother Stanislaus, James Joyce found his identity underwritten by advertising: '[Joyce] in boyhood and youth was of such a cheerful and amiable disposition that in the family circle he was given the nickname (borrowed from an advertisement for some patent food) of "Sunny Jim" '.[12]

When Joyce was fashioning his portrait of Dublin, advertising provided a key layer in his shaping of that vivid urban scene; it too, to borrow Leonard's metaphor – itself, appropriately, simultaneously commercial and literary – was 'underwritten by advertising'.

'Sunny Jim's' preoccupation with the self-presentations of commerce is perhaps unsurprising given his status as a master of high modernism, which is generally seen as an artistic phenomenon inextricably linked to commercial print culture and its self-presentations, a consensus characterised by Jean-Michel Rabaté in *European Joyce Studies* as one which 'see[s] modernism as the art of a period dominated by the publicity campaigns of journalism and advertising'.[13] One of the ways in which the modernist sensibility addressed the vibrancy, vigour, and sometimes the corruption of city life is through its allusions to brand names and to advertising. That Bloom and the advertising agent Hugh 'Blazes' Boylan are advertising men is certainly indicative of modernity, but that modernity is, at least in part, a specifically *Irish* modernity, located in the midst of a cultural Revival in which, as we shall see, advertising played a significant if often unacknowledged part, and positioned within a cultural business, so to speak, which had grown steadily in Ireland from the 1850s onwards, though it had begun even earlier.

Joyce studies is one place where literary critics have begun to engage with historical advertising in Ireland, at least in the first decades of the twentieth century. Prompted in large part by Jennifer Wicke's *Advertising Fictions: Literature, Advertisement, and Social Reading* (1988), which discusses the relationship between advertising and the twentieth century novel, with *Ulysses* granted a central place, and a 1993 special issue of *James Joyce Quarterly* which addresses 'Joyce and Advertising', there have been a number of recent studies of the author of *Ulysses* and consumer culture, most notably, perhaps, Leonard's monograph *Advertising and Commodity Culture in Joyce* (1998).[14]

For James Joyce, advertising was part of 'the velocity of modern life', and in this book we track that velocity within the wider context of Irish culture. Though there has been much recent work on the social meaning of consumer culture and advertising in late Georgian and Victorian Britain, there is little in the way of major research on these topics in Ireland in the same era,[15] despite the fact that in that country, perhaps even more so than in Great Britain, such cultural practices were politically suggestive. Prompted by Neil

McKendrick, John Brewer and J. H. Plumb's *The Birth of a Consumer Society* (1982), there have been important books on British consumer culture, from Brewer and Roy Porter's *Consumption and the World of Goods* (1993) through to Judith Flanders's *Consuming Passions: Leisure and Pleasure in Victorian Britain* (2006). There has also been important research in Victorian studies on the specific subject of the semiotics of advertising in Britain, notably Thomas Richards's *The Commodity Culture of Victorian England: Advertising and Spectacle, 1851–1914* (1990) and Lori Anne Loeb's *Consuming Angels: Advertising and Victorian Women* (1994). Similarly, Anne McClintock's *Imperial Leather: Race, Gender and Sexuality in the Colonial Contest* (1995) presses readings of advertisements into the service of a postcolonialist examination of late nineteenth-century imperialism (though Ireland is not covered in her study). John Strachan's *Advertising and Satirical Culture in the Romantic Period* (2007) takes the story of the cultural history of British advertising back into the 1780s. This all said, there is as yet no equivalent study of advertising's cultural, literary and ideological resonance in Ireland during the Revival, that momentous period for the country. This study provides one. To borrow the words of an 1853 essay in Dickens's *Household Words*, 'Irish advertisements all seem to have a curious character of their own',[16] and our study sheds new light on the literary and commercial culture of Ireland in the decades during which the nation slouched towards Bethlehem.

III

This book attends to the impact of advertising on aspects of Irish print culture between the 1890s and the 1920s. After a prologue and first chapter which survey the Irish advertising scene from the 1850s to the 1910s, it goes on to offer a series of case studies that deal with certain highly significant moments in the cultural history of Revival-era Irish advertising, and with literary reactions to advertising, notably by Oscar Wilde and W. B. Yeats. Though this is a book of over 100,000 words, comprehensiveness is not possible here, given that advertising is a subject which intertwines with almost all aspects of modern western culture. Our study pays little attention, for instance, to such matters as advertising aimed at children or the importance of advertising in that politically charged arena the Irish theatre.[17] Nor does it cover in great detail the commercialisation of religion and the resonance of advertising in such important aspects of Irish culture as music and dance. Though we pay some attention to the use of the Irish language and the deployment of 'Irish' fonts and typefaces in advertising, more research also needs to be done in these areas. Our hope is that that this volume will prompt further critical discussion of what seems to us to be a fascinating and rich part of Irish culture.

The prologue to this study sets the scene for the rest of the book in examining the rapid growth of the Irish advertising business from the 1850s onwards. The period immediately following the Great Famine was, curiously, one in which consumer culture established itself more fully in the island of Ireland than ever before, as the country recovered after the scourge had visited. Indeed, there were some Irishmen who saw blessing in a very ugly disguise in the Famine. John Francis Maguire's *The Industrial Movement in Ireland* (1853), for instance, boasts of Ireland's economic resurgence – symbolised by the holding of the Irish Exhibition in Dublin in that year – and optimistically declares that 'that dread visitation of Providence, which filled our streets and our highways with mourning and desolation, has been followed by the most salutary results'.[18] Advertising fuelled this economic development, becoming an important driver in the rebirth of the Irish economy. Though the first significant advertising agency in Dublin was founded in the late 1810s, advertising really took hold in Ireland in the middle of nineteenth century. Beginning with an account of the epochal significance of the Irish Industrial Exhibition of 1853, our prologue discusses the development of Irish advertising, examines the structural mechanics of advertising in Ireland (agencies, advertising freesheets, paid newspaper canvassers and so on) and briefly discuss the cultural meanings of mid-century advertising copy.

Chapter 1, 'Advertising and the Nation in the Irish Revival', draws a contrast between the advertising of the 1850s through to the 1870s – in which a genuflection to imported goods (and manners), notably from London and Paris was common (though by no means universal) – and the nationally charged advertising evident in the period from the 1880s and, especially, the 1890s onwards. The chapter, which is particularly focused on the manner in which advertising used the concept of 'Irishness', demonstrates how the 'Support Irish Industries' movement was reflected in Irish advertising, examines the campaigns for national economic integrity epitomised in the Irish Trade Mark and the work of the Irish Industrial Development Association, and discusses the manner in which national sentiment echoed through campaigns for individual companies such as Pierce's Cycles, the Kilkenny Woodcutters and the Belfast and Dublin Tailors Co-Partnerships.

The second part of the book, 'Print Culture' looks at aspects of the cultural history of advertising in Revival-era Ireland. Chapter 2, '*The Shan Van Vocht* (1896–1899) and *The Leader* (1900–1936): National Identity in Advertising', looks at the intersection of nationalism, advertising and print culture evident in two these pivotal nationalist periodicals. *The Shan Van Vocht,* the monthly magazine published in Belfast by Alice Milligan and Anna Johnston (the poet 'Ethna Carbery') and described by Maud Gonne as a 'daring little paper', served an important role in the dissemination of nationalist iconography, and that iconography was also evident in its advertising columns. One of the major features of the paper was the commemoration of the United Irishmen uprising of 1798, and this was prominent, not only in editorial matter, but also in paid copy: for commemorative jewellery, the life of

Wolfe Tone in commemorative edition, and souvenir items of genuine 'Irish' manufacture.

Some of *The Shan Van Vocht*'s advertising material was also heavily gendered as well as nationalistic; the 'chaste' jewellery, for instance, advertised in December 1898, with its clear appeal to the conventional vision of Ireland as virginal maiden. The second part of the chapter addresses what one might call the contrasting hypermasculinity of *The Leader* under its first editor, D. P. Moran, who saw one of the main duties of the newspaper, as Patrick Maume has written, to be 'the publicising of Irish goods'.[19] Irish advertising ran to up to eight pages of the paper, and Moran persistently refused to advertise English products as part of his drive for material independence for Ireland. We examine *The Leader*'s economic principles and its advertising strategies together: its particular form of protectionism, its opposition to publicising 'foreign' goods, its ethos in terms of the Irish language (and how this filters through into advertising copy in terms of typescript and dual language use), and the way in which such advertising material can be contextualised within the broader concerns of the national movement.

As is well known, in the opening decades of the twentieth century espousing specifically 'Irish' forms of sport within what was then the UK was often a deeply political gesture, and it was one which was exploited by canny nationalist advertisers peddling goods and services of, they maintained, a most 'Irish' kind. Chapter 3, 'The Sinn Féin Depot and the Selling of Irish Sport' addresses the remarkable manner in which sports of the Gaelic Athletic Association (GAA) were promoted by the indefatigably nationalist company Whelan and Son (sometimes 'The GAA House'; sometimes 'The Sinn Fein [sic] Depot'), of 17 Upper Ormond Quay, Dublin, from the early 1900s through to the 1920s. Buying a *camán* from Whelan's, the firm implied, struck a blow for Irish freedom, as one of its advertisements put it in verse:

> When comes the day, as come it must
> That England's rule of greed and lust,
> Shall lie, all broken, in the dust
> We'll still have the Irish Hurling Men.

We examine the close connections between the proprietors of this company and radical nationalism. Seumas Whelan, the owner of the store, was a remarkable figure: entrepreneurial capitalist, noisy advertising man, advanced nationalist, publisher and friend of both Patrick Pearse and Arthur Griffith, founding member of Sinn Féin, and manufacturer of hurling balls, soap and prayer books (and eventual stalwart of and – unsuccessful – candidate for Cumann na nGaedheal in the early 1920s). Also closely involved with Whelan's was Brian O'Higgins ('Brian na Banban'), the author of the above verses (which were included in a 1911 advertisement for the company), indefatigable author of a dozen books and more published by Whelan's, participant in the events of Easter 1916, prisoner at Frongoch, and designer of Christmas cards (featuring his own poetry) in both English and Irish (and eventually a Sinn Féin and anti-Treaty Republican party TD in the early 1920s).

Chapter 4, '*The Lady of the House* (1890–1921): Gender, Fashion and Domesticity', offers a specific example – advertising aimed at women – of the manner in which the trajectory of Irish advertising moved from an association with France and England in the middle decades of the nineteenth century to a more domestically Irish set of influences which were evident by the turn of the century and through to the Free State period. The advertising culture of Ireland in the late nineteenth and early twentieth centuries was permeated by discourses aimed at the female consumer, and the chapter is focused upon the most notable of the Irish periodicals targeted at a female readership, *The Lady of the House*. This journal, which included a wealth of advertisements directed at the Irish middle-class woman and her housekeeping budget, and which was founded by the notable Irish advertising agency and publisher Wilson, Hartnell and Co., offers a fascinating insight into the representation and cultivation of the contemporary Irish female in the commercial sphere. Indeed, as a specifically Irish publication, the journal, as well as being a revealing document in terms of contemporary commodity culture, also says much about constructions of femininity in Ireland at the turn of the twentieth century.

'Ireland has never been a Nation. But even if she were entitled to that description, we think it a prouder thing to be members of the Great British Nation, in which the English, Scottish, Ulster and Irish peoples are merged, than to cling to insular nationality.'[20] These words are taken from *The Irish Unionist Pocket Book*, published in Belfast and Dublin by the Unionist Associations of Ireland in 1911. This publication was part of an explosion of print ephemera in which Unionists in Ireland, and particularly in Ulster, fought the spectre of the Home Rule Bill. Chapter 5, 'Unionism, Advertising and the Third Home Rule Bill 1911–1914', examines the part advertising played in this material, in addressing explicitly Unionist advertisements and discussing the way in which the union was sold as if it were a consumer product, and the Ulster Volunteer Force was transformed into a kind of marching advertisement for the Carsonite position. The chapter also looks at songs and satires attacking the bill, such as the spoof advertising handbill from 1912 which represents the Home Rule Bill as bacon which has been slaughtered in the north of Ireland – 'GUARANTEED ULSTER-CURED'. Advertising played a fascinating, though historically neglected, role in the northern Unionist opposition to the Bill.

The third part of our study, which seemingly moves from the popular–cultural to 'High Culture', seeks to argues that these two strands of Irish culture are, in some, though certainly not all respects, closely intertwined. Our initial focus is on Oscar Wilde. In striking contrast to the relative abundance of scholarship on the same topic in Joyce studies, there is relatively little academic writing on the subject of Oscar Wilde's relationship with consumerism and with advertising. Chapter 6, 'Oscar Wilde as Editor and Writer – Aesthetic Interventions in Fashion and Material Culture', attempts to redress the balance. It maintains that Wilde's engagement with commodity culture was equally as large scale as Joyce's, and, indeed, demonstrates that the former had both a practical as well as an imaginative engagement with that culture, given that the 'Divine Oscar' wrote for the *Pall Mall Gazette* on women's fashion and edited *Woman's World* from 1887 to 1889. As Paul L. Fortunato has remarked, he was in some measure 'producing mass culture' as much as 'attempting its critique'.[21] Situating Wilde in the context of Irish commodity culture is one way of identifying the subtle nuances of his artistic and philosophical positions.

In striking language, W. B. Yeats proclaimed in 'A General Introduction for My Work' (1937) that 'When I stand upon O'Connell Bridge in the half-light and notice that discordant architecture, all those electric signs [. . .] a vague hatred comes up out of my own dark'.[22] Despite this rejection of shopkeepers' vulgarity and its concomitant 'electric signs' (dispelling the Celtic mist?), Yeats was more consistently located in the commercial sphere than may at first be apparent. Chapter 7, 'Consumerism and Anti-Commercialism: The Yeatses, Print Culture, and Home Industry', examines the way in which Yeats's stated position regarding consumer culture often differed quite discernibly from his practice, with particular reference to events in 1896, when the poet reformed the Irish Literary Society, with one of his express aims being the promotion of a book series entitled 'The Library of Ireland' (later 'The New Irish Library'), to be published by Fisher Unwin. Yeats explained to John O'Leary that the series would follow 'sound national doctrine', but this was to prove an especially contentious issue in terms of competing versions of the nationalist agenda at the time, and it never came to fruition. However, despite this, Yeats's plan for a popular library – and for the marketing of the same – marks a key moment in the propaganda of the Irish Revival and is one of the most revealing of contemporary Irish literary reactions to the advertising and commodification of books.

The chapter also examines the commercial enterprises of the Yeats sisters, Elizabeth and Lily. While the sisters were overshadowed by their famous brothers, they have a place in Irish history for founding and managing those culturally significant endeavours the Dun Emer and the Cuala Press Co-operatives. In her account of the Cuala,[23] Gifford Lewis has argued that they were modelled on existing aspects of the British Arts and Crafts movements, and while this is undeniably true we particularly situate Dun Emer and Cuala in the light of commercial Ireland. Cuala Press Christmas cards, St Patrick's Day greetings cards, bookplates and business cards all testify to the business acumen and entrepreneurship of the sisters as well as their talent for encouraging Irish art and design. At Dun Emer and the Cuala, the iconography of the Revival, like that of the Arts and Crafts movement itself, ultimately – if to some paradoxically – became a commodity spectacle.

The fourth, and final, part of our book examines 'Advertising in Ireland 1914–1922'. Chapter 8, 'Advertising, Ireland and the Great War' does several things. First, it examines the ingenious manner in which a specifically 'Irish' frame of reference was used in First World War recruitment campaigns. There has been some recent scholarly work on the meaning of Irish recruitment posters[24] but almost nothing on the related matter of the extensive use of the advertising columns of Irish newspapers by government propagandists. These advertisements were highly ingenious. The song of the Manchester Martyrs, the brotherhood of the Irish farmer, a lad's love for his old mammy and for Ireland herself, the nation's pugilistic prowess, Mr Stephen Gwynn, MP, a girl's respect for her young man, the manly self-regard of Dublin shop assistants; all of these were pressed into the service of the British army in Ireland. Secondly, we discuss the manner in which revolutionary nationalists opposed to Irishmen taking the King's shilling went about spreading their own message in posters and in parodic announcements such as the 1914 mock-advertisement published in the *Irish Freedom*, mouthpiece of the Wolfe Tone republicans: 'WHAT THE ENGLISH ARMY OFFERS ... TO IRISH DUPES AND TRAITORS'.

Thirdly, the chapter also examines the extensive campaigns in the Irish press, mainstream and ultra-nationalist, on behalf of products aimed at the Irish Volunteers, most notably in the sales pitch of Thomas Fallon of Mary Street, Dublin, chief supplier to the force, whose shop, formerly the 'Irish Tweed Company', became both gentleman's outfitters and quartermaster's store in 1914. The final part of the chapter looks at the way in which general brand advertising in Ireland evoked the war in ingenious, some would say shameless, fashion. Advertisers frequently indulged in opportunistic advertising copy, and we examine the manner in which products such as cigarettes, beer and corn cures were frequently marketed with reference to the Irish soldiery.

The brief coda to our book, 'From the Armistice to the Saorstát', looks at the manner in which the Anglo-Irish Treaty and the concept of the Free State resounded through contemporary advertisements, and makes the concluding argument that Irish advertising, far from being in a rudimentary state as the 1920s began, was actually a mature and – at least in terms of the ingenious nature of its copy – relatively sophisticated cultural form. Guinness, in beginning direct advertising for the first time in the late 1920s, was drawing on an already developed Irish tradition rather than beginning one.

Writing in 1892, Maurice O'Connor Morris declared that 'the eye of observation will see some quaint advertisements in Irish journals'.[25] Some of the advertisements discussed and reproduced in this book are certainly 'quaint', while others have different qualities. Some are amusing, some beautiful, some humdrum and some, frankly, preposterous. However, all of these advertisements have social meaning and many of them are possessed of political resonance. The 'eye of observation' has been closed for too long; our book examines the neglected history of Revival-era advertising in the island of Ireland.

Part I

Advertising in Ireland 1850–1914

Prologue – The Irish Advertising Scene from the 1850s to the 1880s

> ADVERTISING IS THE ROAD TO AFFLUENCE. If you see a man affluent in the commercial world, his name has become familiar to the Public by the FREQUENCY AND FORCE OF HIS ADVERTISEMENTS. In the present day the Printing Press is the *avant courier* of success, and the Advertising Papers act as an introduction to the 'Order Book'. If we wished to bequeath to our best friend a MOTTO by which to regulate his efforts and to advance his interest, we would say ADVERTISE, ADVERTISE, ADVERTISE!
>
> (*Irish Weekly Advertiser,* 25 March 1863)

I

In 1853, a contributor to the *Irish Quarterly Review* declared that 'the woeful famine years were the epochs from which much social good, and many, very many, great advantages to the prosperity and to the well being of the country, and of the people, may be dated'.[1] Espousing what now seems the rather remarkable notion of the Great Famine as a form of redemptive suffering, the reviewer proclaims that 'we have, amidst famine, poverty, and neglect, advanced in all the old branches of industry, and have opened new sources of employment for our artizans and for our poor'.[2] The essayist's optimism as to Ireland's economic future was not entirely misplaced. Though underpopulation and emigration ensured that Ireland would never come close to rivalling England in industrial terms, the country achieved a measure of economic success between the late 1840s and the contentious establishment of the Free State in the early 1920s. In this period the mercantile centres of Irish cities, notably Dublin, Belfast and Cork, grew apace if unevenly. Belfast became industrialised along the lines of Newcastle or Liverpool, new department stores sprung up, notably in the capital, and a series of enduring Irish companies were founded (among them Murphy's Brewery (1856), the shipbuilders Harland and Wolff (1861), Jacob's Biscuits (1885), Eason's the bookshop, stationers and newsagents (1886), Barry's Tea

(1901) and Lyon's Tea (1902)). In the same period, attempts were made to foster 'home' or 'peasant' industries – of both rural and urban crafts – in an effort to help the poor and dispossessed of both sexes throughout the island of Ireland (some of these efforts philanthropic, some with an eye to the main chance, and, indeed, some with a measure of both), exhibitions and trade fairs proclaimed the excellence of Irish industry and manufacture, and the advertising business developed in a manner hitherto unprecedented.

Much of this development began, it should be acknowledged, before the Irish Revival, in the period between the 1850s and the turn of the 1880s. For the *Quarterly* reviewer in 1853, a nascent national recovery had become evident in Ireland since the catastrophe of the late forties. For him, one thing above all testified to this Risorgimento: the Dublin International Exhibition: 'The Exhibition shows this fact plainly.'[3] The highly successful exhibition, which was held from the spring to the autumn of 1853 on the lawns of the Royal Dublin Society at Leinster House, showcased Irish goods in a manner analogous to London's own Great Exhibition of 1851, which had demonstrated the British Empire's commercial power, strength and ingenuity. In the *Quarterly*'s opinion, the Dublin jamboree was clear testimony to a movement towards economic recovery in Ireland: indeed, in such optimistic accounts, the Irish Exhibition was both spur and symbol of an economic renaissance, a revival, it might be pointed out, which began decades before its cultural equivalent. Dublin, 'the principal city of a kingdom', as the *Illustrated Magazine* put it, 'but lately risen from the slough of famine and despond',[4] had emerged, triumphantly, from the midden into which it had fallen.

Whereas the *Quarterly* saw the Dublin International as the spirit of economic renewal incarnate, the *Illustrated* maintained that it heralded a new dawn for the Irish nation. The exhibition, the contributor asserts, 'cannot but be beneficial to the social, industrial, and political welfare of the people':

> The Dublin International Exhibition may be looked upon as a great hope and promise for the future of Ireland. [I]t is a proud reflection for Irishmen, that they have raised this beautiful building, and filled it with the evidences of skill and the products of industry, by means entirely their own, [w]ithout government assistance of any kind, but by sheer force of perseverance.[5]

Trade and industry, arts and engineering, manufacturing and merchandising; the goings on in the Society's grounds were commonly read and understood in national terms, as something mimetic, as the proud reflection of the new vigour of Ireland.

The Dublin Exhibition, which ran from May to October 1853, was a wooden-jointed advertisement for Ireland, a commercial message on behalf of the nation writ very large. Advertising was, indeed, extremely important to the exhibition. Alongside its substantial advertising budget (£4357) and the promotional copy which coursed through its programme (which sold several thousand copies), all of its stands were de facto advertisements for Irish goods and merchandise. Similarly, the exhibition had many champions in the Irish and British press willing to lead a chorus of 'Three Cheers for Ireland!' on its behalf and, indeed, to bark the excellence of the goods on show therein. The *Quarterly*'s aforequoted essayist, sounding something like a market trader with a literary bent, lingered over the charms of the exhibition: 'its matchless linens – its incomparable cambrics – its superb damasks [–] its infinite variety of coarser but not less important fabrics'.[6] Irish commodities, in 1853, were now displayed in a most elevated market place.

Commenting on the exhibition's opening ceremony, the *Illustrated* declared that 'The 12th of May 1853 was a great day for Ireland, for on that day the triumphant experiment of 1851 [the Great Exhibition] was repeated in the centre of her beautiful metropolis.'[7] Writing about London's own extravaganza, Thomas Richards, in *The Commodity Culture of Victorian England: Advertising and Spectacle, 1851–1914* (1990), argues that 'The real novelty of the Great Exhibition is that it constructed a centripetal space of representation that took the commodity as its center and axis.'[8] The Dublin Exhibition did the same for Ireland, with the Irish commodity there celebrated as the very incarnation of national renewal. Richards was by no means the first commentator to sense the symbolic importance of the nineteenth-century exhibitions. Contemporary forms of cultural commentary, as per the *Quarterly* and the *Illustrated,* also stressed their figurative weight. John Francis Maguire's *The Industrial Movement in Ireland, As Illustrated by the National Exhibition* (1853) is emblematic of this approach in seeing the modern exhibitions as loaded with symbolic resonance: 'What the Olympian games, and other public festivals of Greece, were to the poet, the historian, or the sculptor, of former days, the Exhibitions of modern times are to the inventor, the manufacturer, and the artizan.'[9] Maguire, then the Mayor of that important mercantile centre the City of Cork (which held its own exhibition in 1852), saw nineteenth-century industrial exhibitions as nationhood on display in the manner of the ancient sporting contests. For him, as for many contemporaries, the sale of such products as linens, whiskeys or lace – historically seen as Ireland's totemic goods – could be celebrated as the very symbols of national renewal. As early as the 1850s, the consumer culture displayed and, indeed, advertised in the Dublin Exhibition was linked to a sense of the nation and, indeed, to the very 'future of Ireland'.

II

The Panhellenic Games of ancient Greece, to which J. F. Maguire MP referred in *The Industrial Movement in Ireland*, were celebrated by a series of bards – with Pindar the most notable – who saluted the deeds of the heroic sportsmen of old. In the nineteenth century, mercantile Ireland also had its own, generally more prosaic, panegyrists, the advertising copywriters, the visibility of whose efforts increased greatly from the 1850s onwards, and particularly from the year of the Dublin International. The spring of 1853, the period in which the festivities at Leinster House commenced, was a highly significant moment in the history of advertising in both Great Britain and Ireland. In the month before the opening of the Irish Exhibition, on 15 April 1853, the parliament of the UK had finally abolished the duty on press advertisements which had first been introduced in 1797 as part of William Pitt the Younger's fiscal measures to fund the war against revolutionary France. The tax remained after the end of the Napoleonic Wars and subsequently impeded the growth of newspaper advertising.[10] While the highly unpopular 'tax on knowledge', the newspaper stamp, had been abolished in 1836, it took seventeen more years before advertising duty (initially three shillings but latterly eighteen pence per insertion)[11] was similarly dispensed with.

A leading light in the campaign to abolish the duty was the Manchester MP Thomas Milner Gibson, the President of the Association for the Repeal of the Taxes on Knowledge. In the House of Commons debate on the third and final reading of the bill, Milner argued for the removal of 'every vestige of stamp-duty on advertisements and supplements'.[12] An important part of his argument, it might be pointed out, was predicated on Ireland and its recent history. There were many well-intentioned advertisements for relief, the member noted, which had stemmed from the Famine and its circumstances from 1847 onwards. But every appeal for assistance raised money, he pointed out, for the government as well as for the starving poor:

> But what a monstrous thing it was, that ... when there was an Irish famine, and when it was necessary, by repeated advertisements, to arrest public attention to those calamities, the exciseman required that there should be 1s. 6d. paid upon every one of these announcements; thus converting the advertisement duty into a tax upon calamity, and causing the funds of subscribers, who fancied that they were contributing to an Irish famine ... to pay a portion of their contribution into the Board of Inland Revenue.[13]

Milner's oratory was successful, and almost all the Irish parliamentarians present supported him (indeed, it was an ad hoc coalition of Irish MPs, Tories and Radicals that managed to pass the bill against the wishes of the Whig and Peelite coalition government). This decision led to a rapid growth in the number of newspaper advertisements. In *Advertising in Britain: A History* (1982), T. R. Nevett notes that the result of the abolition of duty 'was a tremendous expansion of the press, coinciding with a vast increase in advertising',[14] and Frank Presbrey, in *The History and Development of Advertising* (1929), sees the 1850s as marking the emergence of a 'golden age' of press advertisements.[15]

This huge increase in advertising was evident both in Great Britain and in Ireland, for the high-mindedness of Arthur Guinness – if that is what one must call the company's attitude towards paid columns – was not shared by a significant number of Dublin businesses, from sole traders to limited companies employing hundreds of people, which were willing to use advertising to promote their goods. These enterprising capitalists, 'Traders of every class who depend on advertisements for the sale of their goods',[16] as the freesheet *Dublin Advertising Gazette* described them in 1858, embraced advertising with varying degrees of enthusiasm. Advertising was instrumental in developing new brands such as Murphy's, founded in Cork in 1856, in the further development of long-established products such as Jameson's Whiskey, first distilled in 1780, and in fashioning the commercial life of late nineteenth- and early twentieth-century Ireland.

Certainly by the 1850s Irish cities had many business people willing to use advertising to promote their goods; 'the Irish Advertising Community'[17] as the *Advertising Gazette* labelled them in August 1858. Alongside this came the further development of the advertising industry, in the rapid growth of agencies, freesheets, increasing number of commission agents (Leopold Bloom's profession), more visible street advertising (on billboard, bus and poster) and so on. This was to grow over the next fifty years into the well-developed advertising culture of early twentieth-century Dublin which is reflected in the pages of Joyce's *Ulysses*. As well as building brands and businesses, advertising also helped to fill the coffers of contemporary Irish newspapers, especially after the hated levy was abolished. Advertiser and medium served each other's interests well. That nationalist journal *The Gael* noted the importance of advertising to Irish newspapers' income in 1903: 'a newspaper may exist upon very little news; but only upon advertisements does it wax fat and prosperous'.[18] Similarly, for many companies puffery was seen as the way to prosperity: the 'Printing Press', as the *Irish Weekly Advertiser* – another freesheet – declared in 1863, 'is the *avant courier* of success, and the Advertising Papers act as an introduction to the "Order Book" '.

In the wake of the abolition of the stamp duty a number of advertising free newspapers such as the *Weekly Advertiser* – now suddenly made economically viable – sprung up in Dublin and the major mercantile centres of Ireland during the 1850s and 1860s. The capital alone saw the opportunistic establishment of the aforesaid *Dublin Advertising Gazette* in 1858[19] and the *Weekly Advertiser*[20] – later the *Irish Weekly Advertiser* – in 1863, both journals seeking to challenge the hegemony of the city's long-established *General Advertiser*, which dated back into the eighteenth century. Such periodicals were not slow in coming forward, making large claims for themselves in terms of reach and circulation.[21] The *Cork Advertising Gazette*, for example, a free paper founded in 1855,[22] which was 'Published every Wednesday, GRATIS', advertised itself in the following unlikely fashion:

> This is the recognised official Organ for all Advertisements intended to reach the Two Million Inhabitants of the large and important district of which Cork forms the centre. Terms moderate. All orders to be addressed to the Proprietor, Samuel M. Peck, Office, 40 South Mall, Cork.[23]

'Advertising papers', gratis and paid for, both took advertisements and advertised themselves as vehicles for commercial messages. The *Drogheda Conservative*, for instance, declared itself in the *Irish Weekly Advertiser* in 1863 to be 'an admirable Medium for business announcements of every character' (although 'particularly useful to Advertisers of anything appertaining to Agriculture').[24] In the same paper, the *Nenagh Guardian*, which continues to this day, advertised its status as an advertising 'medium' thus: 'Any Advertisements requiring *Extensive Publicity* through the Mercantile, Commercial, Agricultural, and the higher classes, will have desirable medium through the NENAGH GUARDIAN, which circulates widely throughout Tipperary, and the adjoining counties in the South and West of Ireland' (indeed, the importance of paid columns to the journal in the mid-nineteenth century was reflected in this paper's title: the *Guardian* then rejoiced in the title of *Nenagh Guardian or Tipperary (North Riding) and Ormond Advertiser*).[25] Later, in the north of the island, the *Belfast Newsletter* announced itself as 'The Reliable Advertising Medium'.[26]

Advertising was vital to Irish newspapers long before the Free State and its champions – like the partisans of the exhibition – claimed that it was a spur to economic renewal. Robert H. Smythe, for example, the proprietor of the *Western Star and Ballinasloe Advertiser* (which promoted itself as 'Circulating in the Counties of Galway, Roscommon, Mayo, King's County [Offaly] and the Metropolis'), wrote of his journal in 1863 that it 'advocate[d] every movement which has for its object the development of the *Industrial and Commercial Resources of the Country*'[27] ('Smythe also declared the paper non-partisan: 'It ranks itself under no political party.') Advertisers, like the philanthropic investors in home industries, claimed that their motivations went beyond mere money grubbing and, indeed, served a decidedly higher purpose in sponsoring the development of the nation.

Even the freesheets of the 1850s and 1860s, with their inflated claims of circulation reach, with their editors possessed of the self-promotional instincts of a P. T. Barnum and a willingness to indulge in fratricidal knocking against their rivals,[28] also claimed to be wedded to that hybrid of commercial and national interest which was so common among Irish capitalism's self-representations in the late nineteenth century. The *Dublin Advertising Gazette*, for instance, was established, or so it maintained, with a national mission, its proprietors declaring in an editorial of August 1858 that 'We started it with the laudable desire to promote Irish enterprise in a manner which we believed would be conducive, not to ourselves only, but to the interests of the whole advertising community.'[29] That said, national interest can also be self-interest, as both British and Irish businessmen well knew in the nineteenth century. Allied to this philanthropic impulse was a fondness for making money and a zealous belief that advertising was a panacea for all financial ills, a belief summed up in a March 1863 banner for the *Weekly Advertiser,* carried in large letters, heavy type and caps, large and small:

> BY ADVERTISING IN THE IRISH WEEKLY ADVERTISER YOU SECURE THE BEST MEANS OF SERVING YOUR INTEREST AND PROMOTING THE OBJECT IN VIEW – ADVERTISE! ADVERTISE! ADVERTISE!

III

During the late nineteenth and early twentieth centuries, advertisements for Irish companies such as Atkinson's Poplins, Kinahan's Whiskey or Murphy's Stout, of for small or sole traders – such as the grocer Alexander Keyes who plays a part in Joyce's *Ulysses* – were written by a number of hands, either solely or collaboratively. They were composed by the tradesmen and service providers themselves, sometimes via advertising clerks acting as copy-writers (the Keyes advertisement in *Ulysses* appears to have been generated in-house by the proprietor). Sometimes they were composed or titivated by the staff of the newspapers in which they were inserted (in the same episode of *Ulysses,* Bloom asks the pressman politician J. P. Nannetti for 'a little par[agraph] calling attention'[30] to the Keyes's ad). They might also be composed by jobbing advertising agents such as Mr Bloom (in the same conversation Bloom suggests some conventional copy to Nannetti: 'the usual. High-class licensed premises. Longfelt want. So on'),[31] or, especially for bigger ticket business, advertising agencies such as the one which houses 'Blazes' Boylan – when he is not attending to matters musical, sexual or sporting – and Miss Dunne. Certainly Boylan's status as an advertising agent is higher in the pecking order than Bloom's as a canvasser, and his is an example of a profession which began, as far as Dublin was concerned, in the nineteenth century.

Just as the abolition of the stamp duty prompted an increase in advertising in Irish newspapers, so, from the 1850s onwards, agencies began to be more important in the Irish commercial scene. This is not to say that they were anything new. Dublin has had advertising agencies for a long time, with the first opening its doors as far back as 1819. In May of that year Captain Alexander Johnston founded Johnston's Newspaper and Advertising Office at Eden Quay, Sackville Street. Johnston conducted the business with his brother J. K. (John Kent) Johnston.[32] The Johnstons were both advertising men and newsagents, writing and placing advertisements in Irish newspapers on behalf of clients but also selling newspapers on their premises in both Ireland and Great Britain. Their business was bought in by the early 1850s by the famous London firm of W. H. Smith and Son, which continued the concern under the Johnston's name; the company declared in the 1852 edition of *Thom's Directory* that business was as usual: 'Advertisements received for, and promptly published in all the Dublin and London Newspapers, Gazettes & Co., as well as every Provincial Paper in the Kingdom.'[33]

After this, and following the abolition of the tax in the following year, Dublin saw an upsurge in advertising agencies (and there were others in Belfast, Cork, Limerick and all of Ireland's principal cities).[34] Though Irish companies could go to London-based agencies if they chose, and, should size and cost allow (the whiskey company Bushmills, for example, established in 1784, used the London firm of Maher and Crowther), there were options close to home. As the century wore on other successful agencies were established in Dublin. One of the most notable was Wilson, Hartnell and Co., which was founded in 1869 and which led many campaigns for Irish companies and for British firms active in Ireland. Initially founded as an advertising agency alone, Wilson Hartnell later developed into a publisher, notably of periodicals, guide books[35] and political works.[36] In 1890, its co-founder Henry Crawford Hartnell successfully established *The Lady of the House*, a journal aimed at middle-class women readers, which is discussed at length in Chapter 4. Advertising agencies wrote copy, but it is important to realise that they were frequently closely intertwined with Irish print culture in a rather wider sense, and that their activities were by no means divorced from the complex ideological resonance of Ireland's civic and national life.

Wilson, Hartnell and Co. were followed by a number of competitors, perhaps the most notable – and certainly the most enduring – being Eason and Sons and J. H. Parker. Eason's of Middle Abbey Street was initially an advertising office, subscription library and newspaper distributor. It was founded in 1886 by Charles Eason (1823–1899; once of W. H. Smith Ireland) and, continued into the twentieth century by his sons, survives as a newspaper wholesaler and chain of bookshops to this day.[37] Similarly, John H. Parker's firm, founded in 1888, remains a going concern in the twenty-first century. Its founding father worked for Johnston's as a young man and also had a stint in London on the *Daily Express* selling advertisements.[38] Parker then moved back to Dublin to work briefly for Eason's before establishing his own agency in the capital.[39] The toing and froing of Parker's career, like that of Eason, was not uncommon in Irish commercial life in the period and is mirrored in Leopold Bloom's own, albeit less illustrious, professional trajectory in Joyce's *Ulysses*. Such men as Parker and Eason are the most successful examples of the trade which Bloom pursues at his own, rather lower, level.

James Joyce visited Eason's shop in the winter of 1902[40] to buy stationery, testimony to the fact that Eason's was another of these Irish firms which mixed press and publishing and advertising alongside the sale of stationery goods for the office and the home. Advertising was but one part of what modern business analysts called their income stream. Eason's was advertising office, stationer, subscription library, bookstore and newspaper distributor all in one. Early Irish advertising agencies did not resemble modern Saatchi & Saatchi-style companies focused solely on advertising. They sold both newspapers and the advertising space within them, and much of the copy which they placed they did not write themselves.

Such companies were frequently closely intertwined with the Irish press in a wider sense than just advertising. Wilson Hartnell was at the centre of a confluence of advertising, printing and book and periodical publishing, like much of the subject matter and stylistic variegation of Joyce's *Ulysses* itself, it might be pointed out. Companies such as this manifested the interconnectedness evident throughout contemporary Dublin's print culture, whether in terms of newspapers, magazines, books and advertisements – a print culture which so vividly informs Joyce's novel – whether in the *mise en scène* or indirectly in Joyce's pastiche of newspaper and magazine copy, or in his advertising puffs and parodies. ('Hello Jones, where are you going? Can't stop Robinson. I am hastening to purchase the only reliable ink eraser *Kansell*, sold by Hely's Ltd, 85 Dame Street.'[41])

The development of advertising agencies evident in the 1850s and 1860s in Ireland grew apace, and especially as the Revival gathered momentum. The early twentieth century, for instance, saw the establishment of Kevin J. Kenny's business. Kenny, an enormously influential advertising man in the first half of the twentieth century, initially made a name for himself by canvassing for nationalist periodicals[42] and he certainly acted as business manager for D. P. Moran's *The Leader*.[43] Kenny was a stalwart of the Irish Industrial Development Association[44] and, from 1907 was on the organising committee for the annual Sinn Féin aonachs, or trade fairs, which were set up to promote the sale of Irish goods.[45]

In January 1907, the *Irish Independent* noted that the fraternity of Dublin 'advertising agents' was a 'rapidly expanding body of business builders', and in that year there were no fewer than fourteen advertising agencies active in the city.[46] As the likes of Wilson Hartnell and Kenny & Co. demonstrate, these agencies, like newspapers, played a significant role in the development of Irish advertising culture before the establishment of the Free State, and their advertising – like much of that discussed in this book – was often charged with ideological significance.

IV

We will conclude our account of Irish advertising in post-Famine, pre-Revival Ireland by considering the cultural significance of advertising copy in the representative pages of the freesheet newspapers the *Dublin Advertising Gazette* and *Irish Weekly Advertiser* in the late 1850s and early 1860s. The range of goods advertised in these journals was large; in its sixteen broadsheet pages, for instance, the *Weekly* carried announcements divided into the following categories: Medical, Lodgings, Houses and Land, Situations Vacant, New Publications, Amusements, Public Notices, Photography, Furniture, Boots and Shoes, Wines, Groceries, Jewellery, Dress, Money (generally pawnbrokers), Chandlery and Oils and Confectionary (it also carried a subsection with the banner 'ADVERTISING', in which regional journals barked their services as media for advertisements). From relatively modest announcements ('*Everyone* should use Letchford's Blacking'), to ornate display (illustrated advertisements), copy in 'jingle' verse, comic advertisements and so on, the business people of Dublin town saluted their products – and many English and French imports – in a variety of ways.

Looking at the general nature of the copy in these newspapers and comparing it to the tenor of advertising discussed in the main body of this study, it becomes evident that there is one principal difference between Irish advertising before the Revival and that which followed it. The celebration – even fetishisation – of all things Irish in advertising copy, which was to reach fever pitch from the 1890s onwards, was by no means as prevalent in the advertisements of the 1850s and 1860s. Though 'Irish' is certainly used as a term of approbation in notices for lace, linen, whiskey and so on, the word does not pulse with half as much vigour through the advertising copy of this period as it did three decades later. And much more common here are advertisements which appealed to a sense of the excellence and exoticism of non-Irish – principally English and French – products. Imported goods, such advertisements implied, possessed a nose-in-the-air cachet which Irish products could not quite muster.

This is evident in contemporary advertisements peddling such stuff as the 'French Surtout Coats'[47] and the 'French Velvet Hats'[48] sold by F. Kellett of Henry Street, Dublin, and the 'Royal Ventilator Hat' offered by 'Le Chapeau Compagnie de Rouen et Londres' of Grafton Street. The latter was advertised thus on 25 August 1857 in the *Gazette*:

> *Le Chapeau Compagnie de Rouen et Londres,* Makers of the Royal Ventilator. Nagel and Co., Commission Agents have opened a House at 34 Grafton Street for the sale of the Magnificent and Beautifully Designed Hat (THE ROYAL VENTILATOR) which shall be supplied at the Maker's price, thereby giving an advantage to the purchaser of 2s. 6d. per hat. OBSERVE! – 34 Grafton Street.[49]

In Ireland consumer goods are far from *soigné,* but in England and France, to borrow the words of Brian's Friel's pretentious Nancy O'Doherty in *London Vertigo* (1990), a character keen to disguise the Irish roots which she despises, 'Everything there is high, tip top, the *grande monde,* the *bun tun*'.[50] In like manner to the ventilated *chapeau,* in the *Gazette*'s next column Stephenson's Soap and Candle Manufactory offered both the temptingly exotic and Frenchified 'Le Grand's Colza Oil' ('which has been refined by a peculiar French process'),[51] alongside the none-too-homely sounding British product 'Young's Patent Non-Explosive Parraffine Oil'. London copywriters had been appealing to an English sense of the sophistication of the French for years, and their Dublin equivalents sometimes did the same, a sprinkling of (none too difficult) French in the copy only adding to the product's allure (in the manner in which, towards the end of the century, a few words of Irish would boost the claims of the 'Irishness' of a product).

This is not to say that this 'cultural cringe' was universal in this period. The scorn felt among Revival-era advocates of 'Irish Ireland' products towards those who genuflected to foreign goods is well known, but this sentiment was of rather earlier vintage. In its 1853 essay on the Irish Exhibition, for instance, the *Irish Quarterly* lamented the fact that despite the compelling evidence of the excellence of Irish goods which was provided by the great event, there were still Dubliners who automatically assumed that English and French goods were best:

> And notwithstanding the evidence of superior skill and taste which have been afforded by the work of some twenty exhibitors, there will be found, even in this city, gentlemen weak enough to believe that nothing can be done in this wretched country – that it is impossible to obtain the same fit, or the same cut, as in England, – and who, in pursuance of this enlightened and patriotic belief, will still have their boots and shoes made in London, or ordered from Paris![52]

Similarly, as Stephanie Rains has demonstrated, the emergent Dublin department stores – 'monster houses' as their critics dubbed them – were not infrequently attacked in the correspondence pages during the 1850s by small traders whose businesses were threatened by their 'importation of "slop productions" from Britain'.[53]

Not everyone was listening to such talk, however. In the 1850s and 1860s, the menswear and boys' outfitters Benjamin Hyam (Figure P.1 shows a display advertisement for this company dating from the early 1860s), which opened a branch on Dame Street in Dublin in 1851,[54] was a constant presence in the advertising columns of the Irish press. In many of its advertisements, the shop saluted the excellence of the goods to be found at its establishment, not because they were made in Ould Erin – as many later advertisers would do – but on account of the fact they were 'made from

Figure P.1 Advertisement for Hyam's, 30 Dame Street, Dublin (1860): 'Hyam's Summer Season'. Courtesy of the National Library of Ireland.

the finest imported cloth from London and Paris', 'sent direct from the Metropolis' or 'fashioned in the latest styles from London'.

In one advertisement for Hyam and Co., 'the very first house in the Kingdom for Fashionable Clothing', which dates from April 1862, the company's copywriter, his enthusiasm so strong, bursts into song in a verse paean to the splendour of the shop's varied summer range of imported finery:

> This summer his extensive stock
> Will every heart entrance
> Composed it is of fabrics rich
> Of England and of France.
>
> For every age, for every style
> For every varied use,
> It is the cheapest and the best
> That Europe can produce.
> B. Hyam, 30 Dame Street, Dublin.

In both verse and prose the Hyam's advertisements genuflected to external style and fashion. Its copywriters were also capable of heroics, as a Popean salute (also published in 1862) to the goddess of fashion personified, then resident at Dame Street, Dublin demonstrates: 'Utility and beauty here are shown / And *Fashion* claims the garments as her own.' The appeal of such striking copy is demonstrated by the prose copy advertisements which preceded and followed one insertion of the summer season poem in August 1863. These are given in full:

> 137 BAGGOT STREET. A GENERAL REDUCTION in all items of CHANDLERY. THOMAS M'EVOY.
>
> [...]
>
> JAMES L. NIXON, late of Messrs John Charley and Co., begs to announce to his Friends and the Public that he has OPENED his office at 31, EDEN-QUAY, where he proposes carrying on in the Coal Trade. J.L.N. promises good value to those who favour him with their orders.

Sober and informative though these announcements might be, the eye is not caught as it is by the Hyam's verse copy. Hyam's tongue-in-cheek verses, however ludicrous they might seem to the modern reader, are certainly memorable.

The fact that Hyam's advertisements often used verse is not as surprising as it might initially appear. During the nineteenth century, Irish copywriters, following in the wake of the remarkable British campaigns for Packwood's Razor Strops which date from the 1780s onwards,[55] began to use verse or 'jingle' copy in metrical salute to products such as Hyam's summer tailoring. For decades, branded English goods such as Warren's Blacking – a shoe polish 'launched on a sea of poetry'[56] – had used light comic verse as an advertising tool[57] and it was this jocular tradition in which Hyam's copywriters offered verse such as the eulogy to the summer season or, indeed, the jovial ballad stanzas of 1860 which saluted its new seasonal range in sentimental manner:

> We love the time of Easter
> For all its special joys,
> We love it for our children's sake,
> Our darling girls and boys.
>
> It is the time when HYAM takes
> The most important care,
> To revel in the choicest styles
> Of summer dress to wear.[58]

What is happening in copy such as this is a form of literary aspiration where advertising, a cultural form fairly low down the ladder of artistic esteem, elevates itself by utilising poetry, a highly prestigious art form (at the same time, it is also done for gently comic effect; humour sells, as the John Gilroy campaigns for Guinness show and, indeed, advertising executives know to this day). Elevation by association is a key strategy in advertising copy, as modern-day celebrity endorsements or testimonials from sportsmen and women demonstrate. It was particularly evident in advertising in Great Britain and Ireland in the second half of the nineteenth century in advertisers' appealing to the patronage of the aristocracy and royalty, through the personal patronage of His or Her Majesty or Lord this and Lady that. (Appeals to royal patronage were not unknown in early twentieth-century Irish advertising copy, but they became much less common as the Revival gathered pace, and there was an increasing stress on the virtues of Irishness and a conscious and concomitant move away from appeals to British patronage and British fashion.)

In 1863, for instance, under a banner which implies that their services were frequently patronised by the highest in society, Kelly's Dance Band offered its services in the *Irish Weekly Advertiser* with reference to its rarefied, even royal, connections:

> TO THE NOBILITY AND GENTRY!
>
> KELLY'S QUADRILLE AND WALTZ BAND, that had the honour of performing before his Royal Highness the Prince of Wales, No 5, Great Brunswick Street. All the newest Music performed, and first class Musicians employed. Town or Country supplied with large or small Bands.[59]

The distillery of Jameson's went further, not only addressing the 'nobility and gentry' of Ireland but also namechecking almost the entire Ascendancy establishment in some of its advertising copy:

> Jameson and Co have the honour of being patronized by His Excellency the Lord Lieutenant; the Irish Government; Right-Honourable the Lieutenant-General Commanding the Forces; the Adjutant-General, &c, &c.; the Right Honourable and Honourable the Judges; the Bars; the Kildare and Sackville Street United Service and Reform Clubs; Friendly Brothers; the Chamber of Commerce; Dublin Library; Nobility and Gentry, &c.[60]

Triumph of all triumphs in terms of elevated patronage was the royal warrant. Figure P.2 shows an 1854 advertisement for R. Atkinson's Poplins, of College Green, Dublin which proudly features Queen Victoria's coat of arms, with English lion and Scottish unicorn. And not only is Atkinson 'Poplin Manufacturer to the Queen'; he also boasts that he is patronised by other members of the 'nobility and gentry of Great Britain and Ireland' (including the Duchess of Kent and the Peelite parliamentarian, the Earl of St Germans, then Lord Lieutenant of Ireland).

In like manner, Figure P.3 show an 1860 advert for Patrick Corbett, purveyor of pianofortes in Limerick at the Apollo Music Warehouse in George

Figure P.2 Advertisement for R. Atkinson, Purveyors of Poplin, College Green, Dublin (1854).

Street, which also features the royal warrant crest (to which the proprietor was not formally entitled). Corbett (d. 1895), a Roman Catholic stalwart of the St Vincent de Paul Society, boasts of his years of experience in London

Figure P.3 Advertisement for Patrick Corbett, George's Street, Limerick, vendor of pianofortes and other musical instruments (1860).

and his acquaintance with the 'First Houses' in the metropolis. The musical entrepreneur, having availed himself of an impressively neoclassical title for his store, both associates himself with royal patronage and boasts of his experience in the metropolis of London.

As well as royal warrants and elevated patronage, also echoing through the Irish advertising freesheets are the cautions which were so common in nineteenth-century advertising copy in Great Britain. Kinahan's of Dublin, for instance, whose whiskey 'retailed at 18s 6d per gallon', warned its customers in the *Irish Weekly Advertiser* of 27 May 1863 against – to borrow a phrase from Horace – a slavish herd of imitators:

> KINAHAN AND SONS, CARLISLE BUILDINGS, DUBLIN
>
> L. L. WHISKEY. To Guard against Imitations our customers are particularly requested to observe the Seals and Labels, *and that the Corks are all branded*

> *with the name 'Kinahan'.* Our Vans deliver Goods in Bray and its vicinity every Tuesday and Friday.

As Thomas Hood wrote in one of his eloquent meditations on nineteenth-century advertising, 'The Art of Advertizing Made Easy' (1825), in such prudential counsel 'The public must be cautioned against every thing on earth but the identical item advertised…The inventor must be "ever anxious", or "always emulous", to check imposition.'[61]

It might also be pointed out that alongside advertisements for such stuff as Kinahan's bargain booze and Jameson's whiskey, salutes to the supposedly non-advertised prince of porters are not uncommon in the pages of the Dublin advertising press. Guinness & Co. did not rush to their lawyers to prevent John Bebe publicising its beers in the pages of the *Irish Weekly Advertiser* in 1863:

> *The Most Wholesome Drinks now in Use*
>
> GUINNESS'S EXTRA STOUT
>
> *The subscriber begs leave to state that he has the celebrated porter in Prime Order*: GUINNESS'S EXTRA STOUT, or XXX PORTER (same as brewed for exportation), made from *pure Malt and Hops*, SMALL BOTTLES (Pints) 2s 4d per Doz.
>
> Bottles wired and tin-foiled.
>
> GUINNESS'S XX PORTER (pure 1s 6d)
>
> JOHN BEBE, TEA, WINE, SPIRIT AND PORTER MERCHANT, 18 THOMAS STREET, DUBLIN.[62]

Though the Guinness company did not loosen its purse strings to advertise its products directly in the nineteenth century, the firm's beers were frequently 'celebrated' in Irish advertisements by second parties.

Also typical of pre-twentieth century advertising copy is the presence of many announcements in the Irish press for those stalwarts of the advertising ranks, the vendors of patent and proprietary medicines.[63] Mid-nineteenth-century Dublin had its own advertising 'empirics' in the manner of the noisy British medicine sellers Dr Samuel Solomon and Thomas Holloway, men such as S. A. Levenston, healer, man-midwife and proprietor of 'Levenston's Golden Specific', a product which was also marketed as 'Life's Invigorator'. Sometimes the Golden Specific was marketed as a cure for the drink habit ('how easy it is to cure drunkards with this remedy') and on other occasions it is was sold as a cure for what were euphemistically described as 'private' or 'secret' diseases. The Dublin advertising freesheets of the late 1850s and the 1860s were full of stuff such as this advertisement for Levenston:

> CONFIDENTIAL MEDICAL ADVISER
>
> In all cases of Nervous Debility use LEVENSTON'S GOLDEN SPECIFIC. It is the most wonderful Medicine ever discovered for the care of Secret Diseases, and must ever be hailed by the human race as the GREAT and GLORIOUS REMEDY for the REGENERATION and RESTORATION OF SUFFERING HUMANITY. It has a pleasant taste, devoid of smell, and is so portable that it can be carried in the VEST POCKET, so that the patient can CURE HIMSELF without even the knowledge of a bedfellow.
>
> OBSERVE THE ADDRESS: S. A. Levenston, Consulting Accoucheur. 42, Kildare Street, Dublin. Midwifery Cases attended to. Fee 10s. 6d.[64]

As Roy Porter has demonstrated,[65] the advertising of quack 'cures' for venereal diseases was decidedly contentious in England in the nineteenth century, particularly on the morally censorious grounds that offering a remedy was seen as encouraging the vice. The same applied to Ireland. One 'Civis Dubliniensis', for instance, wrote to the *Medical Times* in 1862 to attack 'the author of these vile productions' – Levenston's advertisements – and to call for the 'public protection of the Medical Act against the imposition of such *charlatans*'.[66] Levenston, man-midwife and pox doctor, had the cheek, declared the correspondent, to market his wares in the very same street – Kildare Street – as that in which the Royal College of Physicians was based, and his fly-posting was a public nuisance ('the walls of our city are defiled with [his] placards').[67]

Levenston, however, was unabashed by criticism, and his euphemistic copy poured forth in the pages of the Dublin prints, curing alcoholism, venereal disease, even impotence: 'In all cases of nervous debility, whether arising from excess or abuse, use Levenston's Golden Specific or Life's Invigorator. This wonderful agent will restore manhood to the most shattered constitutions in only two weeks.'[68] Despite the importance of both the Roman Catholic church and the Church of Ireland in civil society, Dublin, like all of the major cities in the UK, had advertisers willing to wink away moral laxity and to sell treatments for the consequences of the freedoms lads were wont to take.

Advertisements for such products as pox pills, poplins and pianofortes were part of a widespread culture of brand advertising in Ireland in the middle decades of the nineteenth century. From the period of the Famine onwards – and certainly after the opening of the event at the Royal Dublin Society and the abolition of the stamp duty soon afterwards – the Irish press, from north to south, and from supposedly non-partisan and widely distributed freesheets to paid-for newspapers of various political hues, was inextricably wedded to advertising. Towards the end of the century, however, the nature of that advertising would begin to change.

1
Advertising and the Nation in the Irish Revival

GLEESON AND CO.

STAND BACK, you who doubt Ireland's Industrial Possibilities. We have entered the citadel after having torn down the old wells of prejudice against Irish Goods. We have opened an Irish Drapery Store at 11 Up. O'Connell Street for the Sale of IRISH GOODS ONLY.

Advertisement for Gleeson and Co., Dublin (1911)

The Irish Revival is generally seen as a literary and cultural movement, but it did, of course, have an economic nationalism associated with it. As the nationalist journal *The Shan Van Vocht* declared in 1897, 'literature alone, though it move mountains, will not stir the rank and file of the breadwinners and nerve them for an arduous struggle for self-government'.[1] 'The best thing that could happen', it maintained, was that Irish goods could compete 'in the world's market [and] put an Irish product in the highest place': 'Anything therefore which tends to create new industries and to teach people how to help themselves towards material prosperity should be welcomed as a direct furtherance of the national ideals and aspirations.'[2] Advertising can be seen as, in part, sponsoring, or at least reflecting, this project of national self-improvement, and we would argue that it is worth extending our historical consideration of the print sphere of the Irish Revival to that particular cultural form.

Writing in *The Philosophy of Irish-Ireland* (1905), D. P. Moran declared that 'There will be found a native colour in arts, industries, literature, social habits, points of view, music, amusements, and so on, throughout all phases of human activity.'[3] In the period of the Irish Revival, Irish advertising, like contemporaneous 'arts, industries, literature [and] social habits', took on the 'native colour' of an Ireland attentive as never before to issues of nationality. Advertising is, of course, a matter of image-making, and in Ireland in the Revival years it frequently reflected wider national self-presentations. Advertising became one part of Irish industry which clearly began to reflect the native tint, evolving into a cultural chameleon which was frequently green in hue. A central theme of Irish consumer culture in this period was Ireland itself.

I

In Joyce's *Dubliners* story, 'A Mother', Mrs Kearney sees opportunities for her fortuitously named daughter, Kathleen, in the renaissance of Irish culture which had begun in Ireland in the last decade of the nineteenth century:

> When the Irish Revival began to be appreciable Mrs Kearney determined to take advantage of her daughter's name and brought an Irish teacher to the house. Kathleen and her sister sent Irish picture postcards to their friends and these friends sent back other Irish picture postcards [...] Soon the name of Miss Kathleen Kearney began to be heard often on people's lips. People said that she was very clever at music and a very nice girl and, moreover, that she was a believer in the language movement. Mrs Kearney was well content at this.[4]

Mrs Kearney, as Garry Leonard puts it in his 1997 Lacanian analysis of the story, 'packages her daughter',[5] and she packages Miss Kathleen in terms of her Irishness. She knows that this is a marketable quality in the Revival, and something of which she can take full 'advantage'.

Mrs Kearney's sense that there was now a premium on Irishness is exactly right in terms of middle-class Dublin at the turn of the twentieth century. Irish advertising in the late nineteenth and early twentieth centuries is an often fascinating body of work: diverting, intriguing, suggestive and, indeed, sometimes faintly risible. And within the millions of lines of print copy, one word stands out among all others. The word with the greatest cultural capital of all here is 'Irish', an indisputably good thing in this context. Instead of tempting references to the allure of 'foreign' goods, now the emphasis was, in the Revival, increasingly placed on the excellence of Irish products and the consumer's national duty to purchase them. The remediation of Irishness in key parts of contemporary popular culture, such as dance and sport, is one of the defining characteristics of the Revival, and this phenomenon, we want to argue, was also evident in advertising copy. In a famous 1892 lecture which is perhaps the founding document of the Irish Revival, Douglas Hyde had called for 'The Necessity for De-Anglicising Ireland', and commercial culture, with its frequent genuflection to English products, was one place ripe for de-Anglicisation alongside language, sport and music. Buying Irish-Ireland goods became a key plank of such cultural change; as Jason K. Knirck has written, by the turn of the twentieth century:

> Irish towns and cities teemed with various and sundry nationalist organisations, and, whether one supported political manifestations of Irish nationalism or not, most Irish men and women would have at some point come into contact with a Gaelic Athletic Association-sponsored hurling match, an Irish dance put on by the Gaelic League [Conradh na Gaeilge] or a "buy Irish" advertisement.[6]

In a manner analogous to the contemporary turn to Gaelic games and away from British ones, and from English to Irish, there was a concomitant turn to Irish products from the 1880s onwards. This was one more method of 'de-Anglicising': buy Irish campaigns were a form of introducing protectionism by the back door, a voluntary protectionism which offered a way of resisting the tenets of British Free Trade and the pervasiveness of British imported goods. This offered commercial opportunities for Irish business folk. One could now cash in on Irishness; manufacturers and advertisers could turn a profit while simultaneously paying tribute – whether sincere or meretricious – to the national cause, and they could target a ready market of Irish folk all minded to grant priority to home goods rather than imported products. And one place in which this constituency could be addressed was in the advertising columns. A 1906 article published in the *Independent Review* pointed out the business logic of the canny Irish advertiser: 'He knows that, so far as he possibly can, the Gaelic Leaguer will buy Irish-made goods; and he expects to catch the attention with Irish advertisements.'[7] This fact is indubitable. The Irish Provident Assurance Co. Ltd, for instance, announced in *An Claidheamh Soluis* in 1904 (during Patrick Pearse's editorship) that 'A SPECIAL DEPARTMENT HAS BEEN STARTED FOR THE ASSURANCE OF MEMBERS OF THE GAELIC LEAGUE AND KINDRED SOCIETIES INTERESTED IN THE IRISH REVIVAL.' Customers were invited to 'write in Irish or English' to the society.

This appeal to those 'interested in the Irish Revival', whether they were (relatively) apolitical cultural nationalists, radical separatists or Home Rulers, was frequently evident in contemporary advertising copy. This nationalisation of advertising, so to speak, whether motivated by capitalistic instinct, political principle (Irish Party stalwarts, Sinn Féiners and Unionists are all represented here) or a mixture of both, was apparent throughout Ireland. Some advertising copywriters[8] explicitly tailored their text to what *The Leader* once described as the sympathies of the 'genuine, oppression-hating, Government denouncing, undying-cause-of-our-native-land'[9] reader; others, in the manner of Mrs Kearney, seemed content to ride the crest of the national wave for commercial gain.

The 'greening' of Irish advertising, it might be pointed out, was apparent in the very brand nomenclature of Irish goods and manufacturers; these of hundreds: Bates's Irish Exhibition Razors, E. and J. Burke's Fine Old Irish Whiskey ('Bottled, Corked and Capsuled in DUBLIN'), the Irish Colour

Printers, the Irish Curled Seed Company, Dickson's Pedigree Irish Seeds, the Irish Embrocation, the Irish Farm Produce Co., the Irish Feather Bed Co., Elliott's Irish Poplin Neckties, Mackey's Irish Grown Flowering Bulbs, McDowell's Lucky Irish Wedding Rings, M'Fall's Celebrated Irish Harps, O'Reilly's Irish Boxes, the Irish National Cigarettes,[10] Samuels's Irish Bog Oak Ornaments and D. Towell, the Great Irish Tailor of Great Irish Tailoring. And what say you to the Irish Shroud and Frilling Co. of Belfast ('Telegraphic Address "Shroud", Belfast'), which in 1904 presented itself as the 'manufacturers of Irish shrouds, robes, coffins, trimmings, side sheets, furnitures and all undertaking requisites'?[11]

Contemporaneously with the Revival, the word 'Irish' swam through Irish branding like fish through a river. Figures 1.1 and 1.2 show advertisements for Grappler Tyres ('For Irish Roads... MADE IN IRELAND – BY IRISHMEN') and An Cló-Cumann ('Printing in Irish by Irishmen on Irish-Made Paper'), which described itself as 'The First Printing Company started in Ireland on Real Irish Ireland lines'. Irish goods, all might agree, were superior to the works of foreign manufacturers and, instead of being endlessly desirous of foreign goods from London or Paris, the Irish consumer was now assumed to prioritise the goods of Erin's isle.

Advertisers appealed to national sentiment as never before, both in explicitly Irish brand names and in a predictable paraphernalia of Irishness in such nomenclature as the Blarney Brand Old Irish Whiskey, Emerald Gem Cigarettes, O'Connell's Dublin Ale, Hibernian Manures and Keltic soap, alongside, inevitably, shamrock this, shamrock that and, indeed, shamrock the other. Purchasing Irish brands rather than Sunlight Soap, Bell's Whisky or Burberry coats was, it was implied, one's patriotic responsibility. 'Are you

Figure 1.1 Advertisement for Grappler tyres (1899): 'Made in Ireland – By Irishmen'.

Figure 1.2 Advertisement for An Cló-Cumann, Ltd (1904): 'Printing in Irish by Irish-Speaking Irishmen on Irish-Made Paper'.

Irish?', asked an 1899 advertisement for the jam manufacturers William Vint and Sons, proprietors of the Unity Street Preserve Factory; 'If, so you must help to Preserve' – the reader winces – 'Irish Industries'. 'We do our part', the copy goes on: 'Our famous jams are made from specially selected Irish Grown Fruits.'[12] The patriotic calls continue: 'Support the Irish farmer by buying White's Wafer Oatmeal!'; 'Give a fillip to the wave of prosperity which has started for our country by buying Gaelic Brown Wrapping Paper!'[13]; 'Support an Old Home Industry by buying flour made in the Mills of Walter Brown and Co., Dublin'; 'Support Home Industries by buying your Cycle from John O'Neill' (who offered 'terms from 3s per week' to nationalists without deep pockets)[14]; 'GAELS OF CORK! Do you know where to get the Best Value in Flowers, Vegetables, Sweets, etc?' (the answer to the conundrum being 'Peg Duggan's, 51 Grand Parade Market, Cork').

Unsurprisingly, the economic campaigns for Irish 'home goods' evident from the 1880s onwards were directly echoed in advertising copy, as manufacturers saw the chance to make money from such crusades by stressing their *bien pensant* credentials. Advertisements were topped by banners such as 'Encourage Irish Manufactures', 'Support Irish Industries' and 'Home Goods Only'. For every exhortation by the likes of Hyde and Moran – or, indeed, politicians such as the dual-monarchist, Arthur Griffith, and the leader of the Irish Parliamentary Party, John Redmond – to buy Irish wares, there was an advertising response echoing the same sentiment, and trading on the cultural and ideological sympathies of consumers. One person who was aware of this fact was that advertising man Leopold Bloom, who showed himself to be an acute cultural critic in his interpretation of the advertisement for the house of Keyes in Joyce's *Ulysses*: 'The idea, Mr Bloom said, is the house of keys. You know, councillor, the Manx parliament. Innuendo of home rule.'[15] Keyes's ad, with the crossed keys suggesting the semi-autonomous Isle of Man, is an appeal, in part, to political nationalism of a constitutional cast. Bloom knew this, and Joyce showed himself to be cognisant of the ideological subtexts of much Irish advertising in Revival-era Dublin.

Advertisers began to imply that by partaking of their goods, consumers might thereby assimilate a full-blooded Irishness. Advertisers stressed their thorough-going patriotism and sought where possible to present themselves as 'Home Industries'. In 1903, for instance, Eason's advertising agency and newsagents proudly advertised its Irish stationary – the 'Genuine Irish' and the 'Real Irish' ('YOU CANNOT GET BETTER VALUE!') – by instructing customers to 'Ask your stationer for these if you desire to help Irish Industries.' This was 'PRACTICAL PATRIOTISM', as T. J. Loughlin, the 'Irish Outfitting Specialist' of 19 Parliament Street, Dublin, put it in *An Claidheamh Soluis* in April 1904. Practical patriots, the notice went on, could demonstrate their love of country by trooping to Parliament Street to purchase Loughlin's 'Irish Poplin Scarves, Irish-Made Shirts, Irish Hosiery, Irish-Made Football Jerseys and Cycling Hose'.

The temper of Irish advertising had changed in what one might call, in Hyde's terminology, a 'de-Anglicising' of both product and publicity. Now Irish women were portrayed as being positioned at the height of fashion rather than mere followers of foreign example: 'All the Dublin Beauties use *Leonard's Irish Arsenical Soap*' ('It creates a charming complexion, soothes the skin, and prevents contagion'). Where once Kelly's Quadrille and Dance boasted of their playing before a future king of England, now music lovers had a native monarch of their own, Cathal MacGarvey, the composer of 'The Star of the County Down', who proclaimed himself in *An Claidheamh Soluis* in the early 1900s as the 'KING OF IRISH IRELAND ENTERTAINERS, now available to Gaelic Leaguers'. (MacGarvey, or Mac Garbhaigh (d. 1927), also kept – and advertised – a tobacconist's shop on North Frederick Street, An Stad ('The Stop'), which was frequented by Michael Cusack and luminaries of the Gaelic Athletic Association and Gaelic League, and was the venue for many a session of Irish music; a contemporary once breathlessly described it as the most 'Gaelic spot in all of Ireland'.[16])

The eye of advertisement had turned inwards. Whereas manufacturers still occasionally fawned over the clothing 'of England and of France', as Benjamin Hyam's once had it, more common in the Revival was such stuff as Dunlop and Co.'s 1904 salute to their 'Celtic Suits made to measure' ('39/6'): 'The Cloths are the *choicest range of Irish goods procurable,* in Checks, Stripes, Blacks and Blues, turned out in the very finest style. Motto – Excellence with Economy.'[17] The 'choicest goods' were now Irish ones.

At the end of the period discussed in this book, Urney's Chocolate, founded by Eileen Gallagher in 1919 in Urney, County Tyrone (though it later moved to Tallaght on the outskirts of the capital), boasted in *The Gael* in 1921 that it was 'Entirely Made in Ireland'. The well-polished copy for this product ('every one is a revelation of deliciousness'), which survived until the 1960s, appealed to a heavily romanticised view of Ireland: 'It is as pure, as fresh, as delightful as the mountain breeze that blows over the old Irish demesne in the midst of which it is made.' 'Every piece', the copy continues rather poetically, 'is a mouthful of sheer joy' (and packed in 'boxes bearing quaint old Irish designs'). What is going on in such copy is an appeal to the national imagination which draws on the powerful connotations of the words 'Irish' and, indeed, 'Ireland', an exemplary kind of place in both nationalist rhetoric and advertising copy, and one to which people felt a sense of great rootedness and attachment.

II

During the Revival era, a green-tinged glow began to issue from contemporary Irish products. In the first decade of the twentieth century, grown-ups could puff happily on Emerald Gem Cigarettes while their children read from the volumes in the 'Emerald Series of Books' which were produced by Sullivan Brothers, the educational publishers of Middle Abbey Street, Dublin. A correspondent to Moran's *The Leader*, writing in October 1904, called for the publication of more 'books that might be called Irish, that is, books purporting to be different in "note", or "style", or in something, no matter what, from their English contemporaries'.[18] Sullivan's rose to the challenge, their work directly marketed as inculcating national spirit in the young. 'BOOKS OF THIS KIND' announced a 1909 banner for the series in a *Thom's Directory* advertisement, 'CANNOT FAIL TO DO GOOD AMONG THE RISING GENERATION IN OUR COUNTRY'.

Irish business after the Revival was something of a school for Irishness, and this notion was made incarnate in the Sullivan list. These volumes, metaphorically and literally wearing the green (they were bound in handsome emerald boards), featured historical works such as *The Clans of Ireland* ('2s. 6.'), which featured 'introductory chapters on the Clan System, the Descent, Territories, Castles, Strongholds, and War Cries'). Having practised their war cries, youngsters could then cultivate more cerebral parts of their being with the *Emerald Advanced Literary Reader*, 'Comprising selections of high class literary merit from the writings of famous authors, principally Irish.' Should the youth aspire to grow up an Irish-Ireland entrepreneur, then Sullivan offered *Lessons on Ireland and its Industries*, including notes on 'Peat, Coal, Potatoes... and the Brewing industries'.

This was modernity, but with a long memory, as the company also offered *Old Irish Stories* featuring tales of a very Irish kind, 'including Lia Fail, Cuchulain, Cormac, Grace O'Malley, The Ape of Kildare, Old Laws, Irish Doctors, Fergus Roy, the Poet King [...] Brian Boru, Great Books of Ireland, Historical Women, Finn and his companions, the Ancient Fairs, Children of Usnach, Baile Mac Buain, King Dathi, etc'. These 'memories of Ireland's heroes' – some heroes well documented, others shadowy and some entirely imaginary – betoken a will to folk memory rather than to a dry and literal remembrance. These books and the tenor of the advertising which they represent arguably derive directly from the cultural agenda of the Gaelic League. Hyde's influential 1892 lecture declared that 'the Celtic race... about to largely recover possession of its own country, finds itself deprived and stript of its Celtic characteristics, cut off from the past... It has lost since the beginning of this century almost all that connected it with the era of Cuchulain, [and all] that connected it with Brian Boru.'[19] The Emerald Series was a conscious attempt to reunite young people with that glorious past, offering inspiring examples to the contemporary youth of Ireland.

'"Development from within" is the Irish Ireland motto', declared *The Leader* on 3 October 1903, encapsulating in three words the economic ethos of the Revival, and these words 'Irish' and 'Ireland', alongside various national emblems, became matters of currency in this period. Indeed, as the taste for explicitly labelled 'Irish' goods spread, attempts were made to protect Irish interests from bandwagon-jumping British companies wishing to exploit that appetite. A key task of the Irish Industrial Development Association (IIDA) (founded in 1905 from a coalition of local bodies in Dublin, Galway and elsewhere which had been inspired by the example of the Cork Industrial Development Association established in 1903) was to pursue such miscreants. It did so with great vigour. An appendix to *Modern Irish Trade and Industry* (1920), a book written by the secretary to the association, E. J. Riordan, lists some of the writs, warnings and prosecutions issued by the association in its early years. These are some of dozens:

> A Northampton firm were detected by us selling boots which were branded with the title 'Ould Erin'. On our giving them the option of discontinuing this misleading practice or fighting the matter in the courts they chose the former alternative.
>
> A Birmingham firm gave us an undertaking to discontinue advertising as 'Irish' Dry Ginger Ale, a mineral water made by them in England.
>
> A Bolton (Lancashire) firm undertook to discontinue applying the title 'Shamrock' to tins containing baking-powder of non-Irish manufacture.
>
> A Birmingham firm applied to register a design, as a trade mark, representing an Irish Colleen looking through an Irish Harp, in respect of earthenware and porcelain. We notified them that unless they withdrew this application we should oppose it. They thereupon withdrew the application.

> A Cardiff firm applied to the Board of Trade to register the title 'Slainte' in respect of non-Irish milled flour. We opposed this application, and, after the usual applications, succeeded in preventing registrations.
>
> A Glasgow firm applied to the Trade Mark Office to register the word 'Colleen', and an Irish design, in respect of blouses, etc. made in Scotland. We filed an opposition and after the case had reached a certain point the Glasgow firm abandoned their application.[20]

In Great Britain, as in Ireland, the taxonomy of 'Irishness' was now a valuable commodity, though, as a correspondent for *The Leader* once put it, 'not everything branded Irish [was] the genuine article'.[21] In Birmingham and Bolton, in Cardiff and Glasgow, the same romanticised version of 'Ould Erin' had currency, as it did in Ireland itself. Those partisans of Irish Ireland who scoffed at English 'shoddy' were possessed of an unrequited hate. The British vogue for all things Irish, or at least all things pertaining to the familiar iconography of colleens, harps, leprechauns and shamrocks, manifested itself in this willingness to use an opportunistic brand of counterfeit Irishness.

The association also sternly policed businesses within the island of Ireland itself:

> A Dublin firm of wholesale stationers gave us an undertaking to discontinue using the title 'Dublin' and the words 'Irish manufacture' in respect of writing pads made of imported paper and merely put together in this country.
>
> A Dublin firm gave us an undertaking to discontinue using the title 'Shamrock' in connexion with non-Irish table salt.
>
> [A] Belfast firm undertook to cease using the words 'Support Home Industry' and 'Sole Proprietors', and to substitute the words 'Packed by' in respect of Cocoa which they import in bulk and merely pack in Ireland.[22]

In its enthusiasm for national mercantile purity, from 1 January 1907 the association began licensing firms to use its Irish Trade Mark, *Déanta i nÉirinn* ('Made in Ireland'), issuing more than 700 licenses between then and 1920. Secretary Riordan writes proudly of 'the value which Irish manufacturers have derived from applying the Mark to their manufactures'.[23] The trademark (Figure 1.3) was used on display (that is, illustrated) advertisements, labels, posters and the like, becoming a valuable commercial imprimatur of Irishness.

As contemporary advertisers knew, a line or two of Gaeilge (though generally not much more than that) was good for establishing one's Irish Irishness.

Figure 1.3 Trade mark of the Irish Industrial Development Association (1907): *Déanta i nÉirinn* ('Made in Ireland').

The mark itself, with its neo-Celtic iconography of the collar of Moran (or Morand), owes something to the contemporary arts and crafts movement (Moran was a legendary Irish judge whose collar was placed around the neck of a witness. It would strangle him if he swore falsely but leave him unharmed if he spoke truth – a nice symbol of the trademark's claim to distinguish genuine Irish goods from fakes). It was a signifier of national integrity and it was zealously guarded by the indefatigably litigious IIDA, which reported the following case in 1920:

> A Belfast firm received an order some months ago to supply a quantity of roll admission tickets, each ticket to be branded with the Irish Trade Mark. Instead of passing this order over to an Irish printer of these tickets, who is an authorised user of the mark, they sent it to a firm in Hull to execute, and supplied the latter firm with block of the Irish Trade Mark to use in printing the tickets. We have instituted proceedings in the Dublin Chancery Court against the Belfast firm, applying for an injunction to restrain them from using the mark, and the case will be tried in the course of the present term.[24]

The Irish trade mark, unsurprisingly, became something of a badge of honour for advanced nationalists. On 16 October 1909, *Sinn Féin*, a periodical printed in Ireland by Irish printers on Irish paper using, indeed, Irish ink, announced that it was now newly anointed with the Irish trade mark. Arthur Griffith proclaimed in an editorial that '"Sinn Féin" is the only journal in Ireland entitled to use the Irish Trade Mark', and he explained why:

> The reason why is that 'Sinn Féin' is the only daily journal in Ireland printed on Irish paper. 'Sinn Féin' is printed with Irish ink. All the

> materials procurable in Ireland that go to make up a newspaper are used in 'Sinn Féin'. All other daily journals in Ireland import their paper from England, America, France, or Holland. If they procured their paper and ink at home, at least £100,000 a year would be retained in this country and permanent employment provided for about 2,000 people. 'Sinn Féin' is the only daily paper in Ireland that supports the paper-making and ink-making industries of the country. That is why 'Sinn Féin' alone is entitled to bear the Irish Trade Mark. The Irish Trade Mark distinguishes what is Irish from what is spurious. We bear the Irish Trade Mark.

To use the words 'Irish', and 'Ireland' a dozen times in a single paragraph certainly betokens a national zeal.[25] The journal's vigorous patriotism (to which we will return in Chapter 3) is endorsed by the *Déanta i nÉirinn* mark, the symbol, in more sense than one, of national enterprise.

III

Another early recipient of the *Déanta i nÉirinn* was a County Kilkenny furniture shop and manufactory, the Kilkenny Woodworkers.[26] Figure 1.4 shows a striking display advertisement for the Woodworkers, which features the oval IIDA trade mark prominently displayed underneath the proud boast 'An Irish Industry'. This fine image simultaneously appeals to national spirit and catches at Irish nostalgia for a lost age of rural industry. The past affected the present in Irish advertising of the early twentieth century, as it has much else in the country's culture before and since. Here modern advertising frequently contrived to be nostalgic, patriotic and new-fangled in simultaneity. It is striking how the image, with its clog-wearing becapped worker, implies that this large furniture manufactory and shop, which had more than 100 employees in 1910,[27] was a 'peasant industry'. In envisaging national renewal though industry, the *Irish Quarterly* had anticipated a time when 'the hum of the spinning-wheel and the shuttle will be heard issuing from the door of the thatched cottage, as in former times, when the stout farmer wore on his back the produce of the industry that flourished on his own hearth'.[28] In an early form of heritage marketing, advertisements like those for the Kilkenny Woodworkers drew on this mythical golden age of 'former times', an idealised notion of the dignity of labour, of industriousness rather than heavy industry, and of the days of Irish self-sufficiency.

The Kilkenny Woodworkers, a business that practised a form of homespun capitalism, so to speak, was founded in an attempt to help the local economy and to bring employment in the then newly fashionable old-fashioned skills of rural Ireland. Like several firms which drew on and cultivated the skills of Irish craftsmen, it was established by members of the Anglo-Irish upper classes, in this case Captain the Honourable Otway Cuffe and the Countess of Desart. Cuffe, later the Mayor of Kilkenny and a liberal Unionist, was

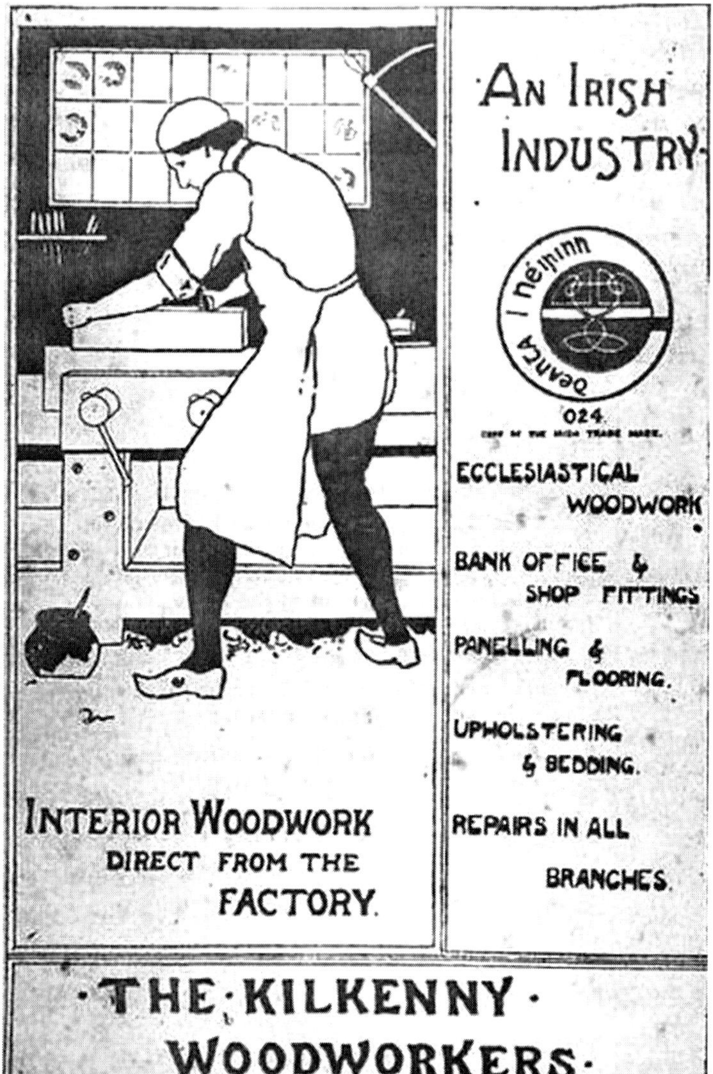

Figure 1.4 Advertisement for the Kilkenny Woodworkers (1907): 'An Irish Industry'. Courtesy of Joseph McBrinn.

one of the most notable of the paternalistic Irish Protestants who saw it as their duty to foster Irish industry[29]; alongside strongly supporting the cultural aims of the Gaelic League, of which he was the local president, he was the first national president of the IIDA.

Despite their portrayal here as modern-day peasantry, the artisans who toiled at the Woodworkers' two premises in Kilkenny and Dublin were tough-minded working men and most of them, indeed, were active trade unionists. They participated in the industrial strife widely evident in Ireland before the First World War, closing down both of the company's workshops in 1910 as a consequence of the management's resistance to their attempt to bring in a cabinet-makers' union closed shop. In October of that year, the *Freeman's Journal* noted that the company's workers had gone on strike because a 'non-society man from Belfast was employed as a cabinet-maker.'[30] (The company's demise in the 1920s was the result of an even more prolonged lock-out as a consequence of industrial action.)

After the Great Famine, and particularly in the final decades of the nineteenth century, home industries such as the Kilkenny Woodworkers became a significant part of efforts towards economic national renewal. These sought to remove the taint of pauperisation from the rural poor, and from the indigents of the cities, by giving them some useful trade. (Many of these organisations were inspired by the existing British co-operative associations and the contemporary arts and crafts movement which had sprung up in England and Scotland.) Though more common from the 1890s onwards, it might be pointed out that such 'cottage industries' had existed for years before. As early as 1879, in a simultaneous appeal to patriotism and to the pocket, a handbill for 'Irish Cottage Industries', published by Desmond Brothers of Royal Avenue, Belfast, sets the tone:

> We earnestly beg to call to your attention these industries, by the manufacture of which we keep many of the poorer class of Irish peasants in employment. Through the partial failure of the potato crop, on which the Irish peasant is principally dependent, owing to the rainy and unfavourable summer, the number of those who are dependent on those industries has largely increased.
>
> In order to in some measure meet demand we have decided to make a reduction in our selling price of goods. The increased sales which we thereby expect will enable us to give employment to more workers, and thus help to relieve distress without the demoralising results attendant in open-handed charity.
>
> Among these goods are Ladies and Gentlemen's Handkerchiefs of all kinds. These can be beautifully embroidered with initials, monograms, & co., thus giving immediate work.

Rather than purchasing imported goods, the ethical consumer should patronise goods made by the 'poorer class of Irish peasants'. The upmarket shop on Royal Avenue presents itself as being imbued with a national mission. It is noticeable that the company's decidedly patronising copy warns of the morally deleterious effects of handouts among the poor – much better the dignity of simple labour. At the same time, as well as appealing to the philanthropic urge, Desmond's also play to their customers' self-interest: 'They are much cheaper than anything to be found in Belfast, and immensely cheaper than can be obtained from any London house, so that as well as assisting the distressed, you at the same time receive a genuine bargain.'

This tradition of 'top down' Anglo-Irish assistance for the deserving poor reached its apogee in the Royal Irish Industries Association, which was founded in the late 1880s by the Countess of Aberdeen (the wife of the Earl of Aberdeen, Lord Lieutenant of Ireland, and a self-styled 'countess with a conscience'),[31] and was associated with a number of other aristocratic society ladies: the Duchess of Abercorn, the Countess of Arran and the Marchioness of Londonderry, among others. A 1907 advertisement for 'Irish Industries of Donegal' was issued on behalf of the association:

> Irish Industries lies in the part of Ireland known as the congested districts of Donegal. In this and in other counties of Ireland, the Irish workers are trained to produce beautiful and artistic woollen and linen fabrics, rich embroideries, and fine laces. These original and beautiful articles make excellent Christmas gifts and at the same time add to the resources of the Donegal Industrial Fund, the proceeds and profits of which are devoted to the furtherance of the industrial work begun and carried on with so much promise in Ireland.

Figure 1.5 shows a 1907 advertisement for the 'Irish Hand Embroidered and Real Lace Robes' available at the smart new showroom of the Royal Irish Industries Association at Grafton Street, Dublin ('By Special Appointment to H.M. King Edward VII and H.R.H. Princess of Wales').

While the Protestant grandee Cuffe, as president of the IIDA, was afforded a measure of (sometimes grudging) respect, Catholic nationalists such as D. P. Moran had no time for the Royal Irish Industries Association. 'Yet another annual meeting of the Society plaything, the Royal Irish Industries Association, was held recently at Lincoln Place',[32] wrote *The Leader* contemptuously of the association in September 1906. In such opinion, this was development from without, and its efforts were dismissed as patronising and infantilising.

IV

The tradition of the philanthropic purchase and the moral bargain informed both the marketing of cottage industries by the social elite and calls to

Figure 1.5 Advertisement for the Royal Irish Industries Association, Grafton Street, Dublin (1907): 'Irish Hand Embroideries and Real Lace Robes'. Courtesy of the Gjenvick-Gjonvick Archives.

buy goods made by members of the urban working class. Advertisements for city co-operatives not infrequently appealed to Irish (and sometimes to class) solidarity. The manner in which the Belfast Tailors Co-Partnership and the Dublin Tailors Co-Partnership pitched their wares in the first decade of the twentieth century is a good example. These organisations, 'set up' – as the *Freeman's Journal* put it in 1908 – to 'provid[e] working men [...] and especially trade unionists with cheap clothes' (and to 'oust the products of the foreign sweating firms'),[33] were productive societies in the manner of the Co-operative Wholesale Society in Great Britain. Their plain-speaking marketing in nationalist journals consistently targeted national economic feeling, particularly among the members of the Gaelic League. An advertisement for the Dublin Co-Partnership which appeared in *The Leader* of 29 August 1903, for instance, directly appeals to the men and women of Conradh na Gaeilge:

> Gaelic Leaguers and all those interested in giving Irishmen employment should patronise the above Establishment, where they will not only get Irish Materials and trimmings, but all orders will be executed by local labour.

In the following January, in *An Claidheamh Soluis*, the Belfast crowd also set out their stall, in addressing devotees of 'Industrial Revival':

> AN APPEAL TO GAELIC LEAGUERS AND ALL THOSE WHO BELIEVE IN A REAL IRISH INDUSTRIAL REVIVAL.
>
> Patronise the Belfast Tailors' Co-Partnership Limited, where all Garments are made in their own specially fitted Workshops where NEITHER SWEATED OR FOREIGN LABOUR is employed...
>
> SPECIALITIES!
>
> Irish Tweed & Serge Suits from 50s. 0d.
> Irish Tweed & Serge Trousers from 13s. 6d.
> Irish Tweed & Serge Overcoats from 40s. 0d.
> NOTE ADDRESS: 5 Bridge Street, Belfast.

Patronising the Tailor's Co-Partnership was one way in which the Gaelic Leaguer could help the honest artisan, the co-operative implied, and expedite a key task of the league – that of making, in the words of the Reverend Joseph Guinan, 'the shop-keeper more business-like and the manufacturer more pushing and self-advertising after the manner of his foreign competitor'.[34]

Moran's *The Leader* declared on 20 February 1904 that 'We want industry in Ireland, but we don't want sweating', and the sentiment was echoed in advertising copy. The Belfast collective declared, as we have seen, that they employed 'NEITHER SWEATED OR FOREIGN LABOUR'. It may be that 'foreign' might be code for 'Jewish' here. Notwithstanding their appeal on behalf of the labours of the Irish working man, less appetising to the modern taste is the twin co-partnerships' xenophobia, even racism. In *The Leader* in 1904, the Dublin company saluted the quality of its 'Suits of Irish material at Moderate Prices'. 'All Garments [are] made in our own Workshops by Irish tailors' it declared: 'Irishmen, help us to stamp out sweated, Jewish labour in the Tailoring Trade in Dublin'.[35] In the same year the Belfast shop boasted that all of its produce was fashioned by Irishmen rather than 'Sweated or Jewish labour', which, they tartly maintained, was 'mostly the case with those advertising Home Manufacture'. The darker side of national economic identity was this forthright prejudice, which echoes contemporary campaigns against Jewish immigrants in the East End of London. It was also evident in a 1904 advertisement in *An Claidheamh Soluis* for another bargain tailors, the Cash Tailoring Company of Capel Street:

> NAILING A LIE. £50 CHALLENGE
>
> Several Gaelic Leaguers and others having complained to us recently that they were informed we employ Jewish labour, we now offer the above to any person who can prove that we are not an exclusively Irish firm, with Irish capital, Irish Management, and employing none but Irish labour.
>
> NOTE – ONLY ADDRESS: THE IRISH TWEED HOUSE
>
> The Cash Tailoring Co.
> 4 Capel Street, Dublin
> And Branch: 50 Upr. George's Street, Dunleary.

The notion of 'sweated labour' in the nineteenth-century clothing industry brings to mind Thomas Hood's famous political poem, 'The Song of the Shirt' (1843), which movingly articulates the suffering of a worn-out seamstress paid a pittance for her piece-meal work:

> With fingers weary and worn,
> With eyelids heavy and red,
> A woman sat, in unwomanly rags,
> Plying her needle and thread –
> Stitch! stitch! stitch!
> In poverty, hunger, and dirt,
> And still with the voice of dolorous pitch
> She sang the 'Song of the Shirt!'

This poem prompted an opportunistic Irish advertiser in the early 1900s to provide a 'New "Song of the Shirt"' (Figure 1.6) to advertise the outfitting firm of A. Leonard, Cavan, which, Leonard declared, were not 'made by any "sweated" labour, but honestly done by the best workers I can find':

Figure 1.6 Advertisement for A. Leonard, Cavan (1906): 'The "New Song of the Shirt" '.

In Leonard's drollery, a poem of political protest is pressed into the service of selling Irish products; the needlewoman's suffering is forgotten in the striking contrast between the images raised by the banner and the comic anti-climax of the puff.

There were other politically resonant but less jocular advertisements for Irish shirts in this period, notably those for a co-operative society founded in late 1901, the Sligo Manufacturing Society Ltd, which began production of shirts in the following year. The next advertisement, a 'puff collateral',[36] or hidden advertisement, dates from 1903:

> EMIGRATION, AND HOW TO STOP IT.
>
> 413,516 persons emigrated from Ireland during the ten years ending 1902. This state of affairs is simply appalling, and if emigration continues at the same rate, within the next 100 years Ireland will then be uninhabited.
>
> The Sligo Manufacturing Society Ltd. started operations as manufacturers of coloured shirts in the summer of 1902, to lend a hand in putting a stop to this drain. It is the plain duty of the people of Ireland to buy

> Shirts made by Irish girls, provided that they are of equal quality and as cheap as imported goods, as we claim that our Shirts are.
>
> All of our Shirts bear our stamped label 'SLIGO FACTORY'. Sligo-made Shirts should be obtainable from Drapers in every town and village in the kingdom. By asking for them, and seeing that you get them, you will lend a hand in putting a stop to the tide of Emigration.
>
> NOTE – IRISH MADE SHIRTINGS A SPECIALITY.

The eye-catching banner offering a cure for the Irish scourge of emigration, though plainly intended to arrest the reader's attention, nonetheless accurately reflected the aims of the Sligo Manufacturing Society, which was explicitly established – as its advertisement put it – 'to lend a hand in putting a stop to this drain' of emigration. Its founder, Sir Josslyn Gore-Booth (who had previously established the Drumcliffe Creamery, Co-operative Agricultural and Dairy Society in 1895),[37] declared in a December 1901 speech that 'Our factory must tend to keep here some of the young people who are at present fleeing to the big cities across the waters.'

Proving that patriotism had different ways of expressing itself among the Anglo-Irish, as, indeed, it did among the Roman Catholic community, the reformist Sir Josslyn was, of course, the brother of Eva Gore-Booth and the revolutionary Countess Markievicz. The society was organised, as Jacqueline Van Voris, one of Constance Markievicz's biographers, notes, 'with the applause of the Trades Union Council',[38] and Gore-Booth recruited numerous small shareholders to it. (The *Celtic Review* described the venture in 1905 as 'a plucky and promising effort to bring co-operative principles into town'.)[39] Gore-Booth, in the Sligo speech, saw mutual good for capital and labour in the principle of 'co-operation', which he declared 'tends to conciliate the conflicting interest of the capitalist and the worker through an equitable division amongst them of the fund called profit'. 'Under the rules' of the manufacturing society, he went on, 'if profit [was] made, they proposed to pay capital a fair dividend, and to divide the balance to workers'.[40] Yet again the hinterland of Irish advertising was charged with a clear ideological resonance.

V

Many miles south of Sligo, in Wexford, there was another Irish company which used striking advertising copy. This was the Pierce Ironworks Foundry, which had been established in the town in 1839 by James Pierce, and which ran memorable nationalistic advertising campaigns in the early twentieth century on behalf of its goods. This firm began as a manufacturer of farm machinery ('If you desire perfection in any class of Machine or Implement required on a Farm, Go Straight for PIERCE'S!' ran a 1906 advertisement), and for decades it was one of the most notable of the country's newly emergent industrial companies. (At the celebrations held at the company's centenary in April 1939, Dr James Ryan, then Free State Minister for Agriculture, praised 'the firm's high position in the industrial life of Ireland'.[41])

In 1903, a sister company, the Pierce Bicycle Works, was established alongside the agricultural implements workshop, and this produced and sold bicycles until 1941. The new vehicles were launched in a flurry of advertising which saluted the excellence of Pierce's products and stressed their status as Irish goods. Either way, Pierce's copy firmly, if unsubtly, positioned the company within the Irish industries continuum. A 1904 advertisement, for instance, saluted its Victor bike: 'The voice of intelligent Ireland trumpets the Pierce Victor! – The Pierce Victor has no equal!' The same notice pillories 'a few backboneless shouting supporters, not of Irish industry, but of American Shoddy, which lasts a year of two and is gone'. Buyers of imported goods are here derided as industrial fifth columnists rather than as consumers exercising a choice, and Irish sportsmen loyal to foreign bicycles portrayed as spineless traitors to the noble cause of Ireland. In effect, filling the coffers of the Pierce family is presented as a patriotic duty.

Perhaps it was this winning self-confidence in the superiority of their products that took Pierce's to the Irish Industrial Exhibition, which was mounted as part of the World's Fair held in the land of inferior bicycles

Figure 1.7 Advertisement for Pierce's farm machinery and bicycles (1904): 'Pierce's Stand, Belfast'.

at St Louis, Missouri, in 1904.[42] Alongside a display of agricultural machinery ('Mowers and Reapers, Threshing Machines, Horse Gears, Patent Steel Two-Fork Rakes, Turnip and Mangle Seed Sowers'),[43] where every one was a prize-winner – at least in the company's account – Pierce's displayed its range of bicycles. These were 'IRELAND'S ONLY IRISH-MADE BICYCLES', as a banner, reinforced by a pointing finger, has it in Figure 1.7, which shows a May 1904 *Irish Independent* advertisement for Pierce's shop in Belfast (which also crows about the American success of the company).

'Not Cheap Rubbish', said the copywriter; no, only the best and most Irish of bicycles, sporting machines now so fashionable that they had seen off the 'shoddy' produce of the USA. Indeed, Pierce's, with their successful Parisian shop, could even teach the French themselves new levels of sporting sophistication. In copy such as this, the Irish cultural genuflections of the 1850s and 1860s were no more.

Three years later, in April 1907, Pierce published an advertisement which explicitly appealed to the constituency of 'Irish Ireland Industrial Revivalists' (Figure 1.8).

Figure 1.8 Advertisement for Pierce's farm machinery and bicycles (1907): 'Pierce's, Wexford... Irish Ireland Industrial Revivalists Take Special Note'.

'All that can be done by the people has not yet been achieved'; the phrase reads like a contemporaneous banner in *The Leader* or *Sinn Féin* or, later, a call-to-arms for the Irish Volunteers. Pierce's, while appealing to 'Irish Ireland Industrial Revivalists', here simultaneously invokes national revival in an explicitly ideological manner. Irish advertising has said 'all that can be said about Irish Manufacture'. The shift from the previous decades' valorisation of 'foreign' goods is clearly evident here. In his speech 'The Necessity for De-Anglicising Ireland', Douglas Hyde recalled that, formerly, 'if the products of Irish hands and Irish brains were to find a market they had to come back with the hall mark of London or Paris on them'. 'Today', he declared enthusiastically, 'we are rearing and raising a race of men whose one object will be that the article that they buy shall bear the hall mark of "Made in Ireland" '.[44]

Part II

Print Culture

2
The Shan Van Vocht (1896–1899) and *The Leader* (1900–1936): National Identity in Advertising

A good newspaper... is a nation talking to itself

Arthur Miller (interview in the *Observer*, 26 November 1961)

In late nineteenth- and early twentieth-century Irish newspapers and periodicals, we can identify a relationship between contemporary print culture and the sense of an emerging nationhood. As we saw in Chapter 1, various permutations of nationalist support filtered into consumer culture during the Irish Revival, informed by the Home Rule campaign, the Literary Revival, the Gaelic League, constitutional nationalism and more militant separatism. Such advertising, indeed, offers an insight into the subtle variances at work under the umbrella of the national cause. During the 1890s and early 1900s, when cultural nationalism was at its zenith, with debates surrounding Irish Ireland and the Gaelic League highly topical, there was a perceptible preoccupation with national identity in many Irish periodicals and, indeed, the advertising material present in those publications. This chapter offers a comparative study of two of the key journals within the nationalist tradition: *The Shan Van Vocht* (1896–1899) and *The Leader* (1900–1936), the former much preoccupied with the role of women in nationalism and the other characterised by a certain hypermasculinity.

I

The Shan Van Vocht ('The Poor Old Woman') was a relatively short-lived but influential advanced nationalist journal published in Belfast, under the editorship of Alice Milligan and Anna Johnston (the latter wrote as a poet under the pseudonym 'Ethna Carbery'). The periodical was described by Maud Gonne as 'that daring little paper',[1] and, more recently, it has come to be seen as 'a pivotal nationalist newspaper'.[2] Though the notion of the virtuous old woman as a symbol of Ireland goes back to medieval Irish traditions, such as the Cailleach Bhéirre,[3] according to Richard Harp the journal took its title from a patriotic song 'written on the occasion of the French fleet sailing for Ireland in 1796 to support local uprisings'. The masthead of *The Shan Van Vocht* was – again in Harp's words – 'a sunrise, suggestive of a new beginning in Irish independence'.[4] The journal was established in 1896 by these two Belfast literary women: Milligan, whose father was a Presbyterian minister, and Johnston, the Catholic daughter of a Belfast timber merchant.[5] Literary in nature, it featured stories, serialised fiction and nationally inflected poems (such as the verses in honour of 'Kathleen Ny-Houlahan' published in March 1899).[6] *The Shan Van Vocht* (in English and – some – Irish),[7] alongside its journalism and explicitly political content, featured a select number of advertisements, often relating to Irish themes. Few advertisements featured in the early issues, but gradually they expanded to fill approximately three pages at the rear of the paper. By 1898, the journal's advertisements had diversified; alongside simple announcements of new publications and stockists of *The Shan Van Vocht,* there were also themed United Irishmen centenary commercial features, including 'The '98 Calendar', which was iconically 'harp-shaped' (and available for purchase from 'L. McKay, The Irish Depot, 4 Bridge Street, Belfast'),[8] and 'The Gaelic League '98 Handkerchief', which featured a 'harp, Celtic border and motto in Gaelic'.[9]

In mythological terms, the figure of the Shan Van Vocht is representative of the iconic, virtuous and nationalist old woman, part of a set of images of a feminised Ireland prevalent during the nineteenth and early twentieth centuries. Indeed, L. Perry Curtis Jnr maintains that the golden age of Erin or Hibernia's representation was the late nineteenth century,[10] where she adorned 'every kind of artefact including commercial cards, china, silverware, harps and monuments or memorials honouring the heroes and martyrs of the long struggle for independence from Brian Boru to Wolfe Tone and beyond'.[11] This focus on ideal Irish womanhood, which 'possessed all the qualities associated with male fantasies of the ideal wife or lover for whom any patriot should be prepared to die',[12] was not enacted only in literature or on the stage.[13] It was also present, as Curtis's list demonstrates, in consumer products, and was evident in the advertising columns of *The Shan Van Vocht.*

The paradox here, in some critical opinion, is that such iconographies are in direct contrast to the actual power women wielded in Irish society. Anne McClintock writes that 'Excluded from direct action as national citizens, women [were] subsumed symbolically in the national body politic [...] Women are typically constructed as bearers of the nation, but are denied any relation to national agency.'[14] As we will see, this notion of a disempowered Mother Ireland was crucial to *The Shan Van Vocht*'s intellectual position.

The feminised image of the nation's struggle reflects *The Shan Van Vocht* itself, and not simply its title. Alice Milligan's main agenda in the journal was not to agitate for female suffrage but, rather, to discuss how women in their existing roles could contribute to the cause of Ireland. She was convinced that male-led agitation and action were not always effective, and that a more feminine approach to conciliation might have a better effect: 'To [women] is entrusted the moulding of the minds of the growing generations of the Irish race, and they should exercise their influence so that [...] those who are to work for Ireland in the new era should be able to do so untrammelled by old feuds and hatreds.'[15] Clearly, in common with much conventional nationalist iconography of the period, Milligan viewed women as inherently 'more spiritual and less worldly than men',[16] and she implied that they were above party factionalism and petty divisions.

However, one of the ways in which Milligan envisaged women making a practical contribution to the nation was through consumer culture, as she wrote in *The Shan Van Vocht* in 1898: the 'native housewives of Ireland could do more for the revival of trade and manufacture than any Government or titled patronesses' by purchasing Irish-made goods to support the home economy.[17] A woman in the home, although disenfranchised from the vote and the constitutional process, would be able to contribute to the national cause by shunning goods of English manufacture. At the same time, however, there is some irony in the fact that while Milligan was advising the rejection of English commodities, her journal occasionally took advertisements from British companies, such as the London-based Tower Tea Company ('Tower Tea. 1/6, 1/8. 1/10. 2/-. 2/4. 2/6. 2/8. The Best and Cheapest Tea in the World at the Price. Ask your Grocer for it. Agents appointed by Tower Tea Ltd, 5 Jewry Street, London EC'). Should Ireland co-operate with England when it suits her to do so, or reject the country completely? Constitutionalism or open rebellion? Though Alice Milligan was separatist and republican by conviction, the tactical need for a consensus nationalist politics was another matter and the journal never settled such issues, representing instead a plethora of opinion on national concerns. Karen Steele sees this as a sign of its inherently dialogic status: '[it was] marked by an unstable discourse to which editors, authors, and the public could speak and respond'.[18]

In terms of readership, the journal had a predominantly middle-class following, with subscribers from Belfast, Dublin, New York and London.[19] Its advertising had a clear bourgeois register that reflected this particular audience: in 1898, for instance, visitors or 'tourists' in Belfast were invited to visit 'Wightman & Co' at 5, Garfield Street, Belfast, to scrutinise their 'Irish Marble and other Souvenir Jewellery'. At the same time there is a clear ideological resonance here as the souvenirs depicted were for the celebration of the centenary of 1798 (Figure 2.1).[20] The appeal to disposable income, and to

Figure 2.1 Advertisement for Wightman & Co. (1898): 'Irish Marble and other Souvenir Jewellery'.

leisure time as a 'tourist', in such advertising clearly signals the middle-class consumer.[21] Similarly, in *The Shan Van Vocht*, 'Ristona' paints, in gold, silver and lustre, were advertised by the Belfast firm M'Caw, Stevenson and Orr, Ltd as having been used 'with splendid results on Costumes used in Tableaux Vivants, &c.'[22] Again the appeal to a leisured class with a disposable income. In 1897 *The Shan Van Vocht* carried an advertisement for 'Imperial & Windsor Hotels',[23] names which seem to jar with the declared nationalist ethos of the journal, but were completely in accord with the consumerist and class discourse of the paper. As Steele has noted, 'Whereas the *Irish Worker*, in 1911, advertised thrifty or union-allied venders, such as Larkin's Little Shop for Good Value, *the Shan Van Vocht* featured notices inviting readers to stay at the Imperial & Windsor Hotels or the "Prince of Wales Hotel and First-Rate Restaurant".'[24]

While the readership of *The Shan Van Vocht* extended beyond Ireland to the Irish diaspora abroad, one significant feature is how frequently Belfast companies were represented in it (in sharp contrast to *The Leader*, for instance). Indeed, much of the consumerist focus related to Ulster. Among the advertisers taking space in the journal were the Belfast Gaelic League, 'Abraham Neill, Castalia Mills, Belfast', purveyor of flours and oatmeals; Andrew Macguire of 15 North Street, Belfast (who sold 'sashes, badges, band caps, band uniforms' of 'Genuine Irish Manufacture'); the Belfast bookseller J. Shone and Co.; and John Magee & Co., The Homespun Depot, Donegal (in the province of Ulster but to become part of the Free State under Partition), who advertised under the banner 'encourage home industry'.[25] Conversely, E. & W. Pim (of Belfast and Bangor, Co. Down) made a point of stating that they supplied 'customers in England, Scotland and Wales', for which carriage might be paid weekly, fortnightly or monthly,[26] suggesting a very different set of geographical alliances. Even the relatively short advertising pages of *The Shan Van Vocht* present a multivocal array of political and national allegiances, competing for the reader's attention and the buyer's loyalty. This accommodation of differing ideological viewpoints was the cornerstone of the journal's own political ethos.

II

Alice Milligan published *The Life of Theobald Wolfe Tone* in 1898, and one of the foremost aims of her newspaper was to heighten awareness of the centenary of 1798. As the declared aim of *The Shan Van Vocht* was to revive and maintain interest in revolutionary nationalism in the context of the centennial celebrations, Milligan's vision of 1798, which frequently informed the advertising and the articles of her newspaper, was, in Karen Steele's opinion, 'a popular, if selective memory [...] one shared by other Protestant nationalists such as Yeats and Gregory. In Milligan's mind, the eighteenth-century society united patriots and poets, Catholics and Protestants, southerners and northerners, the wealthy and the poor.'[27] As her aim was a measure of national unity, Milligan often edited out the more contentious aspects of the nationalist agenda. Virginia Crossman has noted that this tendency towards inclusivity meant that when Milligan published the eighteenth-century version of the song which gave her journal its name, a song which anticipates a French invasion to aid Irish republicans and destroy the Orange Order, she removed references to the Orangemen, and foreign intervention was represented in less inflammatory terms (America, not France, is the 'land of liberty').[28] But perhaps this was itself Toneian, given that Wolfe Tone's declared national ethos, as Declan Kiberd has pointed out, was founded in contradiction:

> He found in the nation a concept to reconcile individual energy and transcendent tasks, a notion vast enough to hold contrasting elements. He could conceive of Ireland as a nation uniting Catholic, Protestant and Dissenter because he himself had in a few years traversed society: a coachmaker's son turned gentleman-scholar of Trinity College Dublin, a Protestant lawyer turned Catholic propagandist, a former empire man become a republican militant.[29]

In essence, Milligan and *The Shan Van Vocht* itself were delicately trying to negotiate several competing forms of Irish nationalism: radical republican, constitutional, northern, southern, socialist and provide a platform of expression for each of these without necessarily committing to their principles (beyond the very broad aspiration of a free Ireland).

As a number of critics have remarked,[30] the aims and aspirations of the 1798 centenary were belied and undermined by the heterogeneous and divergent loyalties of many of the participants. As Steele noted, 'The beliefs and methods of the non-sectarian United Irishmen strongly shaped the editorial content of *The Shan Van Vocht*.'[31] Often, however, the practice seems distinctly more complex than the theory. In July 1898, as Crossman has shown, Milligan herself, despite her Presbyterian upbringing, commented that the Presbyterians of Derry are 'not Irish [...] they are colonists from

England and Scotland [...] there were all sorts of people in Ireland who had no right to be there'.[32] Such contradictions were also something to which others were subject. For instance, the author of the famous 'Who Fears to Speak of '98?', the Young Irelander John Kells Ingram, while not repudiating his own poem, declared that he had 'no sympathy with those who preach sedition in our own day, when all the circumstances are radically altered'.[33] Such subtleties and ambiguities are essential to understanding the ensuing tensions and hostilities which complicated the 1798 centenary celebrations. Timothy J. O'Keefe has written that:

> The United Irishmen centennial became the subject of political controversy which demeaned the nationalist cause and imperilled the celebration itself [...] this patriotic manifestation soon became the object of intense squabbling among Ireland's contending political factions. Instead of demonstrating the unity and commitment of the nationalists, it was to illustrate vividly the divisions and rancor of Irish political life at the end of the nineteenth century.[34]

John O'Leary, the president of the provisional committee for the centenary, initially introduced a strong advanced nationalist flavour to that body, but it soon became such a seductive and, indeed, powerful organisation that the Parliamentarians (of both Parnellite and anti-Parnellite inclination) attempted to flood the movement with their own men.[35] In the meantime, a London branch of centenary celebrants, chaired by W. B. Yeats, maintained that the Dublin committee 'violated basic democratic principles'[36] and, indeed, Alice Milligan herself waded into the foray by claiming that the Dublin organisers were 'in the contemptible position of making the '98 Executive the basis of a Redmondite and Healyite alliance'.[37] Milligan found that women were often excluded from centenary meetings and as a consequence founded the Women's Centenary Union in Belfast in 1897, asking in *The Shan Van Vocht*: 'Is it too much to ask [...] that the women of Ireland, who are not called on to have any opinion whatever as to who has the right to speak for Ireland in the British Parliament, should form that Union which a historic occasion demands?'[38]

Milligan argued that the United Irishmen saw 'the future liberty of Ireland depended upon the abolition of creed distinctions and the promotion of union amongst all whose homes were in the land'.[39] However, despite the idealist appeals to unity and anti-sectarianism both in her role in the centenary of 1798 and in her journal, the commemoration events in Ulster to some extent heightened divisions in the community.[40] However, for many nationalists the 1798 uprising remained 'a powerful symbol of Ireland's melancholy history under British rule'.[41] One of the cornerstones of the celebrations was the cult of the dead: processions to the graves of dead heroes, the erection of monuments, the public presentation of wreaths, all fed into the Irish nationalist trope of memory. Indeed, 'the clubs engaged in a series of ritualized patriotic activities that imitated Roman Catholic religious devotions'.[42] Veneration of a patron or fallen hero,[43] attention to his martyrdom, focus on relics and pilgrimages to his grave all became a part of centenary practice.[44]

The various consumerist tokens sold for the 1798 commemoration events, as advertised in *The Shan Van Vocht*, reflect this much broader cultural impetus. The role of memorial, which was central to the philosophical ethos of the 1798 celebrations, also informed the advertising culture and memorial paraphernalia which surrounded the event. Wightman & Co.'s advertisement for Centenary Jewellery in *The Shan Van Vocht* is a case in point. The copy promises that such items will be 'a substantial and lasting Memento of the Centenary'. Rings in silver and gold were inscribed with the famous invocation 'Remember '98', with the name of the club affiliation, while the 'Wolfe Tone' coin charm also venerated the heroic dead.[45] Consider the 'Wolfe Tone Souvenir', also produced by Wightman & Co. (Figure 2.2).[46] Here the jewellers noted that they had received a few pieces of the block of stone from the sculptor, O'Neill, who cut the foundation stone of the Wolfe Tone monument in Belfast, and had fashioned them into commemorative charms, pins and brooches. Time and again the reader was invited to purchase a 'relic' of the event in order to demonstrate veneration of the fallen hero. (More generally, another advertisement from the same firm invited purchasers to buy Christmas presents of crosses, shamrock scarf pins and Gaelic name brooches (with variants featuring a round tower, a harp or shamrocks) under the sales pitch of 'Special Value and Chaste Jewellery'.[47])

The political inflection of the Wolfe Tone pendant and brooches is reminiscent of Miss Ivors in Joyce's short story 'The Dead', who wears a 'large brooch' on the front of her dress bearing an 'Irish device',[48] a commodity which aligns her with nationalist politics and implied refusal of participation in the English market. Indeed, some 1798 clubs (such as the Oliver Bond Club in Dublin) encouraged the wearing of Irish clothing, and the

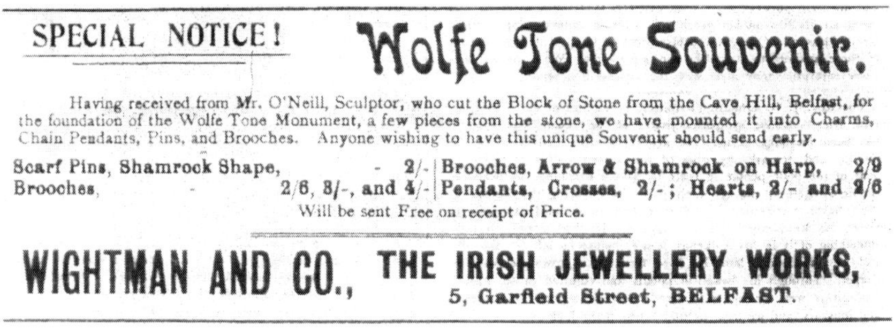

Figure 2.2 Advertisement for Wightman & Co. (1898): 'Wolfe Tone Souvenir'.

use of Irish music, airs and language, at their functions and commemorative events in order to curb English influence.[49] Such practice suggests how advertising material in *The Shan Van Vocht* sometimes shared the ideology of the 1798 celebrations.

III

The Shan Van Vocht also carried Irish language material; a poem by 'Mac' (probably Seumas MacManus), '*Is binn beul na thosdh*' ('The silent month is melodious'), from a Gaelic aphorism, featured in an early issue of 1896,[50] as did Irish-language advertising for *Fainne-an-Lae,* a bilingual penny weekly published under the auspices of the Gaelic League.[51] The very title *The Shan Van Vocht* is an anglicisation of *An t-Sean Bhean Bhocht,* as the Irish subtitle of the journal made clear on the title page of each issue. Of course, in itself, this is a central irony of the Gaelic League's campaign to rejuvenate the language: to ensure that Irish cultural nationalist material appealed to a wide audience, the dominant language (English) had to be employed alongside Irish until such a time as the nation spoke the 'native' tongue. Douglas Hyde touched on this issue tangentially in 'The Necessity for De-Anglicising Ireland' (1892): 'The Irish race is at present in a most anomalous position, imitating England and yet apparently hating it. How can it produce anything good in literature, art, or institutions as long as it is actuated by motives so contradictory?'[52] *The Shan Van Vocht* declared, in an article entitled 'The Irish Language', that 'the preservation of the language of the Nation would under ordinary circumstances be a National duty – under existing circumstances it is an imperative national duty'.[53] In part, this issue of language usage negotiated various problems of audience as Ireland approached the turn of the century – how was it possible to sell a nationalist, Irish language newspaper or journal if only a select number of Irish Revivalists and *Gaeltacht* speakers could realistically purchase and consume such material?

Despite its declared nationalist aims, *The Shan Van Vocht,* as we have seen, was not above accepting advertising copy from English firms. The plain text advert quoted above for 'Tower Tea' (so named because the company's business address, Jewry Street, was in close proximity to the Tower of London) offered 'The Best and Cheapest Tea in the World'[54] and competed for attention with other Irish-made items on the same page. Karen Steele maintains that *The Shan Van Vocht*'s advertisements 'especially appealed to consumers who viewed each simple purchase as a political act aimed at Irish economic and cultural independence from Great Britain',[55] but this advertisement is clear evidence that more complex economic and political issues were also at work. As Steele notes, the maintenance of solid revenue for the newspaper was a constant concern, and 'moderate advertising' was sought to keep *The Shan Van Vocht* afloat.[56] Essentially, a complex nexus of competing nationalisms (cultural, moderate, separatist, advanced or militant), accompanied by simple financial need, meant that, ultimately, the advertising pages of *The Shan Van Vocht* became an ideologically contentious space.

This notion of competing ideologies informed the enterprise of the whole newspaper. Consider its handling of James Connolly, the socialist and working-class campaigner whose memory was secured in nationalist mythology by his prominence in the 1916 Easter Rising. When he contributed to *The Shan Van Vocht* in 1897, the journal qualified his opinions by adding the following separatist and parliamentary abstentionist coda to his piece: 'Whilst in full sympathy with Mr Connolly's views on the labour and social questions, we are absolutely opposed to the scheme he puts forward for the formation of an Irish Republican Party in the British Parliament. Any conscientious Republican would stick at the oath of allegiance.'[57] Here, as per the advertising pages of the newspaper, the editorial material of *The Shan Van Vocht* clearly articulates a dialogue regarding competing nationalisms. One of the central focuses of this issue was how far political and economic negotiation with Britain could be countenanced; the advertising pages of *The Shan Van Vocht* carefully stage the conflicts and dialogues inherent in the precarious post-Parnell nationalism of the time, when supporters were re-evaluating their strategies and tactics for independence.

IV

In 1899 *The Shan Van Vocht* ceased circulation, and its subscribers thenceforth accepted delivery of Arthur Griffith's *The United Irishman* instead.[58] In some ways, this might be seen as marking a transfer of gendered ideology from the feminine 'Poor Old Woman' to the 'Irishman' of Griffith's title, a masculinity which was also the cornerstone of D. P. Moran's variety of nationalism, which is found in *The Leader* (1930–1936) and elsewhere.

Moran had a gift for publicity. From its early days, *The Leader* portrayed itself as a great success, frequently reporting that it had sold out and that its print run was increasing. The journal attracted a wealth of advertisers (the *United Irishman* attracted far less revenue), and even carried advertisements for the Abbey Theatre while berating Abbey productions in its editorial columns. (As Patrick Maume points out, this success was initially due in no small part to Kevin J. Kenny, who was later to build one of the largest advertising agencies in Dublin, acting as Moran's business manager.[59]) While many nationalist journals were suppressed during the First World War,[60] *The Leader* escaped this fate until 1919, when it published an advertisement for Dáil Éireann bonds. Papers featuring this advertisement were suppressed, and publication was only allowed to continue if Moran agreed to refrain from such behaviour in future. He refused, and *The New Leader* was launched six weeks later.[61]

In the first edition of *The Leader*, published on 1 September 1900, Moran set out his prospectus for the journal:

> Today, for the first time, we present the Anglo-Irish public with an independent weekly, review, written from first to last from exclusively Irish standpoints [...] To us [a nation] means a self-governing land, living, moving and having its being in its own language, self-reliant, intellectually as well as politically independent, initiating its own reforms, developing its own manners and customs, creating its own literature out of its own distinctive consciousness, working to their fullest capacity the material resources of the country, inventing, criticising, attempting and doing [...] We do not desire to go back to the past: we simply want to re-establish our communications with it in order that we may go forward in a manner racy of the soil.[62]

Moran's definition of 'racy of the soil' here warrants attention. It was a phrase taken from Thomas Davis, who set out the objectives of *The Nation* thus: 'to create and foster public opinion, and make it racy of the soil'. In Moran's logic, to be 'racy of the soil' would not imply a union of Catholic and Protestant (which was Davis's declared aim). For him, Irish identity was indivisibly Gaelic and Catholic, and quite plainly did not include what he referred to as 'the Planter': 'we must allow at once that an aristocracy and society, more or less alien in blood and almost exclusively alien in feeling, is a great stumbling block to the growth and development of character racy of the soil'. There is a clear and arguably reductive alignment here between the non-'Gaelic' community, illegitimacy and 'alien' influences.[63] Irishness was an essential category in this account, and had to be rooted in the land. Being explicitly Gaelic (unadulterated by the 'coloniser'), it had also to assert a Catholic devotional identity. Daniel Corkery, using the pseudonym 'Lee', summed up this monocultural point of view in *The Leader* in 1906: 'I hold Catholicism to be a quality essential to Irish nationality [...] when the Irish nation comes to stand four-square up before the world, it is a Catholic nation that the world will behold.'[64] In July 1901, Moran himself declared that 'any genuine non-Catholic Irish nationalist must become reconciled to Catholic development or throw in his lot with the other side [...] The Irish nation is *de facto* a Catholic nation.'

The union of Catholic religion and Irish nation endorsed by *The Leader*[65] also featured in its advertising columns. C. Bull, Ltd, of Suffolk Street, Dublin, for instance, advertised in *The Leader* in 1921 their 'Irish Manufactured Prayer Books. Catholic Piety, Garden of the Soul, Imitation of Christ, Kingdom of God, Key of Heaven.'[66] Similarly, Catholic notices in *The Leader* frequently advertised lectures, or novenas of masses and prayers dedicated to Our Lady of Lourdes, or clerical tailoring from the Henry Street Warehouse.[67] Missions to China, or women's retreats, also featured extensively in the paper's pages.[68] Another advertisement – bearing a large Celtic cross – announced a 'Grand Fete in Aid of Our Lady's Hospice, Harold's Cross, July 8th to 15th, 1920'.[69] The advertising agency and publishers Eason and Son marketed devotional books to readers, such as *The Manual of Catholic Piety*, which was 'printed and bound in Ireland',[70] while the Kelly Brothers offered the finest 'Pure Altar Wine, Sweet, Medium or Dry'.[71]

As Lisa Godson remarks, the nineteenth century in Ireland saw the mass consumption of devotional items, 'with the growth of wholesale and retail businesses dedicated to selling these objects'.[72] These businesses publicised their wares in nationalist journals, with *The Leader* carrying many such announcements. In 1904, for instance, the periodical carried advertisements for 'The Catholic Scholar's Introduction to English Literature by A. H. Mathew', published by James Duffy & Co., Ltd.[73] The Catholic Truth Society announced its second annual conference in the pages of *The Leader*, clearly perceiving a captive Catholic readership in its audience,[74] while the oculist, Patrick Cahill, proudly proclaimed in 1904 that he had 'the sole privilege of supplying his late Holiness, Pope Leo XIII for many years with Spectacles' and 'had the further honour conferred on him of receiving a command from Rome to make Glasses for His Holiness Pope Pius X'. Finally, the Christian Brothers sought attendance at their 'Tailltean Bazaar & Fete, in aid of Christian Brothers Schools, James Street and Golden Bridge, August 9th to 15th, 1904' with more than a hint of Gaelic Catholic nationalism marking the event.[75] In the context of *The Leader*'s advertising (which soon filled up to eight pages of the paper), these religious items also acquired a political context. Here Christmas cards were marketed as 'Topical, National, Religious', being 'Gaelic and Bilingual' and 'Produced in Ireland'.[76]

This tripartite alignment of Irishness (Catholic religion, Irish language and nationalism) was something for which Moran campaigned indefatigably. Both his editorial and his advertising pages mark a departure from Alice Milligan's bid to bring together all the differing permutations of nationalism and religion under a broader campaign of national good. There were other important divisions between the two editors. Unlike Milligan and her valorisation of 1798 in *The Shan Van Vocht,* Moran was quite explicit about his censure of Irish nationalism's recourse to history. In *The Philosophy of Irish Ireland* (1905), he expressed his chagrin as follows: 'The '98 processions are a grand intoxication and no more. What, after all, was the great Wolfe Tone demonstration significant of?'[77] He continued his objections in forthright manner. Wolfe Tone, it seems, was no Irishman:

> The United Irishman Movement was organised and led by men of the Pale. It produced many noble men. When we consider his opportunities there are few more masculine characters than Theobald Wolfe Tone. But the truth remains that he was not an Irishman. He was a great Irish rebel; not more extreme, however, than the Bishop of Derry, who was English

> born and bred. If I were asked to define Tone's nationality I should say that he was a Frenchman born in Ireland of English parents.[78]

Here the nationalist canon is rewritten to accommodate Moran's notion of authentic Irishness. He also quite plainly rejected physical force nationalism – 'Fenianism did a lot of damage to Ireland. It implanted the secret society virus into the national blood'[79] – preferring to support, with qualifications, Home Rule and the development of Irish agriculture and industry alongside that of Gaelic culture. Indeed, Moran was keen to show that the Gaelic Revival alone could not renew the nation. Economic development was needed as a simultaneous goal, and this is, as we will see, clearly reflected in the advertising material of *The Leader.*

V

D. P. Moran's solutions to Irish ills were economically inflected. In common with Yeats, he saw the peasant as the repository of authentic Irishness, saying that 'the ignorant peasants are the most interesting portions of the population'.[80] However, at the same time he also advocated, at least in part, an awareness of market-driven forces and the need for pragmatic economics. His metaphors are sometimes filtered through this discourse, as in *The Philosophy of Irish Ireland,* where he claimed that Ireland's relationship to England was like 'a huxter's shop in competition with a monster store'.[81] He goes on:

> Economic tendencies sway the world now. The highest aim of the English and other statesmanship is to find new markets. What is known as the industrial revolution has changed the face of the world and fundamentally altered the forces that make the figures move. The new forces have driven Ireland into an ugly economic corner.[82]

Moran was also outraged by high rates of emigration, ongoing since the Great Famine, and was dismissive of Irish inventiveness, claiming that Ireland had invented nothing of importance (except 'the Dunlop tyre').[83] Part of his pragmatic solution for the rejuvenation of Ireland was not just in arts, literature and Irish language, but in commerce. Moran argued against the development of foreign industry in Ireland, and the lack of buyer's loyalty to home goods, seeing them as key factors underpinning the economic woes of the nation:

> The economic ills of Ireland can be traced to many diverse minor causes, but if you follow them up you will arrive at the great common source – the lack of Irish heart. Ireland has not the courage to say – I will wear this, or I will not wear that. So the draper from Ballyduff goes to London – sometimes he gives out as far as Paris – and a hideous poster in three

> colours announces that the latest novelties from London and Paris have arrived. This sends a thrill through the households of the village. The greasy draper rubs his hands and dilates on 'the circulation of money', and the moss on the still wheel of the village mill weeps for the native heart of other days. Ireland, because she has lost her heart, imports today what on sound economic principles she could produce for herself.[84]

He insisted that Ireland had to reject imports and prioritise Irish products. One key way in which Moran's advocacy of buying Irish, while refusing English products, was expressed was in what one might label a deliberate and considered consumer combativeness. As we have seen, early twentieth-century Irish buyers were encouraged to show their allegiance through commodity, and in *The Leader* this phenomenon often took a specific form. What emerged was a discourse in Ireland of what we will call the 'belligerent consumer', the ideal purchaser who is invited to buy Irish commodities through a variety of strategies – the linguistic, typographical and pictorial – and who has no truck with the Saxon, his culture or, crucially, his products.

Moran, in common with other nationalists, such as Arthur Griffith and Michael Cusack, rejected what some saw as the dreamy 'femininity' of the Irish Celt (and, implicitly, in Moran's case, of the Literary Revival): 'He wanted [the Irish people] "masculine" – strong, confident and assertive... Then, instead of crawling after West Britons and imitating their vices, the native Irish would take pride in their (Catholic) religion and develop their sense of identity.'[85] In an early piece in *An Claidheamh Soluis,* entitled 'The Lighter Side of It', Moran identified the battle between England and Ireland as perceived through a schoolboy's argument, and endorsed this new-found 'Gaelic' and 'boyish' form of masculine expression:

> But wait till the schools of the country have their leaven of Gaelic boys – that is, boys who have been told by their fathers and other big people to stand up for the Gael – and we will witness an interesting development. I almost think I hear the shrill-voiced abuse already going on, and I see two fierce little faces too near one another to be pleasing to the angel of peace. When a new boy makes his appearance the first question will be – 'Is he a Gael or a Sassenach?' If he say the latter! There will be eating of words and blubbering by and bye [...] there may be plenty of bloody noses painting the play-grounds red.[86]

The development of specifically masculine Gaelic culture is here jovially offered in the form of Sassenach-bashing.

Let us remain with *An Claidheamh Soluis*[87] to discuss a 1902 advertisement for the Gaelic League which encapsulates the belligerent consumer. 'Declare War on Anglicisation', 'The Great Invasion of Galway' (Figure 2.3)[88] metaphorically engages with martial ideals and, indeed, is emulative of the

Figure 2.3 Gaelic League advertisement (1902): 'Declare War on Anglicisation'.

aggressive masculinity of British imperialism. Here there is a clear move from the feminised Ireland of Alice Milligan to the military force of Erin. The consumer, the dedicated reader of the Gaelic League weekly, is invited not only to support such events but equally to marshal his or her own 'belligerence' against the English. The martial logic of such metaphorical referents creates an easy binary opposition of 'us' and 'them' – them, of course, being 'the English'. Galway was being 'invaded' in order to bolster Irish identity, 'war' was being declared on English influences.

In the 'Invasion of Galway' advertisement, the *Gaeltacht* is portrayed as a repository of Irish identity and authenticity. During the revival, as Seamus

Deane has argued, 'The west became the place of Irish authenticity.'[89] (This form of Western Irishness became commercialised as a key archetype of the national character and persists in the selling of Irish identity in tourist board visions to this day.[90]) Conversely, in contradistinction to the implications of the advertisement, Moran himself, acutely aware of the need for economic and social development, was keen on the modernisation of Ireland rather than on nostalgia for the past, declaring that 'Ireland cries out for very many of the modern mechanical inventions'.[91] Nonetheless, he shared the assertiveness and the distrust of the 'foreign' evident in the Gaelic League advertisement, and so did many advertisements in *The Leader*. The opposition of native versus foreign was very common in its pages, in such stuff as 'Boland's Bread. NOT made of Foreign Flour. Support Irish Milling',[92] and 'Emerald Gem: We Fear no Foreign Competition! Our products are as Good and as Cheap as any Foreign Ones'.[93] White's Wafer Oatmeal offered 'A Comparison: Irish Industry v. Foreign', maintaining that they were 'cheaper and of better quality than imported goods'.[94] National superiority was frequently proclaimed.

The masculinity in press and paid column evident in *The Leader* is even apparent in the semiotically complex advertisement for the Irish-manufactured 'Gladiator' and 'Titan' soaps (made by the 'progressive' firm James Crean & Co., Dublin) evident in its pages (Figure 2.4).[95] The image of the Irish washer-woman contrasts drolly with the humorously classical nod to Ancient Rome and the machismo of the 'powerful' soaps' nomenclature. At the same time, what this advertisement also achieves – apart from its martial, masculine and warlike brand designation (rather comically, considering the subject matter of household soap and the feature of a jovial Irishwoman washing her clothes) – is a subtle appeal to the classical traditions of Irish education, going all the way back to the Greek and Latin sometimes taught in the hedge school. While *The Leader* featured many addresses to the female reader (including advice on shopping, where to buy Irish-branded goods and such like), there is an overwhelming sense in its advertising columns that the masculine consumer was the focus of appeal. Adverts for pipes, cigarettes, gentlemen's hats, fertilisers, farming implements and wares suggest a very different view of (gendered) Irish consumerism than that represented in *The Shan Van Vocht*.

As part of his campaigns for economic protectionism and material independence, Moran persistently refused to allow advertisements for English products. Essentially, all goods publicised were to be of Irish origin. That said, despite its strong anti-English stance, *The Leader* occasionally featured royal warrants, such as a half page advertisement for 'The Lucan Dairy' in December 1919, which bears the King's crest and the statement: 'By Royal Warrant to His Majesty the King.'[96] While the dairy is Irish, it is quite clear that it holds the monarch's custom to be in high regard. Given the context of the Anglo-Irish War, this might be seen as a politically fraught

Figure 2.4 Advertisement for James Crean & Co., Dublin (1921): 'Gladiator' and 'Titan' soaps.

advertisement. However, in *The Philosophy of Irish Ireland,* Moran maintained that 'Irishmen take a keen delight in making good livelihoods out of their enemies. At present, there is nothing stopping the march of Irishmen to the best markets, and every market in these English speaking countries is open to us.'[97] Broadly, Moran endorsed the stemming of imports, while maximising exports in order to bolster economic and eventual political independence. Selling to the king was not necessarily, under these terms, selling out.[98]

Like *The Shan Van Vocht,* on close inspection it is clear that *The Leader*'s editorial matter also had a somewhat ambiguous relationship to the advertising which it carried in its pages. Take the issue of emigration, of which Moran was particularly censorious throughout his career. This was the reason why Ireland lacked skilled workers: 'Nearly all young men keep one eye on the possibility of emigrating... The eye is always on America or somewhere else.'[99] Nonetheless, his journal carried advertisements which seem to encourage a measure of emigration. A July 1921 full-page advertisement for the Colliery Investment Trust of America Inc. (Figure 2.5) featured the iconic Statue of Liberty against the New York skyline – the epitome of opportunity

Figure 2.5 Advertisement for the Colliery Investment Trust of America Inc. (1921).

and development for all diasporic communities – against a dockside view of Ireland, with the statement: 'The United States message to Ireland: Let there be Peace. And in the words of Abraham Lincoln, An Everlasting Peace.' Aside from the very obvious manipulation of the recent political turmoil in Ireland,[100] the advertisement simultaneously presents solidarity with Ireland, but also a message of hope which implies the possibility of emigration in its image of the Statue of Liberty. The USA as a land of opportunity is juxtaposed against the depressing industrialised docklands landscape. Positioned next to the emphatic iteration of 'peace' which seeks to appeal to popular sentiment following the Anglo-Irish War, the advertisement implicitly offers emigration as a real alternative to Ireland at this time. And the fact that the USA is commercially addressing Ireland (with the position of the USA at the top of the page, and Ireland at the bottom) gives the whole piece an air of American superiority, despite the presence of a company office in Ireland.

The contemporary anxiety over emigration extended to advertising copy. Dowdall, O'Mahoney & Co., Ltd, a margarine manufacturer, headed a plain text advertisement of 1921 in *The Leader* with 'Unemployment! Starvation! Emigration! PREVENT THEM – By buying Irish-made goods'. This exactly mirrors Moran's own perception of Irish economics: he saw one of the main duties of *The Leader*, as Patrick Maume has pointed out, to be 'the publicising of Irish goods'[101] and defended 'Buy Irish' campaigns, on the basis not of sentiment but of competitive pricing.

After the Anglo-Irish Treaty, which Moran supported, *The Leader* publicised the Irish Industrial Development Association's (IIDA's) 'Buy Irish' campaigns[102] and the Belfast trade boycott.[103] After the Dáil Éireann had refused to introduce protectionism, Moran was a key supporter of the IIDA's post-treaty economic nation-building and the need to buy Irish was once again reiterated in his journal. Indeed, *The Leader* carried a satirical poem on exactly this subject in 1921.[104] The poem, by A.M.W. (John Swift – the initials stand for 'A Man Without [a name]') registers a critique of the 'huckstering shops' which sells imported shoddy, while outlining the ideal Irish consumer experience with a description of the perfect Irish-Ireland shop (a cartoon, 'The Irish Stores', which illustrated this nirvana is the cover image for this book):

> A shop of perfection is here for inspection,
> In picture reversing conditions well known,
> Where goods of the nation are foremost in station,
> And dumps of necessity kept but not shown.
> No Irish week merely, but fifty two yearly
> We'd have if such places were here multiplied,
> And normal conditions changed huckster's positions
> And hauled them all over to the national side.

In 1921 the Irish-Ireland campaigns rolled on. The Dublin Metal and Galvanizing Co. Ltd, for instance, asked readers: 'Why buy imported buckets when the world's best are made in Ireland?' (Figure 2.6).[105] Moran's

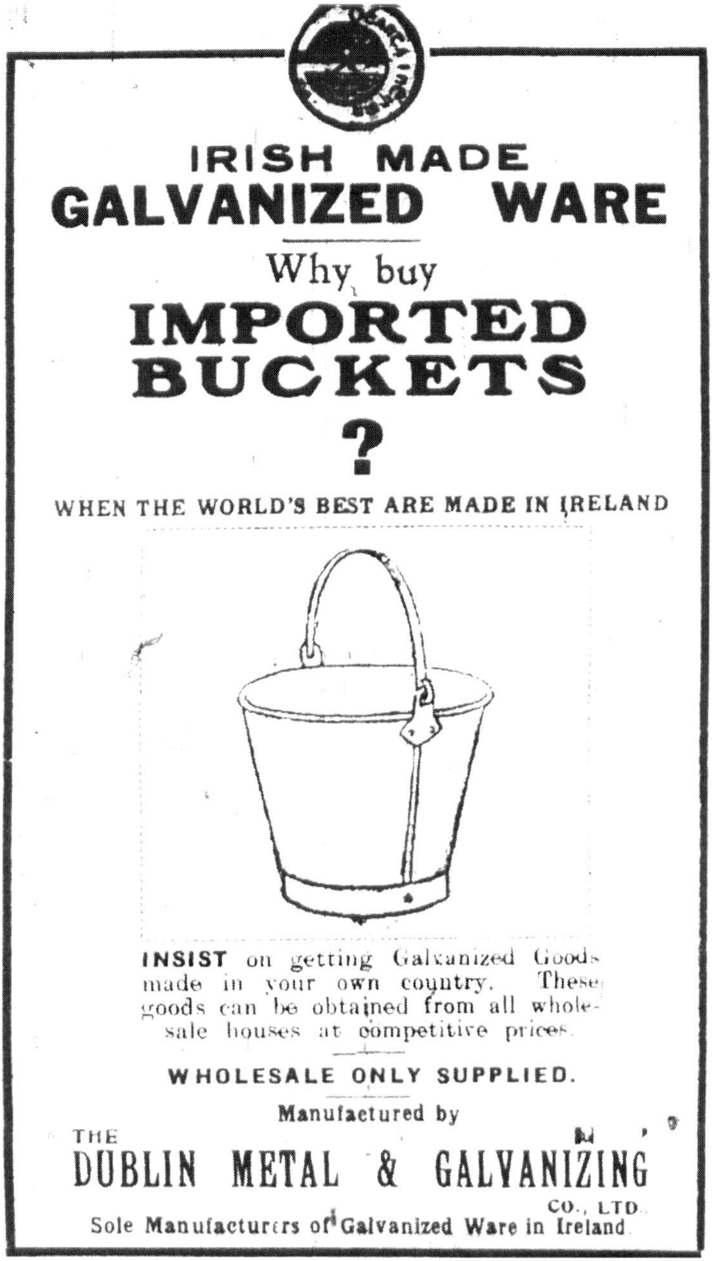

Figure 2.6 Advertisement for the Dublin Metal and Galvanizing Co. Ltd (1921).

advertisers, like his journal, stuck to the line which they had adopted before the First World War and the emergence of the Free State.

VI

While one example of consumer 'belligerence' was to encourage the purchase of Irish goods rather than 'foreign' imports, another strategy used to foster a measure of political resistance, as 'The Great Invasion of Galway' makes clear, involved the employment of the Irish language together with Irish fonts and typography. George Bornstein has written that a text consists not only of words but also of 'material instantiations' – what he calls its 'bibliographic code' – page layout, design, typefaces and spacing.[106] In the light of this, various advertisements from *The Leader* can be seen as illustrating the ideological contrasts and contradictions inherent in competing forms of Irish nationalism in terms of their physical appearance on the page. Typefaces are especially significant here, as they are often resonant of ideological and national convictions. Matthew Staunton, in a perceptive article on Irish Gaelic typography, has written that 'script nationalism', the employment of visual codes and markers to display the individuality of a language, is frequently aligned with 'linguistic nationalism', such as that espoused by the Gaelic League:

> Script nationalism, using the visual uniqueness of a language to express national difference, often goes hand in hand with the linguistic nationalism of emerging nations. In Ireland, it comes as no surprise that typography played an important role in the propaganda of the Gaelic League and Sinn Féin in the first decade of the 20th century… The political revival of Ireland's culture by militant nationalists in the early 1900s convinced both British and American companies like Figgins, Monotype and Linotype that there was money to be made in designing and manufacturing Gaelic fonts, even before the independent Irish state had come into being.[107]

In the words of Simon Loxley, 'A case could be made for a nation expressing its national character through typography',[108] and the use of the Irish language and typographical styles in advertising material can be understood as an assertion of individuality and cultural independence. However, having said this, the specifically typographical design of many nationalist periodicals is sometimes less a clear expression of national character than a site upon which contested ideas about nationality were debated.

The sudden rise in the number of Irish language publications in the early twentieth century makes this an especially suggestive aspect of *The Leader*'s advertising pages. One of the major choices which faced Irish language publications[109] was the decision as to the use of roman or Gaelic type.

It was felt in some quarters that Irish Gaelic fonts preserved 'authenticity' and were free from English influence.[110] This was a complex issue, involving not only 'an assertion of a distinct Irish mode of thought and writing, but [also] a formal rejection of the notion that English, or any other linguistic system, could successfully enclose or translate the Irish mode'.[111] The assertion of cultural distinctiveness, of course, accords very strongly with Moran's notion of an 'independent' nation, and commentators who supported Gaelic fonts, and argued that they had their origins in the ancient scribal tradition and therefore suggested more of a continuity of cultural ethnicity, often saw them as a signifier of nationhood.[112] Criticism of roman type was founded in the abundance of 'h's' which it produced. Roman type lacked the *síneadh fada* (vowels with an acute accent), as well as possessing a (historically unfounded) association with 'Englishness'.[113]

However, the story was by no means straightforward. Some pointed out that the notion of Gaelic type was complicated by the fact that Queen Elizabeth I initially commissioned the first typeface to be cut in Irish in a bid to convert the Catholic nation to Protestantism.[114] Indeed, many Gaelic Leaguers supported a roman font, suggesting that publication in Gaelic fonts would alienate any Scottish allies, as well as potential Irish readers who understood the Irish language phonetically (as it would supposedly be easier to follow in a roman typeface). In 1899, *An Claidheamh Soluis* reported that a Gaelic League meeting, chaired by Patrick Pearse, considered the use of Irish fonts, with advocates on both sides of the typographical fence.[115] Essentially, the debate focused on the issue of whether Ireland was a historically inflected, potentially insular and backward-looking nation, or one which should develop a cosmopolitan and modern identity (a debate which was a concern of Irish literature more generally – Yeats, Joyce and Beckett all engaged with this dilemma in their own particular fashion). Brian Ó Conchubhair summed up the arguments thus:

> The (post-colonial) crux for nativists was to embrace the modern world, to be European, cosmopolitan and outward looking without jettisoning all they held dear and true, their distinctive language, literature, and culture. Abandoning Gaelic fonts risked losing their distinctiveness on the written page, but retaining the font risked isolating them from the outside world and submitting to intellectual and cultural suffocation.[116]

According to Conchubhair, the Gaelic League eventually adopted a pragmatic position on the controversy: it 'did not definitively side with the Gaelic font over the Roman font...its primary objective was to promote and popularize the language as a spoken language. This aspiration required attracting as large a number of active members as possible and making the language accessible to them.'[117] It is this logic which operated in many advertisements of the period. Almost all of those in *The Leader* which either promote the Irish language (books, classes, summer schools) or feature it are bilingual. 'Píobaire' cigarettes (meaning 'Piper'),[118] clearly employing a Gaelic font, for instance, also advertise themselves simultaneously and phonetically as 'Peebra' in brackets underneath the main headline. Tellingly, the advertisement thereby registers a hierarchy: the Irish name precedes its English version. That said, the advertisement's endorsement of the Irish language is also thwarted by the fact that the presence of the English language in the text underscores the fact that, despite the best efforts of the Gaelic League and others, most urban dwellers in Ireland of the period spoke English as their first language; and the use of Irish, in roman or Gaelic font in advertising, was very much a gesture of solidarity and did not assume fluency in the majority of its audience.

A similar case can be made with much of the Gaelic League's own advertising. An 'Oireachtas' in 1920 employed both roman and Gaelic type in Irish, as well as the English language, which seems to testify to the diverse, and indeed contentious, ways in which Irish was employed in the broader culture (Figure. 2.7).[119] The Gaelic League, as we have seen, was far from being settled on the issue. It seems that for pragmatic and purely economic reasons (appealing to a wide readership), many advertisers during the early twentieth century – including the Gaelic League – sought to have it all ways: the

Figure 2.7 'Oireachtas'. Gaelic League announcement (1920).

Figure 2.8 Advertisement for the Gaelic League (1904): Gaelic League 'Irish Language Week'.

inclusion of a Gaelic font in advertising copy marked a particular national allegiance, while the frequent recourse to English signified accessibility and commercial aspirations.

Similarly, in 1904 Conradh na Gaeilge advertised using Gaelic type, during Irish language week, for a house-to-house collection in aid of the cause. A linguistic hierarchy is also perceptible in this advertisement. 'Irish Language Week' features in smaller letters, in brackets, beneath an Irish language headline in Gaelic type ('Seachtain na Gaeilge') (Figure 2.8).

More-commercial advertising was quick to pick up on language as a strategy for appealing to a specific strain of the nationalist community. Paterson's Irish Matches, 'Made in Dublin', for instance, reserved the centre of a 1904 advertisement for the Irish language, claiming 'Solus na nGaedheal déanta imBaile Átha Cliath' (translated as 'Light of the Gael, Made in Dublin'), but the text is flanked by English text featuring the brand name (Figure 2.9).[120] Similarly, P. B. Hay & Co. (Figure 2.10) advertised their Braces and Belts in English but with a Gaelic font used for taglines, such as 'féach anseo' ('look here').[121] Dartry Dye Works advertised in 1904 with two Gaelic-type phrases flanking the English text (though the main informative text is in English (Figure 2.11)).[122]

The Irish Co-Operative Clothing Manufacturing Society ran a full-page, elegantly illustrated advertisement in *The Leader* in 1921 (Figure 2.12), which was in English with the exception of an Irish banner, stating 'Deuntuísí Gaedhlacha do Ghaedhlaibh' with a translation in brackets below – 'Irish Industries for Irish People'.[123] Despite this frequent scattering of Gaelic, the advertisement for the National Land Bank (Figure 2.13) is one of the few examples of Gaelic type in *The Leader* which provides more than a phrase or two in Irish.[124]

Advertising in *The Leader* clearly operated on several levels. It engaged with Moran's 'Buy Irish' economic policy, sought to foster greater manufacturing investment in Ireland, and, in its use of typeface and linguistic strategies, engaged with some of the most important issues surrounding what Irish

Figure 2.9 Advertisement for Paterson's Irish Matches (1904).

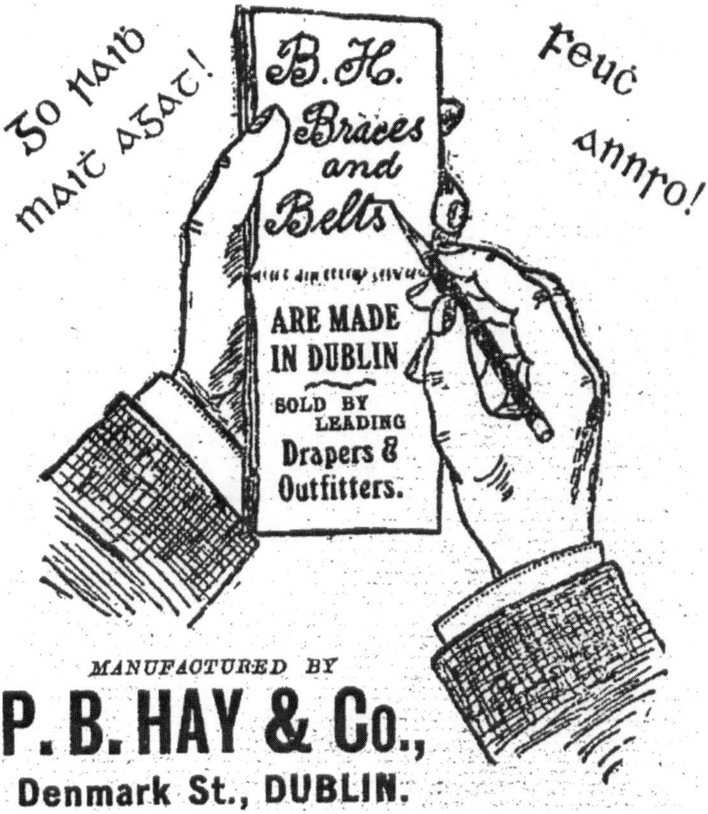

Figure 2.10 Advertisement for P. B. Hay & Co., Denmark Street, Dublin (1905).

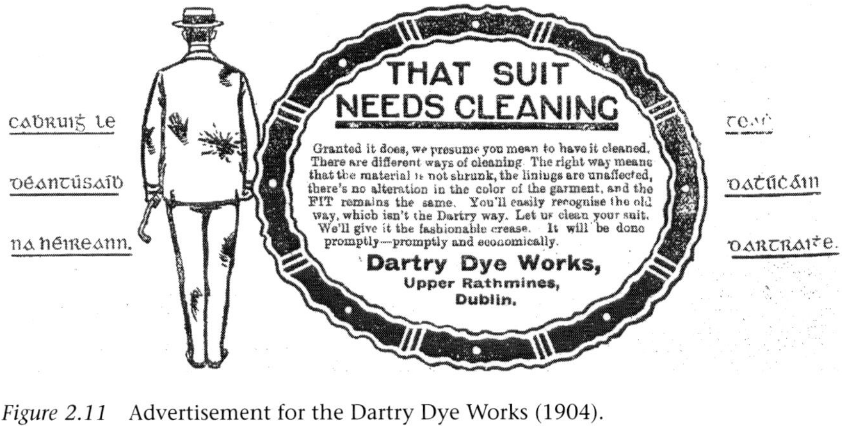

Figure 2.11 Advertisement for the Dartry Dye Works (1904).

Figure 2.12 Advertisement for the Irish Co-Operative Clothing Manufacturing Society (1921).

Figure 2.13 Advertisement for the National Land Bank (1921).

identity meant in the early twentieth century. For many commentators, critics and supporters, this issue was still very much in flux, and this ongoing debate was revealed, in part, in advertising copy and graphic design. On the one hand, various strategic uses of typeface harked back to a pre-twentieth-century typeface, which broadly coincided with Irish cultural nationalism's literary aspirations (the recovery of, and nostalgia for, a golden age of Irish writing), while also supporting the Gaelic League's broad campaign of reviving the Gaelic language. On the other hand, the equally strategic use of English in such advertisements suggests that advertisers and companies were very much aware of the pragmatic need to communicate to the widest range of consumers in order to sell goods, and that this simply could not be achieved exclusively in Irish at the turn of the century.

3
The Sinn Féin Depot and the Selling of Irish Sport

> When comes the day, as come it must
> That England's rule of greed and lust,
> Shall lie, all broken, in the dust
> We'll still have the Irish Hurling Men.
> 'Brian na Banban, 'The Irish Hurling Men',
> from a 1916 advertisement for Whelan and Son,
> GAA suppliers, 17 Upper Ormond Quay, Dublin

One of the defining characteristics of the Irish Revival was its preoccupation with popular-cultural forms of national expression. Industrial renaissance in Ireland was followed by cultural change, and in ways which fundamentally changed that country's life and manners. Dancing at the céilí, learning Irish at a Gaelic League class and patronising well-advertised home industries were important parts of what Douglas Hyde called the 'de-Anglicisation' of Ireland. So, too, was participating in or attending contests of Gaelic sports. Reviving activities such as hurling, which had lain fairly low for several decades, and sponsoring other, specifically Irish, forms of sport were important parts of the national validation of Irishness and Irish culture.

This chapter examines sports-related advertising in Ireland in the later nineteenth and early twentieth centuries. It draws a contrast between the selling of Irish sport *before* the foundation of the Gaelic Athletic Association (GAA) and the Irish Revival – exemplified by the paid columns of the *Irish Sportsman*, established in 1870 – and *after* it, as represented by the combative nationalism evident in the advertising copy of Whelan and Son of Upper Ormond Quay, Dublin (also known as the 'GAA House', the 'Sinn Féin Depot' and the 'Old Sinn Féin Shop'). It pays attention to the marked ideological differences between these two manifestations of Irish commercial culture. The *Sportsman*, which was entirely happy to cover non-Irish forms of sport, declared itself to be non-partisan and apolitical; Whelan's, on the other hand, shared the nationalist agenda of the GAA, scoffed at all things English and, indeed, was arguably the most radical of all Irish-Ireland companies. We discuss the close connections between Whelan's shop and Sinn Féin, notably in the careers of the two men who were most closely associated with the company. They are Brian O'Higgins, incendiary nationalist bard (in the guise of his pseudonym 'Brian na Banban'), republican prisoner, publisher of the Wolfe Tone annuals and greeting cards salesman; and the shop's proprietor Seumas Whelan, successful capitalist, intimate of Arthur Griffith, co-publisher of a series of separatist newspapers, republican prisoner and one-time secretary of Sinn Féin.

I

In December 1885 John L. Dunbar, secretary to the newly-established Irish Amateur Athletic Association (IAAA) wrote to the only slightly older Gaelic Athletic Association[1] – founded in the previous year – to initiate a dialogue to discuss matters of common interest and to see if the disputes between the two organisations might be mediated.[2] The founder of the GAA, Michael Cusack, promptly wrote back, with the cheerful contempt which seemed to come so naturally to him:

> Dear Sir,
> I received your letter this morning and burned it.
> M. Cusack.[3]

Cusack had history, as they say, with Dunbar and his renowned sporting family, who owned the influential weekly the *Irish Sportsman*. He had initially been friendly with the Dunbars and had contributed to their paper several times in 1881,[4] notably in attacking the contemporary elitism of contemporary Irish sport, before falling out with them in spectacular fashion (he contrived to do likewise with the association itself in 1886, leading to his resignation as secretary of the GAA in July of that year).[5] Cusack conducted a quarrel with the *Sportsman* throughout 1885, attacking it in his weekly column in W. O'Brien's *United Ireland* and suing the journal in June of that year after it had published a satirical poem attacking him in its pages.

The quarrel between Cusack and the *Irish Sportsman* is something of a symbolic moment; a challenge to the existing Irish sporting hierarchy by the combative celebrant of the Gaelic games which were – in large part – to prevail over the latter's preferences for non-native pastimes such as hunting, cricket, racing, cycling and athletics. It was also a dispute between pressmen. Jack Dunbar, the secretary of the IAAA, was himself a professional journalist, and was then the editor of the *Athletic and Cycling News*, an offshoot of the *Sportsman*.[6] His family, and its version of Irish sport, with its emphasis on 'imported' pursuits, was to lose out, in no small measure, to that of the GAA with its 'native' ones. Nonetheless, it has an important place in the history of the print culture of Irish sport. John Leopold Dunbar's father

William J. Dunbar (d. 1888), nicknamed 'Nimrod' (after both the scriptural 'mighty hunter' of the book of Genesis and the pseudonym of the pioneering English fox-hunting journalist C. J. Apperley (1773–1843)), was the founding editor of the *Irish Sportsman*, Ireland's first dedicated sporting periodical. This weekly newspaper was established in 1870 (son succeeded father as editor in 1888, before dying himself in April 1891 at the relatively early age of 34).[7]

The *Irish Sportsman* was an attempt to Hibernise – so to speak – what had been for decades a lucrative niche within the British publishing market.[8] Indeed, compared to England, Ireland came comparatively late to sports journalism. Though Britain's first periodical devoted to sport, the *Sporting Magazine*, was founded in 1793 (and was followed by a host of monthly and weekly rivals: the *Annals of Sporting, Bell's Life in London,* the *New Sporting Magazine* and *The Field,* among others), Ireland had to wait seven decades and more before William Dunbar of North Great George's Street, Dublin, established an Irish equivalent. Indeed, in its first issue the *Sportsman* explicitly referred to the widespread taste for sports print across the water: 'Amongst the most notable features in the history of the Newspaper Press has been the gradual but steady progress of Sporting Literature in England.' The new journal would do the same for the mother country, it declared, and was intended to 'form a complete record of all the sports of the week in Ireland'. Its range was wide, though equestrianism and various forms of hunting loomed particularly large. Certainly the *Irish Sportsman* was by no means limited to Hibernian sports, with what some in the GAA would later denominate 'foreign' sports looming large in its prospectus's list of promised subjects: 'the Irish turf, steeplechasing, racing, hunting, coursing, aquatic sports, yachting, cricket, rowing, croquet, shooting, rifle shooting, athletic sports, pedestrianism, running', and – almost as an afterthought – 'hurling' (rather than the latter sport, the journal maintained that 'steeple-chasing appears likely to become the National Pastime').

The *Irish Sportsman* claimed a form of ideological innocence to itself which might seem surprising to the modern eye, given how politicised Irish sport has been since the 1880s. It explicitly argued in the manifesto published in that first issue, which appeared on 19 February 1870, that it would be non-sectarian and conducted 'without leaning to any political party'. Underpinning this was a conviction, or at least a hope, that sports could be set apart from politics, and were capable, indeed, of providing a beam of light in a sometimes dark national history. Indeed, the *Sportsman* maintained that 'the sunniest aspect of [the] history' of Ireland was its sporting life. Not there a turbulent history of war, rebellion and famine, or a testimony to a fractured nation. Sport was one place, according this optimistic account, where the nation – Catholic and Protestant alike – could unite in a common ideological space after the horrors of the 1840s. 'Ireland', it declared, 'emerging from her miseries, is boldly arraying herself in the brightest of Emerald Greens', and the country's sporting life could be a force for national unity, bringing together all 'the genius and talent of our Native Land'.

From the first, the *Irish Sportsman* carried a large number of advertisements. Indeed, in 1878 the *Irish Law Times* declared that the 'advertising public should bear in mind that the best medium for their announcements is the *Irish Sportsman*'.[9] The *Sportsman* was especially to be recommended, the journal continued, because it steered clear of politics, being supposedly 'a non-political and non-sectarian Weekly'. So, what of the nature of those announcements? In its early days the paid columns of the *Sportsman* were principally a mixture of advertisements for both Irish and British goods. As we have seen, before the 1880s much Dublin advertising manifested a genuflection to imported goods – and manners – in stressing the excellence of goods from London and Paris in particular. The *Irish Sportsman* was no different. In its first decade the same trend was visible: much of the paper's advertising was mail order, announcements placed on behalf of London manufacturers of sporting goods based in the Strand and such like. Irishmen could copy the fashions of the English sporting gentry and avail themselves, via the *Sportsman*'s columns, of their fashionable accoutrements. Indeed, in the third edition of his 1868 treatise *Modern Athletics* (1877), Henry Fazakerley Wilkinson explicitly noted the attraction of the journal to advertisers from England: 'Enjoying a monopoly on its own soil, it presents the best channel through which the English advertising public can reach their Irish brethren. It is read weekly by over 100,000 persons.'[10]

Dublin sportsmen scanning the pages of the *Irish Sportsman* could order the finest English dog foods, French wines, smoking accessories and sporting equipment of all types. That said, there were also many Dublin manufacturers therein, all offering sporting requisites to the Irish middle classes. Furthermore, as well as tempting consumers with goods from over the water, the *Irish Sportsman* also simultaneously featured its own kind of commercial patriotism, its paid columns imploring readers to 'Use only Irish manufactured manures', and endorsing such stuff as Irish riding tackle, Irish cricket bats, even Irish lever trusses – protective padded belts for sportsmen with hernias ('the most effective invention ever in the curative treatment of HERNIA'). However, nowhere in its pages is found the subversive nationalist manner later evident in the commercial pronouncements of Whelan and Son.

In the first year of the journal's publication, 1870, the *Irish Sportsman* published some jocular anapaests saluting the shooting, hunting and racing equipment to be found at the premises of M. Mahon and Co., of Henry Street, Dublin. 'To the Sportsmen of Ireland' is another example of the nineteenth-century poetical advertisements – the contemporary term is 'jingle' – which appeared so frequently in the period. It captures the journal's sense that sport was an innocent, manly and light-hearted diversion, with little to do with politics:

> TO THE SPORTSMEN OF IRELAND
> When you go out to shoot, with your dog and your gun
> Determined through heather and bogs to have fun,
> Then come to M. MAHON'S and Co.;
> They are famed for knit stockings of *the* very best
> Which thousands of sportsmen have put to the test
> And praise on their worth did bestow.
>
> When you go out to hunt on your old gallant grey,
> Procure Riding Trousers, without delay
> M. MAHON and Co. keep these prime.
> In those you may ride, without fear of a fall
> You may jump over gates, over fences and walls
> And be in at the death in good time.
> [...]
> When you mount your fast racer, the Prize to secure,
> From M. MAHON you can a silk jacket procure
> And a cap that will Victory crown.
> With his Gloves made of buckskin, and breeches to match,
> The Devil himself your great speed could not match,
> And *echo* will give you renown.

In this account, Irish sport was an entertaining – though not perhaps a serious – business, and the 'sportsmen of Ireland' were portrayed as a laughter-loving, prosperous crowd who did not see it as their job to challenge the prevailing state of affairs.

II

The *Irish Sportsman*'s 1870 claim that Irish sport was ever innocent of politics – a highly debatable premise – would shortly be put under severe question. Indeed, within a decade of the *Irish Law Times* boasting that Irish sport could be 'non-political and non-sectarian', the Gaelic Athletic Association – about as political a sporting body as it is possible to imagine – had been established. As is well known, the GAA, founded in 1884, had a clear nationalist agenda, one which has influenced the nature of sport in Ireland ever since. Indeed, Richard Holt has written that 'the formation and early history of the GAA is arguably the most striking instance of politics shaping sport in modern history; it is certainly the outstanding example of the appropriation of sport by nationalism in the history of the British Isles and Empire'.[11] The association in its early days, and certainly in the form of

Michael Cusack, had no truck with the political quietism and the implicit status quo-ism of the views encapsulated in the pages of the *Irish Sportsman*, seeing them, indeed, as implicitly unionist. Cusack, in his forthright manner, dismissed the Dunbars as exactly the type of 'Anglomaniacs' and 'voluntary slaves' whom he despised, and colourfully labelled their IAAA as a 'ranting, impotent West British abortion'.[12] Twenty years later, *Sinn Féin* (on 29 September 1906) sustained the attack on the IAAA when the Gaelic Athletic Association was once again in dispute with the Irish Amateur Athletic Association (and with the International Cycling Association):

> There is no room for compromise and no grounds for compromise. There can only be one national athletic organisation in Ireland and its existence now depends not on the good will or support of a few score of crack athletes or cyclists, but upon the national spirit it displays and upon the masses of Gaeldom which a vigorous Irish policy and programme can alone attract.[13]

The 'National Pastimes' and the GAA must be endorsed over the values of the IAAA and its residual affection for outsider games.

Cusack and Griffith's attack on the supposed West Britishness of the IAAA is best understood as part of a wider cultural campaign against imported manners in favour of what was seen as the national heritage of Ireland. As they had with other aspects of the island's culture – language, music, dance and so on – from the 1880s onwards, both mainstream nationalists and purist republicans – notably the Irish Republican Brotherhood (IRB), who were so important in the early history of the GAA[14] – took the opportunity to examine the Irishman's sports. Their rhetoric offered for comparison two kinds of activities, one of which was decidedly more 'Irish' than the other. On the one hand there were the sports of the Gael: handball, Gaelic football, camogie (eventually), and, especially, hurling; on the other there were the pastimes of the Saxon: association football, rugby and cricket, all cuckoos, in this line of thought, in the Irish sporting nest. A correspondent to D. P. Moran's *The Leader*, for instance, declared in February 1904 that 'The GAA is the regenerator of our national pastimes. The GAA it is which is to expel and stamp out for ever those foul pastimes that have come into this land to the almost total annihilation of our own.'[15]

The history of the GAA and its national mission have been well documented by a number of cultural historians.[16] However, there is little attention in this impressive body of writing to the way in which the association was marketed, how ingenious advertisements served its ideological purpose, and there is nothing at all about the remarkable manner in which the sports of the Gaelic Athletic Association were promoted by the indefatigably nationalist company Whelan and Son, of 17 Upper Ormond Quay, Dublin, a shop which described itself variously as the 'GAA House' and the

'Sinn Féin Depot', and whose copy endorsed the excellence of Irish sport, and of its own 'Irish-Ireland' sporting merchandise, while simultaneously repudiating the shoddiness of English goods, the inadequacy of English sport and the black perfidy of English rule. We shall now turn to the history of this remarkable company, and to its noisy advertising.

III

> GAELS!
> The GAA House is WHELAN AND SON, 17 Upper Ormond Quay, Dublin.
>
> (Advertisement for Whelan and Co. (1908))

The same national sentiment evident in the rhetoric surrounding the establishment of the Gaelic Athletic Association was, unsurprisingly, also apparent in commercial announcements related to Irish sport from the late 1880s onwards. Take this 1898 advertisement (Figure 3.1) for Robert Day and Son, GAA suppliers in the City of Cork, which proudly declares its goods 'Home Manufactured', as well as 'Gaelic' and 'Irish', both now adjectives of the highest approbation after the post-Revival demise of what one might call the 'cultural cringe' of the 1850s onwards, in which imported goods had been praised to the very skies. Whereas the *Irish Sportsman* in its early days was full of advertisements placed on behalf of London manufacturers of sporting goods, and those of Dublin shops in which one could buy the finest English-made sporting requisites, now the emphasis was on Irish goods and, indeed, on Irish sports: the *Sportsman*'s emphasis on 'the Irish turf, steeplechasing, racing, hunting, coursing' and so on has given way to a patriotic concentration on what were seen as 'genuine' Irish sports.

Robert Day and Son, despite their evident national passion, were outshone in the fervour and frequency of their Irish-Ireland advertising by another supplier of GAA requisites, namely Whelan and Son, of 17 Upper Ormond Quay, Dublin, shopkeepers and, indeed, culture warriors. This company was founded in the early 1900s as a tobacconist and newsagent, but soon diverted into a sports shop, publishing house and, indeed, vendor of all manner of odds and sods. However, alongside the sale of cigarettes, greeting cards, books, Gaelic League publications, sheet music, items of furniture and fancy goods, Whelan's principal business was sporting merchandise for those participating in pastimes endorsed by the Gaelic Athletic Association. However, these were tradesmen with an explicitly nationalist – and republican separatist – agenda. Certainly Whelan's maintained the spirit of Michael Cusack, who in Paul Rouse's words 'wrote of hurling as an act of freedom, of hurling as a game which was inherited from the heroes of Irish history and which a new generation was duty bound to revive'.[17] A poetic advertisement for the company of the 1910s, which implies that buying a camán from Whelan's of Ormond Quay struck a blow for Irish liberty, put it this way:

When comes the day, as come it must
That England's rule of greed and lust,
Shall lie, all broken, in the dust
We'll still have the Irish Hurling Men.

In nationalistic thought about sport, writes Richard Holt, 'The hurley stick became a symbol of Irish freedom, a "weapon" to drive out the British', and certainly Whelan's saw it that way. This was, in the words of Joyce's Stephen Dedalus (however satirically he meant them), 'rebellion with hurleysticks'.[18]

Figure 3.1 Advertisement for Robert Day, GAA Suppliers, Cork (1898): 'Home Manufactured. The Gaelic'.

Whelan and Son's was one of the earliest recipients of the 'Déanta i nÉirinn' – Made in Ireland – mark, established by the Irish Development Association on New Year's Day 1907.[19] A 1907 advertisement for Whelan's declares that ' "There's nothing like Irish leather" for Hurley balls; the Irish Trade mark on Whelan's Hurley balls says something! 17 Upper Ormond Quay. *Sinn Féin Amhain*.' These last words are suggestive, and not just because of their echo of James Joyce's parody of the sportsman journalist Michael Cusack, in the form of the Citizen, who also uses them ('Sinn Fein! says the citizen. Sinn fein amhain! The friends we love are by our side and the foes we hate before us').[20] As we will see, the founder of the shop, Seumas Whelan, was associated with Sinn Féin from its foundation in 1905 and began explicitly associating his company with the organisation fairly soon after its foundation. Indeed, by 1908, Whelan's had begun to use the term 'Sinn Féin Depot' as an alternative title for its premises. The proprietor's friend Arthur Griffith, whose party was perfectly capable of promoting itself in its eponymous newspaper and in press advertisements elsewhere[21] ('the Sinn Féin party seems to live by advertisement'[22] commented one weary Royal Irish Constabulary source in 1919), did not seem to mind.[23] Nor did his organisation exercise itself to prevent commercial organisations from associating themselves with it. Indeed, Whelan and Son's was not the only Sinn Féin shop in Ireland's capital in this period. In 1907, a 'Sinn Féin Limited' opened a furniture store in Camden Street, Dublin, and boasted (Figure 3.2) of its superiority over 'foreign companies' (and its innovative hire purchase terms).

The Sinn Féin Depot's use of ingenious and highly politicised advertisement served the ideological commitments of its proprietors to Gaelic sport and to Irish freedom. The prose copy for its products frequently manifested a polemical style which aped the tone of the GAA's more combative

Figure 3.2 Advertisement for Sinn Féin Limited, Camden Street, Dublin (1907): 'We Furnish Irish Homes'.

pronouncements. Indeed, the company declared in several advertisements that 'As *Gaels* ourselves we know the spirit of the *G.A.A.*, its aims and objects'. The 'spirit of the *G.A.A.*' is certainly evident in a 1910 salute to Whelan's 'Hurling Balls, Camans, Football Boots, Balls, and Handballs':

> DON'T PLAY IRISH GAMES WITH FOREIGN REQUISITES!
>
> The *G.A.A* typifies an Ireland active, enterprising, self-reliant, willing to essay, fit to endure, independent, resurgent, insurgent if you will. We are specialists in GAA requisites and give the best value in Ireland. We stock only *Irish* Athletic goods, and all are branded with the *Irish Trade Mark*.

The three adjectives, 'independent, resurgent, insurgent', tell their own story, in echoing the rhetoric of separatist nationalism, with the last even suggestive of a physical force brand of nationalism, the military separatism which culminated in the events of Easter 1916, in which Whelan's premises, as we will see, played their own small part (Figure 3.3).

As the First World War approached, nationalist advertising in republican journals became even more clear voiced and unequivocal in its tone, with Whelan's one of the most clamorous of Irish-Ireland firms. In journal-of-the-ultras *Irish Freedom*, for instance, alongside such stuff as 'The Only Tobacco Dealer in Dublin who does not stock Foreign Manufactured tobacco is J. C. LARKIN, 36 Wexford Street', an advertisement which implies that not stocking Benson & Hedges is a patriotic obligation, we have overtly republican

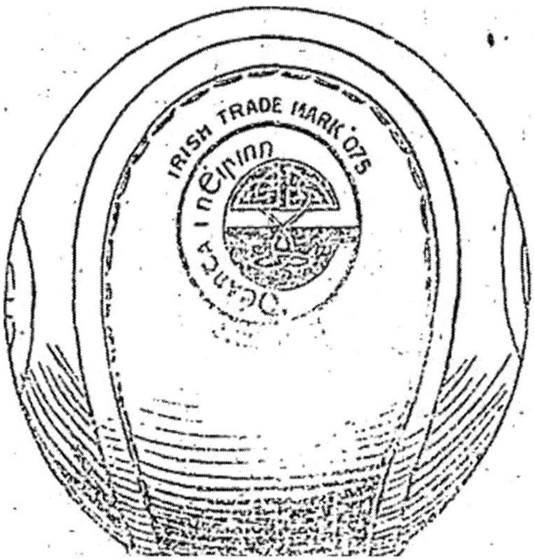

Figure 3.3 Gaelic football. Detail from a Whelan's advertisement (1910).

copy in this disguised advertisement[24] for the house of Whelan, published as the Christmas of 1910 approached:

> STRIKE ENGLAND!
>
> ... this Xmas in her trade. £. s. d. is the Englishman's God. England keeps Ireland in her grip principally for her trade. *Loosen that grip*; be true to your country and to your principles. *Strike a blow for Irish freedom* by buying Irish goods this Xmas. This list of Irish Xmas presents will help you in the Good Work.

There follows a long and eclectic list of 'Made in Ireland'-marked goods. Alongside the sporting paraphernalia – the customary hurling balls, camáns and 'Irish Made Hand-Stitched Footballs (10/6)' – the following are also announced:

> Irish Xmas cards (1/- and 2/-), Irish Shaving Outfits (5/6), Prayer Books printed and bound in Dublin (6d to 5s), Complete Works of Brian na Banban (3/6), Fully Upholstered Irish-made Pear-Shaped Settee (27/6), M'Clinton's Irish Colleen Perfume and Soap in Fancy Box (2/3), Irish-made Punch Balls (11/6).

Whelan's, as we will see, were very fond of this Brian na Banban, and his patriotic verses were traded alongside perfume, soap and punch balls.

In July 1911, in the month of the newly crowned King George V's royal visit to Ireland, Whelan and Son indulged in some more sharp-elbowed copy in the columns of *Irish Freedom*, the 'Wolfe Tone Clubs' (IRB) organ whose readers were doubtless receptive to its dismissive tone: 'We are *Irish*, and so have no need for Union Jacks and Royal Visits. Our motto, as far as possible, is *Boycott English Goods*'. Indeed, Fenian-inspired journals, as well as carrying Whelan's advertisements, also wrote editorial copy in its favour commending the fervour of their shopkeeperly activism. *The Gael*, which back-scratched advertisers of like-minded political conviction in a series on nationalist merchants and shopkeepers,[25] wrote approvingly of Whelan's in February 1916:

> Whelan and Co., Ormond Quay, Dublin are well known as the premier Irish-Ireland firm. Readers of the *Gael* needing books, pamphlets, Irish made cutlery, Irish-made jewellery, Irish-grown as well as Irish-manufactured tobacco, camans, hurling balls and footballs, and other GAA requisites [and] boys scouts' outfitting, could not do better if they want Irish-made goods at the right prices, than order their supplies from them.[26]

As well as selling boy scout uniforms, tobacco and Gaelic footballs, Whelan's were also a publisher, in particular of politically agreeable material which served the cause of advanced nationalism. In 1916, they reprinted Patrick Pearse's 'series of studies of the English education system in Ireland'[27] as *The Murder Machine.* They also published the majority of the same author's Irish Volunteer pamphlets. A contemporary intelligence report on the (MacNeill/Pearse) Volunteers noted that they 'took every opportunity of spreading disloyalty by means of seditious pamphlets'[28] and the most notable of these were the 'Tracts for the Times' which were published by the Irish Publicity League (the IRB publicity organisation) and by Whelan and Son. Pearse's pamphlet 'Ghosts' was published for the first time at Ormond Quay in 1915, price one penny, and was swiftly followed by others under the Whelan imprint: the 'Spiritual Nation', the 'Sovereign People' and the famous 'The Separatist Idea' (all 1916). Also in 1916, the company brought out the third edition of Arthur Griffith's dual monarchy thesis *The Resurrection of Hungary: A Parallel for Ireland* (1904). Whelan's developed a reputation as a trader in revolutionary literature and, according to a 1924 letter in the *Irish Independent*, in the week after the Easter uprising of 1916, its premises at Ormond Quay were raided by the soldiery and '8,000 of these [pamphlets] were seized by the military'.

As well as Volunteer pamphlets and much of the advanced nationalist newspaper press, Whelan and Son's also published songs and patriotic poems to inspire the heart of the patriot. James Connolly's rousing verses 'Watchword of Labour' (first published in the *Irish Worker* in 1913), for instance, were republished, with music, by the company in 1916 after the poet's execution:

> Oh, hear ye the watchword of Labour, the slogan of those
> who'd be free,
> That no more to any enslaver must Labour bend suppliant knee,
> That we on whose shoulders are borne the pomp and the
> pride of the great,
> Whose toil they repay with their scorn, must challenge
> and master our fate.
>
> Then send it aloft on the breeze boys,
> That watchword the grandest we've known
> That Labour must rise from its knees, boys,
> And claim the broad earth as its own.[29]

So, indeed, was one of the most notable early publications of 'The Soldier's Song', which appeared as sheet music published by Whelan's in 1916, also in the aftermath of the Rising, and is described as 'The Soldier's Song. *First Edition* with Music.' First edition or not, this is certainly one of the earliest separate publications of Peadar Kearney and Paddy Heeney's battle-cry, which first appeared in the separatist *Irish Freedom* in September 1912 and is now sung in translation, of course, as the Irish national anthem, 'Amhrán na bhFiann'.

Connolly and Kearney notwithstanding, the poet most closely identified with Whelan's in this period was the aforementioned Brian O'Higgins (1882–1963), who wrote under the more mellifluous Gaeilge pseudonym 'Brian na Banban' (na Banban was himself a kind of walking brand of Irishness, his name meaning 'Brian of Ireland'). O'Higgins's verse, indeed, was directly used in jingle advertisements for Whelan's. In 1916, for instance, in the republican journal the *Spark*, Whelan's inserted a display advertisement showing a muscular sportsman clutching a hurl and waving it above his head as if it were indeed, in Holt's phrase, 'a symbol of Irish freedom'. The verse copy which accompanies this we have quoted previously:

> When comes the day, as come it must
> That England's rule of greed and lust,
> Shall lie, all broken, in the dust
> We'll still have the Irish Hurling Men.
>
> Camans 36s, postage 4d extra. Hurling balls 3/6, 3/- & 2/9. Jerseys, footballs and all G.A.A requisites stocked.
> WHELAN'S THE G.A.A HOUSE. 17 Up. Ormond Street, Dublin.

'THE G.A.A HOUSE' explicitly anticipates the day in which England's reign will 'lie, all broken, in the dust', its jingle copy borrowed from O'Higgins, the majority of whose books and pamphlets it had published. The advertisement, it might be pointed out, is a truncated version of a longer poem by O'Higgins, first published in 1907, 'The Irish Hurling Men'. The poem opens thus:

> Who say our country's soul has fled?
> Who say our country's heart is dead?
> Come, let them hear the marching tread
> Of twice five thousand Hurling Men.
> They hold the hopes of bygone years,
> They love the past – its smiles and tears
> But quavering doubts and shrinking fears
> Are far from Ireland's Hurling Men.
>
> *Chorus*
> When comes the day, as come it must
> That England's rule of greed and lust,
> Shall lie, all broken, in the dust
> We'll still have the Irish Hurling Men.[30]

'They love the past' is a striking half-line. This poem is characteristic of the Revival's simultaneous appeal to the past and its anticipation of a glorious future. As it did for Cusack, or for the Gaelic League's Douglas Hyde who wrote the GAA anthem 'Dan Mairseala na nGaodhal', the 'Marching Song of the Gaelic Athletes' ('Different from the creeping Saxon/ We are men of other minds'...), the sporting past – or at least a Gaelicised version of it – mattered greatly to O'Higgins. For him it could both inspire the present and shape the future. The poem continues by proclaiming that hurling, with its glorious history, could inspire a new generation of warriors against the English, and 'fire the blood of fighting men':

Hurrah! Hurrah! The stout caman
Not English steel can match its blow;
Hurrah! The arms of might and brawn
And hearts with Freedom's flame aglow!
They sing the songs their fathers sung,
When to the breeze the Green they flung-
They speak their own sweet Gaelic tongue,
That fires the blood of fighting men.
When all around was dark as night,
With scarce a gleam of cheering light,
When traitors fled their country's fight
She still had hope in Hurling Men!
Chorus[31]

The poet O'Higgins, who made his living at the turn of the twentieth century giving instruction in Irish as a múinteoir taistil (travelling teacher) for the Gaelic League, eventually developed business sidelines as a printer and as a designer and manufacturer of greetings cards (he wrote many of the ditties published in Whelan's aforementioned 'Irish Xmas Cards', which appeared both in English and in Irish).[32] Brian na Banban first published his poetry in book form in 1907 as *The Voice of Banba: Songs and Recitations for Young Ireland*. Some of O'Higgins's work is anodyne and sentimental stuff, as per his *Christmas Stories and Sketches* (1917), *Hearts of Gold* (1918) and *Songs of the Sacred Heart* (1921). According to a 1921 Whelan's advertisement, some verses in the latter were 'written in Birmingham Jail' during one of O'Higgins's spells as a political prisoner and commended by the Bishop of Killaloe, the Sinn Féin-supporting Michael Fogarty, as full of 'simple and profound religious feeling'. Other parts of the na Banban canon are sharper and highly satirical. In advance of the 1911 royal visit of King George, for instance, O'Higgins penned his own ironic tribute, 'The Song of the Loyal Irish' (1910) in which he envisaged Irish rebels 'welcom[ing] George with a slavish smile/ Greet[ing] him in real colonial style':

Boys, O Boys! Listen here to me,
We're going to live in a State that's Free,
Good English citizens all we'll be;
And friends of the Princess Royal;
If we only flop on our hands and knees
And swear by George of the lands and seas
To wipe the green from the Irish trees
And for evermore be loyal.
[...]

We'll curse the name of the rebel Tone,
And of every rebel our land has known
And all who hated the English throne,
And fought for the Irish Nation,
We've torn up every oath and vow,
We're part of the civilised Empire now.

In an advertisement for his anglophobic, bilingual volume *Signal Fires* (1912), Whelan's boasted that 'Slaves and Saxons would be hit hard' by na Banban's verse, but for nationalists, 'the dominant note will be one of hope and cheer and courage'. In his book O'Higgins reinforces his notion that Irish sportsmen playing Irish sports were the avant-garde of the struggle against 'Sassenach thrall' in another of his rebel-rousing sporting poems, 'The Athletes of Erin':

God strengthen the athletes of Erin,
To free her from Sassenach thrall,
To stand as the guard of her honour,
And march to the fight at her call.

When honour we give to the toilers,
Who strove through the gloom of the night
To combat the wiles of the Saxon,
When crushed was the cause of the Right,

Let us think of the athletes of Erin,
Who vowed by the graves of her dead,
To win back the light of her freedom
And raise up her sorrow-crowned head.

Though slavelings kneel down to the tyrant
And kiss every link of her chains,
The old hope still lingers in Erin
Of a fight for her mountains and plains.

And whenever the red light of battle
O'er town and tochar shall glow,
In the vanguard the athletes of Erin
Shall crash through the ranks of the foe.[33]

Patrick Maume has pointed out* that O'Higgins's 'The Athletes of Erin' is based on William Rooney's 'Men of the West', just as the 'Hurling Men', previously cited, is modelled on Thomas Davis's 'Clare's Dragoons'. O'Higgins' ballads share with advertising jingles the quality of being modelled on pre-existing and well-known poems in order that they can piggyback on those texts' associations. This imitative strategy of elevating one's cultural product by exalted association is one which informs both the pages of O'Higgins's volumes of poetry and the advertising copy of the Sinn Féin Depot.

In 1916, Brian O'Higgins, then secretary of the O'Curry Irish College at Carrigaholt (in County Clare), did indeed 'march to the fight'. Though too short-sighted and sickly to take direct part in the fighting during the events of Easter week, O'Higgins was present in the General Post Office, tending to the wounded and encouraging doubters to the fight. Following the execution of the ringleaders of the rebellion, he was interned, with many of the republican survivors, at Frongoch in North Wales (where he 'wrote a poem a day', each with 'a patriotic or anti-British flavour')[34] before being released in 1917. Continuing his radical politics, he was afterwards imprisoned in Birmingham Jail (in 1918) and was elected a Sinn Féin TD for Clare West in the First Dáil while still in prison. On the Anti-Treaty side in the Civil War, O'Higgins ended up being gaoled again in the early 1920s, this time by Irishmen, enduring spells in the Curragh and Mountjoy prisons.

O'Higgins finally lost his parliamentary seat in 1927, after which he went back into publishing, issuing Christmas cards, calendars and devotional materials, most of which were sold in Whelan's, though, as the veteran Sinn Féiner Maire Comerford commented in *Survivors* (1980), he found himself making unpleasant compromises in his business: 'Even a purist like Brian O'Higgins was forced to sell his Christmas cards under a *Saorstát Éireann* trade insignia,'[35] she recalled ('he was', she comments, 'a very bitter man').[36] From the 1930s to the early 1960s, O'Higgins published the Wolfe Tone Annuals, volumes intended to cheer and inspire those true to 'the Separatist Idea and [devoted to] the vindication of all of those who have sacrificed themselves for the full Independence and Gaelicisation of Ireland'. He died in 1963.

We will conclude our account of Whelan's by returning to the subject of its owner, Seumas, sometimes James, Whelan. Figure 3.4 shows a photograph of

*Private correspondence.

Figure 3.4 Photograph of Seumas Whelan (*Irish Independent*, 1924).

this individual. Poor in quality though this is, it does at least have a kind of pleasingly Conradian conspiratorial air to it. This man Whelan was personally acquainted with the contemporary titans of Irish ultra-nationalism. He was at the Dublin Christian Brothers School with Patrick Pearse, claimed to have taught at Rockwell College with Thomas McDonagh and was a friend and particular admirer of President Griffith. In the year after the latter's death Whelan argued, in the *Irish Independent* of 20 April 1924, that 'in the writings of this great man, Arthur Griffith – now almost forgotten – will be found the soundest advice on all the complex questions in Ireland to-day'.[37] Whelan, who published Pearse, also edited Griffith, notably *To Rebuild the Nation* in 1919 (in 1917 he had also published the splendidly named *Golden Moments with Arthur Griffith*).[38] In a fine phrase in a letter to the *Independent* in April 1923, Whelan described him as 'the father, the teacher, and the great brains carrier of the Sinn Fein movement'.[39] Whelan was an enthusiastic advocate of the protectionism which the government of Saorstát Éireann had denied him,[40] writing in the same letter that 'the Irish people should afford voluntary protection for Irish goods' and quoting Griffith to that end.

Whelan was a fairly close personal ally of Griffith it would seem, especially before the First World War. By 1908, according to *Sinn Féin*, he had been appointed Secretary of the organisation. On 4 January of that year, Griffith writes thus in the newspaper:

> With the New Year is born the Sinn Féin stamps. The Sinn Féin stamp is intended to be affixed to all correspondence of Sinn Féiners as a visible sign that this is Ireland. We recommend it to be placed on the envelope in the opposite corner to that of the revenue stamp. The revenue will carry the correspondence, the Sinn Féin stamp added will spread Sinn Féin propaganda and will help to bring about the one thing Sinn Féin needs to make it win the land from end to end – a daily paper.

Griffith goes on to identify 'James Whelan' (that is, Seumas Whelan), of 17 Upper Ormond Quay as 'Chief Agent for sales of the Sinn Féin stamps' (Figure 3.5), which, he added, 'retail four for a penny'. In the same year Whelan stood unsuccessfully for Sinn Féin in the Dublin North City council ward (1908, as we have seen, was also when Whelan started to describe his shop as the Sinn Féin Depot).

Whelan also played a key role in the separatist press as the co-proprietor, with the better-known Joseph Stanley, of the Gaelic Press, based at Upper Liffey Street.[41] The Press published many of the ultra-nationalist papers during the opening years of the First World War: *The Gael*, (Arthur Griffith's) *Nationality*, *Republic* and the *Spark*.[42] In the heated period before the Easter Rising, the Press was raided by the authorities on 24 March 1916 as the result of a particularly provocative article in *The Gael*. From within the Dublin General Post Office in the following month Joe Stanley, 'printer to the Rising'[43] published Pearse's four-page newspaper *Irish War News* and ended up in

Figure 3.5 Sinn Féin stamp (1908).

Frongoch for his pains. We have been unable to ascertain if Seumas Whelan took an active part in the events of Easter week 1916, but certainly his shop had its place in those proceedings. In Frank Henderson's *Easter Rising. Recollections of an Irish Volunteer* (1996), Henderson makes it clear that 17 Upper Ormond Quay was selling illicit arms and equipment to the rebel Volunteers:

> The arming went ahead. Small arms, including revolvers and a few automatics, were imported secretly and distributed. Rifles became available in different ways, sometimes by bribing soldiers in barracks. Arms and military equipment were all on sale to a limited extent at Lawlor's, Fownes Street, and at Whelan's, Upper Ormond Quay.[44]

Whether it was for activities as a soldier or, more likely, the consequence of his role as quartermaster and incendiary publisher, Whelan ended up in British custody, first at Stafford Jail and, eventually, at Frongoch alongside colleagues O'Higgins and Stanley.[45]

Unlike Brian O'Higgins, Seumas Whelan was in favour of the Anglo-Irish Treaty and stood for election in the summer of 1923 as a Cumann na nGaedheal candidate for North Dublin. He is announced as one of the 'Pro-Treaty Official Parliamentary Candidates' for Dublin, Clare and Kildare in the *Irish Independent* for 4 August 1923, alongside such luminaries as Desmond FitzGerald, W. T. Cosgrave, Daniel McCarthy, Eoin MacNeill, Seumas Hughes, Margaret Collins-O'Driscoll and the ill-fated Kevin O'Higgins. He was influenced in his decision to advocate the Treaty by the example of Griffith, and in an election address (with fellow candidate – and fellow ex-Frongoch prisoner – Sean McGarry, the IRB veteran) at Manor Street, Dublin on 17 August, in the week after the president's death, Whelan lamented the loss of 'the great noble-hearted Arthur Griffith' and told his audience that his was 'the policy he came to advocate'.[46] Whelan failed to win a seat in the fourth Dáil, unlike Brian O'Higgins, who was elected in Clare for De Valera's Republican party, and, by 1926, when he had begun to announce his premises as the 'Old Sinn Féin Shop', he had quarrelled with Cumann na nGaedheal and with Kevin O'Higgins in particular, writing several vituperative letters to the papers accusing the minister of betraying Griffith's legacy.

In the Free State period, Whelan's began to abandon its purely Irish roster of sports, selling equipment for other popular, but not specifically Irish, pastimes. Boxing gloves were available for the first time, as were (association) football jerseys and athletics equipment, notably running kit.[47] That said, its owner's commitment to Irish nationalism and its history and traditions remained undimmed. One of his last political acts was a letter to the *Irish Independent* published in 1929 on an Ancient Wrong, in which Whelan questioned the fact that the street on which he had ploughed his trade for nigh on thirty years was named after an oppressor:

> SIR – As business people on Ormond Quay for over a quarter of a century, we desire to join whole-heartedly in the demand to have the name of Ormond Quay changed to Oliver Plunkett Quay. It was in the very district now known as Ormond Quay that Blessed Oliver Plunkett was seized by the Duke of Ormond's agents and cast into a dungeon at Dublin Castle.
>
> Surely the time has come when the names of the streets in the capital of Ireland should be of those who have done honour to their country by lives of noble service and sacrifice rather than those who have dishonoured and tyrannised over her.
>
> WHELAN AND SON.

As Dubliners know, this plea went unheeded, and Ormond Quay it remains, with number 17 now occupied by Sharon's Coffee Shop, where no trace of its incendiary past remains. However, Seumas Whelan's letter is testimony to his lifelong and indefatigable advanced nationalism; something evident not only in his orthodox literary work as editor, speech maker and correspondent but also in the advertising copy used to endorse the wares of the Sinn Féin Depot.

4
The Lady of the House (1890–1921): Gender, Fashion and Domesticity

> IRISH OATMEAL is far superior in every way to that made in America, the home-grown oat being larger, better-developed, and more succulent than the dried-up American grain. FINDLATER'S IRISH OATMEAL. Findlater's Finest Quality Pinhead or Flake, per 5lb linen bag, 1/-.
>
> (Advertisement for Findlater's Irish Oatmeal (1909))

Irish advertising culture in the late nineteenth and early twentieth centuries was pervaded with discourses aimed at the female consumer. Periodicals aimed at a female readership, such as *The Lady of the House* (later to become, in the 1920s, the *Irish Tatler and Sketch*), are particularly valuable when considering the representation and cultivation of the female consumer in the commercial sphere. *The Lady of the House* might signal itself (through its very title) as a traditional journal that marks out women's roles in the specifically private sphere (the home), but in fact, it demonstrates a complex engagement with normative values for Irish women. This chapter examines its fascinating paid columns.

I

Founded in 1890, *The Lady of the House*, one of a very few mainstream Irish journals of the period aimed at a female readership, was owned by the large food and drinks company, Findlater's, which had eleven branches in what is now the greater Dublin area (three in the old city between the canals, and one each in Rathmines, Sandymount, Kingstown, Blackrock, Dalkey, Bray, Howth and Foxrock).[1] The journal derived advertising revenue from English companies (such as Fry's Cocoa, Bovril and the Lever Bros' 'Sunlight' and 'Lux' soap brands), but also from Irish brands (including, most obviously, Findlater's own-brand goods but also 'Irish Cambric Pocket Handkerchiefs' and ladies outfitters' such as Lowry and Co., Belfast and Robert and Co.,

Dublin). *The Lady of the House* promoted itself as non-partisan, and as the product of a female hand, as an early prospectus demonstrates:

> Written by Gentlewomen for Gentlewomen, exquisitely illustrated, and published on the 15th of each month. Sold everywhere. Post free for one year. Two shillings. Each issue contains the current fashions, finely illustrated by leading French artists; Portraits of Leaders of Society; Interviews; an instalment of a novel by a popular writer; Articles on various charities, household matters, health and the toilet; Delineations and Portraits of our Readers' faces; gossip, valuable prizes, etc. Non-sectarian and non-political.[2]

Despite the claim that the *Lady* was written 'by Gentlewomen for Gentlewomen', the editor and founder was in fact male – the pressman and advertising agent H. Crawford Hartnell (see the 'Prologue'), who worked on the journal from 1890 to 1935.[3] Nonetheless, *The Lady of the House* was based on the notion of a female community, of women speaking to women, and 'ladies' contributed both occasional journalism and to various reader pages, even though the ultimate authority for the journal rested in male hands.

The use of the noun 'lady' in the journal's title represented a long-established magazinist tradition. As Margaret Beetham has noted, 'of fifty "female" titles published [in the United Kingdom] between 1800 and 1850, twenty-seven included the word "lady", but none included the word "woman" '.[4] *The Lady of the House* carries an overt gender distinction in its title and it also registers a very specific audience in terms of social class, being for those who considered themselves 'ladies' of a certain rank in life (we will return to this taxonomic distinction with regard to Wilde's editorship of *The Woman's World*). Those who read the magazine kept servants, or if they did not, they aspired to such a state. Even a cursory glance at its 1909 advertisement for Findlater's hire of vacuum cleaners indicates that the actual use of such an item will be delegated to the hired help. The picture reveals a boy who 'winds' the machine, and a female servant who conducts the cleaning, while the caption reads: 'Housekeeping a pleasure instead of a worry.'[5] Indeed, as *Findlater's Ladies' Housekeeping Book* (1890) testifies, it was assumed that the lady reader would have some form of housekeeper or servant: 'No mistress can hope to have her house in order, her servants under her command, her wishes promptly attended to, and yet leave plenty of time for the prosecution of the social duties which is demanded by society of the present day.'[6]

The implied reader of the journal is also distinctly metropolitan, and assumed to have easy access (both financial and geographical) to Dublin and Belfast as shopping districts.[7] And the register of many of the adverts in *The Lady of the House* suggests a level of disposable income in its readers. A frequent advertiser is the furriers J. M. Barnardo & Son, whose shop was (and still is) located on Grafton Street, opposite Trinity College. They maintained a prominent advertising presence throughout the late nineteenth and early twentieth centuries (in theatre programmes, journals, magazines and specifically *The Lady of the House*). (The shop was well situated for the trade of affluent customers, as the vice-regal residence was just up the street.[8]) Much of *The Lady of the House* was a vehicle for marketing to a strongly middle and upper-middle class set of consumers, and Barnardo's was a good example of this tendency. One of their advertisements, from 1920, advises: 'To express the warmth of your Friendship it is doubtful whether you could select a more memorable means than through a gift of fur', suggesting a luxurious token of excess (a gift which is gratuitous and signifies its difference from *quotidian* living requirements).[9] Another, earlier, Barnardo's advertisement, of 1890, continues the appeal to the aristocracy and the landed gentry which was such a feature of pre-Revival Irish adverting (and which did not evaporate entirely after the Revival): 'they invite with confidence the continued patronage of the Nobility and Gentry & all purchasers of Furs in Ireland'.[10]

During the nineteenth century, the women's magazine evolved as a very specific site of gender discourse, and one which had a clear, double investment in commodification: the purpose of every journal is not just to advertise, of course, but to sell *itself*[11] and, in this case, its proprietor's branded goods. As we have seen, *The Lady of the House*'s ownership rested in Findlater's hands, and at every turn, their brands – jams, alcohol, household wares, teas and so on – are heavily marketed, with especial attention to their catalogue or 'Grocery List', which often appeared at the back of each number.[12] *The Lady of the House* became a vehicle for cross-promotion of Findlater's products.

Findlater's everyday goods apart, the *Lady* also ran advertisements addressed to the luxury end of the market, as per Barnardo's furs, promoting the fashionable items which were available in Dublin department stores and elsewhere. As Erika Rappaport argues, 'there is no question that department stores promoted and defined female pleasures in order to sell their goods'.[13] At the same time, as well as fashion and beauty products, domestic purchases featured heavily in the advertising columns of women's journals. Adverts for vacuum cleaners (as sold by Findlater's), Singer Sewing Machines,[14] 'Frame Food', offering 'a nursing mother's testimony'[15] and even features on 'Spring Cleaning'[16] clearly envisage the proper place of woman to be in the private sphere (as mother, nurturer, housekeeper or clothes-maker).

So, alongside the promotion of luxury items, *The Lady of the House* also addressed matters of household economy. Tellingly, it included a feature entitled 'Our Household Corner', with tips and advice for the household manager, from what to do with parsnips and how to economise your coals, to dealing with childhood consumption and making evening blouses.[17] Perhaps this is unsurprising. In general terms, at the risk of stating the obvious, Irish housekeeping (as in most other nations in this period) was maintained almost exclusively by women, and small wonder that many journals featured advertising which endorsed such 'normative' womanhood to their readers. In her study of women in Revival-era Ireland, Joanna Bourke notes that:

> Single women performed housework, free of charge, for fathers, brothers, and uncles. Or they emigrated. Married women nursed their children and strove to improve the standard of services that they provided to their family, while widowed women competed with their children's spouses in the production of goods. Female labour came to be dominated by housework.[18]

By 1890 the rural economy in Ireland was in a far better position than it was mid-century (despite the persistent threat of famine), and economic growth necessarily entailed a greater desire for consumer goods. Historians have tracked the impact of technological and industrial development on the home, arguing that with mass production of goods and appliances, women's household labours altered dramatically.[19] Bourke argues that, perhaps paradoxically, this did not mean less work for the average woman in Ireland at the turn of the twentieth century; indeed, the average amount of time spent on housework increased with technological developments, as possession of domestic goods grew and standards of living improved.[20]

Of course, in general the access to such goods centred on the towns and cities, and in Ireland, as late as 1911, less than a third of the population lived in such places, by contrast to four-fifths in England and Wales.[21] But Irish towns and cities were subject to great change from 1890 onwards. Bourke gives an illuminating anecdote:

> Innovations were noted by the priest and novelist the Reverend Joseph Guinan in 1915, when he revisited his first parish in Rathmore. On entering the parlour/drawing-room of the parochial house, he discovered that, during his twenty years' absence, the hearthstone fireplace and turf-barrel had been replaced by a grate and a coal-box, and a piano stood in the place of the old chest of drawers.[22]

Improved living standards meant an increase in consumer purchases: once thought luxuries, such items became more and more popular. Consumer expectations, and women's expectations, were rising; in the women's page of the *Irish Homestead*, one columnist pointed out in jocular fashion:

> Honest Tommy Traddles felt himself compelled to defer his marriage with the dearest girl in the world (prepared to wait for him twenty years if necessary), when he counted what plenishings would cost – the sheets

> and pillowcases and tablecloths, and the gridirons and saucepans and salamanders. Of course, you may talk about artificial wants![23]

In this march towards what the columnist calls, ironically, a new 'civilisation',[24] the nature of women's housework also changed, although the plethora of material possessions did not necessarily mean less work for the average woman. Ninety per cent of all married women claimed their occupation as 'houseworker'[25] and this continued through to Irish Dominion status and beyond.[26] Unmarried women were frequently employed as servants in larger and more prosperous households (in 1911, for every thirty people in the Irish population, there was one paid domestic servant).[27] Women's lives were also under increased pressure from the religious community: by the time a married woman reached the age of 45, she would (on average and again according to Bourke), have given birth to five or six children.[28]

There were also very clear social and moral expectations placed on a woman, in Ireland, in common with the rest of the United Kingdom at this time. Dympna McLoughlin characterises late nineteenth-century Irish womanhood in the following manner:

> There were essentially three main characteristics of a respectable woman, regardless of class. The first was that she have an overwhelming desire to marry, remain faithful in a lifelong union, and remain subordinate and publicly dependent in that relationship. Second, that the woman's natural sphere was the domestic, where she engaged in reproductive and not productive tasks. Mothering became newly defined and confined and the widespread practice of wet-nursing became severely curtailed. Thirdly, and most significantly, women's sexuality was totally contained in marriage.[29]

The conventions placed upon a woman were sometimes seemingly resisted in the commercial sphere, however. In some ways, commodity culture was at odds with prevalent social and religious ideologies about the proper role of middle-class women, while, at the same time, consumerist discourses maintained that the world of the commodity spectacle was overtly a feminine sphere.[30] Despite Theodor Veblen's claim that patriarchal tradition heavily influences the purchase of 'leisure' goods (a married woman's luxurious display – on her person, or in the home, is based on male consumption of the woman as chattel)[31] both shopping and consumer culture has been seen as ultimately promoting a degree of female liberty. Rachel Bowlby sees the very act of shopping in such a manner: 'the "shut-in" place of women's lives, and then more generally of "home and work", presumably for men as well, is contrasted with release or freedom in the street, associated with its windows and with the activity of walking'.[32] In *The Lady of the House*, there is also shopping in the home itself: the journal might be said to have allowed the female consumer to engage with a world of commodity culture from the comfort of her own home, to risk a cliché of the advertiser, and in this way, it might be argued, the female magazine reader transgressed the more established boundaries of the public and the private sphere.

A maternal tone of motherly advice is frequently invoked in the housekeeping and cosmetic advertisements in such journals as *The Lady of the House*. This is a voice within advertising discourse which, as Diane Barthel notes in her study of gender and advertising, 'is nurturing, protective, gently encouraging, and born of experience. It is used exclusively in women's advertisements; in men's advertisements, mother is anathema. It is often found in skin-care advertisements, reminding women, as mother did, to wash their faces and clean their teeth.'[33] This is clearly revealed in both the advertising copy and the editorial material from *The Lady of the House* at this time. For instance, a full page article written by 'Meg Hunter' offers warm and friendly advice on 'Social Amenities' – how to conduct afternoon tea, how to dine out or be a successful hostess, how to behave at a concert or what to wear for the theatre (note the use of the French term 'demi-toilette' which adds to the atmosphere of high sophistication):

> If you have a dinner gown that requires remodelling, design it as a demi-toilette, with elbow sleeves and without a train, suitable for theatres and concerts... Do not appear on such occasions in a ball dress or tea gown. The former would be bad taste, and fortunately, is not often seen, though he latter is a constant offender... Should the play not be to your taste, do not chatter to your chaperone or companion, because it may be of the greatest interest to your next door neighbour.[34]

A similar advisory voice is obvious in the advertisement for Findlater's 'Ladies' Housekeeping Book' (Figure 4.1). Clearly the audience for the journal is not a post-famine rural mother, but an urban middle-class lady of leisure, who has enough disposable income in her housekeeping budget to avail herself of 'Fashionable Fancy Work', 'Laces and Fine Things' and 'Titbits from Breakfast, Luncheon and High Tea'.[35]

Interestingly, some feminist critics have argued that the materials advertised in such stuff as the Housekeeping Book provided one way in which women may have exerted some degree of freedom of control in their lives. Lori Anne Loeb makes this case in *Consuming Angels*:

> Even with limited or unequal resources, Victorian women had some control. As society moved from an ethic of production to an ethic of consumption, the role of women as household purchasers acquired new social significance. In the commercial forum the woman exercised

> a considerable degree of free choice. It is probable that, especially for expensive items such as furniture or appliances, husbands contributed to the decision to purchase [and] a household allowance may have limited purchasing latitude. But within these constraints each woman had freedom of action. She could, for example, emphasize her superior understanding of taste, status, or utility as applied to the domestic sphere [...] Although she did not earn the money, the woman of the house could significantly control the way that it was spent.[36]

In choosing from the surfeit of goods available at the turn of the twentieth century, the woman of the house, Loeb argues, was exercising some measure of economic control.

The Lady of the House is a useful guide to advertising to women in Ireland in the Revival period. Though Irish-Ireland firms are as not as common or as clamorous in its pages, alongside salutes to a wide range of imported English goods (such as Fry's Cocoa and Monkey Brand polish) the journal offered many advertisements for Irish-branded goods that proudly declared their Irish provenance, such as the puff for Findlater's Irish Oatmeal which provides the epigraph to this chapter (an illustrated version of

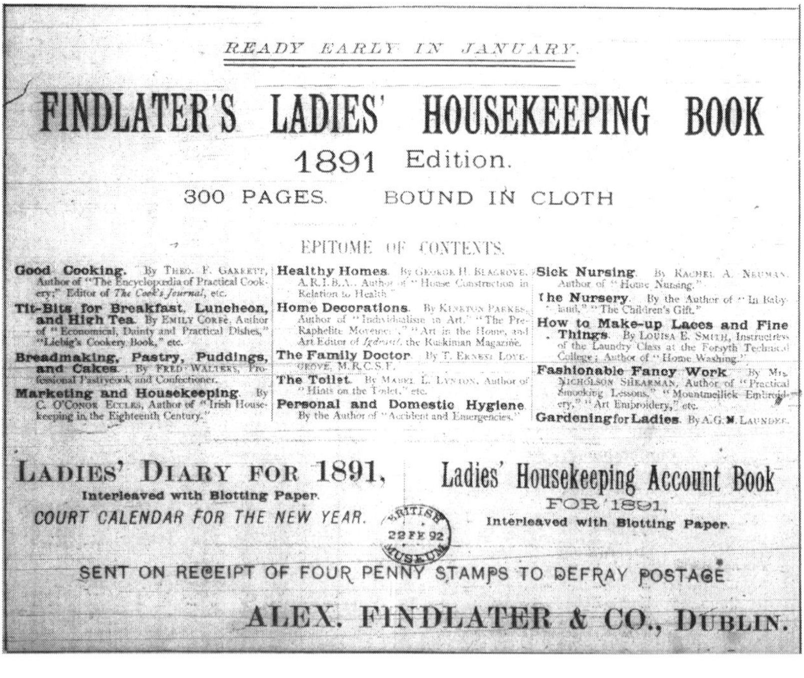

Figure 4.1 Findlater's 'Ladies' Housekeeping Book, 1891' (1890).

this advertisement is reproduced as figure 4.3 below). An 1891 advertisement headed 'A Delightful Present', another example, declares that:

> Among the nicest and most welcome presents that can possibly be given in the family circle, or from one friend to another, are bottles of Scent, done up on dainty parcels, such as the exquisite "OSOSWEET" that hails from Ireland, and is declared by many people to be the sweetest and more durable perfume of the day and is prepared exclusively at TATE'S MEDICAL HALL, 9 Royal Avenue, Belfast.[37]

The periodical also addresses such issues as court fashions, cookery, iconic Irishwomen, the management of the home and indeed 'Scientific Cookery' as well as a 'Prettiest Child Prize' which asked readers to submit photographs of their children and 'Our Little Darlings' (the children's page).[38] Despite these fairly conventional appeals to the Irish domestic middle-class female, there were also such non-conventional features as 'The Women's Parliament' and coverage of female university graduates, which suggest some potential for more unconventional thinking. *The Lady of the House* included debates on 'What do suffragettes deserve?' (which proposes the next debate as 'What are women's rights?').[39] Topics covered also include 'How well do we treat our menfolk?' (this alongside 'Is early rising beneficial?').[40] The female graduates of the Royal University of Ireland are pictured in a full page spread of 14 November 1891, although their diminutive designation as 'sweet girl graduates' tends to suggest that young women were still to be indulged rather than taken entirely seriously.

The journal's articles and, indeed, advertisements constructed a particular vision of womanhood as caregiver, mother and wife, but, additionally, they also endorsed commercial desire. Indeed, numerous articles in *The Lady of the House* confirm how commodities and commercial goods were represented as legitimising consumer 'desires' in women. Witness, for example, an article by Meg Hunter on 'Shopping' published in 1890:

> It is here that a woman's faculty for organisation will prove valuable to her, a faculty, by the way, that should be cultivated to the greatest possible extent and not allowed to rust, for it will stand her in good stead many a time and oft [...] It is a good plan to ascertain which shops are the best, and as much as possible stick to them, as this invariably ensures better attention. Draw up lists before you start, because it makes one so dissatisfied with one's day's work to discover something forgotten. As far as possible, know what you want before you enter a shop, and do not be persuaded to take an alternative, unless, as often happens, it will answer the purpose equally well.[41]

The overarching principle at work in this advice is that of rationality. Hunter emphasizes the need for careful planning (lists), rigorous knowledge of the field (which shops are best), and to refuse impulse purchases unless they are actually needed. The 'rational' household manager is celebrated (as opposed to the 'irrational' impulse buyer, excessive spender or even shoplifter).[42]

In common with European practices, department stores in Dublin employed advertising, competitive pricing, lavish interiors, winter and summer sales and the developing use of window display and electric lighting in the latter part of the century.[43] Indeed this 'staging' of consumer goods emerges in the advertising pages of *The Lady of the House*, and it is part of a wider phenomenon in Dublin. As Stephanie Rains argues:

> The picture of early department stores in Dublin [...] is easily comparable to that in other large European cities. Consisting of up to thirty different departments, displaying a wide range of goods for fixed and clearly displayed prices, they were employing up to two hundred workers, most of whom were living in dormitory accommodation attached to or near the shop, and receiving above-average wages for their profession [...] even so soon after the Famine as 1851, Dublin contained a professional and commercial middle class with sufficient disposable income to have acquired the habits of modern consumer culture.[44]

The shop window itself functioned as an advertisement, as Rachel Bowlby has argued, insofar as it is 'supposed to attract attention [...] it is clearly framed, set off behind its exhibiting glass, and draws spectators to it as something designed to be looked at. Its three-dimensional space, on the other hand, can additionally or alternatively make it appear as a stage.'[45] The dressed shop window has immediacy; while being offered a fantasy realm of goods and purchases through a framed, aesthetic pictorial vision, the potential shopper is invited inside to render that vision her own possession.[46]

Women (sometimes accompanied by children) feature heavily in illustrated advertisements for Irish department stores. McBirney & Co., for instance, offered a seasonal advertisement of their 'Great Winter Sale' in *The Lady of the House* in January 1909 in which all of the customers portrayed are female. Such advertisements support Bowlby's argument that shopping was often construed as a middle-class woman's responsibility, especially after the development of the department stores in the nineteenth century:

> The history of shopping is largely a history of women, who have overwhelmingly been the principal shoppers both in reality and in the multifarious representations of shopping. This history began to gather momentum in the middle of the nineteenth century, when department stores entered the world. Their splendid new buildings and permanent exhibitions of lovely new things brought middle-class women into town to engage in what was historically a new activity: a day's shopping.

> They were places of leisure and luxury, offering women the image of a life that they would then, in fantasy if not in substance, take home with them.[47]

In like manner, Elaine Abelson comments that:

> With the ability to exploit a vast array of goods, the large stores educated people to want things, and they played a crucial part in determining the essentials of middle-class life and aspirations [...] Assuming responsibility for consumption, women shopped. Notwithstanding its fundamental place in women's work, shopping was linked in the public mind with pleasure and personal freedom.[48]

Or as Mouret in Zola's *An Bonheur des Dames* shrewdly claims: 'Get the women [...] and you'll sell the world.'[49]

So how were women encouraged, for good or ill, to desire and purchase particular goods, and how were these items advertised in *The Lady of the House*? One particular way was through the cultural cache of a particular nation – France. While advertisements in Irish-Ireland periodicals and for Irish-made goods had generally turned away from the previous genuflection towards that country, this manoeuvre is still evident in *The Lady of the House*. This is in part because many of the *Lady*'s advertisements were placed on behalf of British companies that still frequently enlisted the notion of French sophistication to their sales pitches. It might also be seen as a consequence of the nature of Findlater's status as an Anglo-Irish company owned by (liberal) Protestants. Appeals to Irish-Ireland goods and to economic patriotism, though not unknown in *The Lady of the House*, are much rarer than in the Dublin newspapers and certainly less common than in the prints associated with nationalist political organisations of whatever kind. *The Lady of the House*, as a bourgeois, consumerist periodical was a very long way from contemporary nationalist journals such as *The Shan Van Vocht* or *Bean na hÉireann* ('The Woman of Ireland'), which was founded in 1908 as a nationalist counterbalance to journals, whether British or Irish, which endorsed 'foreign' fashion (Maud Gonne's complaint about 'the frivolous and degrading effect of English women's magazines in Ireland'[50] is exemplary).

Numerous advertisements in *The Lady of the House* employ pseudo-French names in a bid to exoticise their wares, to associate themselves with a prestige culture (the 'Louvelle' corset, or the 'Forme Naturelle' corset), and indeed to infer the possibility of a luxury lifestyle associated with the purchase of a particular product. This is explicitly the case with 'The Parisian Diamond Company', advertising in *The Lady of the House* in 1909, which emphasises that even the most 'fastidious people' are pleased with their jewellery.[51] Invoking the jewellery as 'a suitable present for a lady', the company in fact makes *imitation* pieces, perhaps intended to appeal to the journal's aspirational middle-class readership rather than the *haut ton* who do not generally wear costume jewellery. Interestingly, apart from the title of the company concerned, there is no other French signifier in their copy. The merest suggestion of 'Paris' as correlated with luxury purchases such as 'diamonds' speaks for itself.

More generally, but not less effectively, an advertisement for 'Jaques and Jaques' (based in Darlington in northern England) establishes a somewhat spurious claim to exclusivity and prestige. Claiming they are 'French dress specialists', Jaques and Jaques declare that 'To dress well it is necessary to "Feel the Pulse of Fashion" – know what French people are making, selling, and wearing.'[52] In such copy Paris resounds through the pages of *The Lady of the House*. The 'Paris Letter' feature (by the appropriately named 'Olivette') identifies the latest fashions and practices, ostensibly from the continent.[53] The use of Parisian chic in advertising such as the examples above also suggests a rarefied sense of feminine sexuality. Since Balzac, sexuality and French fashion had been closely aligned: the 'elegant, coquettish Parisienne'[54] achieved status with women across the fashion world. The Parisienne potentially offered a fantasy of a liberty to the Irishwoman.

II

Advertising aimed at Irish women provides insights into this transitional period in Irish consumerism, the changing nature of women's fashion itself, and the shifting ideology of woman's place. The promotion of the corset is perhaps one of the most interesting aspects of advertising aimed at a female audience, imbued at it is with a number of potentially contradictory and ideologically complex cultural meanings. As Leigh Summers notes, 'the corset remains profoundly under-theorized, though it is potentially the most illuminating icon of the Victorian era, heavily pregnant with feminine metaphors and associations, unavoidably steeped in and expressive of Victorian female sexuality and its subordination'.[55]

Summers argues that the corset constricted the wayward female body in order that it might correspond to the Victorian ideal of feminine decency and decorum. At the same time, though it may have provided such control, it was no chastity belt, inasmuch as it also accentuated the sexual characteristics of the female form: the breasts, the waist, the hips and the buttocks. In this way, it can be seen as a garment of conflicting ideological codes. In many respects, Ireland was no different from the USA, England or the continent in this tendency to bind the female form in boned undergarments. However, as we shall see, the advertising of the garment can be read in terms culturally specific to the Irish nation.

As Leigh Summers remarks, 'Advertising played an integral role in the popularity and longevity of corsetry':

> It often revealed more about prevailing socio-cultural attitudes than about the items that were for sale [...] Moreover, a contemporary analysis of nineteenth-century corset advertisements quickly dismantles prevailing conceptions of them as quaint quasi-erotic trivia, and recasts them as significant documents of social history from which attitudes towards sexuality in general, and female sexuality in particular, can be gleaned. Once seen in this way, corset advertisements can be recognized as major forerunners to the sexual objectification of women in the public realm in the twentieth century.[56]

There was a concerted attempt on behalf of corset manufacturers to inundate the advertising market with copy for their products. By the 1880s numerous corset advertisements appeared in Ireland, not only in women's magazines, but also in regional and national newspapers, as well as theatre programmes and journals. Clery & Co. of Sackville Street, Dublin, for instance, announced on the front page of the *Irish Independent* in 1906 that 'We are the Sole Agents in Dublin for Madame Harcourt's celebrated Corsets, and we naturally wish to promulgate the Harcourt idea in Corsets.'[57] Corsetry was frequently advertised with illustrations, often executed with some degree of care and skill, which can be seen as skirting the parameters of public decency.[58] By representing an invitation to view the most intimate scenes of the boudoir and female dress, conventionally reserved for the marriage bed, corsetieres were essentially publicising a highly private scene. For this very reason, many corset advertisements tended to present a disembodied torso or, indeed, a freestanding corset. For instance, the decorous 'Platinum Anti-Corset', as featured in *The Lady of the House* in 1891, portrays an uninhabited corset, as do the garments announced by 'M. Worth et Cie' and Thompson and Co. (the 'Glove-Fitting Corset').[59] However, despite this sanitising gesture, paradoxically, as Summers notes, these disembodied silhouettes actually accentuated 'every curve of the female torso, and in doing so inevitably hinted at sexual availability. Corsets [...] were never illustrated as folded up, nor were they ever represented as empty, two-dimensional garments. An imaginary but fulsome torso was always apparent within, fleshing them out.'[60]

In Ireland, as elsewhere, the corset was generally perceived to be a middle-class phenomenon: the Irish rural poor, despite some aspiration towards the fashion of tight-fitting gowns in the 1890s,[61] more commonly wore the traditional cloak or shawl, with a petticoat, skirt and high collar blouse.[62] At least in their initial audience, the corsetry advertisements of the nineteenth century in Ireland were aimed at an upwardly mobile, financially comfortable, middle-class female readership. In general, the corsets as advertised in early twentieth-century newspapers and magazines cost anything between seven and eighteen shillings (though there were a few which were a great deal more expensive). As a point of comparison, the average, respectable working family in the UK prior to the First World War had somewhere in the region of twenty shillings a week as an income.[63] Even in the more prosperous urban centres of Ireland, the corset tended to be a middle-class commodity.

In her commentary on nineteenth-century female fashion in Ireland, Mairead Dunlevy notes that the bourgeois lady was especially concerned with her corset:

> It is hardly surprising that the wearers of [...] ornate gowns were concerned about their corsetry. This concern was carried to the extent that different types were worn according to the time of day or the leisure activity, whilst some extremists in 1896 even wore body corsets and foot corsets (strong, laced linen socks without soles) in bed. The devotion to supportive underwear was such that journalists in *Irish Society* took to ridicule in an attempt to persuade women to abandon the bustle, after it had been dropped by fashion at large. The same journalists used arguments of health to encourage women to relax their corsets at the waist.[64]

The issue of health raised by Dunlevy is a particularly pertinent one, and, in Ireland as elsewhere, was bound up with the emergence of what is now labelled the 'New Woman' and the development of sporting activities for women, and the emerging emphasis on women's freedom. All of these issues are implicitly addressed in the columns of *The Lady of the House*.

Physicians may have railed against the practice of tight-lacing, but rarely did they claim that the corset needed to be abandoned altogether[65] (indeed, some doctors maintained that a corset was requisite because womankind was not physically strong enough to dispense with such support).[66] Advertising copy responded to such debate by harnessing a pseudo-medical discourse, stressing the healthsome benefits of a particular corset, especially when compared with the inferior products offered by a firm's rivals. The Irish advertising columns offered corsets claiming to cure the very ailments which some argued the garment caused or exacerbated. For instance, the 'Invigorator Corset' (Figure 4.2) from *The Lady of the House* is advertised as being recommended by eminent doctors; 'health [is] insured by Reast's Patent'.[67] It supposedly boasts a number of illustrious patrons and supporters: Thomas Gambier MD, Physician to the Hospital for Consumption, Dr Neville, Medical Officer of Health, and numerous other medical personnel, as well as the Countess of Suffolk (appealing to the aspirational Anglo-Irish reader of *The Lady of the House*). A Dr Kelly of Edinburgh claims that 'it is the best invention of the kind for improving the carriage and appearance of the figure without the injurious effects of the ordinary Corset, even when tight laced'. The Invigorator is actually beneficial to health, and thereby differentiated from other models on the market, mere 'Ordinary Corsets'.

Figure 4.2 Advertisement for the Invigorator Corset (1890).

Such branded nineteenth-century corset advertising can be read as offering a clear message in terms of male authority over female fashion. Her grace apart, it is a male medical establishment which salutes the Invigorator, a voice of authority which can be seen as constructing femininity according to accepted conventions: as physically weak, with a body needing constant maintenance and, indeed, the metaphorical reproof of a corset's figuration. Indeed, several advertisements in *The Lady of the House* offer to 'cure' women of feminine 'ailments': a full page advertorial narrative of 1891, for instance, offers a medicinal cure dubbed 'Mother Seigel's Curative Syrup'[68] for that feminine complaint of 'nerves'. Similarly, advertisements also offer to solve problems with 'weak hair' (April 1891), or anxiety over plain features: 'Good looks: have you got any?' (May 1891). In the latter number women who are lacking in embonpoint – 'LADIES TOO THIN in the BUST, wishing to obtain a good figure' – are told to 'send 3 stamps for [a] Pamphlet' on this interesting subject (such products are reminiscent of the earlier nineteenth-century 'quack' doctors who populated the advertising market of the day with their bogus claims of hair-restorers for the entirely bald and cure-alls for the sick).[69]

The debate surrounding corsetry continued in *The Lady of the House* into the twentieth century, notably in a advertorial feature of 1909 spanning several issues entitled 'The Evolution of the Corset'. The ordinary 'stock corset' is described as having 'evolved' for 'the strong and healthy housewife as well as the young and undeveloped miss'.[70] The article dismisses tight lacing, however, as 'the actual abuse, and not the use, of that most useful and healthful garment [...] Nature did not intend that the body she has created should be distorted out of all resemblance to its natural self; neither was it intended that woman should neglect lending such aid as nature requires in order to make perfect that which she has created.'[71] Instead, the modern miss needs a more free-fitting garment, which is to be found, the piece helpfully informs its readers, only from the good offices of William Pretty and Son, whose corsets are to be found in all good retail outlets in Dublin and via mail order from the firm's manufactory in Suffolk.

The fact that the feature, masquerading as a piece of journalism, is actually a disguised advertisement for Messrs Pretty and Son should not blind the reader to its ideological resonance. While the wearing of corsets had sometimes previously been attributed to ill-health, the article notes that now 'the single strip corsets' of the contemporary moment are both 'hygienic [and] comfortable'. The appeal to 'comfort' clearly reflects developing dress reform (discussed later in this chapter), founded on the free movement of the body, and articles of clothing which can accommodate bicycling, sports and the requirements of the modern young woman.

In May 1909, *The Lady of the House* announced an essay competition on the subject of 'Are Corsets Injurious?' Again, the text turns out be a hidden advertisement,[72] noting that 'Most ladies are of the opinion which we ourselves expressed, that corsets, properly worn and properly made, after the style of those produced [of course] by Messrs Wm. Pretty & Sons of Ipswich, are indeed necessary and beneficial.' While the published prize essays do indeed support the corset as indispensible to the modern woman (in no small way influenced by the prize, supplied by Pretty & Son themselves), one successful writer, writing under the pseudonym 'Miss Viking', deserves some notice. Though not rejecting the corset entirely, she advocates the development of the feminine 'trunk muscles' through exercise: 'I know of many weakly corseted neurasthenics transformed [by exercise] into strong healthy girls, with a beauty of figure and carriage that cannot be obtained by corseting'.[73] In this, we can perhaps see a reflection of the nascent move away from the corset – even from Pretty and Co.'s 'comfortable' corset – and of the emerging figure of the 'New Woman' (see below), as she was manifested in 1920s Ireland.

III

In the late nineteenth century, elevated 'high' art prints proliferated in the commercial realm, with reproductions of classical statuary reaching a wide audience. In like manner, advertisers and magazine editors also began to produce fashion plates and advertisements with classical themes.[74] In terms of advertising, the effect of this was twofold. First, an otherwise 'low' cultural product such as advertising could borrow legitimacy from its use of classical paradigms. Secondly, the 'draped' female body, as represented in visual culture (as opposed to the fully clothed subject), allowed a public eroticisation of the female form. There was a recurrent appropriation of the traditions of high art (including Grecian and Roman models) in Irish advertising, as elsewhere. Discussing this phenomenon, Lori Anne Loeb remarks that:

> Classicizing imagery aggrandized the feminine image in advertisements. Draped in timeless Grecian costume, hair loosely knotted and frequently adorned with flowers or a laurel wreath, feet bare or in sandals, the classical commercial goddess contrasted dramatically with the elaborate reality of late Victorian and Edwardian feminine appearance. Within the context of innumerable fashion advertisements that attest to the seemingly endless variety and artifice of Victorian fashion, her simplicity is more dramatic.[75]

To give but one example, the magazine *Photobits* (which features in Joyce's *Ulysses*) was noted, as Tess Marsh has written, for 'a marked interest in the classical. The models [in its pages] are frequently compared to Greek statues and their attire noted for its Grecian style.'[76]

This cultural phenomenon was also evident in the pages of *The Lady of the House*. In an 1891 advertisement for 'Koko for the hair', a martial figure with streaming hair is mounted on a horse, carrying a banner labelled 'Koko'[77] in honour of the noble hair tonic. Here, images of strength, and warlike heroism, combine in the classical iconographic manner of David's Liberty, in the female form. Similarly, in Findlater's full page advert for their own brand 'Irish oatmeal' (Figure 4.3), the goddess Ceres is pictured with an armful of cereal and a sickle, band of flowers in her hair, barefooted and attired in classical costume. As the protector of the harvest and agriculture, Ceres was a potent symbol for the product, implying both fertility and a pastoral vision of Irish nationalist mythology (this oatmeal is 'far superior every way', the copy maintains, to imported 'American grain').

Another *The Lady of the House* advertisement, 'Venus Soap' (Figure 4.4), actively exploits classical association.[78] This brand belonged to Joseph Watson and Sons, who had one of the largest soap works in England, situated in Whitehall Road in Leeds. The Venus de Milo is used in a number of their adverts in the UK and Ireland, and, indeed, the company offered a picture of the original statue in exchange for 25 soap wrappers (for 60, the picture would be framed). The soap itself is advertised as follows: 'Sweet and Pure', 'Purifies Everything and Delights Everybody', 'Saves money, labour, time, and temper', 'Goes farther than any other soap'. The implied addressee is (of course), the female housewife or housekeeper, who is appealed to in terms of financial thrift and labour saving. More significant, however, is the association between household cleanliness and moral hygiene – the

Figure 4.3 Advertisement for Findlater's Irish Oatmeal (1909).

emphasis on purity not only correlates with gradual improvements in living standards and sanitation, but also the policing of the sexual wholesomeness of femininity, for which soap provides a neat metaphor.[79] The figure of Venus herself, like Ceres in the Findlater's advert, demurely averts her gaze while simultaneously revealing breasts, curves and even the hint of genitalia. Simultaneously she is virgin and whore, sexually available and morally incorruptible. Perhaps in her case, as Loeb puts it, 'The classical goddess suggests only a pretence of purity. Breasts partly exposed, arms and feet bared, the goddess seems half-dressed in a costume that is often unashamedly diaphanous.'[80]

Figure 4.4 Advertisement for Venus Soap (1891).

An 1890 advertisement for 'Snowflake' soap reveals the female subject looking directly at the viewer, but from the vantage point of concealment *behind a fan*, on which the following caption may be read: 'Always wash flannels with "Snowflake".'[81] A clear and modest division is placed between the gaze of the consumer and that of the female body. In a contemporaneous advertisement, Martin & Mumford's clothing makers (18 & 19 Suffolk Street, Dublin) portray a splendidly but discreetly attired female figure who stares intently to her left. As Gillian Dyer has remarked in her study of advertising's symbolic meanings: 'The aversion of the eyes and the lowering of the head can indicate withdrawal from a scene and symbolise dependency and submissiveness [...] Women may focus their attention on the middle distance, on some object (like the product).'[82]

Such representations of the female form are not uncommon in the period under discussion here. Barnardo & Son, for instance, placed an advert in *The Lady of the House* in 1891 in which the female subject coyly averts her gaze from the viewer. Likewise, an advertisement for 'Hinde's Hair Curlers' (carrying the possibly spurious testimony 'Mrs [Lily] Langtry writes: "I find them invaluable" ') shows a woman before her toilette, admiring her hair in a classically submissive pose (one arm behind her head).[83] The 'Invigorator Corset' puff reproduced above shows a woman before a mirror, hands ruffling her hair, and subtly glancing over her right shoulder. While in some senses such advertisements may appeal to the male gaze, there is in fact great ingenuity behind them when they are reproduced in women's magazines: the female form, male desire and shopping are closely and firmly linked in a way which implies, as Margaret Beetham puts it, that 'they assumed the reader was an agent, who could enjoy deploying her skills and knowledge in self-creation'.[84] The female reader situates herself in that nexus of desirability, sexuality and commodity.

IV

In many ways, *The Lady of the House* and the advertising culture therein illustrates the competing social and ideological ideals surrounding contemporary women in Ireland. Niamh O'Sullivan argues that enshrined in the nation were 'the "Victorian" nationalism of the Catholic church, and the official Victorianism of the state'.[85] Indeed, the very specific iconography of both the Virgin Mary and Irish nationalist representations of feminine Ireland invoked a figure of benevolence, obedience and passively suffering womanhood. As Timothy P. Foley notes:

> Women were the keepers of tradition, the exemplars of morality as traditionally defined, the disinfecting element in a morally dissolute society. The Irish national character was represented as feminine and as unsuited to modern life... Home was seen as an oasis of selflessness, self-denial, community, indeed of virtue as traditionally understood. Women, as guardians and transmitters of tradition and morality, were held to be naturally moral and self-sacrificing.[86]

Patrick J. Keenan, then an Irish school inspector (though later Sir Patrick, Commissioner of National Education in Ireland (1871–1894) and the chief educational administrator in Ireland), exemplifies such opinion, commenting in 1855 that, 'after marriage, home is the abiding place of woman, the natural centre and seat of all her occupations, the cause of all her anxieties, the object of all her solicitude, and it is a deranged state of society that encourages her to seek employment beyond its precincts'.[87]

This near-indissoluble link between marriage, 'normative' womanhood and home is also evident in Irish consumer culture, as per a forthright advertisement for J. M. McDowell, 'The Happy Ring House' Jewellers, which sports the caption: 'If you want to be Happy, get married' (Figure 4.5). Women were granted equal citizenship in 1922, as part of the new Free State, but essentially the rights of women in terms of not just gainful employment and voting rights, but also liberty outside the home, were often quite restricted: 'While modern, fashionable young women were castigated from the altar, the self-sacrificing Irish mother was elevated to a national symbol.'[88]

Despite this, the late nineteenth and early twentieth centuries were crucial periods in terms of women's rights. The emergence of what has been identified as the 'New Woman' is closely correlated with such issues. The New Woman, frequently stereotyped as a smoker, a bicyclist and an advocate of rational dress, evolved from earlier nineteenth century appeals for women's rights in terms of greater social freedom, the right to equal education and the reinvention (rather than outright rejection) of conventional female roles.[89] The ideological dimensions implicit in a nascent feminine independence and ability to earn a living are also evident in the pages of *The Lady of the House*.

The greater freedoms afforded by developments in working life, for instance, prompted an article for the journal in 1919 in which dressmaking, architecture, estate agency, secretarial employment and other white collar jobs such as typing and shorthand, are all seen as suitable for the middle class woman seeking work[90] (more remarkably, game-keeping, policing and

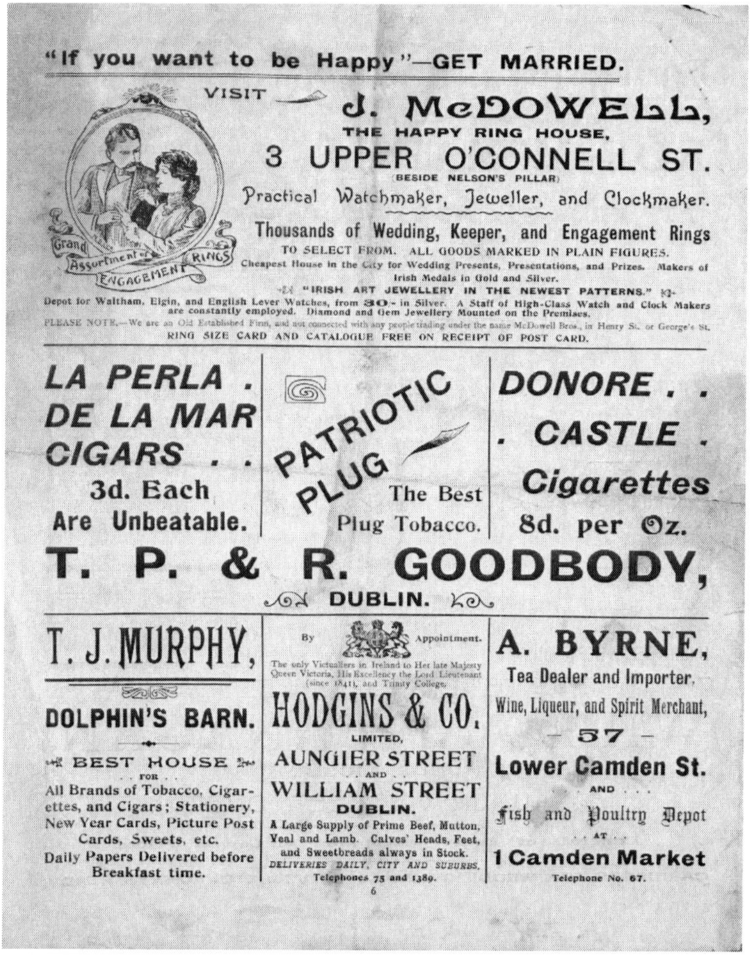

Figure 4.5 Advertisement for the Happy Ring House Jewellers (n.d.). Courtesy of the National Library of Ireland.

chauffeur work are also suggested *en passant*). Indeed, 'The Irish Girl' – as heralded in a subsequent issue of August 1919 – explains how the 'wave of interest' in physical training and gymnastics for the Irish girl has promoted physical well-being and correlates physical health with female employment:

> Now that women are taking their places in ever-increasing numbers in the ranks of the workers, and that 'daily labour's dull Lethean toll' is no longer looked upon as something to be ashamed of, 'the survival of the fittest' has an even more pregnant meaning than some few years ago,

> and it is, naturally, to be anticipated that girls' clubs and associations for physical training will become more numerous and even better patronised than at present, for the physically unfit will speedily be relegated to the scrap heap by the employer whether the daily bread be earned in the 'professions' or among the more humble ranks of 'the toilers'.[91]

Emerging from the 'House' to the world beyond, the New Woman is signified here through an appeal to work and to physical well-being. Indeed, the issue of women and the private sphere of home and family was particularly pertinent in one area of advertising: outdoor life.

Consider the example of cycling. Cycling for women in the late nineteenth and early twentieth centuries was somewhat controversial issue. An early form of bicycle, known as a velocipede, appeared in France in the 1810s, and cycling itself had emerged as a popular innovation throughout much of Western Europe by the 1890s.[92] However, while some supporters of this new mode of transport maintained it would strengthen the female body, the cycle was also attacked by others, sometimes on such preposterous grounds as its supposed tendency to encourage masturbation: 'The act of riding', says Ellen Gruber Garvey, 'was seen as essentially masculine. Women's riding therefore posed a threat to gender definition. It was also perceived as threatening women's sexual purity [...] and when unmarried men and women rode together, cycling threatened chastity and order.'[93] In some contemporary opinion the bicycle was seen as being in direct conflict with the religious and social ideology prevalent in Ireland, which sought to confine women to domestic roles.

The bicycle was frequently castigated in some Irish periodicals. 'In some cases people were run down by these "ladies" and these women miscalled "ladies" actually sometimes rode two abreast.'[94] Ostensibly concerned with road and pedestrian safety, the register of this report from *The Impartial Reporter* in 1901 sees bicycle riding as compromising a woman's gentility and respectability (here a 'District Inspector' notes the 'insolence' of a 'lady offender who rode on a footpath only three feet wide').[95] In Ellen Gruber Garvey's opinion the bicycle threatened the established moral order: 'the new mobility the bicycle allowed offered freer movement in new spheres, outside the family and home – heady freedoms which feminists celebrated'.[96]

Advertisements of the period reflected these developments. For instance, J. W. Elvery & Co.'s 1891 advertisement (Figure 4.6) in *The Lady of the House* portrays a woman riding astride on her bicycle in what appears to be bad weather, but nonetheless bravely sporting her waterproofs. However the advertisement, implying an exclusive audience of women, also notes for sale 'Waterproof Bed Sheeting, Nursing Aprons, Air Cushions, Water Beds, Enemas etc.' alongside waterproofs for children. The advertisement is

Figure 4.6 Waterproofs advertisement for J. W. Elvery & Co. (1891).

complex. While seemingly offering the possibility of freedom and independence, it also situates the female reader in her traditional role as caregiver and mother, neatly encapsulating the contradictions and debates surrounding a woman's role in society. This ambivalence is perhaps in contrast to the oft-vaunted notion that women's magazines simply reinforced 'women's subordinate and secondary social status by putting pressure on them to conform to particular ideals of womanhood'.[97] In fact, as the Elvery & Co. advertisement demonstrates, sites of advertising and women's reading matter were sometimes rather more ambiguous.

An advertisement for Robert and Co. Ltd, of Grafton Street, Dublin seems to offer a vision of independent womanhood. Featuring in a Queen's Theatre Playbill (for 1 June 1914), the advertisement appeals to a middle-class market. Headed 'This Holiday Girl', the image presents a bold representation of both luxury and independence (she is escorted with a large array of luggage behind her, and a well-bred dog). Robert & Co. seem to correlate sporting activities with freedom for women, declaring that their goods included 'Sports Coats, Tennis Frocks, Golfing Hats, Bathing Costumes'. Indeed, there is a hint that the 'Holiday Girl' is in complete possession of her own economic affairs: 'she practices *real* economy; and this means more [...] money for the holidays.' The absence of male authority is notable here, suggesting the possibility that a monied woman could sometimes supersede the traditional order of Irish society. On the other hand, the copy also might be said to invoke very traditional identifications of women with frivolity, and indeed with the construction of the self according to the male gaze: her purchases of hats and blouses, in a turn of phrase more resonant of Joyce's Gerty McDowell, 'will enable her to look fresh & dainty on all occasions'. Here again the ideological ambiguities of *The Lady of the House* are evident.

There are clear differences between the representation of fashionable women in *The Lady of the House* in the late nineteenth century and those of the 1920s, notably in the relative freedom evident in dress in the later period. One example, 'The Lowry Girl', for Lowry & Co. Ltd, Belfast (Figure 4.7), demonstrates this. The young woman's skirt is calf length, demonstrating the rise in hemlines of the period, and the rest of her apparel is designed with practicality and fluidity of line (no corset here): 'To-day the Lowry Girl is wearing a Panama Hat trimmed with Petersham ribbon, an artificial silk sports coat with wide contrasting stripes, a sports skirt in hopsack with neat side folds, and white ribbed all-wool sports stockings with coloured clocks – all Lowry Garments, excellent for Tennis.' She is also unchaperoned (two players conduct their game of tennis behind her), and seems to be hailing the viewer with a direct gaze and a hand jauntily held aloft in greeting.

This 'progressive' style of women's clothing was revealed not just in sportswear. During 1919–1920, *The Lady of the House* carried a series of adverts for Brown Thomas & Co. Ltd (the department store on Grafton Street and Duke Street in Dublin which merited a mention in *Ulysses*)[98] in which this is also apparent. Brown Thomas had, in 1919, joined the Selfridge's franchise, which itself was burgeoning under the auspices of Gordon Selfridge (having made his name under Marshall Field's chain of businesses in the USA (formerly 'Field, Leitner and Company'), Selfridge first opened his landmark store in London in 1909). Here Brown Thomas

Figure 4.7 Advertisement for Lowry & Co., Donegall Place, Belfast (1920): 'The Lowry Girl'.

celebrated their 'anniversary' with Selfridge's by an advertisement which identified their 'high ideals', 'Integrity in every transaction in the public service' and which recollected 'the phenomenal Sale which signalised our entry into the Selfridge Organisation: how it "fired the imagination" of the Irish shopping public and marked the launching of a new selling policy which has won for this House its accredited position as Dublin's

Shopping Headquarters'.[99] Similarly, another announcement claimed that Brown Thomas was 'Dublin's Progressive Merchandise Headquarters'.[100] The advertisements for the department store were as inventive as Selfridge's renowned marketing.[101] While they employ the more traditional pose of the model gazing mid-distance or focusing on a particular item (umbrella, hand-bag), there is the consistent emphasis on the 'new' urban fashions[102] of the twenties, and again, the hemlines going north.

We might also view the rise of women's clubs, such as Dublin's 'Welcome Club for Ladies', as synecdochic of women's new-found freedoms, however limited these might have been. Indeed, some critics have gone so far as to see these clubs as mounting a direct challenge to the confining of woman-hood in the domestic sphere; Erika Diane Rappaport, for instance, maintains that 'urban women's clubs had become socially acceptable symbols of female independence and emancipation [...] clubs were championed for having brought the suburban woman into the public sphere [...] women founded and joined clubs to satisfy their physical, economic, social, and political desires.'[103] The club, in this account, was near to the centre of the modern urban economy and a woman's relationship to it: 'many feminists', says Rappaport, 'supported clubs and other female resting places because they assumed that comfort in the public spaces of the metropolis influenced one's relationship to the public sphere'.[104]

The club – and the teashop – addressed women as consuming entities, as well as urban dwellers. Facilities for women, such as lavatories, respectable dining rooms and even teashops or other 'resting places', became common and with that development, the cityscape and its consumer delights became more open to women. Findlater's was quick to capitalise on this development with its 'Welcome Club for Ladies' (Figure 4.8). Headed with the image of a packet of Findlater's brand tea, the full-page advertisement in *The Lady of the House* (April 1909) obliquely refers to how exhausting and physically demanding a day's shopping could be. The references to an 'invigorating' and 'refreshing' beverage confirm this, while a 'cup of *choice* Tea' implies a certain exclusivity. This is extended by the clubland rhetoric which permeates the advert: 'Here you can meet friends by appointment before, after, or during intervals of shopping in the city. You can also write a note or, happy thought, leave a parcel in safe keeping.'[105] The Tea Rooms, which were damaged during the Civil War and were open at least into the 1930s, were situated in the basement of the premises in O'Connell Street (formerly Sackville Street), under part of the extensive shop premises.[106] Clearly, this aspect of consumer culture in Ireland was as developed in Dublin as in London where, in Rappaport's account 'Harrods, Selfridges, and Whiteleys included ladies' clubs and advertised that their stores freely offered clublike amenities'.[107] This appeal to the specifically female shopper was not without its critics, however, inasmuch as the store, and its Tea Rooms, meant that respectable ladies could go about unchaperoned (Dorothea Findlater used

Figure 4.8 Advertisement for Findlater's Welcome Club for Ladies (1909).

to meet her husband Dermot, proprietor of the Findlater group of stores, in the Tea Room, prior to their marriage in 1932).[108] According to Rappaport the consumer sphere presented a degree of liberty: 'commercial culture was becoming associated with a new type of heterosexual culture in which young men and women could flirt without fear of the watchful eye of the Victorian chaperone.'[109] In her account, the Tea Room represented a new-found liberty for women outside the home.

So how did the Irish clergy, media and general public respond to such fashions? Some were not keen. Writing in *The Irish Monthly* in 1913, Nora Tynan O'Mahony (1865–1954) remarked how the emergence of a new type of modern woman was leading to a neglect of hearth and home:

> The regrettable lack of femininity, of sweet, gracious, dignified womanliness, not only in modern woman's manners but in her dress, all tend to bring her down to a lower level in masculine eyes than she ever sank before. The mannish cut of the modern woman's scanty garments, the short skirts, the liberal display of ankle, the often bared throat and neck (even in the street), the jaunty set of her hat jammed down to one side, and completely covering her hair and eyes – it may be convenient and comfortable, but certainly is not womanly or dignified or nice.[110]

Diarmaid Ferriter has recently argued that sexual morality in Ireland kept the ethics of Victorian England deep into the Free State era[111] and there was a contemporary backlash against 'modern' forms of dress for women. In June 1927, for instance, *The Limerick Leader* reported that '[Short] feminine garments [...] are not so numerously or brazenly evident in Limerick as they were a year or two ago. This gratifying evidence of a return to decency and sanity is largely attributable to the modest dress crusade [...] The craze for nudity was catching on to a disgusting extent all over Ireland.'[112] The author refers to the Limerick Modest Dress and Deportment Crusade, founded in 1927, which received support from the Catholic clergy.[113]

When compared with nineteenth-century modesty, 'the modern woman' seemed to present a very different, more liberated and, to some, more threatening image of womanhood. Conservative commentators of the period saw modern fashions as unsexing young women. As early as 1914, one writer argued:

> The flapper of to-day is the flopper of tomorrow. Girls, after all, will be boys... She plays golf – or rather talks golf (it makes no difference), her brothers tremble beneath her Girton sarcasm. She it is who, in one fell blow, can crush father by saying; 'Dad, you cannot wear that style of collar now' [...] Father doesn't wear that style of collar after. He dare not. The flapper's guide for life is that 'Fathers and brothers should be seen and not heard.'[114]

The 'flapper' was a common antipathetic construction during the period. Louise Ryan has remarked that:

> Concerns with flapper immorality and immodesty usually focused on her clothes. Her short skirts and sleeveless dresses symbolized not only her modernity but also her vanity. In exposing so much of her flesh, the flapper was a danger to all decent society [...] It was common for the flapper to be set up in direct opposition to the modesty of Mary the mother of God [...] Flappers were constructed as wild and uncontrolled daughters but also as poor prospects for marriage and motherhood.[115]

Ryan is right to invoke the contrast between modern hussy and the Mother of God. In the 1920s one Father Deegen, offering a sermon on 'womanly perfection', asked 'Would you really prefer your daughters to imitate the daring sartorial suggestiveness of the modern flapper rather than the modesty, sweetness and gentleness of Our Blessed Lady?'[116]

Urban fashion, as represented in the various advertisements explored in this chapter, was construed by some as being in direct conflict with both the Catholic faith and with nationhood. It was also read in terms of national identity and Ireland's difference from the decadent 'Brits' or 'Yanks', or the morally suspect French. The support of such 'imported' fashions was seen as a betrayal of Irish values: 'Usually disreputable cinema influences came from Hollywood, salacious magazines and papers came from England, jazz was described as African, immodest fashions came from Paris.'[117] But why was such fashion considered so threatening? While religious commentators were claiming such apparel was enslaving women both to consumerism and to foreign influence, the shorter skirt, the abandonment of the strictly corseted form in favour of fluidity and comfort, all meant greater ease of movement. As such, women's emergence from the private domestic sphere into the public realm (be it simply shopping unaccompanied or travel, sports, agitation for voting rights and education) were all signalled by the promotion of modern fashion. As Caitríona Beaumont has noted, 'Despite the prevailing image of Irish woman as wives and mothers, an ideal fostered by both church and state, the 1926 census revealed than 24 per cent of women in the Irish Free State remained unmarried by the age of forty-five.'[118] Accompanied by the gradual emergence of women into the workforce, such developments were seen as a threat to authority, order, and the ideology of the Free State itself, especially in its rather precarious early years. Indeed, this sociological development may be closely correlated with the anxieties of the early nation state in terms of women's fashions: 'In her Parisian short skirts and Hollywood hairstyles, [the flapper] visibly embodied all the dangers of foreign influences on the delicate and fragile essence of Irish womanhood and hence on the newly established Irish nation.'[119] As Maryann Valiulis puts it, women, as symbols of the Irish nation and conventional Catholic morality, were at the forefront of political debate: 'The conflict over women's roles was a theme in Irish society throughout the years of the Free State. Respective government brought in gendered legislation which restricted women's access to the public sphere and increasingly curtailed their freedom.'[120]

Unlike the nineteenth century, twentieth-century fashion progressively moved away from class-based signifiers, as well as strict gender coding. The frequent accusation that flappers were 'boyish' suggests that the anxiety of many conservative commentators was founded in a real fear of transgressing established boundaries: political, sexual and hierarchical. Advertising copy spanning the period from mid-nineteenth century to the Free State not only enunciates such concerns, but furthermore presents the inherent conflicts in Irish society at that time: how and in which ways ecclesiastical criticism focused on fashion and attire; how the changes in clothing and shopping practices relate more broadly to consumerism and women's role in such a development; how the expansion of women's roles in the period was reflected and finally how politics and national loyalty came to be closely aligned with brand loyalty. In this respect, *The Lady of the House* is exemplary of the contested site of womanhood and her role in the home in Revival-era Ireland, and it can also be seen as testimony to the rise of the New Woman in that country as of the shifting nature of Dublin societal codes.

5
Unionism, Advertising and the Third Home Rule Bill 1911–1914

Hail Star of Freedom, hail,
Day-Star of honour hail,
All Hail our Queen!

Hail, England's Glory, hail,
Hail, Scotland's Pride, too, hail;
Hail, Ireland's hope, all hail!
Long live our Queen.

MR DWYER's 'Ireland's Ode to Her Queen' is available now. Fifth edition.

(Advertisement, *Dublin Weekly Advertiser*, 11 March 1863)

In 1933, Northern Irishmen of loyalist convictions could avail themselves of a new product, one through which they could simultaneously signal their political allegiances and guard against unsightly ink stains. This was the 'Ulster Blotter', price two shillings and sixpence, an unusual artefact which featured many advertisements for businesses of the counties Antrim and Down, which were printed at the bottom of the sheets of blotting paper, which were otherwise blank. Loyal folk could be reassured, on the evidence of their blotters, that many of the traders of Belfast shared their ideological sympathies, as the advertisements all featured banners of a political – and proudly pro-Union – nature. The Morris Commercial Vehicles franchise in Belfast, for instance, announced itself therein as 'Loyal to Crown and Empire'. In like manner, the tobacconists Auld and Pemberton endorsed 'Ulster's Aim – Unity of the Empire', and the Silk Shop of 19 Castle Arcade, Belfast proclaimed itself 'A British Stronghold', as well as a repository for pyjamas. W. Mills, monocultural tailors, expressed their enthusiasm for 'One Throne, One Flag, One King'. Murphy and Orr, loyalist Linen Manufacturers, declared that 'We Stand Our Ground', and the Ulster Menu Company were equally unyielding – 'The Ulster Slogan – Not an Inch!' The blotter's advertisers line up to advertise their politics. Joseph Bradwell, purveyors of sporting guns to the social elite of Belfast, saluted his wares under the sententious banner 'Our Future lies in the Future of the Empire', Triumph Cars renounced the business of fifth columnists – 'Beware of Traitors and Empire Wreckers!' – and Melville the Funeral Directors remained implacably Orange: 'Hands off Ulster and the British Empire!' The exuberant hortatory chorus in the Ulster Blotter was concluded by a final salute to White's Wafer Oats, a full-page colour figure advertisement complete with the Union flag of the UK, which was printed on the back cover of the blotting book. This patriotic porridge offered 'A Call to Ulster Men and Ulster Women!' to 'Support Home Industries'. In particular, the copywriter had in mind the support of White's Wafer Oats, a product 'made in Ulster from Home Grown Oats' ('It retains, to a degree unequalled by any other make, all vitalising elements and sustaining power').

Much of the advertising discussed in this book was nationalist in character, whether possessed of Redmondite or advanced nationalist tendencies. However, as the Ulster Blotter demonstrates, Irish advertising in the late nineteenth and early twentieth centuries was a coin with two faces. Ireland was part of the UK in the period under discussion here, and not everybody who lived there lamented the fact. The blotter was by no means the first advertising in Ireland to be linked to sentiments of a Unionist kind or to Irish business people possessed of the belief that their country should remain in the UK. This chapter looks at the polemics surrounding the slow passing of the third Home Rule Bill in Ulster, arguing that the popular-cultural resistance to the bill among Unionists can be seen to represent the advertising of the union itself.

The Ulster Blotter is testimony to the way in which Unionist politics permeated into popular culture, and its rhetoric was part of a pervasive culture of resistance and patriotic flag-waving. The Union Jack on the back of the blotter was part of the widespread display of the flag in what is now Northern Ireland in the first decades of the twentieth century. In the period between 1911 and 1914 this was no empty show. As the Unionist politician and historian of the Ulster Volunteer Force Ronald McNeill put it in *Ulster's Stand for Union* (1922), 'If there is a profuse display of the Union Jack, it is because it is in Ulster not merely "bunting" for decorative purposes as in England, but the symbol of a cherished faith.'[1] Amusing though the blotter might be, there was nothing comical about flying the flag in Ulster in the period between 1911 and 1914. The flag, and the wider iconography of unionism, was a key part of its response to what Sir Edward Carson called in 1912 'the pressing and urgent danger to civil liberties involved in the unconditional surrender of the Government to the intrigues of a disloyal section of the Irish people'.[2] This was a message reflected in parliamentary and extra-parliamentary rhetoric, in speech, rally, book and newspaper, but it was also remediated in the wider print culture, in populist pamphlets, in satirical squibs and parodies, and, not least, in the culture of advertising.

I

However central were religious division, historical injustice and political controversy about the best future for Ireland – and the merits or demerits of republicanism, socialism and unionism therein – in the debates about Home Rule which preoccupied Ireland from the 1880s onwards, it should be acknowledged that much anti-self-governance, pro-Union polemic and propaganda in the decades before the partition were predicated on what were presented as soberly pragmatic, economic grounds. Ireland, the argument went, would flounder as a separate nation from Great Britain and would not be able to stand on its own financial feet, especially if it drew its leaders from the Catholic community, whether they be constitutional politicians from the Irish Party, southern farmers or – worse – the impractical zealots and pedagogues in charge of Sinn Féin and the like. Aided by its connection to the British industrial powerhouse, it was argued, the country was beginning to establish itself as a modern economy. The Protestant north, with its heavy industries and vigorous capitalism, had shown the way forward for Ireland as a whole and Home Rule would only damage the emergence of a thriving national economy. Indeed, the opening words of the Ulster Covenant itself, appealing as they do to the material rather than to the religious, testify to this economic anxiety: 'Being convinced in our consciences that Home Rule would be disastrous to the material well-being of Ulster as well as the whole of Ireland ... '.

One contribution to the cause of union was *The Irish Unionist Pocket Book*, published simultaneously in Belfast and Dublin in 1911 as the parliamentary and non-parliamentary controversies about Home Rule started to boil to their hottest. It encapsulates such arguments and is testimony to the importance of popular-cultural print ephemera in the propaganda effort against a Dublin parliament. This opinionated volume, written 'for the Use of Unionist Workers', dismissed what it saw as Fenian bleatings about the island's supposed poverty and its oppression at the beastly hands of the Saxon, and in memorable style. Ireland, it declared, was prospering under the union: 'This country, humiliated by being represented by separatist politicians as a mendicant grovelling in rags and misery, is in reality urging onwards to prosperity.'[3] Ireland, led by Belfast's example, was set fair to become a modern industrial nation and the business sector needed to stress a pan-Irishness within the union rather than be damaged by unilateral southern moves towards self-governance.

Nationalist and Unionist Irish business folk – though divergent on most ideological grounds – both endorsed the need to buy home goods rather than those from overseas. Belfast had hosted the 1909 annual conference of the Irish Industrial Development Association and the Unionist *Belfast News-Letter* commented afterwards that:

> the industrial revival is a fact, though much remains to be done, and the Industrial Development Association is helping to do it. If the demand for Irish goods grows [...] our existing industries will expand, and new industries will be founded. More employment will follow and the drain of emigration will grow less. Ireland will become more prosperous than it has been for centuries if the industrial revival is allowed to go on peacefully. An Association which is striving to increase the material prosperity of Ireland may fairly appeal to the patriotism of the public to support it.[4]

The patriotism of the Irish people, of course, expressed itself in different ways. But all parties – Irish Parliamentary Party (IPP) nationalists, separatists and republicans, the southern Anglo-Irish elite and the northern Unionist alike – could stress the need to purchase Irish goods and for businesses to employ local workers rather than foreigners (the 'Ulster Blotter' itself declared that 'No part of the wages paid to foreign workers ever does you a half pennyworth of good!').[5] The difference between them was the divergent understanding of British connection. To the Unionist it could only sustain and encourage Irish development. The union should remain; while Home Rulers and advanced nationalists alike bellowed choruses of Thomas Davis's great anthem of the 1840s, 'A Nation Once Again', the *Pocket Book* forthrightly declared that 'Ireland has never been a Nation. But even if she were entitled to that description, we think it a prouder thing to be members of the Great British Nation, in which the English, Scottish, Ulster and Irish peoples are merged, than to cling to insular nationality.'[6]

The *Pocket Book* was part of a populist effort to counter nationalist propaganda evident in print ephemera, in short, cheap books such as *The Home Rule 'Nutshell'* (1912). Pamphlets such as the widely distributed 'The ABC of Home Rule' (issued in three parts in 1911) also proselytised British liberty to the Irish. The latter argued that national 'prosperity' was at stake: 'Let Ireland be preoccupied, happy, prosperous and free. She can be all this under the present rules of the Government of Great Britain and Ireland. British justice, British freedom, British law is good enough for the best of the King's subjects.'[7] The *Pocket Book*, part of this vigorous polemical reaction to the prospect of self-government, predicted that dire economic consequences would stem from such an unwelcome eventuality: 'English capital would be withdrawn from Ireland should the Nationalists extort from Parliament a measure of Home Rule. The result would be that tens of thousands of labourers would be thrown out of employment and crowded into the already overcrowded Irish market.'[8]

Abandoned by British capital, the country would be incapable of prospering under the stewardship of radical politicians in some putative new Irish parliament. When Dáil Éireann actually came to pass, the republican polemicist Aodh De Blácam optimistically declared in *What Sinn Fein Stands For* (1921) that 'In the Dáil will sit the good, the wise and the brave – men chosen not for their expertness in economic matters, nor for their learning or technical skill, but for character, for Kingliness.'[9] However, this lack of 'expertness' and 'technical skill' among republican leaders was explicitly faulted in some Unionist quarters during the Home Rule controversies. Here the separatist leaders were portrayed as shadowy professional intriguers rather than hard-headed men of business, dismissed as ideologues who possessed no practical ability in terms of economic leadership. The programme notes to 'The Ulster Unionist Demonstration of 1912', a gathering of thousands which was held in the 'Royal Agricultural Showground, Balmoral, Belfast, Tuesday 9th April 1912', predicted a bleak future for an independent Ireland should such unsavoury characters prevail:

> To deprive her of equal citizenship in the United Kingdom, and to hand over her interests and destiny to the control of an Irish legislature endowed with a bankrupt exchequer, and composed of men and women not leaders in economic enterprise, but political agitators nominated by secret societies and salaried by foreign gold, would be equivalent to putting back our material prosperity one hundred years.[10]

This was by no means a new argument. As early as 1893, Robert John Buckley's *Ireland as it is and as it Would Be Under Home Rule* made a similar point: 'Judged by classification of its friends and enemies, Home Rule comes out badly indeed. The capitalists, manufacturers, merchants, industrial community [and] professional men are against it.'[11] 'On the other hand', Buckley continues, enthusiasts for Home Rule are by no means men of business:

> amongst those who are for it, and allied with them, we find the dynamiters of America, the Fenians and Invincibles, the illiterate voters of Ireland, the idlers, the disloyal, the mutilators of cattle, the boycotters, the moonlighters and outragemongers, the murderers, the village ruffians, the city corner boys, and all the rest of the blackguards who have flourished and been secure under the Land League's fostering wing. Are we to stand quietly aside and see the destinies of decent people entrusted to the leaders of a movement which owes its success to such supporters?[12]

'Those who have studied the thing on the spot', writes Buckley in his exasperation, 'will excuse a little warmth'.[13]

Returning to the events of April 1912 at Balmoral, Figure 5.1 shows the multicoloured cover to this programme, an iconographic celebration of

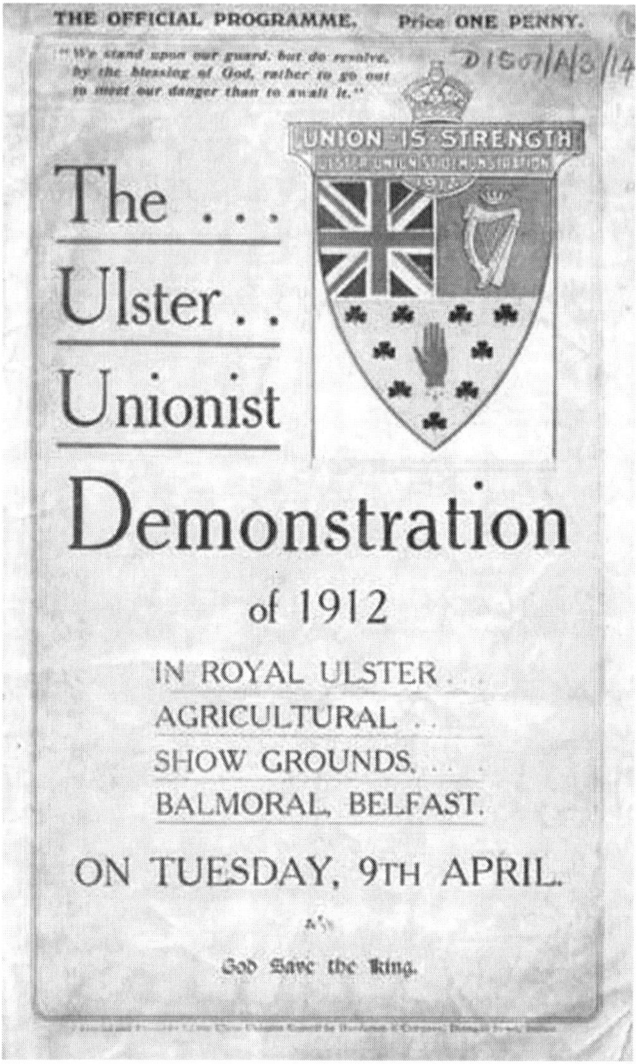

Figure 5.1 Cover, official programme to 'The Ulster Unionist Demonstration of 1912' (1912). Courtesy of the AS Team.

the link between the UK and Ulster and a celebration of the notion that 'Union Is Strength', complete with a shield featuring a Union flag on the top hoist, the gold harp of Ireland (with the crown in this case, of course) on the fly, and the Red Hand of Ulster with shamrocks below. The words of inspiration at the top of the programme are from Gustavus Hamilton's oration at the Williamite Defence of Enniskillen in 1689: 'We stand upon our guard, but do resolve by the blessing of God rather to go out to meet our danger than to await it.' A similar symbolic cavalcade appeared on the cover of the later, January 1914 Ulster Unionist Council demonstration against Home Rule at the Ulster Hall (Figure 5.2), with its shields, flags, red hand

Figure 5.2 Cover, official programme, 'Ulster Unionist Council Demonstration against Home Rule' (1914). Author collection.

and photographs of luminaries of the movement: Carson, the Marquis of Londonderry and Walter Long MP, former parliamentary leader of the Irish Unionists. As in the illustrated advertisements of the time, image and text complement the delivery of the message.

Another of the 'monster demonstrations'[14] of 1912, 'The Ulster Unionist Demonstration of September 1912', held at the Ulster Hall and called to promote Ulster's Solemn League and Covenant ('to defeat the present conspiracy to set up a Home Rule Parliament for Ireland'), which by some accounts was eventually signed by over 200,000 people, roused the faithful in song. Attendees were issued with a hymn sheet of British anthems and stirring Unionist songs such as the 'Orange Tree':

> The Orange Tree stands evergreen,
> The fruit so golden fair
> Mid fragrant blossom hangs on Bough
> O! Union past compare,
> You might conceive its secret is
> Hope, Labour, Praise and Prayer.[15]

The importance of song in Irish politics is well known, and the Unionist campaign also had its musical side. Most commonly, the waving of the flag, literally or metaphorically, was accompanied by the singing of the national anthem. Ronald McNeill argues that there were very good reasons why this should have been so:

> The ordinary Protestant . . . of Ulster is by nature as far as possible removed from the being who is derisively nicknamed the 'noisy patriot' or the 'flag-waving jingo'. If the National Anthem has become a 'party tune' in Ireland, it is not because the loyalist sings it, but because the disloyalist shuns it.[16]

In his important account of the Ulster Volunteer Force, Timothy Bowman quotes another Unionist song, a rather more martial effort than the 'Orange Tree', this time deriving from the Balmoral parade of September 1913. 'The Ulster Volunteers', by Ada Shaw,[17] was republished in the *Northern Whig* on 30 September:

> And if they meet a soldier's fate,
> And die in fair freedom's name,
> Then deathless glory shall be theirs
> Honour and Lasting fame.
> And never shall their memory fade
> In the midst of crowding years
> God in his kindness guard and keep
> Our Ulster Volunteers.[18]

One is reminded of Sean O'Casey's Captain Boyle in *Juno and the Paycock*: 'If they want to be soldiers, well, there's no use o' them squealin' when they meet a soldier's fate.'[19] As in the martyrological utterances and strategies of contemporary advanced nationalism – Patrick Pearse's being the most notable – the author sees sacrifice to the cause of the nation as the most noble and enviable of fates for a patriotic Irishman.

There were also satirical squibs and cartoons[20] dealing with the Home Rule Bill controversies. One little-known example, which enlists advertising to the service of the union, takes the form of a parodic advertisement for Ulster bacon. This is part of a long tradition of using mock-advertisements in British and Irish satirical writing, one which stretches back to the moment of the English Civil War, if not before.[21] This satirical subculture was evident in Revival-era Ireland (Republican anti-recruitment examples of this literary subgenre are discussed in Chapter 8) and one fascinating example of the use of this form of print ephemera is this 1912 satirical squib, prompted by the travails of the third Home Rule Bill in parliament, which echoes the tone of the huge extra-parliamentary resistance to the bill led by Sir Edward Carson.

The mock-advertisement, a double-sided small handbill, celebrates what it optimistically calls the 'death' of the bill. Playing on the well-known contemporary advertisements for Ulster bacon, one side of the satire features a cartoon of a dead pig which – like the problem of Home Rule – has been slaughtered in Ulster (the reference to the pig also has obvious derogatory implications about nationalists). This animal is, in the satire's mock-advertising copy, 'GUARANTEED ULSTER-CURED'. 'Says John to Joe', goes the accompanying jingle copy, 'it'll have to go / And Ulster won't surrender'.

This pasquinade also features a parodic 'death card' on the reverse. In 'Antrim at the end of the nineteenth century', as W. H. Crawford and Robert H. Foy have written, death cards 'were a popular means of announcing deaths and the times and venues of funerals' ('Indeed, attendance at a funeral almost required the receipt of a card').[22] The anonymous satirist writes his own spoof death card:

> IN MEMORIAM.
>
> In Loving memory of the Joyful Death of the Home Rule Bill, Killed by the *Hand* of *Ulster*, and *Buried* for *All Time*. Interred to the *Sound* of Fife and Drum and lamented only by those whose aim was a *GOOD JOB* at a *BIG SALARY*. R.I.P.

The pernicious bill – personified in the satire as 'Mr William Bill' – is deceased and its body taken to the grave yard:

> We've Buried the body of Home Rule Bill
> Which was choked to Death by a Carsonite Pill,
> A compound of Grit and Steel, Bayonets and Rifles,
> And which you'll agree, are no mere Trifles.

On the top of the bill is reproduced the Red Hand of Ulster, as so often in more orthodox attacks on Home Rule, surrounded by concentric ovals through which run the words 'WE WILL NOT HAVE HOME RULE'. In such satire, advertising parody sings from the same ideological songbook as more orthodox polemic against the prospective Dublin government.

II

The events at Balmoral and at the Ulster Hall, where loud if decorous public protest was allied to patriotic song and prose polemic both in impassioned speeches and in the written word, testify to the fact that early twentieth-century Unionists began to utilise, if not copy, the tried and tested methods of Irish nationalists to defend their cause (though their efforts might also be modelled in part on contemporary British political advertising campaigns such as those surrounding the Free Trade and Tariff Reform campaigns). From the onset of the Revival, nationalists had used a variety of media to promote their ideas, and their political opponents eventually began to borrow their clothes. Where Seumas Whelan had marketed Sinn Féin stamps from 1908 onwards to raise funds for that organisation, now, in 1912, there appeared anti-Home Rule fund-raising – and morale-raising – stamps, some featuring the banner 'We will not have Home Rule' under Ulster's Red Hand, and others under a portrait of Sir Edward Carson looking suitably resolute and immoveable (Figure 5.3). Buttons, medals and commemorative coins appeared featuring the Union flag and the tripartite shield of the Ulster Unionists. A widely distributed series of picture postcards advertised the cause of union in displays of the flag, political slogans, Ulster scenes and pictures of Ulster Volunteer Force (UVF) drilling (the monster rallies were also remediated in postcards showing the events at those occasions, both outside and inside the demonstrations). One of the best known of these features the arm of a uniformed militiaman holding up a rifle against the background of a Union Jack, with a banner of 'No Home Rule' and these lines, unattributed, from Swinburne's political verses 'A Song in Time of Order' (1852), an attack on Napoleon III and the Pope which celebrates those who resist despotism:

> Let our flag run out straight in the wind,
> The old red shall be floated again
> When the ranks that are thin shall be thinned,
> When the names that were twenty are ten.[23]

In pamphlet, songbook and satire, a noisy Unionism was manifested in much of the north of Ireland as the First World War approached and as Home Rule and a measure of Irish self-government became increasingly likely. What these polemicists were doing was selling the union. From being an unshakeable – if certainly not unquestioned – fact of life, the union now

Figure 5.3 'We will not have Home Rule'. Anti-Home Rule stamp (c. 1912).

needed to be marketed. In effect it became a brand capable of being advocated and advertised in many different fashions. There is no necessity to market fresh air, but now the union of Ireland with Great Britain was no longer as ineluctable as the circumambient breeze. It was now under threat from the Irish Party, and from worse. It now needed to be sold, and to be advertised as if it were a consumer product.

The cover and contents of the programme for the April 1912 Ulster Unionist meeting at Balmoral – which mixes stirring songs of a most Orange kind, prose polemic, and striking visual iconography – is a case in point, testimony to the tendency for Ulster residents constantly to be taking ocular doses of Ulster Unionism, and, from January 1913 onwards, the Ulster Volunteer Force. Indeed, the UVF itself was a kind of marching advertisement, indicating to British public opinion that Ulster could offer more than elaborate set-piece demonstrations and rallies, and that, should the day come, the people would fight 'for God and Ulster' if necessary. Once again McNeill's contemporary testimony is useful in this context. Writing of preparations for the UK general election expected to take place in 1914 or 1915, McNeill portrays the UVF as an extension of the propaganda effort of

Ulster's Unionists, a move from the orderly demonstration to the show of force:

> Propaganda to the extent possible with the resources at the disposal of the Ulster Unionist Council was carried on in the British constituencies in 1913, the cost being defrayed chiefly through generous subscriptions collected by the energy and influence of Mr Walter Long; but many were beginning to share the opinion of Mr Charles Craig, M.P., who scandalised the Radicals by saying at Antrim in March that, while it was incumbent on Ulstermen to do their best to educate the electorate, 'he believed that, as an argument, ten thousand pounds spent on rifles would be a thousand times stronger than the same amount spent on meetings, speeches, and pamphlets'.[24]

The propagandising of the Ulster Volunteer Force extended to street display in march, drill and rally, alongside the print ephemera of poster, handbill, postcards and more.[25] Take Figure 5.4, the symbolically rich badge of the Motor-Car Corps of the Ulster Volunteer Force. One contemporary American journal wondered at it: 'How deep into the past the feelings of the Irish people reach in the present Home Rule contest is indicated by the sign carried by the motor-car corps of the Ulster Volunteer Force. On the sign are the shamrock, a crown and the "Red Hand of Ulster".'[26]

Anti-Home Rulers used a variety of ingenious methods of visual display and print ephemera to serve their cause, in the manner adopted by their opponents before them. As Jim MacLaughlin has written, 'political pamphlets, posters and placards, perhaps more so than Unionist history books, fostered a sense of unionist identity that rendered the north-east of Ireland a Protestant homeland, one that had its own Protestant capital in Belfast city'.[27] The all-Ireland appeals to southern Protestants and to some residual Catholic affinity with the British nation become silenced in Unionist rhetoric, and the desire to exempt northern Unionists from Home Rule or to build an Ulster nation within the union becomes increasingly clamorous.

One review of McNeill's *Ulster's Stand for the Union* described its author as someone who, 'though he represents an English constituency in the House of Commons, is an Ulsterman born and bred, and pre-eminently "racy of the soil"'.[28] We have seen this phrase, the motto of *The Nation*, before, in D. P. Moran's setting forth the solely Catholic nature of Ireland in *The Philosophy of Irish Ireland*.[29] Thomas Davis's aim in *The Nation* was 'to create and foster public opinion, and make it racy of the soil', aiming for a union of Catholicism and Protestantism (the 'Prospectus' to the journal characterises its aim to achieve 'a nationality which may embrace Protestant, Catholic and dissenter, Milesian and Cromwellian'). However, by the second decade of the twentieth century, with McNeill's own soil being Unionist and Protestant on the one (red) hand, and Moran articulating an indivisibly

Figure 5.4 Badge of the Motor-Car Corps of the Ulster Volunteer Force (1913). From *Popular Mechanics* (1914).

Gaelic and Catholic sense of nationhood on the other, the hopes of such a rapprochement were fading. In north and south, attitudes were becoming polarised.

III

Part of the defence of Protestant Ulster and of what we have called the selling of the union manifested itself in the advertising columns of Unionist newspapers. Paid advertisements played their part in the campaigns for 'British justice, British freedom [and] British law'. The struggle against the bill was sometimes remediated – from platform and pulpit oratory, and from pamphlet and parliamentary speeches – into the advertising columns, which became recruitment offices for the Solemn League and Covenant, for the large-scale public demonstrations in favour of union, and for the Ulster Volunteer Force.

Perhaps this is unsurprising. Some northern Unionist newspapers resembled the partisan advanced nationalist press in their forthright display of political allegiance. Take the *Belfast Weekly News,* press stablemate of the *Belfast News-Letter*. In the first decade of the twentieth century, even before the third bill controversies, the *Weekly News* overtly, and frequently, advertised itself in terms of its Protestantism, its defence of the faith, and its status as the 'recognised organ' of the Orange Order, as per this visually striking, near-catechetical advertisement of the time:

THE BELFAST
WEEKLY NEWS
FOR PROTESTANTS

IT WATCHES THEIR INTERESTS
IT WATCHES THEIR INTERESTS
IT WATCHES THEIR INTERESTS
IT WATCHES THEIR INTERESTS
IT DEFENDS THEIR ATTITUDES
IT DEFENDS THEIR ATTITUDES
IT DEFENDS THEIR ATTITUDES
IT DEFENDS THEIR ATTITUDES
IT CHAMPIONS THEIR CAUSE
IT CHAMPIONS THEIR CAUSE
IT CHAMPIONS THEIR CAUSE
IT CHAMPIONS THEIR CAUSE
IT IS THE RECOGNISED ORGAN OF THE ORANGEMEN
IT IS THE RECOGNISED ORGAN OF THE ORANGEMEN
IT IS THE RECOGNISED ORGAN OF THE ORANGEMEN
IT IS THE RECOGNISED ORGAN OF THE ORANGEMEN
FOR FORTY YEARS IT HAS
FOR FORTY YEARS IT HAS
FOR FORTY YEARS IT HAS
FOR FORTY YEARS IT HAS
STOOD BY THEIR PRINCIPLES
STOOD BY THEIR PRINCIPLES
STOOD BY THEIR PRINCIPLES
STOOD BY THEIR PRINCIPLES
ON SALE
THURSDAYS
ONE PENNY

Sometimes the advertising columns of the *Weekly News* and the *News-Letter* offer explicit priority to the Protestant. Take the matter of recruitment advertising. There was, of course, no legislation against discrimination in the work place in those days, whether for large employers such as the Belfast shipbuilders Harland and Wolff or in personal employment, and a significant minority of the advertisements in the *Belfast News-Letter*, for instance, are religiously specific in the first decade of the twentieth century. Take the issue for 31 December 1900. In the 'Situations Vacant' column, we see the following: 'DRESSMAKER. Wanted. A thoroughly competent dressmaker (Protestant)....' Lower down is an even choosier notice:

> BAKER. Wanted, a young unmarried man, must be strong, clean in his habits, no smoker, accustomed to horses and must be a member of some Protestant church...None need apply whose character will not bear the strictest investigations.

In the 'Situations Wanted' on the same day, the advertisers line up to categorise themselves by their faith:

> MRS MAXWELL
> Housekeeper (Scotch), disengaged. Protestant. Would go companion to an elderly lady...
>
> MRS MACAULAY
> House and Parlour Maid for re-engagement, excellent discharges, Protestant...
>
> MR ELLIOTT
> Land Steward (working). Protestant. Thorough knowledge of buying and selling cattle...
>
> NO SALARY
> Protestant lady having small income would give her services as companion and useful help to Widow or Single Lady in return for comfortable, quiet home.

That said, the picture is not univocally Protestant. In the same number in which Mr Elliott and Mrs Maxwell sought positions we see the following: 'House parlour maid wanted. Immediately. Experienced Roman Catholic preferred. £13. Must understand her business.' And the *Weekly News* was also capable of a more inclusive temper, as in the sister advertisement to the one quoted above, which declares that it was a paper 'for everybody':

> THE BELFAST
> WEEKLY NEWS
> FOR EVERYBODY
> FOR EVERYBODY
> FOR EVERYBODY
> FOR EVERYBODY

FOR FACT OR FICTION
FOR FACT OR FICTION
FOR FACT OR FICTION
FOR FACT OR FICTION
FOR ARTICLES OR ILLUSTRATION
FOR ARTICLES OR ILLUSTRATION
FOR ARTICLES OR ILLUSTRATION
FOR ARTICLES OR ILLUSTRATION
FOR PROSE OR POETRY
FOR PROSE OR POETRY
FOR PROSE OR POETRY
FOR PROSE OR POETRY
IT CONTAINS THE BEST
IT CONTAINS THE BEST
IT CONTAINS THE BEST
IT CONTAINS THE BEST
BY THE BEST WRITERS
BY THE BEST WRITERS
BY THE BEST WRITERS
BY THE BEST WRITERS
ON THE BEST SUBJECTS
ON THE BEST SUBJECTS
ON THE BEST SUBJECTS
ON THE BEST SUBJECTS
ON SALE
THURSDAYS
ONE PENNY

In the *News-Letter* in the 1890s there were also a significant number of advertisements for the Gaelic League, though admittedly in the period in which it was frequently seen as being above politics, and the newspaper also carried advertisements on behalf of the League's Irish Language movement and for individual tutors of and lecturers in Irish (the Gaelic Athletic Association is nowhere to be seen in these pages, however; whether it never sought admission or was turned away as a matter of policy we do not know).

That said, the paid columns of the *News-Letter* in the Revival period through to 1911 and the start of the third bill controversies do possess more than a tinge of Orange. A pointed silence is observed during the United Irishmen centenary in 1898, for example; not there the souvenirs and trinkets of Wolfe Tone remembrance advertised in *The Shan Van Vocht* at the time.[30] But in the same period there are dozens of advertisements for such events as meetings of the Presbyterian Unionist Voters' Association, the Belfast Conservative Association, the Protestant Alliance and the Ulster Loyalist Union. There are also numerous announcements made on behalf of the Loyal Orange Lodges and the Orange Institution, publicity for grand openings of Orange Halls and special offers for discount excursions to the anti-Home Rule demonstrations in Great Britain, in London, Liverpool and elsewhere.

The *News-Letter* carried a deal of advertising for southern-based companies in this period, though often for enterprises in Anglo-Irish ownership such as Jameson's 'Celebrated Dublin Whiskey' and, via second parties, the beers of Arthur Guinness and Co. (Bushmill's and Kavanagh are also in evidence). Aspirational companies still trade on the allure-of-beyond-the-sea, as per John Hanna's 'French and English Dress and Costume Cloths', which were available at The Ladies' Emporium, High Street, Belfast. Some northern advertising copy stressed the British nature of the Irish producer (the (English-owned) Clarence Engineering Company of Belfast, for example, proudly proclaimed itself 'The Pick of Britain's Motor Production'), and the royal warrant was highly prized, exemplified in a 1902 advertisement for W. Abernethy, who announces himself as 'Photographer to his Majesty the King. By Royal Warrant. 29 High Street Belfast.' Abernethy was a business man with an eye to the political main chance who also possessed a clear sense of his and his customers' loyal political sympathies. In 1895, for instance, Abernethy was selling souvenir photographs of the Grand Orange Lodge of Ireland in the pages of the *News-Letter*, 'taken at Holyrood by W. Abernethy (3s 6p per copy)'. Five years earlier, in 1890, he had announced a 'Grand Group of 500' portraits of the 'Ministers of the General Assembly' of the Presbyterian Church. In 1893 Abernethy opportunistically offered a series of prints of the huge Arthur Balfour demonstration in Belfast against the second Home Rule Bill, including likenesses of 'the Procession passing through Donegal Place to Linen Hall Grand Stand', a 'Splendid Likeness of Mr Balfour' and a portrait of the 'Orange procession'. Abernethy, who did 'all sorts of outdoor photography' ('football, cricket, wedding or garden photography') also aligned himself with high society (offering sets of photographs of the County Down stag hunt and hounds at work) and boasted of the patronage of the 'Marquis of Londonderry [former Lord Lieutenant and later stalwart of the Ulster Unionist Council], Marquis of Ormonde, Lord Arran, Countess of Antrim, Lieutenant-Colonel Alexander' and all 'the leading nobility and gentry'.

In a time of turmoil and conflict, in Ulster, as in the other three provinces, the commercial messages were not infrequently charged with an ideological resonance, and the columns of the *News-Letter* and elsewhere in Ulster become even more politicised from 1911 onwards than they had been previously. Announcements in the paid columns were testimony to the momentous events of the time. The monster rallies at Balmoral and the Ulster Hall were extensively publicised, as were trips to English anti-Home Rule rallies in London, Liverpool and Tyneside. Many polemical contributions to 'the cause of Ulster' and against the Home Rule Bill are announced, from the pithy 'ABC of Home Rule' through to Simon Rosenbaum's weighty *Against Home Rule: The Case for the Union*, with its introduction by Ulster's hero and its roster of parliamentarian contributors such as Arthur Balfour, Austen Chamberlain and Andrew Bonar Law. The establishment of the Ulster Volunteer Force is publicised and sound men are invited to join the ranks. Tailors offer uniforms, and drills, rallies and meetings are announced.

Though there were opportunistic hidden advertisements in the manner of 'SUPPORT THE UNION... Of quality and value to be found at W. Mills, Tailor', the most basic form which this advertising took was in direct political advertising. After the campaign turned, in Carson's words, to 'warrior mood',[31] 'between the first and the second readings of the Home Rule Bill', as Geoffrey Lewis notes in his biography of the politician, 'the *Belfast News-Letter* carried advertisements for rifles and for drilling instructors. The paper called for an association of all Loyalists and a solemn League and Covenant.'[32] Mass signings of the Covenant were publicised in the Unionist newspapers, alongside the text of the document itself. In the *News-Letter*, in the *Weekly News*, in the *Londonderry Sentinel*, in the *Ballymena Observer* and in the *Coleraine Constitution*, the covenant itself became advertising copy:

ULSTER'S SOLEMN LEAGUE AND COVENANT

> Being convinced in our consciences that Home Rule would be disastrous to the material well-being of Ulster as well as of the whole of Ireland, subversive of our civil and religious freedom, destructive of our citizenship and perilous to the unity of the Empire, we, whose names are underwritten, men of Ulster, loyal subjects of His Gracious Majesty King George V, humbly relying on the God whom our fathers in days of stress and trial confidently trusted, do hereby pledge ourselves in solemn Covenant throughout this our time of threatened calamity to stand by one another in defending for ourselves and our children our cherished position of equal citizenship in the United Kingdom and in using all means which may be found necessary to defeat the current conspiracy to set up a Home Rule Parliament in Ireland. And in the event of such a Parliament being forced upon us we further solemnly and mutually pledge ourselves to refuse its authority. In sure confidence that God will defend the right we hereto subscribe our names...

GOD SAVE THE KING

When the Home Rule Act became law on 18 September 1914, the UK was at war and its implementation was suspended. By then the Ulster Volunteer Force had been reoriented to the war effort. Both John Redmond (see Chapter 8) and Sir Edward Carson now proselytised for the ranks of the British army in the effort against the 'Hun'. In the opening days of the Great War Carson refocused Ulster Protestant military masculinity on the coming conflict. 'Quit yourselves like men' he urges Ulstermen in the Unionist presses' advertising columns, and demonstrate your support for your 'fellow Britishers':

> TO THE MEMBERS
> of the
> ULSTER VOLUNTEER FORCE
>
> I greatly appreciate the action of our Volunteers in rallying so enthusiastically to my call for Defenders of the Empire. To those who have not already responded to that call, and are eligible and can go, I say – QUIT YOURSELVES LIKE MEN AND COMPLY WITH YOUR COUNTRY'S DEMAND.
>
> Enlist at once for the Ulster Division in Lord Kitchener's Army for the period of the war.
>
> You were formed to defend our citizenship in the United Kingdom and the Empire, and so preserve our civil and religious liberty. Now the UK and the Empire are threatened we must fight with our fellow Britishers until victory is assured.
>
> . . .
>
> NO SURRENDER
> GOD SAVE THE KING
> EDWARD CARSON
>
> Old Town Hall, Belfast
> September 7th, 1914.

Part III

'High' Culture

6
Oscar Wilde as Editor and Writer: Aesthetic Interventions in Fashion and Material Culture

> Indeed, properly speaking, there is no such thing as Style; there are merely styles, that is all.
>
> Oscar Wilde, 'A Note on Some Modern Poets', from *Woman's World* (1889)

In the declaration on 'Style' which provides the epigraph to this chapter, Oscar Wilde might not be making a solely aesthetic point in gesturing towards the way in which the aesthete's ultimate commitment to art involves a plurality of postures (or 'Masks', something which he developed in his later essay 'The Truth of Masks' (1891)). He might also be seen as making a point about human identity, the author's words reflecting the complex and suggestive manner in which he set forth his own multifaceted and sometimes contradictory notions of subjectivity.[1] We argue here that Wilde's notion of the multiplicity of style is closely linked to issues of consumption and consumer culture in the author's work and thought; tracing some of the subtle nuances of Wilde's artistic and philosophical position regarding the relationship between art and commerce demonstrates how far Wilde and his various self-representations were invested in commodity culture.

This chapter also discusses the implications of Wilde's practice as well as his theory, in examining the author's editorship of *Woman's World* (1887–1889) and the fascinating engagement with both Irish and British consumer culture evident in the years in which he oversaw the journal. Wilde once wryly meditated on the 'reproduction' of types in literature: 'A great artist invents a type, and Life tries to copy it, to reproduce it in a popular form, like an enterprising publisher.'[2] We also demonstrate how Wilde's own image circulated in contemporary advertising copy produced on behalf of entrepreneurial capitalists by ingenious copywriters, how it was reinterpreted as a walking advertisement for goods as diverse as cotton and cigarettes.

I

Oscar Wilde, poet, novelist and dramatist, but also – less seamlessly – Irishman and Englishman, husband and homosexual, artist and consumer icon, is rightly held to be one of the pre-eminent figures of the Aesthetic Movement. The contradictions inherent in the oppositions noted in the previous sentence are telling.[3] Critics have noted Wilde's supposedly effortless ability to occupy several subject positions simultaneously, and this, in part, also seems to reflect the paradoxes which the author often gleefully included in his essays and journalism. Let us take, initially, the last of these apparently contradictory pairings, between artist and consumer icon, and consider the relationship between art and commerce in Wilde's life and work. A key spokesman and advocate of aestheticism, Wilde is often presented as being in dialectical opposition to market forces, and certainly there is evidence to support such a position. In 'The House Beautiful', for instance, which formed part of his lecture series delivered in America during 1882, Wilde repeatedly counsels against mass-produced decoration. 'Have no machine made ornaments' he declares, adding that 'all ornaments should be carved, and have no cast iron ornaments, nor any of those ugly things made by machinery'.[4] Wilde also stresses the need to rebel against 'the tyranny of materialism' in order to foster independent art.[5] Here the mass-produced, the (regrettably) popular is set in contradistinction to the individual and the independent.

In 'The Decay of Lying', Wilde also ploughs the same idealistic furrow, declaring that 'In literature we require distinction, charm, beauty and imaginative power'. 'We don't want to be harrowed and disgusted', he goes on, 'with an account of the doings of the lower orders.'[6] This is not only a reaction against the naturalism of Zola and others but also part of a lordly artistic posturing which takes no heed of the popular and of the people.[7] In like manner, in 'The Soul of Man Under Socialism' (1891), Wilde sought to distinguish between popular and high art by explaining that 'A true artist takes no notice whatever of the public. The public are to him non-existent. He has no poppied or honeyed cakes through which to give the monster sleep or sustenance. He leaves that to the popular novelist.'[8]

On the other hand, as this is Oscar Wilde we are dealing with, contradictory evidence is also available. The sentiments above might be seen to be in studied contradistinction to his humorous declaration in 'The Critic as Artist' that 'Cheap editions of great books may be delightful, but cheap editions of great men are absolutely detestable'.[9] The rise of literacy and popular publishing tentatively endorsed here ('may be delightful'), with its attendant production of mass produced, cheap literature for the entertainment of the middle and lower classes, seems somewhat in contrast to Wilde's rejection of cheap machine-made objects in 'The House Beautiful'.[10] And Wilde is also capable of stating, quite openly and in an unqualified manner, that commerce need not be opposed to art: 'I do not regard the commercial spirit of the present age as being opposed to the development of art, and I look to our merchants to support the changes we seek to make'.[11]

This tension between Art and Commerce in Wilde's *oeuvre* – and ultimately in his own literary personae – might usefully be contextualised against the opinions of Wilde's literary peers. Walter Pater, for instance, the chief English exponent of *l'art pour l'art* and a man to whom Wilde paid tribute as 'the most perfect master of English prose now creating amongst us',[12] celebrated the role of art as entirely autonomous from social incidentals. In his 'Conclusion' to *The Renaissance* (1873), for instance, Pater advocates espousing 'such wisdom, the poetic passion, the desire of beauty, the love of art for its own sake [...] For art comes to you proposing frankly to give nothing but the highest quality to your moments as they pass, as simply for those moments' sake.'[13] Such a statement underpins much of Wilde's own aesthetic theory, as in the 'Preface' to *The Picture of Dorian Gray* where the author notes that 'The artist is the creator of beautiful things... it is the spectator, and not life, that art really mirrors.'[14]

Despite such posturings, we might also note how complex and untenable such a dislocation of literature and art from the everyday can be. As Regina Gagnier has argued, 'late-Victorian aestheticism was embedded in popular culture, everyday social life, and common experience'.[15] Certainly Wilde based his early career on journalism, that popular-cultural and heavily socially inflected mode of writing, and he was also much concerned with consumer culture in that career, especially when he was the editor of *Woman's World*. And perhaps there is not such a distance between consumer culture and the aesthetic world view. Indeed, the cult of 'surfaces' and the 'sensuous' which became instrumental to the aesthetic mode of artistic appraisal, has much in common with the discourse of commodity itself. Pater's sinuous prose delights in the role of the senses, maintaining that 'all art has a sensuous element, colour, form, sound – in poetry a dexterous recalling of these, together with the profound, joyful sensuousness of motion'.[16] This was also something to which Wilde sometimes subscribed, as when he declares in the preface to *Dorian Gray* that 'All Art is at once surface and symbol. Those who go beneath the surface do so at their peril.'[17] Though this might seem a distance away from commodity culture, this pursuit of sensation, of an appeal to sensory desire, is arguably comparable to the strategies of the marketplace itself. Consumerism is nothing if not sensuous, in its looking, touching and desiring. Rachel Bowlby, for instance, has written of consumer culture, with specific reference to the department store, as appealing to the 'exorbitant private pleasures to be got from sniffing and seeing and touching'.[18] These seemingly oppositional forces, the place of art and the place of commerce, are sometimes closely connected. Consider Bowlby's shop window. The critic maintains that the window display of many modern retailers 'is framed, aesthetic, for looking at; and it is just the things as they are, making a direct appeal to the potential purchaser. It is for contemplation and it is for action. You can admire at a distance, and you can go in and get it right now.'[19]

In the light of what we want to argue is aestheticism's complicity with materialism and the functions of the everyday marketplace, it is useful to consider Theodor Adorno's discussion of supposedly autonomous art such as aestheticism. The philosopher, who claimed that the phenomenon first emerged in the eighteenth century, reaching a culmination in *l'art pour l'art* philosophies, argued that it involved an ostensible rejection of commodity forces and the rejection of social mission: 'Insofar as a social function may be predicated of works of art, it is the function of having no function.'[20] Ross Wilson glosses Adorno's position well: 'Autonomous art is emancipated from having to perform any specific, pre-established social role. Simply by existing as something unique, by obeying its own law autonomous art stands in contradiction to a society in which everything must be exchangeable for everything else.'[21]

Autonomous art thus casts itself as dialectically opposed to market forces (and to 'pre-autonomous' art which is often marked by the gesture of aristocratic patronage). Adorno returned to the subject in his fine essay 'Culture Industry Reconsidered' (1963) where he undercuts the self-presentations of aestheticism in arguing that, however artistic idealism might have it, 'cultural commodities [...] are governed [...] by the principle of their realization as value, and not by their own specific content and harmonious formation'.[22] He maintains that 'the autonomy of works of art [...] rarely ever predominated in an entirely pure form', in essence acknowledging that autonomous art is often imbricated with mass commodity, despite its ostensible status as its conventional opposite.[23] As Andy Hamilton puts it, 'Adorno's key claim is that although autonomy and commodity status are in tension, yet each requires the other.' 'Socially autonomous works', writes Hamilton, 'have no choice but also to be commodities. According to Adorno, high art's claims of autonomy – the implicit claim of artworks to be more than a mere thing, to have a non-exchangeable dignity – are strictly illusory.'[24]

Adorno claims that most artistic objects lodge in between pure commodity and pure aesthetic, and Wilde's pragmatic relationship with the economic demands of publishing and his meditations on style, art and fashion seem to confirm this notion. Gagnier maintains that 'Wilde was one of the last celebrities to be identified in the public domain with autonomous art'[25] and while this is a valid point, it also seems to us that Wilde's own engagement with autonomous art was accompanied at all points by a careful attention to, and engagement with, market forces and consumer culture.

The Hegelian notion of dialectical opposition, and the relationship between seeming antitheses, was a key plank of Wilde's own aesthetic theory.[26] The critic maintained in 'The Truth of Masks' that 'in art there is no such thing as a universal truth. A Truth in art is that whose contradictory is also true [...] It is only in art-criticism, and through it, that we can realize Hegel's system of contraries. The truths of metaphysics are the truths of masks.'[27] Wilde embraced, as Yeats did after him, the power of oppositional logic. Indeed, Richard Ellmann has suggested that this philosophical attachment was responsible for Wilde's capacity to maintain simultaneous allegiance to seemingly incongruous positions.[28] In terms of the art/commerce dichotomy, these de facto contradictions in Wilde's thought became a way in which he could negotiate the demands of his desire to adopt an aristocratic/aesthetic/artistic posture and, simultaneously, to deal with the realities of the literary marketplace.

One of the most interesting tensions or oppositions explored in Wilde's philosophy is that between late nineteenth-century consumer capitalism and the role of the artist – as expounded by aesthetic theory – as an individual set apart. Despite Wilde's avowed rejection of utility as a measure of assessing artistic value, in the preface to *The Picture of Dorian Gray* – 'All art is quite useless'[29] – the novel itself outlines something quite different. Lord Henry Wotton, though the ostensible spokesperson for aestheticism in the novel, possesses a linguistic register which he couches in explicitly economic terms; 'Conscience and cowardice are really the same things, Basil. Conscience is the trade-name of the firm. That is all.'[30] Wotton also sees modern poetry as deeply complicit with the need to find both publisher and audience: 'Poets are not so scrupulous as you are. They know how useful passion is for publication. Nowadays a broken heart will run to many editions.'[31] Returning to the subject of the relationship of the sensual to both art and commerce, Lord Henry's espousal of the 'new Hedonism' is crucial here. Wotton urges Dorian to 'Be always searching for new sensations. Be afraid of nothing [...] A new Hedonism – that is what our century wants. You might be its visible symbol.'[32] He also remarks, in that brilliantly Wildean epigram, that 'The only way to get rid of a temptation is to yield to it.'[33] This pursuit of new sensations, of new experience and the thrill of pursuing such a goal, is also central to modern commodity culture. What Henry describes is analogous to the modern psychopathology of consumption. Shoppers in late nineteenth-century department stores experienced simultaneously the cult of the new (the fashionista's – to use the modern phrase – need for *this* season's handkerchief, collar or muff), and the lure of what might be called the commodity machine – the encouragement of the consumer's desire through impulsive purchases, the need for acquisition, irrational buying and material possessions being seen as definitive of status.

Rachel Bowlby has read *The Picture of Dorian Gray* in terms of commodity culture. Citing Lord Henry's description of the cigarette as 'the perfect type of the perfect pleasure. It is exquisite, and it leaves one unsatisfied',[34] she notes the way in which other commodities operate to generate but not to fulfil desire: 'The enjoyment of the "perfect pleasure" results not in satisfaction but in a lack of it, leaving open the demand for more, the search for the next (or the same) short-lived and necessarily incomplete pleasure.'[35] Developing this notion, we might note how *The Picture of Dorian Gray* is replete with descriptions of the domestic interior. What emerges in the novel is not only a concerted engagement with the idea of surface and appearance which is central to aestheticism but also a clear attention to the meanings of the modes and fashions of late nineteenth-century consumerism. Consider the opening scene:

> From the corner of the divan of Persian saddle-bags on which he was lying, smoking, as was his custom, innumerable cigarettes, Lord Henry Wotton could just catch the gleam on the honey-sweet and honey-coloured blossoms of a laburnum, whose tremulous branches seemed hardly able to bear the burden of a beauty so flame-like as there; and now and then the fantastic shadows of birds in flight flitted across the long tussore-silk curtains that were stretched in front of the huge window, producing a kind of momentary Japanese effect, and making him think of those pallid jade-faced painters of Tokio who, through the medium of an art that is necessarily immobile, seek to convey the sense of swiftness and motion. The sullen murmur of the bees shouldering their way through the long unmown grass, or circling with monotonous insistence round the dusty gilt horns of the straggling woodbine, seemed to make the stillness more oppressive. The dim roar of London was like the bourdon note of a distant organ.[36]

The reference to Japanese goods and Japanese products in this scene is worth further discussion. The rush of imports from Japan to the Western markets from the mid-nineteenth century onwards had an influence upon the aesthetic movement. As Rachel Teukolsky writes, 'Japanese imports, in particular, greatly influenced the visual styles of aesthetic art'.[37] However, as well as exerting a formal influence, this artistic influence was also evident in some of the higher-end commercial establishments in London. Arthur Liberty, to give one notable instance, who founded his shop in Regent Street, London in 1875 as a mercantile venture with its roots in the Aesthetic Movement, was an admirer of Japanese goods. Initially, the store focused on domestically produced fabrics, but, according to Judith Flanders, 'in less than a year he had added Japanese goods, as well as fans, wallpapers, fabrics, screens, lacquerware and other exotica from the Far East more generally'.[38] By the 1880s, Liberty's offered goods for every part of the modern home, boasting a Decoration Studio, Eastern Bazaar and a Paper Hanging Studio. As Judith Flanders puts it, 'Now both a house and its owner could be entirely "done" by Liberty. Liberty had created a space where – in a very modern fashion – one could acquire a lifestyle.'[39] Liberty's focus was on the high-end artisan nature of the London market and it is in this emphatically commodity-driven and urban context that Wilde sets the scene for his novel in Wotton's 'Eastern' saddle-bags and his exquisite silk curtains with their hint of Japan. Lord Henry's surroundings are seen as exquisite and testimony to his avant-garde taste, but a more popular version of his finery was available at Liberty's of London by the 1880s. Even if Wotton as an aesthete might aspire to the condition of artistic 'autonomousness', the 'roar of London' surrounds him as surely as the hum of commerce resounds through the aesthetic world view itself.

The fine products which surround Wotton are signifiers of an elevated form of consumption. But while upper-class folks like Basil or Lord Henry might command high quality and artisanship in the materials for their mansions, a similar aesthetic, albeit rendered cheaper, might be available in any number of lower-middle-class homes. Indeed, the appropriation of Japanese aesthetics is also featured in Wilde's *Woman's World.* An anonymous piece from the journal, an 1888 essay entitled 'Japanese Art Wares' noted the ubiquity of Japanese-influenced design:

> There is now hardly a drawing-room in the kingdom in which the influences of Japanese art are not felt. Walls are draped and tables covered with the rich brocades of the Land of the Dragonfly; brilliant enamelled plaques have been found a cheap and effective substitute for china, always costly and often of doubtful antiquity. We put our flowers into Japanese bowls; serve tea from Japanese trays; and in the hot summers that have become the fashion fan ourselves, without regard to sex or condition, with Japanese fans. Some of us hang our snuggeries with Japanese pictures; others collect the beautifully illustrated books filled with 'figures strange and sweet, all made out of the artist's brain' that have come down from the Nippon of the Mikados.[40]

By the time *The Picture of Dorian Gray* was published three years later, in 1891, the Japanese craze had already become part of popular commodity culture. Indeed, while the author of *The Woman's World* piece carefully distinguishes between high-end and lower-quality Japanese imports, the nature of *fashion* and taste is at all points emphasised. From expensive shops such as Liberty's to less up-market commercial concerns, Japanese 'influences' are felt in both aesthetic theory and mercantile practice.

In Wilde's *Woman's World,* references to modern designer products, whether *japoniste* or otherwise, abound, and the journal is of crucial significance to our discussion, uniting as it does the principles of aestheticism and consumerism. Indeed, Paul Fortunato notes that through the 'New Journalism' of *Woman's World,* 'aestheticism was very palpably tied to consuming' in Wilde's journal. This was 'evinced', he argues, 'by the references to identifiable brand names' in *Woman's World,* such as 'those of interior designer E. W. Godwin, the department store run by Messrs Liberty, and other "leading houses of business" '.[41] The rise of the popular press's preoccupation with feminine fashion, and its relationship to the modern marketplace, was something to which Wilde contributed, both in his writings in *The Pall Mall Gazette* on women's fashion and, most notably, in his editorship of *Woman's World* from 1887 to 1889.

Wilde's first gesture in 1887 as the new editor of the journal was to change its name, from *Lady's World* to *Woman's World*, an act which properly distinguished it from its competitors, such as the *Lady's Pictorial* and the *Lady*. When Wilde took over the periodical it was a six-shilling monthly, which had commenced publication in November 1886, the year before Wilde assumed editorial control. Though he considered that the journal was already a sufficiently aesthetic concern to be granted his notice, it was, he declared, 'too feminine' and 'not sufficiently womanly'.[42] While the magazine was not radically transformed, even after Wilde's change of nomenclature, the editor did introduce more consideration of dress design and of art. Perhaps most importantly, Wilde adjusted the cover of the magazine; from carrying the subtitle 'A Magazine of Fashion and Society' it was now described as being 'Edited by Oscar Wilde'. Plainly aware of market forces, and the way in which his name was already associated in fashionable circles with the Aesthetic Movement, Wilde commodified his own literary status. Alongside the brand names of Liberty's, Godwin's or Debenham and Freebody's, Wilde's status on the cover of *Woman's World* operated in a similar fashion, as an identifiable 'brand'.

Wilde also carefully rebranded and situated the journal in terms of the 'New Journalism' of the 1880s, which is often discussed in terms of the opportunities which it afforded women to write journalism for the literary marketplace.[43] As one female contributor to *Woman's World*, Mary Frances Billington, explained in an article on 'Journalism as a Profession for Women', a new form of journalism was giving attention 'to social functions, to dress, to decorative novelty, to women's domestic interests, to philanthropy, to bazaars, and countless other questions which may well fall under the easy, pleasant touch of an observant woman's pen'.[44] In asserting the importance of shopping, decoration and the domestic interior, the journal accorded with Wilde's own aesthetic philosophy, as set out in his 1882 American tour, while simultaneously clearly engaging with a commercial ethos which might seem at odds with the more idealistic artistic pronouncements of that era. In 1889, for instance, Wilde published 'Shopping in London' (by A. E. F. Eliot-James) as well as frequent essays and articles on fashion by diverse hands, including a number of female contributors. Art and fashion are here closely aligned. 'Dress is now a fine art', claimed a Mrs Johnstone in a Christmas 1889 meditation on 'December Fashions', 'on which artists and artificers do not disdain to expend all their talents, all their experience, and all their research'.[45] Wilde's aesthetic theory, with its focus on colour, form and sensory appeal, correlates with the emphasis in *Woman's World* on fashion as a 'fine art' product as well as a commodity.

In his editorship of *Woman's World*, Wilde vacillates between his appropriation of an English persona,[46] as he had done during his US lecture tour in which he presented himself as a spokesman for 'what we have done in England',[47] and his deployment of his Irish-born identity. His Irishness was certainly not forgotten. Nor were his roots. Using her pseudonym 'Speranza', his mother Lady Wilde, the noted Irish nationalist who wrote poetry and also tales from Irish folklore, featured in the 1889 edition of the journal, writing 'Irish Peasant Tales'.[48] In an 1889 'Some Literary Notes' column, Wilde as editor reviewed W. B. Yeats's *Fairy and Folk Tales of the Irish Peasantry*, as well as *The Wanderings of Oisin and Other Poems*. Reflecting the way in which 'Irishness' and its concomitant expression in 'Celticism' was marketed in England, Wilde notes that Yeats 'is essentially Celtic, and his verse, at best, is Celtic also'.[49] From the 'Literary Note' which Wilde devoted to the art of Irish lace making[50] to his comments on Yeats, the *Woman's World* is a useful document in determining how Irishness was marketed to the English during the late nineteenth century in terms of Celticism, folklore and peasant culture.

In the same year, 1889, as he reviewed Yeats, Wilde published an interesting piece of cultural criticism by Richard Heath called 'Politics in Dress', which reads Irish costume in political terms, notably in Heath's discussion of a 'Fenian hat' which had supposedly been banned by the Irish authorities and 'square-toed boots' (American army boots worn by veterans of the US Civil War who had returned to Ireland to take part in the 1867 Fenian Uprising):

> The Fenian hat [is an illustration] of the fact that the expression of political opinions in dress is perennial, only requiring the stimulus of popular excitement to become really portentous. The last named article of dress accompanied by square-toed boots seems at one time to have awakened the fears of Dublin Castle, and the police notice issued was thus scoffingly alluded to in a Nationalist song:
>
> Their hats caved in and shapeless to slight the Crown are meant;
> Their knickerbocks and gaiters show a desperate intent,
> Their beards look all seditious from the tips unto the roots,
> But there's mischief beyond all measure in their square-toed boots.[51]

The journalist declares that dress is symbolically meaningful. By the same token, Oscar Wilde's own costume, as we shall see, was not without sociopolitical meaning. But for now let us develop the fact that the nationalist song in Heath's article is a de facto corrective of a national stereotype.

This was not the only time that Wilde published an article condemning easy Irish caricatures. H. E. Keane's 'Lace-Making in Ireland', which appeared in 1888, does the same in terms of Irish manufacturing and peasant industries. Keane laments what he sees as the fact that Irish design was uninspiringly devoted to a few lazy signifiers of national identity:

> Unfortunately, in this country [Ireland] the traditions regarding design have been more inspired by sentiment than knowledge of art. A distorted harp, a few caricatured shamrocks, occasionally an Irish deerhound, with a round tower placed beside him, as though it were his kennel – these oddly sorted emblems furnished the stock-in trade of many a designer.[52]

While offering a critique of these hackneyed images, Keane also offers a clear rejection of the machine-made: 'As margarine is to the butter-maker, an oleograph to an artist, or a cast-iron cover to a Quentin Matsys, so is the machine-made lace to the lace-lover.'[53] However, the rejection of the machine in the particular craft of lacemaking does not imply a rejection of commodity culture per se, for the writer, in the manner so common during the Revival era, sees commercial development as crucial to Ireland's development as a nation. He praises the innovation in Irish arts exemplified in the women's section of the Glasgow Exhibition of 1888, and draws attention to the role of exhibition culture in marketing and selling various forms of Irishness and Irish products. Keane's quarrel, like Wilde's in 'The House Beautiful', is with 'ugly things made by machinery'.

During his editorship of *Woman's World*, Wilde not infrequently drew attention to Irish commercial themes. Mary Jeune's article, 'Irish Industrial Art' (1888), to give another example, addresses the convergence of Irishness and commodity evident at the Irish Industrial Exhibition at Olympia of that year, and stresses the importance of home and peasant industries in Irish economic development. Jeune pays especial attention to the support given to Irish home industry's role by another woman, Alice Rowland Hart, who had been instrumental in aiding economic recovery after the 'Donegal Famine' of 1879–1883:

> Mrs Hart, full realising that the real cure for the apparently chronic distress existing in Donegal lay in providing work and developing some industry by which the people could reckon on constant employment, turned her attention to the revival of the weaving industries which had once flourished there successfully [...] Debenham and Freebody, among other large houses, promised at once to give large orders for hosiery if Mrs Hart could provide socks exactly to size and shape.[54]

Hart was one of those Irish philanthropists who, as Janice Helland puts it, 'determined to have Irish textiles accepted by an English market and understood the need to shift the perception of objects and makers as well as to make the material available to a consuming public'.[55] In Wilde's journal, therefore, we see the end point of Hart's efforts in the display of Donegal lace in London town, testimony to the way in which the English marketplace was marshalled to serve the interests of the Irish poor.

In *Woman's World*, Wilde's awareness of commodity, both in terms of his discussions of the home, décor and furnishings, as well as fashion and the persona of the artist himself, registers his very clear affiliation with modern commercial practice. But does it repudiate his earlier meditations on the subject? In 'The House Beautiful', Wilde suggested that 'the first necessity is that any system of art should bear the impress of a distinct individuality; it is difficult to lay down rules as to the decoration of dwellings because every home should wear an individual air in all its furnishing and decorations'.[56] The notion of individuality, which Wilde counsels as crucial to the décor of any interior, is considerably difficult to attain in nineteenth-century décor or, indeed, any other art form, rife as the age was with reproductions and commodification. (Walter Benjamin, in 'The Work of Art in the Age of Mechanical Reproduction', claims 'that which withers in the age of mechanical reproduction is the aura of the work of art'.[57]) Indeed Wilde himself acknowledges the problems inherent in commercial reproductions when he urges his audience in 'The House Beautiful' to 'Put no photographs of paintings on your walls – they are libels on great masters; there is no way to get a worse idea of a painter than by a photograph of his work.'[58] Historical context, the notion of tradition and provenance, is eroded by the nature of the modern photographic reproduction (though Wilde is also censorious of the imperfection of reproduction: 'there is no colour of worth for decorative purposes in photographs').[59]

Despite his leeriness about photographic reproduction of the work of art, Wilde, in the same lecture, also celebrates photography as 'an art that will be a democratic art, entering the houses of the people'.[60] The tension here, between the celebration of fine art for the masses, and a resistance to replicas or copies, is central to Wilde's own philosophy. Arts such as photography, woodwork or weaving can be popular, but they must also strive to find the beautiful in the everyday. The way to square the circle between market values and artistic products is found in the notion of the craftsman endorsed in 'The House Beautiful': 'the real basis of all art is to be found in the application of the beautiful in things common to all and in the cultivation and development of this among the artisans of the day'.[61]

II

In her study *Advertising Fictions* (1988), Jennifer Wicke makes an important point about the historical relationship between literature and advertising: 'Post-Gutenberg literature has always had advertisement as a shadow partner, but what is more remarkable is that advertisement was a concomitant of the early printing industry, and needed literature for *its* first appearances'

('Literature and advertising are composite, heterogeneous language practices', she maintains, 'which need to be read off each other to gauge their respective outlines').[62] By the modern period, writes Wicke, the advertising of books had begun to exploit the 'celebration of individual authors'[63] as if they were literary brands.

The post-Romantic stress on 'individual authors' also prompted the later nineteenth-century culture of literary celebrity that was closely associated with the development of modern print culture and its attendant sales techniques. Alexis Easley writes in her study of Victorian authorship that 'with the proliferation of new media – travel guidebooks, mass-market newspapers, illustrated periodicals, and gossip columns – came a corresponding obsession with the lives, homes, and bodies of literary celebrities'.[64] Oscar Wilde's life and body certainly became a preoccupation of literary culture, both before and after his fall from grace. And, before his catastrophic libel action, Wilde's personae and literary celebrity were also frequently co-opted by consumerism.

The increased visibility of such figures as Wilde had itself a strong basis in the marketing of literary commodity to a wider literate market. As Gagnier writes, 'The commercialization of [Wilde's] "genius" amounted to channelling this spontaneous intelligence into a marketable "talent". This commercialized talent, in turn, leads us to consider his life's political economy, which again supports the case for the concrete embeddedness of Aestheticism in a late-Victorian market economy.'[65] Wilde, as we have seen, presented himself – marketed himself is not too strong a word – in several different and contrasting ways. During his travels in America he could use the first person plural pronoun when referring to what 'we have done in England', and call the USA 'our colonies',[66] but that tour was certainly not disengaged from the notions of Irishness or Irish politics. Wilde also presented himself in explicitly nationalistic terms. In his lecture 'The Irish Poets of '48', delivered in Platt's Hall, San Francisco in 1882, he refers with great approval to his nationalist mother, 'Speranza', and rhapsodises about Young Ireland: 'As regards the men of '48, I look on their works with peculiar reverence and love, for I was indeed trained by my mother to love and reverence them as a Catholic Child is the saints of the calendar.'[67] He goes on to praise William Smith O'Brien, John Mitchel and Charles Gavan Duffy, among others (the currency of Irish nationalist figures had immense impact in America, occasionally featuring in promotional material for stateside businesses, as per a 1904 calendar for the vintners M. H. Crehan of Boston, Massachusetts – see Figure 6.1, which features a photograph of the Irish Party luminaries John Redmond, John Dillon and Edward Blake, alongside Michael Davitt and several of the mainstays of the United Irish League of America).

Wilde's American audience, who lived in a land rid of its former colonial rule, provided a coded way for Wilde's nationalism to be paraded, for the

Figure 6.1 Calendar for M. H. Crehan of Boston, Massachusetts (1904). Courtesy of the National Library of Ireland.

author to market himself strategically as an Irishman. Indeed, nowhere is this more apparent than in his lecture 'Personal Impressions of America', in which Wilde states 'It is well worth one's while to go to a country which can teach us the beauty of the word FREEDOM and the value of the thing LIBERTY.'[68] Here his representation of himself as an Irishman in a sympathetic geographical space is overt. As always Wilde's public persona in his lectures shifts according to his stratagem of the moment and line of attack. While seemingly willing to portray himself as the consummate Englishman abroad, Wilde also presented himself as a very Irish literary celebrity in the Unites States.

In terms of Wilde's own engagement with popular and material culture in the context of marketing, we might consider a few examples of the way in which his image and literary celebrity filtered into contemporary advertising. One example is a trade card of the 1880s for 'Aesthetic' cigars, drawn from the 1882 photos taken by Napoleon Sarony (discussed below). Here Wilde's eminently elegant physique in the foreground is matched by the sunflower which features on the cabinet beside him, the curtains in the background, and in the advertising copy itself: 'Straiton and Storms. New Cigar. Aesthetic Sunflower. Capadura Patience. Dealers Supplied by R. B. Brown & Co, New York.' The cigar, itself a high-end commodity (Capadura was a boutique-level premium cigar), is promoted by an allusion to the elevated world of the Aesthetic Movement, both in the figure of Wilde and in the pre-eminence of the sunflower, the symbol of the Aesthetic Movement (in part because of its ease of stylisation and boldness of colour). In like manner, Oscar Wilde, in caricature form, appeared on another trade card from the Duval Litho Company of Philadelphia in 1882, in which the text reads 'Strike Me With A Sun Flower'. Finally, the unlikely and here surprisingly petite figure of Oscar Wilde was paraded with P. T. Barnum's famous Jumbo the Elephant (sporting a sunflower in his buttonhole), in a tradecard entitled 'Jumbo Aesthetic' (Figure 6.2), advertising 'Clark's Trademark O.N.T Spool Cotton'. Richard Ellmann has established that P. T. Barnum, the American entertainer and showman, did in fact attend one of Wilde's lectures in New York, occupying a front seat,[69] and here the great self-publicist is implicitly associated with Oscar Wilde, simultaneously avatar of high art and accomplished self-promoter, of all of his various 'masks'.

Each of these examples demonstrates the congruence of advertising, commodity culture and aesthetic principles in the visual signifier of Wilde himself. As Talia Schaffer points out, 'Aestheticist ideas, images, designs and fashions permeate the culture [and] Wilde became the visible embodiment of the movement'.[70] This, of course, is something which the author did not discourage. Indeed, this signifier of the aesthete which Wilde epitomised became widely disseminated in the stereotypical 'aesthete' easily recognisable in popular culture. One cherishable example is the Warner Bros. Coraline Corset, as advertised in the USA in the 1880s and dubbed 'the latest aesthetic craze'.[71] In the advertising image reproduced as

Figure 6.2 Trade Card, 'Jumbo Aesthetic', for Clark's Trademark O. N. T Spool Cotton (late nineteenth century). Courtesy of the National Library of Ireland.

Figure 6.3 (a), the coraline corset is held aloft by a naked cherubic figure, in a nod to the aesthete's valorisation of ancient Greece, and presented to a man in aesthetic dress (eighteenth-century knee breeches and hose, long hair, loose jacket with the suggestion of velvet fabric), who sports similar attire to that which Wilde wore on his 1882 lecture tour of the USA (featured in the famous photographs by Sarony), and who, of course, sports a sunflower button-hole.

The aesthetic style of clothing had been lampooned in Gilbert and Sullivan's satire on the aesthetic craze, the 1881 operetta, *Patience*, which was first performed at the Savoy Theatre in 1881. The character of the 'fleshly

Figure 6.3 (a) Recto of advertisement for Warner Bros.' Coraline Corsets. 'The Latest Aesthetic Craze' (early 1880s). (b) Verso of advertisement for Warner Bros.' Coraline Corsets. 'The Latest Aesthetic Craze' (early 1880s).

poet' Reginald Bunthorne, a composite of Swinburne, Whistler and Wilde, appears in the opening scene of the opera moustachioed, clad in a velvet knickerbocker suit and carrying a sunflower, and proceeds to talk of love to a gathering of twenty maidens. It is Bunthorne as first played by E. Ward Symmons, who is portrayed in the corset advertisement, but more important is the fact that the opera also had a direct influence on Oscar Wilde himself. It was the idea of the theatre manager Richard D'Oyly Carte, as part of the high-profile publicity campaign for the opera's American tour, to ask Wilde to accompany *Patience* as it toured the USA, lecturing on the aesthetic movement which the opera was gently sending up. In effect, D'Oyly Carte engaged Wilde – the 'English Poet' as he called him – as a representative of aestheticism, contracting him to a lecture schedule of ten months across the USA. A letter of 8 November 1881 tells the story:

> I have lately had a correspondence with Mr Oscar Wilde, the new English Poet, with reference to a tour in the U.S. during the winter. My attention was first drawn to him for the reason, that while we were preparing for the opera 'Patience' his name was often quoted as the originator of the aesthetic idea... It was suggested to me, that if Mr Wilde were brought to this country with the view of illustrating in a public way his idea of the aesthetic, that not only would society be glad to hear the man and receive him socially, but also that the general public would be interested in hearing from him a true and correct definition and explanation of this latest form of fashionable madness.[72]

Figure 6.3 (Continued).

We have noted the public's increased fascination with the physical body of the literary celebrity, and D'Oyly marketed Wilde as the physical representative of aestheticism. Wilde represented aestheticism in 'a public way', not only through his intellectual arguments regarding 'The House Beautiful' or 'The Decorative Arts', but through the physical presentation of himself on the stage. The poet himself becomes a commodity in the service of his art.

In part, this is why Wilde's costume during the lecture tour was so carefully considered, so that he could quite literally embody the ideas he was propounding. It was D'Oyly Carte who directed his aesthetic star to Napoleon Sarony for the publicity shots in which Wilde was captured, in twenty-seven different poses, in aesthetic dress purchased in London for the lecture tour. These, in the modern term, went viral as the tour progressed and were purchased in large numbers (and also used piratically). Indeed, as Joseph Bristow writes,

> [By] early 1882 it was possible to purchase the series of images in different sizes, and each shot confirmed for the American public what was already familiar to British viewers. Attired in silken hose, knee-breeches, a sumptuous velvet jacket, and a fur coat, Wilde stood before the camera. Within weeks advertisers would produce engravings of these images to promote such commodities as "aesthetic" ice cream and "aesthetic" wallpapers.[73]

Wilde's deployment of the Sarony photographs as part of his lecture tour in 1882 is testimony to the ways in which identity can be seen as elective, even multifarious, in commodity culture. The photograph, Shawn Michelle Smith claims in her study of American visual culture, was used 'to create new images and to posit new identities, proliferating the possibilities of representing and circulating the self [...] The proliferation of variously performed identities was intricately linked to the status of the photographic portrait as a commodity.'[74] It is the oscillation between opposing poles which was also the foundation of the journalistic commentaries on art and materialism in Wilde's lectures.[75] Wilde's visual staging of himself, whether through photography or through his 'variously performed identities', reproducible and adaptable in the commercial sphere, is testimony to both commodification and what one might call the elusive nature of human identity. Perhaps this is most clearly demonstrated in *The Picture of Dorian Gray* (1891) where the eponymous anti-hero is seen to be – arguably like Wilde himself – a model for emulation which is constructed entirely from an ironic pose in terms of apparel and fashion:

> His mode of dressing, and the particular styles that from time to time he affected, had their marked influence on the young exquisites of the Mayfair Balls and the Pall Mall Club windows, who copied him in everything he did, and tried to reproduce the accidental charm of his graceful, though to him only half-serious, fopperies.[76]

So the *Patience* version of the composite aesthete, in part but not exclusively modelled on Wilde, became decidedly ubiquitous in the 1880s (even appearing on a tea pot in 1882).[77] Let us return to the trade card and the Warner Bros. Corsets hero, with the aesthetic subject sporting the sunflower in the company of an exclusively female court. This alignment of femininity and the aesthete is overt in the trade card's portrayal of the female audience, and in the very object it sells, as the aesthete is mobilised to market a woman's garment. There are interesting resonances here. As Talia Schaffer writes:

> The male Aesthetes, especially Oscar Wilde, were often condemned for effeminacy, both because they worked in fields traditionally associated with women and because they borrowed elements of women's attire. In the Aesthete's desires to beautify everyday life, they moved into areas that had historically been associated with women: the decoration of homes and bodies.[78]

In the Warner Bros.' advertisement the future editor of *Woman's World* is explicitly co-opted to market 'women's attire'.

Wilde's celebrity status was exploited in *Woman's World*, which, as we have seen, carried the prominent subtitle 'Edited by Oscar Wilde' (this perhaps brings to mind Henry's famous axiom in *Dorian Gray*: 'There is only one thing in the world worse than being talked about, and that is not being talked about').[79] It was also an important part of the lecture tour of the USA in 1882, the brainchild of a promotional genius, D'Oyly Carte, who was a leading light in what we would now call the culture industries. The lecture circuit and the popular press were two of the major ways in which Wilde's publicity was fostered. Joe Moran has argued that Wilde, like 'Boz' before him, was a forerunner of the modern-day celebrity: 'Certainly the kind of hysteria that authors [...] like Dickens and Oscar Wilde experienced on their lecture tours of the US – overnight queues, packed theatres, huge box office receipts, ticket touts and the use of police reserves to control the crowd – anticipated the treatment meted out to contemporary celebrities.'[80] Moran's maintains that Wilde was a key part of the growing publicity 'industry': 'The principal reason for these writers' popularity is that it did not just emerge out of publishing books, but "operated in and on a relatively new context – the world of commercialized print and the burgeoning industry of publicity".'[81] The relationship between the artist and consumer culture, therefore, is at the very centre of Wilde's own US tour in 1882 – both in the subject matter of several of his most important lectures, and also in the way in which the author actively rendered himself a commodity for literary audiences, providing the foundation for much of his subsequent career.

7
Consumerism and Anti-Commercialism: The Yeatses, Print Culture and Home Industry

> You gave, but will not give again
> Until enough of Paudeen's pence
> By Biddy's halfpennies have lain
> To be 'some sort of evidence'.
> (W. B. Yeats, 'To A Wealthy Man who promised a Second Subscription to the Dublin Municipal Gallery if it were proved the People wanted Pictures' (1913))

W. B. Yeats's stated position regarding consumerism and commercial culture often differed quite discernibly from his practice. The poet loudly proclaimed in 'A General Introduction for My Work' (1937) that 'When I stand upon O'Connell Bridge in the half-light and notice that discordant architecture, all those electric signs [...] a vague hatred comes up out of my own dark',[1] but despite this lofty rejection of the modern world and its concomitant 'electric signs', we want to argue that his work is more consistently located in the commercial sphere than may at first be apparent.

In this chapter, we problematise the notion of W. B. Yeats, and indeed the Irish Revival enterprises of the Dun Emer and Cuala Presses, as avowedly and uncomplicatedly anti-consumerist. We demonstrate how Yeats's play *The Countess Cathleen*, one of the key texts of the Irish Revival, is not without critical engagement in terms of economic and commercial concerns. Similarly, despite the poet's anti-materialist positionings, as the editor of his sisters' press, alongside the business acumen of the sisters, Yeats also demonstrated an awareness of publishing practices and the status of literature as commodity. Dun Emer and Cuala were enterprises which were both aesthetic and cultural endeavours, but they were also deeply linked to trade and to high-end retail.

I

We are perhaps accustomed to thinking of W. B. Yeats in terms of his avowed antipathy to materialism and to 'base' economics: in his polemical essay on the Irish Literary Theatre, 'The Theatre' (1900) he declares his aspiration to move away from a mercantile, even meretricious, commercial theatre:

> We must make a theatre for ourselves and our friends, and for a few simple people who understand from sheer simplicity what we understand from scholarship and thought. We have planned the Irish Literary Theatre with this hospitable emotion, and, that the right people may find out about us, we hope to act a play or two in the spring of every year; and that the right people may escape the stupefying memory of the theatre of commerce which clings even to them.[2]

This entrenched conflict between the theatre of commerce and the theatre of art was one which also pervaded Yeats's own work in the drama. We will examine this dichotomy by examining the tensions evident within his play *The Countess Cathleen*, a work which arguably marks the start of the Irish Revival in the theatre. In this drama, written in 1892 but first performed on 8 May 1899 in the Antient Concert Rooms, Dublin, Yeats presents the Irish people, 'in old times', in the midst of a terrible famine, being forced to sell their souls to mercantile devils in order to save their lives. Eventually the countess herself, in a move which simultaneously highlights Yeats's distrust of mercantilism and his reverence of the aristocratic class, sells her property to gain much needed food for the peasants. She then offers her – much more valuable – soul to free them from their dark bargain (her soul is valued at five hundred thousand crowns, while the soul of an ugly old woman weighs in at but a thousand).

The play was subject to some scandal predicated upon its economic Faustianism and its portrayal of an Irish peasantry participating, however unwillingly, in such diabolical contracts. Yeats's willingness to depict a peasantry with moral flaws conflicted with the idealising evident in much Revivalist rhetoric, with one reviewer maintaining that 'the Irish peasantry in this play are, and always were, totally incapable of the acts and sayings attributed to them'.[3] F. Hugh O'Donnell went further in his condemnation, publishing a pamphlet, *Souls for Gold: Pseudo-Celtic Drama in Dublin* (1899), which labels the *Countess Cathleen* 'blasphemous' and which excoriates Yeats, in Adrian Frazier's words, for producing 'a play that presented the Irish as a people eager to sell their souls for gold, that said souls came at different prices, and that illustrated as features of Irish life some peasants who stole, some who committed sacrilege, and one woman hell-bent on fornication'.[4]

One of the major problems for Yeats here, of course, was the competing values within Irish society. The idyllic Ireland presented and portrayed in much nationalist discourse (something which was to cause later, bitter contention in the theatre in 1907 with the production of J. M. Synge's *The Playboy of the Western World*) did not include a peasantry with failings like those evident in any other part of society. Frazier rightly suggests that *Cathleen* caused such outrage because 'an ideal Ireland would not be so richly populated with sinners'.[5] One of the cornerstones of nationalist ideology during the Revival was the presentation of 'the Irish' as a people of spirituality, in opposition to the materialism of 'the English', living in a religious land populated by poets and dreamers. So Yeats's representation of the Irish soul as being subject to commodity exchange and base coinage, however desperate the motivations behind it, was something which some among the audience found hard to stomach. It is telling that O'Donnell's pamphlet thunders that 'Mr W. B. Yeats is entitled to construct any "drama" he pleases and to people it with as many thieves and devil-worshippers as he may please... Only he has no right to lay the scene in Ireland.'[6]

Whatever the contemporary controversies which surrounded Yeats's play, it is perfectly possible to view his drama, with its imperialist, money-minded diablerie, in nationalist terms. As David R. Clark observes in his discussion of the play:

> Universal spiritual values are represented by the Christian God and spirits, who are at home everywhere. They struggle with universal material values, represented by Satan and his demons, who, wherever they go, are foreign exploiters. The plague-smitten land, the starving peasants, and the enslaved gods of ancient Ireland represent the Irish land and people, individual targets of temptation by material values.[7]

According to this line of argument, the play clearly engages with Yeats's nationalist and anti-commercial ethos and echoes some very clear tenets of nationalism – Adrian Frazier, for instance, maintains that the malign supernatural elements of the play clearly represent the British as the natural enemy of the Irish, 'the strangers with good manners who operate on principles of Free Trade even in times of Famine'.[8] Therefore, one ideological aspect of the play lies in what can be seen as its focus upon the demonic nature of English commercialism. Indeed, in depicting the English mercantile character as a source of corruption and disapproval, Yeats is engaging with a much broader debate about the construction of Irishness on the one hand, and the supposedly pernicious nature of Englishness itself on the other. As R. F. Foster has written, contemporary 'Anti-materialism was often a code for anti-Englishness'.[9]

In his 1897 essay, 'The Celtic Element in Literature', Yeats offers a definition of the ancient Irish race that grants it the intrinsic characteristics of spirituality, otherworldliness and affinity with nature: 'They had imaginative passions because they did not live within our own straight limits, and were nearer to ancient chaos, every man's desire, and had immortal models about them.'[10] Similarly, Yeats's vision for the Irish Literary Theatre was idealising: it would be 'remote, spiritual, and ideal'.[11] Offering a qualification of Ernest Renan and Matthew Arnold's previous analyses of Celticism, Yeats sees the literature of the Irish Revival as built upon 'the life beyond the world':

> Certainly a thirst for unbounded emotion and a wild melancholy are troublesome things in the world, and do not make its life more easy or orderly, but it may be the arts are founded on the life beyond the world, and that they must cry in the ears of our penury until the world has been consumed and become a vision.[12]

The supposedly unworldly nature of the Revival apart, Yeats's use of 'penury' here is significant in the context of our current argument. He sees contemporary cultural poverty as something which must be resisted, rather than stressing the simplicity and moral superiority of the Irish peasantry as a way in which Ireland might define herself in opposition to English material principles (this is very much counter to certain other strains of Irish nationalism, such as D. P. Moran's emphasis on economic independence and native modes of production).[13] Yeats carefully deflects the question of the economic and social deprivation suffered by the Irish peasantry and also deftly avoids a critique of the aristocratic class by uniting the peasant and the landowner in resistance to the British.[14]

Despite what one might see as Yeats's gesture towards decolonisation here, his position was not without its attendant problematic. Alongside its perceived slighting of the Irish people (it 'offers as a type of our people a loathsome brood of apostates' declared the 'Dublin Catholic students of the Royal University'[15] in a letter of protest to the *Freeman's Journal*), what some saw as the implicit anti-Catholicism of the play was another source of contemporary disapprobation. Lionel Pilkington has argued that the drama, whether intentionally or not, endorsed the view that 'Catholic Ireland is, by definition, not fully modern and therefore not ready for political or administrative independence.'[16] Pilkington maintains that 'the anti-Catholicism of the play's thematics threatens to expose the Irish Literary Theatre's dehistoricizing of Irish culture'.[17] Part of the tension in the reactions from the play's first audience, in this account, centres on the competing ideas and priorities within Irish nationalism as a whole.

It might also be argued that there is a carefully delineated class discourse in Yeats's play that serves to valorise Anglo-Irish values. The monetary value of the countess's soul, for instance, with its hint of the 'innate' superiority of the Protestant elite, might be seen as suggesting the placing of ascendancy culture at the foreground of the Irish Literary Theatre movement (again, this was something which was to cause much contention throughout the theatre's early history).[18] Indeed, in the first act, when Cathleen enters the cottage, the explicit notion of class distinction immediately becomes apparent. Mary identifies the countess's demesne as 'A place that's set among impassable walls/ As though world's trouble could not find it out.' Clearly, these lines reveal the literal and physical boundary between the peasant tenant and the landlord class. But, interestingly, the countess says she has lost her way in her own lands: 'Although we've wandered in this wood this hour/Have lost it too, yet I should know my way/For I lived all my childhood in that house.'[19] While this seems rather implausible, in the context of absentee landlords and a garrison mentality, as Frazier points out, 'there were plenty of Irish lords and ladies [...] who could not have found their way around their own property, had they ventured into it'.[20]

While *The Countess Cathleen* was billed as a nationalist play, and – as we have seen – it can certainly be read as such, in many respects it is just as revealing in terms of Yeats's preoccupation with class. Famously, George Moore satirised the poet's approach to his ancestry and gleefully remembered George Russell's put-down:

> [W]e laughed, remembering AE's story, that one day whilst Yeats was crooning over his fire Yeats had said that if he had his rights he would be Duke of Ormonde. AE's answer was: I am afraid, Willie, you are overlooking your father – a detestable remark to make to a poet in search of an ancestry; and the addition: we both belong to the lower-middle classes, was in equally bad taste. AE knew that there were spoons in the Yeats family bearing the Butler crest, just as there are portraits in my family of Sir Thomas More, and he should have remembered that certain passages in *The Countess Cathleen* are clearly derivative from the spoons.[21]

The poet was a veteran self-mythologiser, and in his endorsement of aristocratic values, as well as in his studied posturing of upper-class affiliation, he carefully disregarded the legacy of one half of his family – the Pollexfens, who gained prosperity through that very same vulgar commercialism he claimed to despise. As Roy Foster writes, 'The Sligo Pollexfens...by the early nineteenth century were established in Brixham, Devon, where they had shipping interests; through an unprotected entail their fortunes had declined...'[22] William Pollexfen (the poet's grandfather) married Elizabeth Middleton in 1837, herself part of a large shipping and milling family.

This union of two families which had developed commercial interests is a far cry from Yeats's public declaration of his aristocratic lineage. As Foster states: 'The Middletons were country businessmen, comfortably off members of the local Protestant bourgeoisie with odd "squireen" offshoots. The Pollexfens fitted this mould.'[23] While the Yeatses and the Pollexfens had relatively distant aristocratic connections, and some land ownership, by the late nineteenth century they were largely what snobs would call 'trade'.[24] Yeats's suppression of this commercial heritage in his writings and public declarations largely went without question until relatively recently, and is part of a wider assumption of a supposedly self-evident lack of a bourgeois culture in Ireland.[25] In many ways, Yeats actively sought to resist any real association with the commercial classes of Ireland. Significantly, he declared in his 1909 journal that 'Style, personality – deliberately adopted and therefore a mask – is the only escape from the hot-faced bargainers and money changers',[26] suggesting an awareness of the close link between his own carefully mythologised personality and the denial of his money-making close relations. These relations were so sardonically highlighted in George Moore's *Hail and Farewell*, in which he recollects Yeats shuddering (in a speech on the Lane controversy mentioned below) at the very thought of the bourgeoisie: 'It is impossible to imagine the hatred which came into his voice when he spoke the words "the middle classes".'[27]

Having said this, whatever Yeats's personal antipathy to commercial values, it was frequently accompanied by a keen awareness of the need to find an audience for his work, and a pragmatic attitude towards sales and reviews. In the opening of 'Ireland and the Arts' (1901), first published in Arthur Griffith's *United Irishman*, Yeats explicitly addresses the relationship between the arts and money, claiming that 'The Arts have failed; fewer people are interested in them every generation. The mere business of living, of making money, of amusing oneself, occupies people more and more, and makes them less and less capable of the difficult art of appreciation.'[28] Suggestively, the beginning of the essay polarises artistic integrity and commercial gain (in the same way as 'September 1913' would years later, in response to the controversy surrounding Sir Hugh Lane's offer of his art collection to the nation, as long as a building was erected for that purpose).

Despite his polarisation of high art and the marketplace, it should be pointed out that Yeats also had an eye on commercial success and often dwelt on his pressing need for cash as he first began to make his name as an author. As Yug Mohit Chaudhry points out, 'To a very large extent, and more so early in his career, Yeats had to write for money and therefore produce work that would sell with publishers and editors.'[29] Indeed, he advised one young poet in 1889, before the Revival's de-anglicising kicked in, that Irish culture was both the best topic for Irish poets and the way to stand out from the versifying crowd: 'You will find it a good thing to make verses on Irish legends and places and so forth. It helps originality and makes one's verses sincere, and gives one less numerous competitors. Besides, one should love best what is nearest and most interwoven with one's life.'[30] The mixture of the preoccupations of the cultural Revival ('Irish legends and places and so forth') and the market place ('competitors') is striking here.

In like manner, in writing to Katherine Tynan in 1888, Yeats exclaimed that, while his first priority was not to produce a 'saleable story', nonetheless everything he was writing had 'a practical intention'.[31] Indeed, we might note that Yeats's poem 'The Lake Isle of Innisfree' was composed, as the poet explains, in response to a feeling of homesickness prompted by *a shop window display*: 'when walking through Fleet Street very homesick I heard a little tinkle of water and saw a fountain in a shop-window which balanced a little ball upon its jet, and began to remember lake water. From the sudden remembrance came my poem *Innisfree*'.[32] Inescapably, the poet's work, despite his distaste for the commercial marketplace, often arises directly out of it.

The initial publication of the poem 'September 1913' provides a good example of how Yeats himself persistently engaged with the market forces evident within the social and political diversity of contemporary Irish print culture. It was first published in the *Irish Times*, suggesting that its submission to that paper was tailored to a Protestant audience, with an awareness that the reader of the *Times* would, like Yeats, feel the decline of the ascendancy class most poignantly, alongside a strong awareness of the encroachment of Catholic middle class sensibilities. Indeed, Chaudhry's reading of 'September 1913' goes so far as to argue that the poet was clearly agitating, in these famous words, against a particularly mercantile type of bourgeois Catholic rather than the mercantile class in general; his intention, she maintains, 'to attack middle-class Catholics'[33]:

> What need you, being come to sense,
> But fumble in a greasy till
> And add the halfpence to the pence
> And prayer to shivering prayer, until
> You have dried the marrow from the bone.[34]

To Chaudhry, whatever his literary idealism, Yeats knew that he was working in a literary marketplace; he 'knew the importance of targeting a readership that was likely to receive his work favourably and in the manner he wished it to be'.[35] Alternatively, as the poet himself put it in a letter of June 1906, 'I don't believe it is possible to make a good magazine without making up your mind who it is for whom you are making it and keeping to that idea throughout.'[36] Chaudhry argues that Yeats was strategic in his placement of his poems and articles, which were most often published for the first time in periodicals: 'Periodical publication, albeit sometimes unpaid, was the cheapest and most practical way of publicising [new writers'] work, garnering a readership and establishing their literary credentials [...] Succeeding in the periodical marketplace was [Yeats's] only hope of survival.'[37] Yeats knew how to market himself. D. P. Moran's portrayal of the author in *The Philosophy of Irish Ireland* (1905) as a self-advertiser whose Celtic antics were devised to help him sell his literary wares more profitably is a brutally reductionist view of the author's complex and ambivalent relationship to the market, but it has some truth to it. Moran saw opportunism in such works as *Cathleen ni Houlihan*; when he saw that play in 1905, he dismissed it bluntly: 'the poor old woman has gained admittance to the scented drawing room where they take a little green sentimentality with their coffee and gossip. "Kathleen ni Houlihanism" makes Irish patriotism quite harmless.'[38] Yeats's work is politically quietist and marketed as a product for the genteel, like the coffee served in the salon.

Despite his expressions of antipathy to the marketplace, therefore, Yeats was entirely – and consciously – complicit with it. As Anthony Bradley observes:

> One might think Yeats shared the modernists' contempt for newspapers and other manifestations of mass culture. Certainly he had little good to say about journalists or newspapers, and records his distaste for both on a number of occasions... [Yet] he was, moreover, like many Irish writers and intellectuals in the Irish nationalist tradition, a part-time newspaper journalist for many years.[39]

Yeats's statements on art, politics, contemporary affairs, as well as numerous other subjects, were published in a variety of journals with competing interests (with an equally wide-ranging political and social inflection in terms of readership). Indeed, Chaudhry wittily points out that Yeats's publication record was spectacularly contradictory in terms of its affiliations:

> [It was] high-brow (*Yellow Book*) and low-brow (*Girl's Own Paper*), Catholic (*Irish Monthly*) and Protestant (*Leisure Hour*), intellectual (*Academy*) and athletic (*Gael*), populist (*Bookman*) and elitist (*New Review*), imperialist (*Scots Observer*) and socialist (*Irish Worker*), unionist (*Dublin Daily Express*) and nationalist (*United Ireland*), decadent (*Savoy*) and anti-decadent (*National Observer*), general (*Contemporary Review*) and specialised (*Vegetarian*), celebrated (*Fortnightly Review*) and forgotten (*Lucifer*).[40]

In the light of this conflicted record, we might carefully note how far Yeats's every poetic and political gesture is inflected with his notion of antinomies:

> I had never read Hegel, but my mind had been full of Blake from boyhood up and I saw the world as a conflict – Spectre and Emanation – and could distinguish between a contrary and a negation. 'Contraries are positive' wrote Blake, 'a negation is not a contrary', 'How great the gulph between

> simplicity and insipidity', and again, 'There is a place at the bottom of the graves where contraries are equally true.'[41]

In simple terms, Yeats embraced dichotomy throughout his career, and his negotiation of the conflict between the marketplace and the rarefied field of the arts is no exception to this pattern.

II

Early in his career, in 1891, Yeats played a key role in the organisation of the Irish Literary Society in London, and was later instrumental in the inaugural meeting of the National Literary Society in Dublin, on 24 May 1892. Douglas Hyde became the president of the society, Yeats was appointed one of the two vice-presidents, and his one time mentor the Fenian John O'Leary served on the council. One of the express aims of the two societies in 1892 was the promotion of a book series entitled 'The Library of Ireland' (later 'The New Irish Library'), to be published by Fisher Unwin and edited by Yeats himself. The poet explained in his *Autobiographies*:

> I had definite plans; I wanted to create an Irish Theatre; I was finishing my *Countess Cathleen* in its first meagre version, and thought of a travelling company to visit our country branches; but before that there must be a popular imaginative literature. I arranged with Mr Fisher Unwin and his reader, Mr Edward Garnett – a personal friend of mine – that when our organization was complete Mr Fisher Unwin was to publish for it a series of books at a shilling each.[42]

Though Yeats, like Lady Gregory, was not afraid of telling the Irish people what he thought was good for them, in the case of the Irish Library its conceptualisation was couched in practical terms, in the terms of the 'popular', and in terms of an awareness of the realities of the literary marketplace.

Fisher Unwin was a shrewd choice in terms of publishing Irish works in England. He was certainly aware of a market for Irish writing in Great Britain. Not only had he previously published Yeats's *John Sherman and Dhoya* (1891), as part of the Pseudonym Library (Yeats's moniker was 'Ganconagh'), but he would also go on to publish various other books and editions by the poet in the 1890s: *Irish Fairy Tales* (1892; edited by Yeats and situated in the 'Children's Library'), *The Countess Cathleen and Various Legends and Lyrics* (1892) in the 'Cameo Series', *The Wanderings of Oisin* (reissued 1892), *The Land of Heart's Desire* (1894) and *Poems* (1895). Unwin was part of a developing publishing fraternity in the 1880s and 1890s that saw the decline of the comparatively expensive three-volume novel in favour of a one-volume publication as an opportunity. Along with growing literacy and cheaper methods of printing, there was a sense that books could obtain a much wider audience through lower-priced editions.

Unwin was also, as Troy J. Bassett has demonstrated, strongly aware of a new retail market: he focused on book series such as the 'New Irish Library' as a marketing strategy, with one of his most successful being the existing 'Pseudonym Series' of which Yeats was a part.[43] The books themselves, as Bassett points out, were published 'in an odd, rectangular shape (7 × 3.5 inches [19.05 × 8.9 cm])',[44] designed to fit in a lady's purse or a man's coat pocket, and were sold in railway bookshops and elsewhere. More generally, the notion of a one-volume book in a series was a clear marketing ploy – it generated reader expectations and continuity in terms of quality and style.[45] Yeats had chosen a clever populist, whose existing series, 'the Pseudonym Library', was, in the words of Ford Madox Ford, ubiquitous, 'with its sulphur yellow covers that penetrated like a fumigation into every corner of Europe'.[46]

While series publication was by no means a new development in British publishing, Unwin's innovation was based in the marketing of new works and up-and-coming authors, rather than reprints or issues of older material and classics, as per Colburn and Bentley's block-busting Standard Novels series of the 1830s onwards. It was this issue of original versus old material which was problematic for the 'New Irish Library' and which eventually resulted in Yeats losing the editorship of the series to that skilled politician Sir Charles Gavan Duffy, who had founded the *Nation* in 1842, and who had returned from his emigration to Australia (where he had been Premier of Victoria).

Duffy had very different ideas as to the nature of the Library. Yeats clearly saw the series as an enterprise which would 'have done much for popular education'[47] and he argued for giving 'some representation on its governing board to contemporary Irish writers'.[48] This would be part of a scheme having a general appeal to the public: 'We had planned small libraries of Irish literature in connection with our country branches; we collected books and money, sending a lecturer to every branch and taking half the proceeds of that lecture to buy books.'[49] Yeats had suggested the first books in the series should be a study of Wolfe Tone by T.W. Rolleston, Lady Wilde writing on Patrick Sarsfield, and Yeats himself on 'ballad chronicles'.[50]

By contrast, at least in Yeats's account, Duffy (well over seventy years of age) was backward-, rather than forward-looking, and fairly determined ' "to complete the Young Ireland movement" – to do all that had been left undone because of the Famine, or the death of Davis, or his own emigration; and all the younger men were upon my side in resisting that. They might not want the books I wanted, but they did want books written by their own generation, and we began to struggle with him over the control of the company.'[51] Yeats fought a rearguard action, claiming, in a September 1892 letter to the *Freeman's Journal*, long experience in this market, 'a somewhat considerable experience of the editing of cheap books – I have edited five, some of which were sold in thousands'.[52] However, Duffy prevailed, not least because he had, in Foster's words 'adroitly put himself at the head of the National Publishing Company, set up to produce the books, and now claimed editorial powers as well'.[53]

Essentially, with Duffy at the helm, the project began moving away from the initial plan of a series showcasing new and contemporary material – something much more in line with Fisher Unwin's marketing strategy – to a reiteration of Young Ireland's achievements. Following much heated debate, the first volume published in the series, with Duffy as editor, was Thomas Davis's *The Patriot Parliament 1689* (1893). Yeats noted that there had been ten thousand subscribers to the series, but following the first volume, subscriptions declined and people 'made up their minds to have nothing more to do with us or our books'.[54] If Yeats wanted to market contemporary material, Duffy wanted 'books that by some chance had failed to find publication in his youth, the works of political associates, or of friends long dead'.[55] (Yeats did succeed in securing Douglas Hyde's *The Story of Early Gaelic Literature* (1895) and Standish O'Grady's *The Bog of Stars, and Other Stories and Sketches of Elizabethan Ireland* (1893) in the series, as well as a proposed life of Swift and of Goldsmith.)

However, nothing further came of the series and perhaps one of the reasons for this is the especially contentious issue of competing versions of the nationalist agenda at the time – following the death of Parnell in 1891, the nationalist community of all persuasions was compelled to reflect on, and reassess, its ideology, prompting, as is well known, debate and dissention in many quarters. Despite its failure, Yeats's plan for a popular library – and for the marketing of the same – marks a key point in the propaganda of the Irish Revival and the way in which, despite its declared intention to resist a model of English materialism, it actively engaged with issues of marketing, readership and modern publishing. It this way, it is possible to contextualise Yeats's Revivalist attitudes alongside the broader issue of consumerism and literary commodity in late nineteenth-century print culture. In 1892 Yeats wrote his famous letter to O'Leary declaring that the 'mystical life is the centre of all that I do and all that I think and all that I write',[56] but in the same year his mind was also much preoccupied with marketing and selling, and 'the editing of cheap books'.

III

Correlated to this issue of the Irish artistic marketplace encountered by Yeats is the history of the somewhat less well-known enterprises of the Yeats sisters, Elizabeth (1868–1940, known as 'Lolly' or 'Lollie' to her family) and Susan Mary, 'Lily' (1866–1949). In one of the few book-length accounts of the Dun Emer Guild and Cuala Industries, Gifford Lewis notes that while the sisters were frequently overshadowed by their famous brothers, they nonetheless founded and managed culturally significant endeavours.[57] Joyce satirically refers to them in *Ulysses* when Buck Mulligan exclaims 'Five lines of text and ten pages of notes about the folk and the fishgods of Dundrum. Printed by the weird sisters in the year of the big wind.'[58] While this humorous picture suggests dilettantish ventures organised by two spinsters, more considered analysis reveals that Lolly and Lily were not only rigorously engaged with ideas from the Arts and Crafts Movement, particularly with the work and philosophy of William Morris, but also that their endeavours had a strong business edge. After all, Dun Emer Industries (1904–1908), of which the Dun Emer Press (1903–1907) was a part, was both their chief source of income and an important example of the contemporary home industries movement.[59] Indeed, as Elaine Cheasley Paterson has noted, 'Set against an industrial profile (low wages, sweated work at home for pennies), this artistic revival of Irish industries refined women's crafts as art and provided the women working in them with an alternative to these harsh conditions.'[60]

Part of the enterprise was clearly located against capitalist exploitation of the worker, which again invokes William Morris, who affirmed that nineteenth-century modes of mass production had devalued the experience of the worker who had lost the joy in his or her work, and had resulted in aesthetically inferior products. Morris described the decorative arts as follows:

> To give people pleasure in things they must perforce *use*, that is the one great office of decoration; to give people pleasure in the things they must perforce *make*, that is the other use of it [...] without these arts, our rest would be vacant and uninteresting, our labour mere endurance, mere wearing away of body and mind.[61]

Morris envisages a unity of use value, objects of beauty and socialist respect for the working craftsman or woman.

The Dun Emer Prospectus, issued in 1903, defined its own use value as follows:

> Things made of pure materials, worked by these Irish girls must be more lasting and more valuable than machine-made goods which only serve a temporary purpose. All the things made at Dun Emer are beautiful in the sense that they are instinct with individual feeling and have cost thought and care.
>
> There is no limit to the number and kinds of things that could be well made in Ireland if designers and workers could depend upon a certain market. It is indisputable that the talent of artistic hand-work is widely spread amidst the Irish people.[62]

While Dun Emer obviously saw its role in terms of aesthetic creation and high-end commodity, it was also a part of the contemporaneous move towards economic independence, which, as we have seen, was 'promoted by Irish Revivalists as a necessity for Ireland to become competitive in world markets'.[63]

The prospectus also introduces an inherent dialectic in Dun Emer's philosophy. On the one hand, the rejection of machine-made items in preference for handworked objects is the cornerstone of the Arts and Crafts Movement in the late nineteenth century, but the awareness of Ireland's need for economic development and market forces suggests a subtly different employment of arts and crafts. The discourses of Irish 'authenticity' and 'traditionalism', which were prominent during the Revival,[64] were identified in Dun Emer products and presented in the newspaper press as 'a form of consumable Irishness with its accompanying illusion of uniform national identity'.[65] The remainder of this chapter will address the issue of how far Dun Emer and Cuala were subject to this idea of economic competition through aesthetic design; how far they were modelled on existing aspects of the British Arts and Crafts Movement and, finally, the ways in which it is possible to situate Dun Emer and Cuala in commercial Ireland.

Nicola Gordon Bowe maintains that, while the ideals of the English Arts and Crafts Movement (small industry, workshops, education and societies, as well the need for beautiful objects with a use value which are made by craftsmen with pleasure in their work) might be easily transferable to other countries, the cultural specificities of design varied 'nationally, even regionally'.[66] The incorporation of the Irish Trademark onto the Irish poplin and lace embroidered dress worn in 1907 by Lady Aberdeen, the president of the Irish Industries Association, for instance, highlights the way in which the overall ideology of English arts and crafts was adapted to suit an Irish national economic purpose.[67] In like manner, Dun Emer's education programme included Irish language classes, representing the nationalist inflection in that enterprise.

The Yeatses often visited William Morris (1834–1896) at Kelmscott House, following their relocation to Bedford Park in the 1880s. Yeats records how his sister Susan Mary (Lily) 'became an embroideress under Miss May Morris', the Morrisses' youngest daughter, 'and the hangings round Morris's big bed at Kelmscott House, Oxfordshire, with their verses about lying happily in bed when "all the birds sing in the town of the tree", were from her needle, though not from her design'.[68] Lily had been May Morris's assistant at Morris & Co., in the embroidery department. Elizabeth Yeats also observed May Morris and how women worked printing presses and took a course in printing at the Women's Printing Society, which had been founded in 1876 (all of this was to aid her when she acquired an old Albion Press (as used by Morris) for Dun Emer, following the advice of Emery Walker (1851–1933), who was Morris's typographical advisor at the Kelmscott Press).

We may note at this point that the Dun Emer was from its very foundation a business concern. When Lolly took her course in printing, she also learnt 'not only about composing and proofreading but also about business practices and how to organize the work space for maximum efficiency'.[69] The primary concern of the Women's Printing Society was in fact 'to enable women to earn a decent wage',[70] a more pragmatic economic concern which challenges the conventional image of the Arts and Crafts Movement as being disengaged from the baser realities of finance. If, as Adorno maintains, most artistic objects lodge in between pure commodity and pure aestheticism,[71] then Dun Emer and Cuala were no exceptions. Dun Emer was certainly founded, in the face of the Yeats family's fairly consistent economic problems, as a commercial concern as much as an artistic one.

A key figure in the development of Dun Emer was Evelyn Gleeson (1855–1944), who was acquainted with W. B. Yeats and his sisters through the Irish Literary Society in London. In 1902 Gleeson went to Dublin to take a house, and invited Lolly and Lily to develop an Irish arts industry with her. Lolly was charged with running the publishing wing of the new venture, while Lily would work on embroidery and Evelyn Gleeson herself would take charge of tapestry and carpets. The Dun Emer project was initially funded by Gleeson's inheritance, although the Yeats sisters contributed much in terms of their craft expertise and contacts in the art world.[72] Together they founded their workshop in Dundrum, outside Dublin, on the model used in arts and crafts, training young women in arts and crafts, exhibiting at Arts and Crafts Society of Ireland events, and holding open days in which the buying public came to view the women at work.

The Yeats sisters experienced an uneasy working relationship with Miss Gleeson, resulting in conflicts which eventually resulted in the birth of Cuala Industries and the Cuala Press. In 1904 the Dun Emer Guild split into two parts – the guild, run by Evelyn Gleeson, and Dun Emer Industries, under the Yeats sisters – and matters culminated in Lily and Lolly severing ties with Gleeson, and setting up Cuala Industries in 1908. Here Lily was responsible for embroidery, while Lolly again managed the Press, an arrangement which persisted until her death in 1940.

In the early days of Dun Emer, in 1902, following advice from Sir Emery Walker (Morris's old friend and collaborator), Lolly purchased 120 lbs of Caslon Old Face 14 point. By the late nineteenth century, Caslon was held to be the most readable of typefaces, as well as being commercially accessible. It had been used by William Morris as well as by the influential Doves Press (founded by T. J. Cobden-Sanderson in partnership with Walker himself). It was an eighteenth-century Dutch typeface which the Dun Emer Prospectus described as follows:

> A good eighteenth century fount of type which is not eccentric in form nor difficult to read has been cast, and the paper has been made of linen

> rags and without bleaching chemicals, at the Saggart Mill in the county Dublin. The pages are printed at a Hand Press by Miss E. C. Yeats, and simplicity is aimed at in their composition.[73]

Certainly the use of Caslon had sound arts and crafts credentials, but Lolly's book designs did not employ the intensive decoration used by Morris.[74] The bibliophile W. G. Blaikie Murdoch maintained in 1919 that, while the founder of Cuala was a disciple of Morris, she nonetheless superseded him in certain key respects. Morris's art, he claimed, was 'florid' in his revival of Celtic art: 'the Kelmscott volumes are noble decorative items, rather than genuine masterpieces of typography and it is here they differ with those from the Cuala'. Miss Yeats, unlike her master, had 'realise[d] the beauty of simplicity'.[75]

From the creation of Dun Emer, through to the establishment of the Cuala Press, and until Lolly's death, W. B. Yeats was the two presses' editorial advisor (except for a period in 1906 when he resigned after a quarrel with Lolly). Essentially, his task was to supply recommendations of high quality literary material which his sister would then publish. Unlike Yeats's previous involvement with the 'New Irish Library', his editorial concern was much less about popular appeal. But, as with the Library of Ireland, the press was to publish Irish material (though Yeats departed from with this policy with respect to Rabindranath Tagore's *The Post Office* in 1914 and Ezra Pound's *Certain Noble Plays of Japan* in 1916). On the publication of W. B. Yeats's book *In the Seven Woods* in July 1903, which sold out completely by September, the poet exclaimed that 'My sister's book is [...] a specially beautiful and expensive first edition of certain of my best things.'[76] From such a statement, it becomes obvious that Lolly's material was not destined for a mundanely commercial audience (usually selling by subscription for 10s 6d) and, indeed, Lolly maintained that her books were meant for 'people who really want something rather exclusive and are ready to pay for it'.[77] This 'exclusivity', however, was nonetheless rooted in the marketplace and in the long painstaking work which the sisters undertook, often for uncertain reward. John Butler Yeats was quick to remind his son of this in 1906: 'Lily only sees that they [the Yeats sisters] have to work very hard at a dull and slavish kind of work, and think they get very little reward for what they do, and possibly or probably after all it may end in ghastly failure.'[78]

Jacqueline Genet has argued that 'with the exception of a few advertisements in *The Shanachie*, a quarterly published by Maunsel, the Dun Emer was quite indifferent to publicity'.[79] However, given the status of both sisters' involvement in international exhibitions and promotional work, as well as their constant awareness of making a viable income from the business, this argument seems questionable. As John Butler Yeats wrote to his son in 1906, when Lolly and Yeats were in furious dispute about typesetting AE's book

By Still Waters, 'To make Dun Emer a pecuniary success is a matter of life and death to Lily and Lolly.'[80] The poet's father continued:

> When you advise on books for the press, it should be advice and not haughty dictation [...] After all, *the press is Lolly's business* & it means our means of living & she has other things to consider besides the literary excellence of a particular book – there are questions of convenience & commercial expedience & policy – matter for tactful consideration not to be decided offhand by a literary expert.[81]

Far from being indifferent to publicity, Dun Emer embraced it from its early days, and it often used the appeal to national feeling and national responsibility so common in Revival-era Irish advertising. A publicity campaign in 1904, for instance, gently but firmly encouraged the Irish housewife to 'Decorate your house with Dun Emer tufted rugs, embroidered portieres and sofa backs, put Dun Emer tapestries on your walls and Dun Emer books in your bookcases. This is the duty of an Irish woman.'[82] While many lower class women in Ireland at the time would not have the luxury of affording such decoration, such advertising registers how far the guild negotiated issues of art in the marketplace, national affiliation and self-promotion.

Lily Yeats's responsibility at Dun Emer and later at Cuala Industries was chiefly embroidery (Cuchulain's wife, Emer, of course, was noted for her skill in embroidery and craft). Lily worked not only various domestic items, such as cushions, portieres and sofa backs, clothing and costume, but also vestments and hangings for use in churches.[83] The designs, often traditionally Celtic with zoomorphic motifs and interlacing, also had a political Home Industries aspect, being made with Irish fabrics such as linen and wool. The use of Irish products rather than imported materials was, of course, akin to much of the Revival ethos that Dun Emer espoused, and, as elsewhere, national sentiment went hand in hand with a commercial agenda.

That commercial agenda, however, is a suggestive one. Joan Hardwick has maintained that in the founding of Dun Emer, Evelyn Gleeson wanted to get beyond the philanthropy of the Vice-Regal lodge, attempting 'something a little different from the dabblings of the wives of Lord Lieutenants of Ireland who took to arts and crafts as an occupation which kept them from direct involvement in Ireland's turbulent politics'. 'She had in mind something more along the lines of the Donegal Industry set up in the 1880s by Mrs Ernest Hart, who had wanted to create employment for starving Irish women while at the same time promoting specifically Irish material and designs.'[84]

Alice Hart's Donegal Industrial Fund (founded 1883) had an entrepreneurial motivation alongside its wish for economic improvement, while Lady Aberdeen and the Irish Industries Association (founded 1886, and described, as we have seen as a 'society plaything' by D. P. Moran)[85] advocated a more philanthropic top-down, supposedly apolitical, focus (Lady Aberdeen was one of Dun Emer's supporters). Hart sold her goods through a shop in London and later in larger premises called Donegal House, where she showcased imports from Ireland. She also sold goods through shops in the West End, and did not deny her relationship with industry: 'We employ, as far as possible, the workers we train, and we also work in connection with Belfast and other manufacturing firms for whom we train hands, they supplying them with work.'[86] Similarly, Dun Emer, although it was more strongly inflected by the desire for Irish self-determination, promoted the training of a small coterie of workers in a trade, which would produce financial independence: 'the education of the girls is also part of the idea – they are taught to paint and their brains and fingers are made more active and understanding. Some of them, we hope, will become teachers to others, so that similar industries may spread through the land.'[87]

While the use of handcraft rather than reliance on machine-worked goods was imperative, the development of Irish industry as a gesture resistant of cheap imports from England and abroad was clearly one economic and political motivation informing Dun Emer's origins. One example of this is Lily Yeats's work with ecclesiastical commissions. The large order received from Loughrea Cathedral, for instance, was for Gleeson a triumph over foreign industries:

> Ecclesiastical art-work had until now been mainly supplied from Continental work-shops and it is with great satisfaction that we record the support given to us by a large order from Loughrea Cathedral, where embroidered banners from Dun Emer depicting Irish saints can now be seen. The embroidery is in the mediaeval style which was revived by William Morris.[88]

Edward Martyn, writing in Yeats's *Samhain* in 1901, also identified the new taste for Irish church art, such as that of Dun Emer, as part of a contemporary modern turn away from the imported goods of 'Englishmen and other foreigners', as he tartly puts it, who are no more than vulgar tradesmen:

> There are many movements now for the encouragement of Irish manufacture in all its branches, and for preventing the scandalous outpouring of Irish money into the pockets of Englishmen and other foreigners. Quite recently a movement has been started to turn the enormous demand for church art from the workshop of the foreign *tradesman*, and to get it supplied by the native Irish *artist*.[89]

The twenty-four banners for Loughrea were some of the first larger commissions Dun Emer received. Lily Yeats and her assistant worked the embroidery in silk and wool on linen (during 1902–1903) with designs by Jack Yeats and his wife Mary.[90] AE designed St Patrick and St Lawrence O'Toole for the series, and Lily employed Irish script for titles and banners. Under the aegis of an ecclesiastical commission, Dun Emer clearly articulated a nationalistic and economically inflected art.

The 1880s, as Janice Helland remarks, 'saw not so much a revival of interest in cottage crafts as a new articulation of the display of handmade commodities within a community now responsive to exhibitions.'[91] Following the 1851 Great Exhibition in London, which featured Irish products such as lace and crochet, Dublin hosted the Great Industrial Exhibition in 1853[92] and the Dublin International Exhibition in 1865, and there were many other exhibitions of Irish goods, both at home and abroad. Dun Emer first exhibited at the 1904 World's Fair in Missouri, which marked a clear articulation of national identity. Situated in the 'Irish pavilion', The Dun Emer 'landscape embroideries', designed by Lolly and worked by Lily (*The Orchard* and *The Meadow*), revealed a particular vision of a rural Ireland: 'With a distinctive embroidery technique that used unusually long stitches, the "Irish" colouring of greens and purples of the local landscape, and innovative designs, these works helped originate the style of the Irish Revival.'[93] Dun Emer also exhibited at the annual shows of the Royal Dublin Society, the Oireachtas Exhibitions in Dublin and the Gaelic League in London. Furthermore, they supplied material for the Irish Revival Industries Show in Dublin, 1904, and the Irish Language Week Dublin Demonstration in 1905 (where Dun Emer had a working loom in the procession). Several international exhibitions, including the New York Irish Exhibition in 1907 also lent an expatriate audience to the Dun Emer. Exhibition culture also had a commercial imperative.

In the 1851 Great Exhibition, goods were displayed but were not for sale. However, later exhibitions were more usually founded on commodity exchange. The mixture of art and commerce, and the interplay between literature and the market place, and between the two sides of the Yeatses' artistic and economic endeavours are the subject of a *Daily News* column in 1925, written after its author had seen the Cuala industries stall at the Central Hall, Westminster Home Arts and Industries exhibition in London, where visitors could buy an illuminated version of Yeats's 'The Embroidered Cloths of Heaven' for the sum of 3/6:

> *But I being poor,*
> *Have only my dreams . . .*
> *Tread softly, because you tread on my dreams . . .*
> 'And that will be three shillings and sixpence. Thank you.'
>
> The writer, of course, of the poetry was W. B. Yeats; the speaker of the prose was his sister, Miss Elizabeth Yeats, who was selling the products of the Cuala village industries at the Central Hall, Westminster, yesterday

> during the exhibition of Home Arts and Industries. It seems to me that there was money in this poetry business, in spite of the cynics. The poems were beautifully written and illuminated, but it is odd to think of 'The Embroidered Cloths of Heaven' on an illuminated card sold at three shillings and sixpence. You must be a little richer than your dreams to buy it. But they tell me that the business mind runs strongly in the Yeats family.[94]

The combination of the Arts and Crafts Movement and its critique of capitalist worker exploitation, alongside the need to reinvigorate Irish industry, ultimately produced a Revival ethos which was associated with selling an idea of 'authentic' Irishness; Elaine Cheasley Paterson argues that 'the role of authenticity had shifted from that of signifier of Irish cultural "incapacities", to that of marketable sign of value'. 'The newspapers', she continues, 'presented the products of the Guild as a form of consumable Irishness'.[95]

The UK Home Arts and Industries Association was founded in 1884, with the Arts and Crafts Exhibition Society following in 1887. Both catered to a growing market for arts and crafts products, and both had 'a tremendous commitment to turn local craft into urban fashion'.[96] The Yeats sisters participated in this movement in their distinct, Irish manner, and one way in which they worked in this particular framework of 'urban fashion' was through commissions from London companies. John Butler Yeats notes in a letter to his son that '[Lolly] is not only working all day – but every evening as well till bedtime [is] designing and painting fans which Liberty has commissioned.'[97] Indeed, the Liberty fans are crucial in this regard. As we have seen in Chapter 6, Arthur Liberty founded his shop in Regent Street, London in 1875, with its roots in the Aesthetic Movement. Initially, the store focused on fabrics, but 'in less than a year he had added Japanese goods, as well as fans, wallpapers, fabrics, screens, lacquerware and other exotica from the Far East more generally'.[98] From 1884 the costume department sold dresses made up in Liberty Colours (as the 'Art Colours' became popularly known) and designed by Liberty himself. There was a Tea Room, Decoration Studio, Eastern Bazaar and a Paper Hanging Studio. To quote Judith Flanders once again, 'Now both a house and its owner could be entirely "done" by Liberty. Liberty had created a space where – in a very modern fashion – one could acquire a lifestyle.'[99] Liberty's focus was on the high-end artisan-focused nature of the London market: it is in this emphatically commodity-driven and urban context that Lolly's fans were commissioned and sold.

If part of the sisters' economic enterprise was selling an avowedly upmarket Irish product to a well-heeled London audience, there was far more to their business than that. Aware of market differentiations, Lolly did not wholly align the Cuala Press with elitism. Rather, she targeted different markets with a variety of products. For instance, the comparatively inexpensive broadsides, greetings cards and other items produced by Cuala were an attempt by Lolly to attract a market which was unable to purchase the expensive books of the press, or the equally costly embroideries of Lily Yeats. As well as targeting London consumers or receiving patronage from Anglo-Irish grandes dames, Lolly advertised her cheaper goods in separatist journals such as *Bean na hÉireann* (the monthly publication of Maud Gonne's Daughters of Ireland or Inghinidhe na hÉireann), founded in 1908 and edited by Helena Moloney. Gonne was herself a regular contributor, and the intended audience comprised not only women, but, arguably, the republican community as a whole. As Joan Hardwick maintains, *Bean na hÉireann* 'recognized the poverty in which most people lived and had a column devoted to offering helpful hints for combating the drabness of life without spending a lot of money',[100] and the Yeatses set out to appeal to this radical, less monied constituency as well as its socially elevated patrons.

Another clear example of this is the development of a printed series of *A Broadside* issued by Cuala from June 1908 to May 1915 (see Figure 7.1). Each *Broadside* included a verse or ballad alongside illustrative material. As William Maxwell noted:

> Every number is illustrated with line drawings by Jack B. Yeats reproduced by zinco blocks [...]. There are mostly two small drawings, hand coloured after printing, attached to a poem or poems in the first two pages, and a full page drawing, sometimes in black only and sometimes hand coloured, on the third page.[101]

The verses or ballads themselves were either derived from older historical material or new verses by contemporary writers. A short survey of the *Broadside* series reveals the following range of authors and works: John Masefield (June 1908), 'Campeachy Picture'; Ernest Rhys (August 1908), 'The Swordsman to his Sword'; James Stephens (November 1908), 'Where the Demons Grin'; Sir Walter Raleigh (March 1909), 'To his Sonne'; Lady Gregory (April 1909), a translation of Douglas Hyde's 'Listen, Young Son, to the Old Man'; Padraic Colum (November 1911), 'Carricknabauna'; and James Clarence Mangan (June 1914), 'Kathleen Ni Houlihan'. The combination of nationalist literary heroes such as Mangan and Hyde, alongside well-known popular classics such as Raleigh, suggest the popular appeal of such material. As Gifford Lewis points out, 'It is interesting to compare the raw vigour of the *Broadside* sheets with the restrained graphics and typography of the Cuala book... They were aimed at two quite different markets, the *Broadside* sheets being evergreen favourites with visitors to Ireland to this day.'[102] The series usually had a print run of three hundred copies, and had a subscription of 12 shillings per year. Notwithstanding the quality and artistic objectives of Lolly's interpretation of such printed ephemera,

NO. 1. SEVENTH AND LAST YEAR OF THE SET

A BROADSIDE

FOR JUNE, 1914

PUBLISHED MONTHLY BY E. C. YEATS AT THE CUALA PRESS,
CHURCHTOWN, DUNDRUM, COUNTY DUBLIN.
SUBSCRIPTION TWELVE SHILLINGS A YEAR POST FREE.

KATHLEEN NI-HOULIHAN

Long they pine in weary woe, the nobles of our land,
Long they wander to and fro, proscribed, alas ! and banned;
Feastless, houseless, altarless, they bear the exile's brand;
But their hope is in the coming-to of Kathleen Ni-Houlihan !

Think her not a ghastly hag, too hideous to be seen,
Call her not unseemly names, our matchless Kathleen;
Young she is, and fair she is, and would be crowned a queen,
Were the King's son at home here with Kathleen Ni-Houlihan !

Sweet and mild would look her face, O none so sweet and mild,
Could she crush the foes by whom her beauty is reviled;
Woollen plaids would grace herself and robes of silk her child,
If the King's son were living here with Kathleen Ni-Houlihan !

300 copies only.

Figure 7.1 'A Broadside'. Verse by James Clarence Mangan. Illustration by Jack B. Yeats (1914).

the broadside itself, first appearing in the sixteenth century, was in fact 'a bill for posting in the marketplace as confirmation of the public crier's spoken announcement'.[103] Indeed, until the advent of newspapers in the seventeenth century, they were also a principal form of advertising: cheaply produced with poor typefaces and print quality.[104] While Lolly Yeats obviously held the form in sufficient esteem (each *Broadside*, in common with Cuala's book production, was printed on Irish paper from Saggart Mills), her tacit acknowledgement of a different literary audience through an adaptation of a commercial and historically populist form of publishing indicates her awareness of market forces.

The production of Cuala bookplates also documents the complex relationship which the Yeatses had with the world of the market. The bookplate originated in the fifteenth century, designed to be displayed inside the front of a book as a declaration of patrician ownership. However, as Martin Hopkinson writes in his discussion of bookplates and their history, 'Originally a mark of prestige and status in society, by the twentieth century the range of people who commissioned or used them had become very wide.'[105] Rather than occupying the exclusive realm of the aristocratic collector and bibliophile who wished to commission a plate in order to display his familial lineage and coat of arms, the bookplate market from the nineteenth century onwards included the middle classes: 'Academics, museum officials, ministers of the church, lawyers and other professional people, along with figures from the literary world, were all attracted by the idea of commissioning bookplates. These men and women were more interested in celebrating their own lives and achievements than in displaying their lineage.'[106] The bookplate commissions at Cuala clearly reflect such a developing market in the middle classes, both in Ireland and the USA. Lennox Robinson's bookplate showed a curtain drawn back to reveal a chair and study, which reveals Robinson's own affiliations as dramatist, poet and Abbey Theatre manager. John Quinn's bookplate illustrated a cottage among the mountains (as a second generation Irish-American born to grocer parents in Ohio, his diasporic nostalgia for Ireland's rural landscape is inherent here), and several bookplates were produced in the Irish language.[107]

Elizabeth began to make up cards early in the Dun Emer days, 'some plainly lettered, some illustrated with floral or landscape designs, printed from woodblocks or zincos and hand coloured by the girls'.[108] The greetings cards continued throughout her printing career, with a long running series of Christmas cards (see Figure 7.2), St. Patrick's Day cards and also business cards, testifying to Lolly's business acumen and entrepreneurship (see Figure 7.3). Such items were both commercially viable and appealing to a wider audience, compared with other, more exclusive, Press items. Joan Hardwick notes that when Cuala was floundering financially in the 1920s, '[Lolly] solved the problem by increasing the number of cards, framed prints and her cardboard cut-out Irish cottage. But more profitable still, and an

Figure 7.2 'Greetings'. Artist Eileen Booth. Hand coloured card. Printed by Cuala Press, Dublin (1914). Courtesy of the National Library of Ireland.

enterprise which kept the Press in the black, was the undertaking of an increasing number of privately printed books.'[109] The iconography of the Revival, like that of the Arts and Crafts Movement, ultimately – and perhaps paradoxically – became a commodity spectacle.

Figure 7.3 'Stay thee awhile, upspringing heart'. Verse by Susan Mitchell and Illustration by Jack B. Yeats. Hand coloured card. Printed by Cuala Press, Dublin (1915). © Estate of Jack B. Yeats. All rights reserved. DACS 2012.

W. B. Yeats, and Lolly and Lily, have frequently been represented as artisans with a declared antipathy to modern industry and commodity. While in some respects that analysis may be viable, it is not the whole story. Yeats's awareness of commercial markets in publishing and his exploitation of this, both in his own enterprises and his editorship of his sisters' Press, suggest a rather more complex position. Artistic products must intersect with the market. As Jaques Attali once put it, 'The artist was born at the same time as his work went on sale.'[110] Similarly, while Lily and Lolly relied on commission and patronage, and while they situated themselves firmly in an Arts and Crafts tradition, they nonetheless employed sufficient business acumen through trade relations and exhibition culture, in order to maintain Dun Emer, and later the Cuala.

Part IV

Advertising in Ireland 1914–1922

8
Advertising, Ireland and the Great War

> Contracts of indemnity against every conceivable risk or contingency including: WAR – REBELLION – RIOTS – INVASION. Persons or property – Land or Sea. Arranged by FRANK GIBSON-LLOYD & CO., LTD, LLOYDS CHAMBERS (Adjoining Stock Exchange), DUBLIN. Telephone: Central 653.
>
> (Advertisement for Gibson-Lloyd and Co., Dublin, taken from the advertising pages of *Dublin and the Sinn Fein Rising* (1916), published by Wilson, Hartnell and Co., advertising agency and publishers.)

The story of Ireland between the outbreak of the First World War in the summer of 1914 and the signing of the armistice in November 1918 is familiar, though certainly not uncontentious, historical territory. Historians have chronicled Irish responses to the opening of the conflict, the initial enthusiasm for and opposition to the war, and the conflicting pro- and anti-positions which were exemplified by the Irish Party and Sinn Féin. They have also, of course, been much preoccupied with the related events which led to the rising of Easter 1916, notably the establishment of the Irish Volunteers and the divisions within that organisation. All of these epoch-changing circumstances continue to echo through historical writing about Ireland. The pages that follow address some relatively little-known aspects of this key part of modern Irish history and culture, examining how the momentous happenings of those remarkable years were echoed in Irish advertising.

I

As early as 1911, three years before the outbreak of the First World War, *Irish Freedom* (*Saoirseacht na hEireann* (1910–1914)), the journal of the 'Wolfe Tone Clubs Committee' (the de facto organ of the Irish Republican Brotherhood

(IRB)) posed an important question for Ireland and for Irish nationalists in the light of what seemed to be the certainty of impending European conflict:

> The question then, for Irishmen, is what are we going to do? Germany and England are going to fight – and we are nominally a part of England. Are we to side with England – supply our young men to face the German guns to be mowed down in thousands or are we going to snatch the independence of our country while England is engaged? That is the issue that Ireland must decide.[1]

'Irishmen', the historical record shows, had different answers to this conundrum, which was to become a defining question in nationalist circles within a very short space of time. It was not only the island's Protestants who 'face[d] the German guns' in large numbers; many men with Roman Catholic and nationalist antecedents joined Irish regiments within the British army. On the other hand, there were those who, with *Irish Freedom*, bitterly opposed the war and saw those Irishmen who enlisted as 'dupes and traitors'.[2]

It is generally accepted that the question of the First World War deepened the divisions which already existed within nationalist ranks. The leaders of the Irish Parliamentary Party (IPP) under John Redmond, with the Home Rule Act enacted but almost immediately suspended until the end of the conflict, advocated and encouraged the notion of Irishmen serving in the army, sometimes at great personal cost, while at the same time various strands of separatist thought strongly opposed the idea, seeing England's involvement as, in the old phrase, Ireland's opportunity. Given the intractability of the issue, propagandists on both sides of the argument presented the case for and against enlistment with considerable vigour. Advertising played an important part in these campaigns, especially on the pro-listing side, with the government spending large sums to persuade young Irishmen to join up. Patriotic posters and newspaper advertisements, both in prose and display, encouraged the men of Ireland to volunteer.

Some of this recruitment material appealed to a sense of imperial loyalty, taking pains to portray Ireland as part of a kingdom united under King George. A recruitment image of 1914, 'Surely You will Fight for your [King] and [Country]' (Figure 8.1), for instance, demonstrates a will to inclusion, a desire to view Britain and Ireland as one coherent nation at the heart of the Empire. The border lines within the UK and the physical separation of Great Britain from Ireland are evident in the image, but are decidedly less important in this account than the four nations' posited unity.

Such appeals to a UK sentiment notwithstanding, copywriters and propagandists, convinced that the patriotic instincts of the majority of Irishmen

Figure 8.1 'Surely You will Fight for your [King] and [Country]'. Recruitment advertisement (1914). Published by the Parliamentary Recruiting Committee, London; printed by James Truscott & Son. Courtesy of the National Library of Ireland.

tended to Ireland rather than to the wider nation, rather more frequently appealed in their campaigns to a specifically Irish brand of patriotism. Indeed, it is noticeable how the widely circulated recruitment materials designed by British government agencies and by both English and Irish advertising agencies marketed the war, so to speak, in terms of a specifically Irish national sentiment. The 'Irishness' constantly appealed to in contemporary advertisements for goods as diverse as whiskey and hurleysticks became a key plank in the enlistment drives. One could still be an Irish patriot and serve in the British army, such campaigns implied. Indeed, it was one's patriotic duty so to do, in the light of difficult present circumstance and what was frequently portrayed – however ironic this seemed to Irish republicans – as the German threat to Irish liberty.

Crucial to attempts to make what was a rather hard sell in some Irish quarters was the testimony of National Party luminaries who supported the recruitment effort and the war (believing that Home Rule would come quickly and relatively painlessly if Irishmen had 'done their bit' in the conflict, rather than showing themselves to be obstructive rebel-rousers). Their sentiments, indeed, became a key part of newspaper advertisements and posters for the army brand. The opinions of John Redmond, John Dillon and Stephen Gwynn became subsumed in advertising:

> Private Stephen Gwynn, M.P., on the duty of Irishmen. 'Every decent Irishman who could go to the War owed it to his fellow-countrymen at the front to go to their assistance and to lighten their desperate burden and risks'. [...]
>
> Are *You* a Decent Irishman? Join an Irish Regiment *Today*.

Dillon's digs at Sinn Féiners and the like, who accused nationalists who joined the British Army of being traitors, were recycled in an advertisement in the *Irish Independent* published in 1915, which denied that 'Nationalist[s] who went into the Army betrayed Ireland' and appeals to Irish racial traditions:

> Mr John Dillon, M.P. on recruiting in Ireland: 'It was a lie to say that any Nationalist who went into the Army betrayed Ireland; on the contrary, the men who joined the army and took their stand beside the Irish Guards, the Dublin Fusiliers, and other gallant Irish Regiments, who had nobly maintained the traditions of our race, were doing a patriotic act. Any man who sought to intimidate anyone from recruiting was doing a wrong act, and acting falsely to Ireland.'
>
> Join an Irish Regiment *Today*.

Redmond, leader of the Irish Party, was himself turned pitchman in a striking 1915 poster which informs Irishmen that 'Your First Duty Is to Take Your Part in Ending the War' (Figure 8.2). This is, of course, an Irish version of Alfred Leete's enduring 'Britons! [Lord Kitchener] wants you!' image of the previous

Figure 8.2 'Your First Duty is to Take Your part in Ending the War... Join an Irish Regiment Today.' Recruitment advertisement (1915). Courtesy of the National Library of Ireland.

year. Enlistment and the war 'first', the image implies, then on to Home Rule and Irish self-determination.

This poster is an example of how canny propagandists adapted existing British recruitment campaigns for an Irish audience. The product advertised – namely the soldiery – remained the same but the selling pitch, so to speak, was adapted. Indeed, the 'Irishification' of propaganda was on some occasions simply a matter of deleting the words 'British' or 'Britain' and replacing them with 'Irish' or 'Ireland'. A 1915 poster published for the Parliamentary Recruiting Committee, for instance, portrays the silhouette of a boy scout asking his papa 'What did You do when Britain fought for Freedom in 1915?' Figure 8.3 shows the Irish equivalent, which was published in the same year.

Recruitment publicity was a multimedia phenomenon that employed posters, advertising pages, postcards, leaflets and other printed materials. The sentiments expressed were not exclusive; the same copy could appear on both billboards and in newspaper columns. Irish periodicals carried a great many recruitment advertisements in 1914 and 1915. That said, whereas a degree of historical and literary-critical attention has been paid to recruitment posters in the first years of the war, both to their propaganda role[3] and to their representation in literature,[4] rather less notice has been taken

Figure 8.3 'What will your answer be when your boy asks you – "Father, What did You do to Help when Ireland fought for Freedom in 1915?" Enlist now.' Recruitment advertisement (1915). Published by the Parliamentary Recruiting Committee, London; printed by Chorley and Pickersgill Ltd. Courtesy of the National Library of Ireland.

of newspaper recruitment advertising in Ireland. Nonetheless, this was a widespread cultural phenomenon, especially in the first eighteen months of the war, and, we would argue, warrants extended discussion here.

First of all, it is instructive to consider the fact that the majority of newspapers with nationalist editorial lines followed the Irish Party lead in taking a great many recruitment paid columns at the commencement of the war. In the winter of 1914, for instance, the whole front pages of both the *Irish Independent* and 'the separatist inclined *Meath Chronicle*',[5] to use Patrick Maume's phrase, carried 'A Call to 50,000 Irishmen' to enlist in the soldiery, a call-to-arms which invoked the proud tradition – or national stereotype, depending on your point of view – of the fighting Irish to drum up trade for the trenches. This notice exploited the more expansive possibilities of newspaper advertisement (as opposed to posters), its 500 words and more combining stirring appeals to patriotism with detailed accounts of conditions of service, training, pensions and so on. The advertisement begins with a direct appeal to national feeling:

> IRISHMEN!
> You cannot permit your regiments to be kept up to strength by other than Ireland's sons! It would be a deep disgrace to Ireland, if all her regiments were not Irish, to a Man.
> A CALL TO 50,000 IRISHMEN
> – Excluding Munitions Workers –
> TO JOIN THEIR BRAVE COMRADES IN IRISH REGIMENTS.

Here the British recruiter-in-chief Lord Kitchener, who happened to be born in Ballylongford in County Kerry to English parents, shortly after his father had bought land in the west of Ireland, is co-opted across the Irish Sea as a thorough-going Irishman – 'Lord Kitchener has told you – his fellow countrymen – that Ireland has done magnificently and all the world knows of the splendid valour of the Irish Regiments, horse and foot'. 'So glorious is the record' the advertisement goes on, 'that it must be maintained by the men of our race – by Irishmen alone'. 'Our race'; the phrase is used here and in the Dillon speech on enlisting (and might it remind some of those other famous words 'ourselves alone'). Like one of Thomas Moore's *Irish Melodies*, these advertisements invoke proud military memory and proclaim the need to maintain the racial purity and masculinity ('Irish to a Man') of the Irish.

The '50,000 Irishmen' advertisement combines appeals to 'proud duty' and a man's responsibility to 'Ireland' ('all must act a man's – an Irishman's – part') with more pragmatic economic and familial considerations. From the farm, from the shop, from the office; all should hasten to the Irish colours, secure in the knowledge that the British state would act *in loco parentis* (the reference is to the separation allowances given to wives and mothers in a soldier's absence):

> It is your proud duty to support your gallant Countrymen who have fought so well. Ireland must stand by them!
> You are asked to SERVE FOR THE PERIOD OF THE WAR ONLY.
> Your relatives, whom you have looked after, will be looked after when you are away – your wife, your parents, your children.
> [...]
> Every famous Irishman urges this duty very earnestly on you. Every Irishman should answer the call – farmers' sons, merchants, men in shops and offices, all must act a man's – an Irishman's – part.

Elsewhere, just as a sprinkling of Irish was frequently used to sell consumer goods in contemporary advertising copy in nationalistically inclined periodicals, so an advertisement of the summer of 1915 for the Royal Irish Fusiliers was headed with the banner 'THE FAMOUS FAUGH-A-BALLAGHS' ('clear-the-ways')[6] in its attempt to recruit for the regiment's eighth battalion based at Tipperary. 'There are still vacancies in this Irish Regiment', the copy declares – as if the military was a job like any other – 'vacancies' for both 'IRISH OFFICERS' and 'IRISH MEN'. The advertisement goes on to tempt recruits with the chance of a trip to the countryside and 'training in Tipperary, amid beautiful surroundings and genial companionship' (and, indeed, 'in comfortable quarters in Barracks'). The rigours of the front line, of course, are nowhere mentioned in such blandishments.

One of the most remarkable of these emerald-recruiting advertisements is a 1915 notice which press gangs T. D. Sullivan's famous 1867 anthem for the 'Manchester Martyrs', 'God Save Ireland!' to whip up business for the army. Irish song, a potent weapon in the nationalist armoury for so many decades, is here co-opted to serve the British empire, the British king and the British army:

> GOD SAVE IRELAND!
> 'God Save Ireland - - - - - - - - - - -'
> When you sing these words you think you really mean them?
> But since the war began what have you done to make them a reality? If you are an Irishman between 19 and 40, physically fit and not already serving your Country as a sailor or soldier, or in the munition factory, there is but one way for you to help save Ireland from the Germans –
> You must Join an Irish regiment and learn to sing 'God Save Ireland' with a gun in your hands.
> GOD SAVE THE KING!
> GOD SAVE IRELAND!

'Sing "God Save Ireland" with a gun in your hands' seems to evoke ultra-Fenian rhetoric, and, indeed, John Mitchel's adaptation of scripture, 'If any man among you have not a gun, let him sell his garment and buy one.'[7] But here it is used for rather different ends.

The coaxing, wheedling and cajoling frequently evident in British recruitment efforts was adapted across the Irish Sea and given a particularly Irish slant. Certainly the emotional blackmail, as one might call it, evident in such stuff as the poster featuring boy scout and pater reproduced above was common in enlistment appeals in the Irish newspaper press. Intimate relationships, both sexual and familial, were frequently exploited in such rhetoric, with women pushed into the role of beskirted enlistment officers. An early 1915 advertisement addressed 'ladies' in their roles as wives and mothers: 'When the war is over and your husband or your son is asked "What did you do in the war?", is he to hang his head because you would not let him go?' There were even appeals to women as lovers: 'If your young man neglects his duty to Ireland the time may come when he may neglect you. Think it over and ask your young man to join an Irish Regiment today.' Just as the child inquires, so the woman implores. An advertisement published in the *Connacht Tribune* in May 1915 exploits similar anxieties: Is a man unwilling to fight worthy of the name of a man?:

> TO THE YOUNG WOMEN OF IRELAND
> Is your 'Best Boy' wearing Khaki? . . . If not don't you think he should be?
> If he does not think that you and your country are worth fighting for –

do you think he is worthy of you?
Don't pity the girl who is alone – her young man is probably a soldier – fighting for her and her country – and for You.
If your young man neglects his duty to his King and Country, the time may come when he will neglect you.
Think it over – then ask him to JOIN AN IRISH REGIMENT TO-DAY!
Ireland will appreciate your help.

Young men were also assailed by advertisements such as 1915's 'Young Man. Is anyone proud of you?', which upped the emotive stakes in appealing not only to a lad's love for his girl ('Is your sweetheart proud of you?'), but also his devotion to his mother, sister and, indeed, to Mother Ireland herself ('Is IRELAND proud of you?'). Guilt, it seems, was an effective recruiting sergeant and young men were nagged and white-feathered into trenches:

YOUNG MAN
Is anyone proud of you?'
Is your mother proud of you?
Is your sister proud of you?
Is your sweetheart proud of you?
Is your employer proud of you?
Is IRELAND proud of you?
If you are not making munitions, get into khaki at once.
Join an Irish Regiment
TO-DAY
and they will all be proud of you.

A great deal of effort was spent on reassuring workers who signed up that their jobs would be kept open if they went off to serve at the front. 'Your employer [will be] proud of you' if you enlist, claims the 'YOUNG MAN' advertisement; sometimes the petitions were directly addressed to the employer. 'An Appeal to Patriotic Employers' (1915), addresses the 'employers of the City and County of Dublin', urging patriotism to the business folk of Ireland's capital:

AN APPEAL TO PATRIOTIC EMPLOYERS
OF THE CITY AND COUNTY OF DUBLIN
As an employer have you seen that every fit man under your control that can possibly be spared has been given every opportunity of enlisting?
Will you call your employees together TO-DAY, and explain to them that in order to end the war quickly we must have more men?
Many more men would enlist if you explained to them what you are prepared to do for them whilst they are fighting for the empire.
They will listen to you – use your influence and help to end the war.

Call your men together – today, and tell them to apply to Recruiting Offices, 24 and 25 Great Brunswick Street and 102 Grafton Street, Dublin.
Your country will appreciate the help you give.
GOD SAVE THE KING.

The pitch is essentially the same in this advertisement as in those aimed at womenfolk, in aiming to manipulate the external influences – in this case richer men influencing poorer men to go to war – who are capable of hastening men through the welcoming doors of the recruiting office.

Implicit in such stuff as the 'Appeal for Patriotic Employers' was the clear implication that petit bourgeois Irishmen engaged in the retail trade, or wielding a pen in an office, were somehow unmanly when compared to their dashing brethren in khaki, that they were wasting their time in such footling activities when there was fighting to be done and when the brave soldiery were risking all to protect the womenfolk of Ireland. How could a real man be 'satisfied' with such unrewarding work when the nation was calling?:

4 QUESTIONS TO CLERKS AND SHOP ASSISTANTS
1. If you are between 19 and 38 years of age, are you really satisfied with what you are doing to-day?
2. Do you feel happy as you walk along the streets and see brave Irishmen in khaki who are going to *fight* for Ireland while you stay at home in comfort?
3. Do you realise that gallant Irish soldiers have been risking everything on the Continent to save you, your children, and your womenfolk?
4. Will you tell your employer to-day that your are going to join an Irish Regiment?
Ask him to keep your position open for you – tell him you are going to fight for Ireland. He'll do the right thing by you – all patriotic employers are helping their men to join.
TELL HIM NOW AND JOIN AN IRISH REGIMENT TODAY.

Those slightly further down the social scale, 'Grocer's Assistants, Waiters and Bar Attendants', warranted even longer interrogations, as an advertisement published in the *Irish Independent* and elsewhere in early 1915 demonstrates. This calls on these men to show fraternal solidarity with the Irish troops who were already fighting and dying in Belgium, and praises the already 'magnificent' numbers of Irishmen who had answered the call of their country:

5 QUESTIONS TO GROCER'S ASSISTANTS, WAITERS AND BAR ATTENDANTS
1 What do you think of your countrymen in this War? Have they not responded magnificently to the cause of Ireland?

> 2 Is it not a fine thing that not only Artisans, Field-Workers, Navvies and other manual toilers have joined, but also, side by side with them, educated men like Heads of Firms, Doctors, Barristers, Accountants, Schoolmasters? Even priests have wanted to go. Is it not magnificent?
> 3 And when other men are responding to the call like this, your country asks you to take your share in the work? There are vacancies for you in Irish regiments where you can earn the honour and gratitude of your fellow countrymen!
> 4 Do you realize that gallant Irish soldiers are risking everything on the Continent to save you, your children, and your womenfolk?
> 5 Will you tell your employer to-day that you are going to join an Irish Regiment?
> Ask him to keep your position open for you – tell him you are going to fight for Ireland.
> He'll do the right thing by you – all patriotic employers are helping their men to join.
> Tell him now and join an Irish Regiment To-day.
> Irish soldiers in Belgium Need Your Help.

Country boys who did not push pens, wait at tables or walk in shops were not neglected by the ubiquitous machinery of recruitment, especially as it became apparent fairly quickly that 'recruiting was particularly unpopular in agricultural Ireland [where] enlistment rates were far from impressive'.[8] In an advertisement published in the *Independent* in August 1915, for instance, a 'Notice' to the rural folk of County Fermanagh announced the chance to enlist in a battalion of the Inniskilling Fusiliers 'consisting entirely of farmers and farmers' sons who would live and serve together in one body'. 'Irish Freedom' (a very different sort from that envisaged by the IRB paper of that name) 'is at stake', the advertisement maintains, as much 'as is the freedom of Belgium; THIS WAR EITHER WINS OR LOSES BOTH'.

'The Farmers of Fermanagh', this advertisement continues, 'are given [a] Special Opportunity to come forward and serve together'. A memorable poster of the day, 'Farmers of Ireland. Join Up and Defend Your Possessions' (reproduced as Figure 8.4) makes a similar appeal. Again we see the echoes of fraternity, fellowship and family, to complement the appeal to the young man's love for his sweetheart, his old mother and for Erin herself. Irish lads could serve with their pals, experiencing war in a soldierly brotherhood of fellow countrymen. 'Comrades in Peace, Comrades in War' as a September 1914 advertisement published in the *Irish Independent* had it. Shamed by Kitchener's supposed 'disappointment' at the enlistment rates among his countrymen in the first few weeks of war, Dubliners were here encouraged both to enlist and to serve 'with their friends' (otherwise the vacancies 'in the Irish Division' would be 'sent in from Scotland and England. This would be a disgrace to Ireland'). In this appeal to young men,

Figure 8.4 'Farmers of Ireland. Join Up and Defend Your Possessions' (c. 1915). Reproduced by permission of the National Library of Ireland.

as so often in the Irish recruitment campaigns, the human context is at the forefront.

II

As is well known, in the period in which European conflict loomed, and during the First World War itself, the separatist Irish press took a strong counter-recruitment position. It dismissed those who enlisted as 'fools', dupes, even 'traitors', and attacked what it saw as the Iscariotism of John Redmond and his IPP cohorts.[9] It also railed against the fact that the King's shillings were pouring into the coffers of Irish newspapers in the colonisation of much Irish advertising by the British Army and its mouthpieces. 'The Press has been corrupted' declared *Irish Freedom*[10] in March 1914, in an attack on what it saw as the meretricious and pro-imperialist willingness of ostensibly nationalist newspapers to carry recruitment advertisements. *Saoirseacht na hEireann* named the guilty parties:

> The following 'Nationalist' papers have been bought with English gold to aid the Army recruiting of a dying Empire: *Dublin Evening Telegraph, Dublin Evening Herald.* The former is owned by the proprietors of the *Freeman's Journal* and the latter by the proprietor of the *Irish Independent.*[11]

The evening papers, it might be pointed out, were by no means the only journals of nationalist conviction to carry recruitment advertisements: the *Independent*, the *Freeman's*, the *Connacht Tribune*, the *Meath Chronicle*, the *Nenagh Guardian* and other papers also carried such materials, especially in the first year and a half of the First World War. As the campaigns to enlist Irishmen grew to their noisiest in 1915, the agents of the Parliamentary Recruiting Committee spent a great deal of money on the Irish advertising columns.

Irish Freedom, however, alongside *Sinn Féin* and the rest of the radical nationalist press, had no space for recruitment tub-thumping in its paid matter. This is not to say that it had any objection to advertising per se. Indeed, the journal considered it nothing to be ashamed of; healthy advertising income allied to a decent circulation, it argued, would help to sponsor the cause of a free Ireland. In the prospectus to its first number, published in November 1910, the paper informed readers precisely how 'How our Friends can Help Us', detailing the practical aid which subscribers could offer: 'asking their friends to subscribe to the paper [...] asking their newsagent to display it for sale [...] purchasing from our Advertisers and stating when doing so that it is done because they advertise in *Irish Freedom*'.

Though recruitment advertisements for Irish regiments were forbidden its pages, *Irish Freedom* carried much in the way of Irish-Ireland and 'Irish Goods Only' advertising[12] for more ideologically agreeable products than the British Army. These products included sporting goods for Gaelic games, radical books and pamphlets, and Irish language-related activities, such as the 1914 puff for the renowned Coláiste Na Mumhan (Munster College) in Cork, which clearly invokes the ideological and conceptual underpinning of the journal's title: 'If you want to be *Free*, if you want to *Learn Irish*, and to spend an enjoyable holiday in an Irish-speaking district come to Coláiste Na Mumhan, Ballingeary, Co. Cork' ('GET THE ILLUSTRATED PROSPECTUS').

Irish Freedom also advertised guns and ammo. Especially after the establishment of the Ulster Volunteer Force (UVF) in January 1913, which was both threat and opportunity to republicans who sought the right to bear arms for Irishmen, the cultivation of riflemen on the nationalist side was seen as a pressing need, and it was one which offered politically sympathetic gunsmiths a commercial opportunity. Targeting that section of the advanced nationalist community willing to take up arms in the cause of the nation, these gunsmiths inserted advertisements for rifles (in particular imported German Mausers) and small arms to guard against Carson's multitudes and to arm the people in the struggle for liberty.

Irish Freedom also carried small ads for its own favoured brand of military and quasi-military activity: the Irish Volunteers (before Redmond's ascendancy), Cumann na mBan and for the Citizen Army. 'The Physical Force Party now had their own organ, *Irish Freedom*', as Aodh De Blácam put it in his 1921 book *What Sinn Fein Stands For* ('the spirit' of this journal, he writes, 'may be summed up in [the nineteenth-century republican John] Mitchel's watchword: *"If any man among you have not a gun, let him sell his garment and buy one"* ').[13] Many 'Gunsmiths' advertisements were published' in its pages, De Blácam notes, and 'Youths began to practise at rifle ranges'[14] with firearms sourced from the journal's columns. Just as surely as in its editorial matter and correspondence, *Irish Freedom*'s paid columns inculcated a martial spirit. And just as surely as in the recruitment advertisements everywhere evident in the more orthodox press, they also endorsed a form of Irish military masculinity: a manliness, of course, which was to be put to severe test over the next decade.

In both imperialist and republican rhetoric the same sentiment is expressed – the bravery and hypermasculinity of the Irishman and of the Irish soldier – though this was, in republican opinion, misdirected in an unworthy cause (even after mass emigration, declared *Sinn Féin*, in a number published just after the opening of the war on 5 September 1914, 'there is more fighting material in the remnant than in England's industrial base'). Revolutionary nationalists who were surrounded by recruitment posters had a nice line in incendiary ripostes, and a 1913 effort by the 'Irish Vigilance Committee' attacks 'the most Immoral Army and Navy in the World' on the same grounds:

> War is imminent between England and Germany. England's cowardly and degenerate population won't make soldiers. Not so the Germans. They are trained and ready. What will England do? She will recruit Irish Fools ... to fight Germany for her Empire ... Irish traitors have ever been the backbone of her Army and Navy.[15]

Irish Freedom and *Sinn Féin,* like several other ultra-nationalist organs (James Connolly's *Irish Worker* and Terence MacSwiney's *Fianna Fáil* among them), were banned in late 1914, in large part on account of their implacable opposition to the conflict, to Irish involvement, and to the recruitment effort. However, such journals – at least in the eyes of the authorities – tended to spring up like molehills. When one incendiary periodical closed, another would swiftly take its place. The short-lived *Scissors and Paste*,[16] for instance, was established by Arthur Griffith shortly after *Sinn Féin* was proscribed in December 1914 (principally for strongly discouraging enlisting). Alongside its mixture of extracts mined from the 'legitimate' press and strategically placed citations from the nationalist tradition, this too carried advertisements, generally featuring the brew commonly served up in such radical periodicals, notably announcements of advanced nationalist pamphlets, notices of public meetings and language classes.

Scissors and Paste also carried messages by sympathetic capitalists; on the evidence of its advertising columns a significant number of Irish-Ireland companies had no hesitation in associating themselves, even in wartime, with rebellious journals which were very likely to be proscribed or prosecuted in fairly short order. The familiar candidates are evident in its pages: the likes of Gleeson and Co., the aforementioned Irish-Ireland drapery store, Loughlin's, the 'Irish Outfitting Specialist' (of 'Practical Patriotism'[17] fame), and, of course, the ubiquitous Gaelic Athletic Association retailer Whelan and Son of Ormond Quay ('You *score for Ireland* as a Nation every time you buy from Whelan and Sons', a *Scissors and Paste* notice informed customers). Gleeson's tailored, if the reader will forgive the pun, their rhetoric to the political convictions of the journal:

> Keep this in your mind – 'Everything that is not Irish must be Foreign'. You must refuse to buy foreign goods. We sell IRISH GOODS ONLY. We give our orders to Irish makers – quantities, not oddments – and consequently can beat the foreigner all along the line. Our Tailoring Department is second to none in Dublin. Clerical Tailoring, Outfitting, Boots and Shoes.

In December 1914, the month in which it was banned, *Irish Freedom* declared that England perpetrated the War, 'not for the cause of religion or civilisation, but for the cause of England's great God-Markets'.[18] Advertising copy such as Gleeson's, in a wartime context and in a context such as *Scissors and Paste*, can be read as a small part of a direct economic challenge to Great Britain by advanced nationalist Ireland.

Periodicals such as *Irish Freedom* and *Scissors and Paste* – like all ultranationalist journals intended to 'beat the foreigner' – strongly disapproved of advertisements for the British Army, and did not allow the recruitment major on to the premises. But they did not, of course, have the deep pockets necessary to compete in the publicity effort, and their own fly-posting of counter-recruitment bills and posters, which began in the year before the death of Franz Ferdinand, was swiftly proscribed under the Defence of the Realm Act (as Benjamin Z. Novick has demonstrated, there were a significant number of contemporary prosecutions of republican posters in this period).[19] Nonetheless, their efforts were striking, as per this effort, perhaps the most inflammatory of them all, which appeared in the opening weeks of the war as both poster and handbill:

> Irishmen – FOOLS!
> Have you forgotten that England is your only enemy?
> Have you forgotten Kathleen-ni-Houlihan, that you are willing to shed your blood to win England's battles?
> Have you lost your wits, that you believe all the ridiculous lies published against the Germans in the Jingo papers?
> Have you forgotten how the English treated the Boers?
> Have you forgotten 'ninety-eight?
> Have you forgotten the Manchester Martyrs?

Have you forgotten the K.O.S.B. murders?[20]
Have you forgotten that the Future lies in your hands?
Have you forgotten that England's difficulty is Ireland's opportunity?
God save Ireland![21]

Here too, as in the army's own pitch, the appeal to Ireland's cultural memory and here too the cry of 'God save Ireland!'

Such posting, part of the ultra-nationalist anti-recruitment campaign, was itself a form of response-by-send-up to the enlistment posters. Indeed, 'Irishmen – FOOLS' can be read as a sharp satirical pastiche of the quasi-catechetical method of contemporary recruitment posters ('Are *You* a Decent Irishman?', 'But since the war began what have you done to make them a reality?' and so on). There were also contemporary counter-recruitment manoeuvrings which were explicitly and overtly parodic, part of the potent use of satire which was frequently evident in the advanced nationalist response to the First World War. Republican journals sometimes ran their own mock recruitment advertisements. One of these, published in *Saoirseacht na hEireann* in March 1914, bluntly declared that Irishmen joining the 'English' army were either fools or knaves:

WHAT THE ENGLISH ARMY OFFERS
– TO IRISH DUPES AND TRAITORS

A Guilty Conscience
An Unclean Life
A Miserable Death

Send for Special Book of Lies!
Join the Most Immoral and Degraded Force in Europe!
Go over to the English Garrison!

[THE ENGLISH GOVERNMENT HAS NOT PAID FOR THIS.]

Striking banners were a stock-in-trade of advertising in this period, and the use of an ironic contrast between headline and text was also not uncommon in contemporary copy, notably in the disguised advertisement or 'puff collateral'.[22] This squib exploits both, and it directly echoes the words of the previous year's anti-recruitment fly poster which attacked 'the most Immoral Army and Navy in the World'; satire – comedy with a moral purpose – and more orthodox polemic went hand in hand during this period.

Another pasquinade – this time in verse – an ad hominem attack on the leader of the Irish party which was published in Seán Doyle's republican scandal-sheet *The Spark* in April 1916, might also usefully be understood as a mock-advertisement:

> Ye Farmers of Ireland, John Redmond commands:
> 'In the trenches in France take your place right away,
> Tis a double-damned shame to be minding your business,
> When the Empire in Ruins ye might find any day'...
> To Hell with your land and your crops and your cattle,
> To Hell with your future, John Redmond obey.
> You may die, but from John you'll get passports to Heaven,
> Along with Home Rule, boys, upon the Last Day.[23]

This is the satirical doppelgänger to the 'Farmers of Ireland' poster reproduced above (Figure 8.4), which it mocks and directly echoes, attacking Redmond's attempt to boost the floundering recruitment drive in rural areas outside Dublin and the principal cities of Ireland.

In the summer of 1918, during the hotly contested conscription crisis, the sainted Douglas Hyde himself joined in the satirical chorus, in a three-part Juvenalian poem which includes a stanza which both parodies the Army recruitment pitch and attacks what it sees as the hypocritical, callous and patronising motivations of the British establishment:

> Now for your sake – more than ours –
> We're giving you this chance
> Come out against the Central Powers
> And bleed with us in France.
> By dying with us you will let
> The whole world see we're Christians yet,
> That you forgive and we forget.[24]

Such vigorous satirical nose-thumbing was not uncommon in the period. That entrepreneurial satirist Brian O'Higgins also joined in the anti-recruitment efforts in 'Eight Millions of English Men' (one of a number of squibs – by Brian na Banban and others – which are quoted approvingly in Margaret Skinnider's memoir of revolution *Doing My Bit for Ireland* (1917)). The following stanza gives the flavour:

> There are plenty of fools in Ireland still,
> Just promise them something soon,
> A Union Jack, or a Home Rule Bill,
> Or a slice of the next new moon.
> And they'll rush to the colors with wild hurroos,
> What price the War Lord then?[25]

As with many Fenians, Skinnider (a Cumann na mBan protégée of Constance Markievicz) saw satire as a key tool in the campaign 'to discourage recruiting for the English army in Ireland'.[26] In this counter-recruitment aspect of nationalist print culture, mockery and more orthodox polemic went hand in hand.[27]

III

The parade of masculinity so common in this period in recruitment advertising, in the paid columns of *Irish Freedom* and, indeed, in publicity material for the UVF, was also apparent in advertisements pertaining to the Irish Volunteers. Take Figure 8.5, a semiotically rich advertisement for Thomas Fallon and Company of Dublin, 'First Maker in Ireland of Special Uniform for Volunteer Officers', which dates from August 1914. In the upstanding figure of the officer stood ready for any eventuality, bandolier laden with ammunition and rifle in his hand, there is a sturdy independence of mien, which might well be seen as symbolising – whether Fallon and Co. intended it or not –

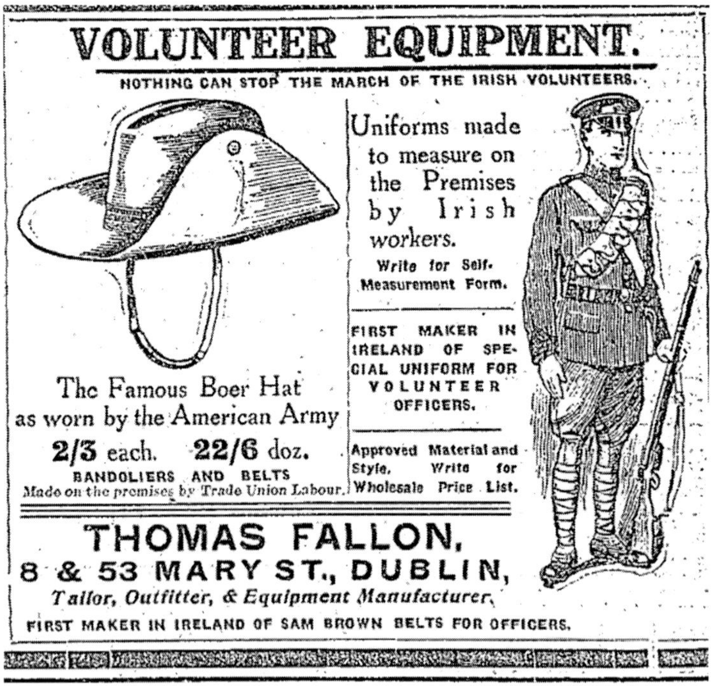

Figure 8.5 Advertisement for Thomas Fallon, 8 and 53 Mary Street, Dublin (August 1914): 'Volunteer Equipment'.

the origins of the Volunteers in the Irish Republican Brotherhood (the proud reference to the union closed shop is also suggestive, invoking another form of brotherly solidarity to match that found among the soldiery itself).

The uniform of this man – and this is one of its key signifiers – is 'Irish', and it is clear at the same time that his outfit is not that of the British Army. It stands alone; it is *different*, and the mark of that dissimilarity, we would argue, is the 'Famous Boer Hat', which may well have been 'worn by the American Army' but also arguably had a nationalist resonance in invoking the campaign, begun in the 1890s, against British military action in South Africa – and Irish involvement in it – which had re-invigorated Irish nationalism after the demise of Parnell, and which was still, of course, in recent memory.[28] Commandant General Pearse, it might be pointed out, wore a green Volunteer uniform and exactly this type of Boer slouch hat outside the General Post Office on Sackville Street when reading the proclamation of the Irish Republic on 24 April 1916.

Before John Redmond's de facto takeover of the Volunteers in the summer of 1914, radical nationalist journals such as the IRB's *Irish Freedom* frequently took advertisements for Volunteer publications, meetings and kit. That said, so did the likes of the *Irish Independent*, the paid columns of which simultaneously featured recruitment materials for the British Army and a significant number of advertisements placed by and on behalf of the Irish Volunteers: announcements of meetings, drill training and parades alongside commercial messages by manufacturers of volunteer equipment, such as Fallon and Co. or Hearne's of Waterford.

Before the September 1914 split of the movement (as a consequence, inevitably, of the Irish Party's support of enlistment into the British military) into the Redmondite Irish National Volunteers and a rump of Irish Volunteers under Eoin MacNeill and Patrick Pearse, which was thereafter frequently and inaccurately referred to as the Sinn Féin Volunteers (and which itself divided before the 1916 rising which MacNeill tried to prevent), the mainstream press took numerous advertisements along the lines of Fallon's 'Volunteer Equipment'. Though Francis P. Jones's *History of the Sinn Fein Movement and the Irish Rebellion of 1916* (1917) maintains that the *Independent* (and the *Freeman's Journal*) refused to take a notice announcing the founding meeting of the Volunteers conducted by Professor MacNeill in November 1913,[29] by the following month the journal was admitting Volunteer advertisements. There were a number of insertions in the paper during 1914, notably for the *Handbook for Irish Volunteers. Simple Lectures on Military Subjects* (1914), published by the leading Catholic publishers M. H. Gill, for the wares of the indefatigable Tom Fallon, and for the 'Volunteer Outfits' which were produced by Hearne and Co. of 63 and 64 Quay, Waterford.[30] Take the September 1914 advertisement for the latter which is reproduced as Figure 8.6 and which boasts of the patronage of John Redmond himself. The National Party leader, it seems, restricted his purchases to some volunteer

Figure 8.6 Advertisement for Hearne and Co., Waterford (1914): 'Volunteer Outfits'.[31]

caps (price '1/6 and 2/3'), but there were far more ferocious goods on sale at Hearne's premises in County Waterford alongside caps, belts and 'Boer shape hats': bayonets, ammunition and rifles (these being the British-made Lee-Metford and BSA (the Birmingham Small Arms company) 30/- 'New Practice Rifle').

Hearne and Co. notwithstanding, the noisiest vendor of equipment for the Volunteers was the aforesaid Thomas Fallon and Co. of 8 and 53 Mary Street, Dublin, a firm which produced numerous advertisements aimed at that band of men, sometimes published under the banner 'NOTHING CAN STOP THE MARCH OF THE IRISH VOLUNTEERS'. Fallon's premises, which had formerly traded as the 'Irish Tweed Company' (though it also used the vigorous-sounding imprimatur 'Eagle Tailoring'), was rebranded in 1914 as the 'Volunteer House'. The shop offered uniforms, 'military marching boots', water bottles, belts, badges and so on – products in 'materials and styles' 'approved', its copy maintained – by the top brass of the Volunteers.[32] Indeed, as the above advertisement demonstrates, Fallon's proclaimed itself capable of supplying 'Everything to Equip an Army in the Field'.

Thomas Fallon was one of those entrepreneurs who, for centuries, have made money out of national feeling and military enthusiasm. Indeed, he candidly admitted in a letter published in the *Irish Independent* in August 1914 that his business did well out of the paramilitaries ('I do a good trade with the Irish Volunteers'). Nonetheless, he was careful to point out that he draped his premises in the flag out of conviction rather than opportunism, as he had 'always been a Home Ruler and supporter of Mr John Redmond', and,

Figure 8.7 Advertisement for Thomas Fallon (1914): 'Volunteer Equipment. Everything to Equip an Army for the Field'.

as such, was one of those dedicated to the cause of 'regaining nationhood for our land' (Figure 8.7).[33]

In May 1914, Fallon's boast that his shops offered 'Everything to Equip an Army in the Field' prompted the *Independent* itself to editorialise on the decided novelty of a tailor's shop turned quartermaster's store: 'The idea of an outfitter supplying Volunteer and military equipment is new, but Mr Fallon goes better, and is prepared to supply everything to equip an army for the field.' The paper noted Fallon's Irish-Ireland credentials; his suits and uniforms were, the firm declared, tailored 'on the premises by Irish workers'. However, it might be pointed out that it was not always thus. When Thomas Fallon began selling Volunteer equipment in late 1913 he was importing goods from Great Britain, a fact which prompted the Irish Industrial Development Association (IIDA) to send him one of its stern letters and, indeed, prompted representation on the subject from within the Volunteers' hierarchy. These actions led the shopkeeper-turned-manufacturer, as he put it in a letter of August 1914 to E. J. Riordan of the IIDA[34] (a letter which was circulated to, and reprinted in, the *Irish Independent*), to have 'plant installed and suitable accommodation made for the manufacture of equipment for the

Irish Volunteers'[35] in early 1914. Fallon's company, which did not have the Irish Trade Mark for its previous incarnation as the Irish Tweed Company – despite its promising name – now negotiated with the IIDA and received the accolade for the Volunteer products in short order. Now Fallon could boast that all of his goods were 'made of Irish equipment in Irish premises by Irish Trade Union labour'. In Fallon's advertising, commerce, militarism, Irish-Ireland goods – and the Irish Party brand of nationalism – walk hand in hand.

IV

Historical advertising has a habit of referring to the events of its day and, unsurprisingly, the First World War and the Irish soldiery were frequently alluded to in advertising copy in Ireland between 1914 and 1918. Recruitment posters, soldiers' letters home, press reports of battles and government propaganda; all became grist to the copywriters' mill, and manufacturers – especially in the first two years of the conflict – often boasted of their popularity with the troops up the line. The most basic of this advertising claimed that a product was, in effect, by appointment to the boys in khaki, a demotic version of the royal warrant. Manufacturers proudly announced themselves as suppliers to the soldiers on the front. Even in 'rebel Cork', for instance, a famous Irish company was willing to align itself closely with 'His Majesty's Forces' in 1916, as Figure 8.8, a display advertisement for Murphy's stout, demonstrates. Here the emphasis was as much on the product's destination as it was on its point of origin – as was more usual in Revival-era Irish advertising. This image, like much else in contemporaneous Irish advertising, was possessed of a national narrative, though not necessarily one to the liking of many radical nationalists of the time.

In a similar manner, in 1915 the Bendigo brand of cigarettes, named after the famous Irish-bred racehorse and manufactured by W. and M. Taylor of Dublin, announced itself as the best 'Tobacco for Soldiers at the Front' (Figure 8.9). That said, at the same time as Bendigo was being shipped to France as the best for the combatants, similar commercial laurels were also being claimed by B.D.V. Cigarettes (Best Dark Virginia),[36] which also maintained that it was the best smoke for the lads and, indeed, saluted the 'Magnificent Gallantry of Irish Troops' in another 1915 advertisement (Figure 8.10). The 'beautiful' cigarette 'silks' mentioned here are printed satin images of Irish regimental badges, which were distributed free with packs of twenty; customers could, with any luck – and even in their very 'first packet' – find a 'copy of the Regimental Badge of a soldier relative or friend'. As per the rhetoric of contemporary recruitment, here the appeal to family solidarity is made explicit in advertising copy.

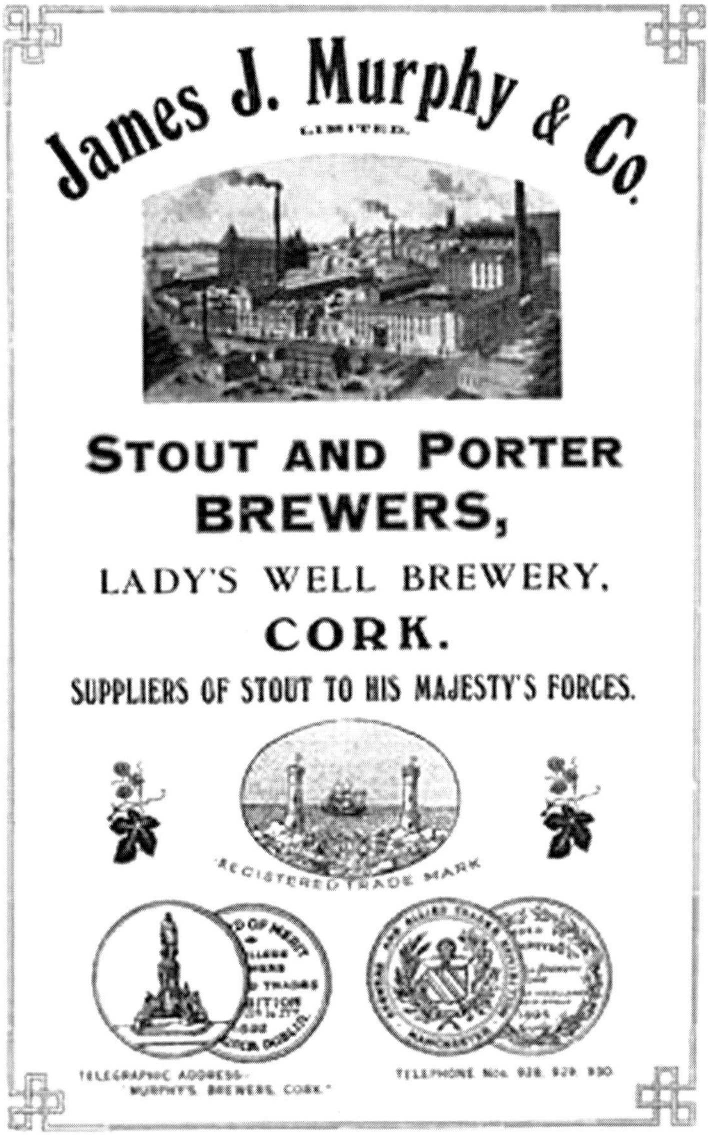

Figure 8.8 'James J. Murphy and Co., Stout and Porter Brewers' (1916).

Notwithstanding their appeal to Irish 'gallantry' and to customers' familial bonds to the soldiers of Ireland, Godfrey Phillips, the firm which owned the B.D.V. brand, was an English concern, established in the 1840s, and the cigarettes themselves were manufactured in Great Britain. This did not,

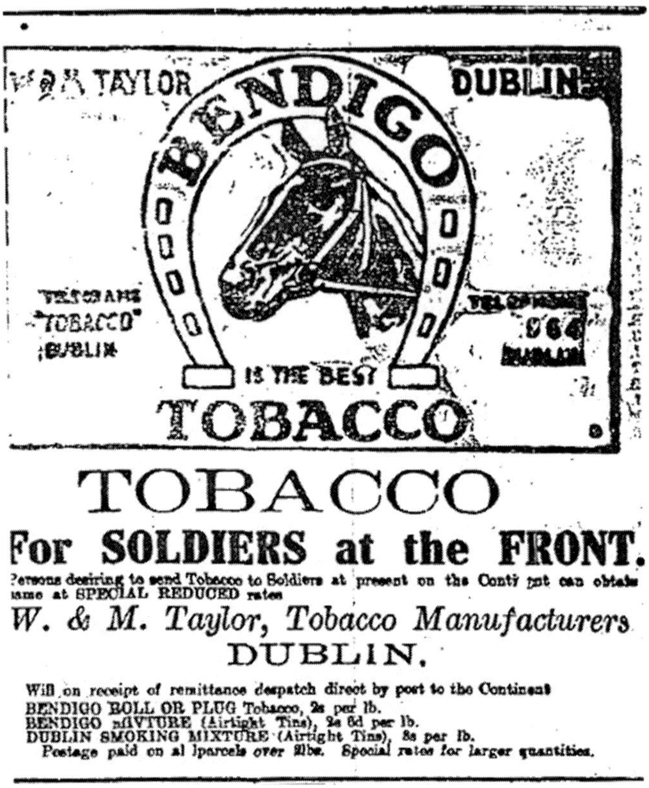

Figure 8.9 Advertisement for W. & M. Taylor, Dublin (1915): 'Tobacco for Soldiers at the Front'.

however, stop the company from echoing Irish-Ireland brand culture by issuing a call to 'Support Irish Industries' (1918; Figure 8.11) on the flimsy if not disingenuous premise that the regimental silks – as opposed than the cigarettes themselves – were made in Dublin's fair city.

Testimonials from the front were also common in First World War advertising copy, as members of the soldiery supposedly put pen to paper to commend manufacturers of cigarettes, porridge, nourishing hot drinks and the like, which had sustained them in their hour of darkness. Figure 8.12 shows an example published on behalf of OXO, dating from 1915, which purports to be from a member of the Second Royal Irish Regiment and which portrays the renowned stock cubes as 'a Godsend to the lot of us' on 'the Front'.

The device of the soldier's testimonial was also utilised by the dispensing chemist and vendor of proprietary medicines Eugene Mac Sweeny of Cork in

Figure 8.10 Advertisement for Godfrey Phillips Tobacco (1915): 'Magnificent Gallantry of Irish Troops'.

his 'A Military Verdict' (1916; Figure 8.13), an advertisement which salutes the efficacy of his then renowned corn cure, 'Tinori' (this also plays on its audience's familiarity with the renowned World War One marching song 'It's a Long Way to Tipperary' (1912), first made famous by the Connaught Rangers). The sergeant enthusiastically recommends Tinori ('discovered' and

Figure 8.11 Advertisement for B.D.V. cigarettes (1918): 'Support Irish Industry'.

solely manufactured by Mac Sweeny) to his 'pals', evoking the spirit of fraternal camaraderie which was evident in such stuff as the 'Dublin Pals Regiment' recruitment advertisement discussed above.

During this period, Mac Sweeny, the Cork chemist, entrepreneurial capitalist and resourceful advertising man, consistently referred to the Great War in

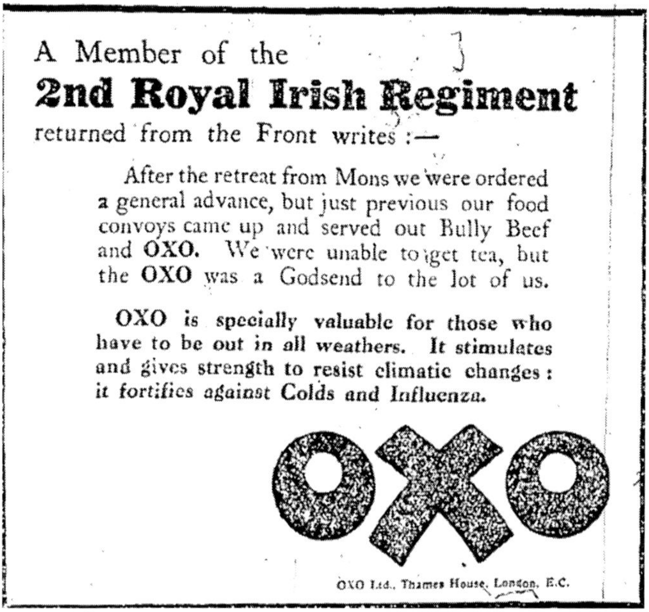

Figure 8.12 Advertisement for OXO (1915): 'A Member of the 2nd Royal Irish Regiment returned from the Front Writes'.

his advertising copy. 'Irishmen Enlist' roars a banner for one of his advertisements of 1915 (Figure 8.14); 'Enlist', that is, 'in your service the wonderful corn-killing power of Tinori'.

At first glance, before the realisation that we are in the presence of a commercial advertisement dawns, this looks like part of the recruitment effort, with its banner evoking the recruitment materials so common elsewhere in the contemporary Irish press. It is noticeable that in an Irish context – although the country's advertising had used the device throughout the Revival – such semi-disguised advertisements, which gesture towards the spirit of the age around them,[37] were especially popular in the turbulent period under discussion here, when readers were hungry for news of war, rebellion and the rebirth of a nation. In early August 1916, for instance, just over three months after the Easter rising and just over one month after the start of the Battle of the Somme, Gleeson's the drapers combined references to both in an advertisement prefaced by some arresting words:

> THE BIG PUSH!!!
> OFFENSIVE RESUMED IN O'CONNELL STREET.
> There is a Sale of Oddments by Gleeson, Drapers, 11 Up. O'Connell Street…

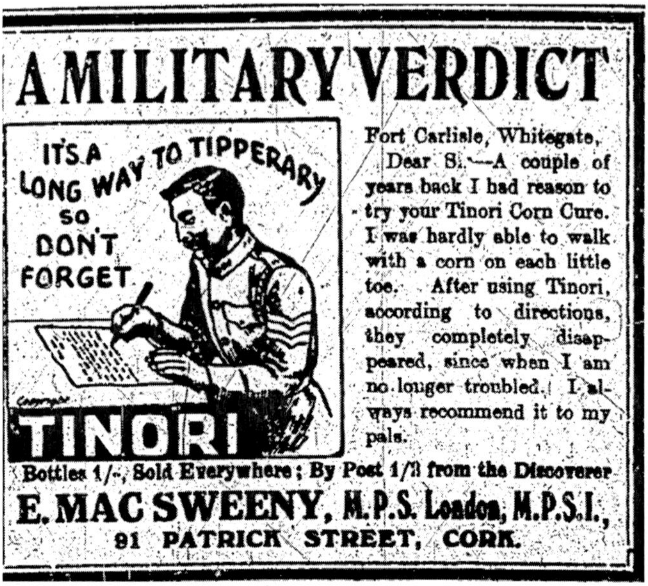

Figure 8.13 Advertisement for Eugene Mac Sweeny, Patrick Street, Cork (April 1916): 'A Military Verdict'.

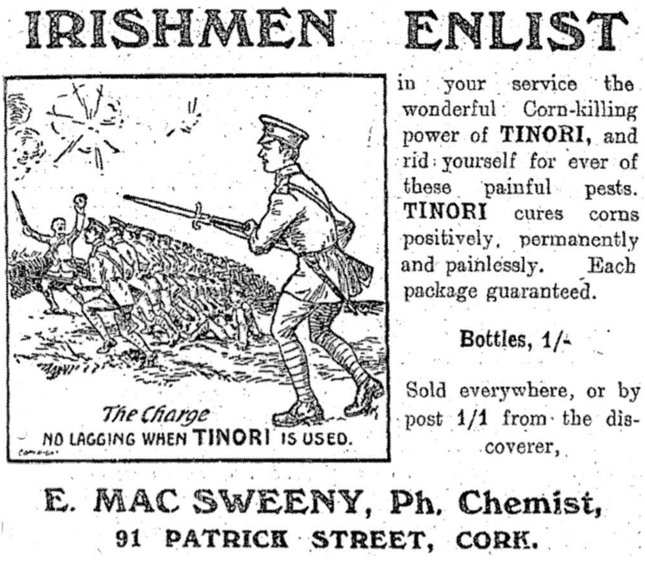

Figure 8.14 Advertisement for E. Mac Sweeny, Cork (1915): 'Irishmen Enlist'.

In like manner, 'IRISHMEN! – DO YOUR DUTY' ran another banner of 1916, one which invoked the contemporaneous recruitment campaigns: 'Buy only Irish-Made Goods', it went on in particular, the 'GRAND NEW RANGE of Irish Tweeds, Suitings and Serges' which had 'just arrived at O'Connell's in Ballynacargy'. Again, 'IN THE PRESENT STRENUOUS TIMES', runs a catchpenny headline in the *Freeman's Journal* published in the same year, 'when you have need of every ounce of energy you can muster, customers are advised to purchase the "Loving Cup Margarine" made by the Shandon Castle Margarine factory in Cork'.

These advertisements are examples of what Sheridan's Mr Puff, in the taxonomy of 'puffery' in the great Irish dramatist's *The Critic* (1779), calls the 'Puff Collateral', the hidden advertisement which appears under a banner intended to catch the reader's eye and gives the impression of being part of the news or editorial sections of a newspaper. Such advertisements, which date back several centuries, 'win their silent way into the recesses of the paper under the mask of general paragraphs',[38] as the poet and radical journalist Leigh Hunt put it in the early nineteenth century.

The puff collateral comes at the reader obliquely, tempting him or her with the promise of something other than a sales pitch. Though Hunt despised the device of the hidden message as a form of advertising 'quackery', it is hard to be too cross with this brass-necked form of advertising as entertainment. Brazenly self-interested though these collateral advertisements might be, they are also ingenious and droll; wit is effective, as modern advertising 'creatives' know (and as Leopold Bloom knows in Joyce's *Ulysses*; the cross keys in the Alexander Keyes advertisement is a weak visual jest, but it is one that he is alert to: 'House of keys, don't you see? His name is Keyes. It's a play on the name').[39] Certainly Eugene Mac Sweeny knew this, and it is worth tarrying over his advertising, not only because of its systematic use of the events of the First World War to sell corn cures, but also because his work features the most sustained used of comic advertising in Ireland before Guinness got into its memorable stride in the 1930s. Figure 8.15 gives another example from the Tinori of Cork publicity, 'Tinori in the Big Push'. Here Mac Sweeny's copy, like that for Gleeson of Upper O'Connell Street in the same year, opportunistically invokes the notion of the big push in a 1916 display advertisement. And here too the soldier's testimonial: 'The Tinori is a bally marvel' ('I could kiss old Mac Sweeny for the relief', he continues bathetically).

As the war continued, Mac Sweeny continued his own particular campaigns. In 1917 his 'Still They Come' (Figure 8.16) portrayed a cart load of corn cures heading up to the front line. Here foot abscesses are portrayed as a resourceful enemy, and crates of Tinori are seen as welcome munitions in the struggle against them. The analogy between the British and Irish soldiery and the implacable 'corn-killers' that are bottles of Tinori – and that between the tin-hatted German army and calluses, scourge of the feet – is made

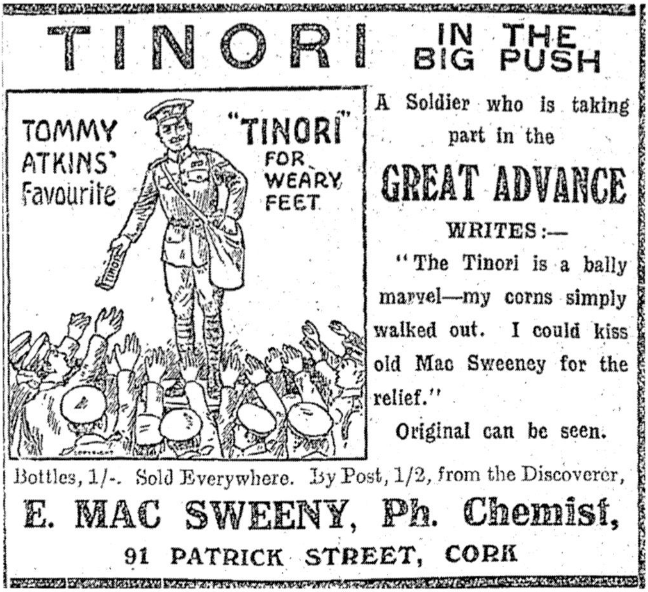

Figure 8.15 Advertisement for E. Mac Sweeny (1916): 'Tinori in the Big Push'.

Figure 8.16 Advertisement for E. Mac Sweeny (1917): 'Still They Come'.

Figure 8.17 Advertisement for E. Mac Sweeny (1916): 'Get a Bottle of Tinori Today'.

explicit in Figure 8.17, 'Get a Bottle of Tinori Today' (December 1916), which triumphantly declares that 'Corns surrender to Tinori'. Finally, in 1918, Mac Sweeny's company brought its engagement with the First World War in display advertising to a logical conclusion in 'The Joy of Peace' (Figure 8.18), which it maintained 'is with the reach of all who suffer from corns', provided they use the 'never failing painless cure Tinori'.

Eugene Mac Sweeny (d. 1937) was a significant presence in the paid columns of Irish newspapers for three decades from the 1910s to the 1930s (and his product lasted two decades more, enduring into the 1950s). After the war he founded and became chairman of the Cork Publicity Association, a body which held annual trade fairs in the city to promote local goods, promoted it as a Christmas shopping destination, and proselytised for the cause of advertising to the businesses of County Cork. Mac Sweeny was convinced of the necessity and commercial utility of extensive advertising, maintaining in the 1930s that 'Ireland could hold its own in publicity with any of the outside countries'. 'The Press was the great publicity agent', declared Mac Sweeny, 'that manufacturers and traders who wanted to market their commodity must turn to' (that said, he also admitted that 'the basic fact was that the commodity must be commendable': 'All the push in the world was a waste if the quality was not right').

Eugene Mac Sweeny, in his forthright manner, informed the businessmen of Munster that 'If they wanted to mould the opinion of the public they must

Figure 8.18 Advertisement for E. Mac Sweeny (1918): 'The Joy of Peace'.[40]

use the Press'. This was advice based on his extensive experience of using public prints in a long series of ingenious advertisements; during the First World War the momentous geopolitical proceedings of the day presented themselves to him as a business opportunity. A politically allusive rhetoric of commerce was clearly evident in this period in Ireland, with the events of the hour evident in advertising copy such as the 'Offensive Resumed in O'Connell Street' oddment sale and, in particular, in the topical gesturings of Eugene Mac Sweeny. The great events of the day resounded, for commercial advantage, through Irish advertising.

Coda – From the Armistice to the Saorstát

> 'Two Murphy's Please!' That was the order as the Republican and the Free Stater finished their argument. Finishing the order, they both agreed that, Free State or Republic, Murphy's (Cork) Extra Stout was the best for either.
>
> Advertisement for Murphy's Stout (December 1921)

In the period between the armistice of November 1918 and the first tentative steps of the Irish Free State in early 1922, Ireland continued in the midst of political turmoil. In economic terms, the efforts to publicise Irish-Ireland goods continued and to a certain extent intensified after the War, with a sense that putting 'Paddy on the shelf'[1] – to borrow a vivid phrase from *The Leader* – was ever more important. Companies such as T. J. Loughlin's of Parliament Street sustained the 'Practical Patriotism' note they had first sounded two decades before ('Keep the Home Industries Going and Buy Loughlin's Irish Outfitting Headquarters. ALL IRISH. ALL RELIABLE') and, in like manner, the Irish Industrial Development Association (IIDA) redoubled its efforts, and began to sponsor direct advertising campaigns for Irish products and manufacturers. At the same time, as had happened during the First World War itself, quick-witted copywriters used the momentous happenings around them to produce eye-catching advertisements. One can trace popular-cultural echoes of the remarkable events of this period in contemporary advertising, with such epochal matters as the signing of the Anglo-Irish Treaty and the establishment of the Free State becoming grist to the mill of commerce.

I

The patriotic card, which had been dealt so many times from the 1890s onwards in the campaigns for home products, was certainly evident in post-war Irish advertising. 'Irish Industries for Irish People means a Prosperous Ireland' declared the Irish Co-Operative Clothing Manufacturing Society in a March 1921 advertisement which calls for 'all Irish people to co-operate in the building up – the reconstruction – of Industrial Ireland'. Advertising, it might be pointed out, was a key plank of efforts to sustain and develop Irish industry in the post-war period. Some copy endorsed home goods and some warned against the damaging economic consequences of imports from Great Britain and beyond. John O'Neill's Lucania Cycle Company of Dublin, indeed, did both, running these twin advertisements simultaneously in June 1920:

> Talking about Irish Industries does not extend them; prove your interest in their extension by purchasing a Lucania Cycle, the Cycle with the IRISH TRADE MARK.
>
> TALK IS CHEAP! Cycles to the Value of £250,000 have been imported into Ireland this year. Have YOU helped with this importation? If so, we would be glad to hear your reason, as we claim that LUCANIA, the cycle with the Irish Trade Mark, is at least as good value as any other.

As Ireland moved towards the Free State its producers maintained the campaigns for home produce and against importation which had been so common from the early days of the Gaelic League. The proprietors of Boland's Bread, for example, a company whose advertising is echoed in Joyce's *Ulysses*[2] and whose premises at Grand Canal Street had seen much of the fighting in the early part of the uprising of 1916, declared in a 1919 advertisement in the *Irish Independent* that their product was 'NOT made of Foreign Flour!' and urged consumers to 'SUPPORT IRISH MILLING'. In like manner, in the *New Leader* for 6 March 1920 Francis Smyth and Co. called for consumers to buy Irish, lamenting the fact of '£65,000 Umbrella Imports! [...] into Ireland each year, while here at 75, Grafton Street, Irish Umbrellas are made'.

The continued need to make such pronouncements was, in part, due to the fact that An Dáil did not, as many had expected, pass protective legislation or introduce preferential treatment for Irish goods in the post-war period. Ernest Blythe, the Ulster Protestant and veteran of the Irish Volunteers who became Minister of Trade and Commerce in 1919, set out the reasons for this in a report to Dáil Éireann of 17 August 1921:

> At the time when this Department was established [in 1919], the postwar industrial boom was in full swing and prices were rising rapidly. In the circumstances, I felt it would not be proper to carry on any propaganda in favour of preferential purchasing of Irish-made goods, since, in most lines, manufacturers had more orders than they could deal with, and propaganda, in so far as it might have been effective, would only have been an incitement to profiteering.

Given this initial refusal of 'preferential purchasing' and the subsequent failure of a scheme to favour a 'schedule' of Irish goods legislatively,[3] the IIDA (funded by subscriptions and levies on the trademark holders), having no qualms about encouraging the sale of 'Irish-made goods', intensified its promotional efforts on their behalf. 'Trade follows the flag', as Blythe's report put it; but it also needed some flag waving.

The Dublin Industrial Development Association was particularly active in the campaigns. It opened a permanent exhibition of Irish Goods at 40 Upper O'Connell Street in December 1921[4] and it also engaged Kevin J. Kenny's agency (the company that had worked both for Moran's *The Leader* and the Royal Irish Constabulary in its time)[5] to assist in the publicity effort. The two organisations jointly placed a series of advertisements headed 'SAY "IRISH" ' and 'HELP "IRISH" ' in the very summer in which the Dáil received its report against formal protection:

> Irish manufacturers desiring to have their names and particulars of their goods inserted in a series of advertisements (appearing widely in leading Irish newspapers), should apply at once to the Dublin Industrial Development Association, 12 Molesworth Street, Dublin or Kenny's Advertising Agency, 65 Middle Abbey Street, Dublin, who have charge of the scheme.

'Will you do this for Ireland?' asked Kenny's, which had, of course, expertise in First World War recruitment publicity, 'Will *you* be able to say "I have done my part towards making my country prosperous?" ' This quasi-military discourse, with its second person pronoun and guilt-inducing rhetoric, urged consumers to fight the good economic fight and, indeed, utilised the trading-in-guilt approach which had been so common in the Great War publicity campaigns.

Those Irish advertisers vetted by the association and by Kenny's were then included in a list of Irish-Ireland advertisers – a private 'schedule', in Blythe's terminology – which included such stalwarts as Loughlin's, Pierce's of Wexford and, of course, Whelan's and Co. of Ormond Quay. Consumers were urged to 'Cut out these lists week by week. Keep them by you and shop from them in future':

> AFTER THE TRUCE
>
> Help now to build up a great and prosperous Ireland in preparation for the peace we all hope is coming. Each one of us can become a nation builder. The prosperity of the country depends on its industries. The prosperity of those industries depends on the support they receive. *Irish Industries will be flourishing, the country will be rich, employment will be plentiful – if only Irish men and women buy goods made at home* ALWAYS. Look down the list

below. Nearly all everyday needs can be filled from it and every item is of proven quality.

This was in effect, voluntary protection when none was forthcoming from above (as a review of *Modern Irish Trade and Industry* (1920) by the IIDA stalwart E. J. Riordan put it, 'the popular preference device is essentially similar to State protection').[6]

Irish goods could flourish, the argument of Irish-Ireland partisans went, if the consumer exercised a positive choice. At the same time, and on the other hand, not all goods made on the island of Ireland were equally favoured. A new, even sharper edge began to emerge in the advertising columns alongside the warnings about avoiding 'foreign' goods. As partition approached, a trade boycott of Belfast goods, introduced in August 1920, gathered pace in the south. The Belfast Trade Boycott,[7] under its director, the Irish parliamentarian Michael Staines TD, was conducted in large part via the paid columns, with Staines and his committee spending significant sums on polemical advertising in newspapers and in nationalist journals. These detailed the various 'atrocities' and 'outrages' perpetrated by Ulster Unionists, from the expulsion of Catholics from their jobs in Belfast to threats and violence against northern Sinn Féinidthe, and were couched in emphatic polemical terms:

BELFAST TRADE BOYCOTT

To the Orange Bigots of Belfast: –
This is your final notice.
When you practice Tolerance and Repudiate Partition you will be allowed to trade with the Rest of Ireland.
To the People of Ireland – Boycott Belfast Goods.
(March 1921)

BELFAST TRADE BOYCOTT

To the Irish People: –
The Belfast Boycott is now being enforced on accounts of the Atrocities of the Orange Bigots. It is to become permanent as soon as the Northern Partition Parliament is elected.
(April 1921)

BELFAST TRADE BOYCOTT

A Protestant Sinn Feiner had his collar and shirt torn. *'If I were a Catholic'*, he said, *'I would have been killed'*.
. . .
Catholic expelled workers going to Lisburn to record their votes were obliged to flee. The windows of their train were smashed.

> ...
> The Orangemen have not Yet Learned Their Lesson
> Teach them Tolerance by Boycotting Belfast Goods.
> (May 1921)[8]

In effect, what such polemic was doing was adapting the previous rhetoric about British goods, sharpening it, and applying it to Belfast ones. Arguably, the boycott weakened the all-Ireland position evident elsewhere in Sinn Féin rhetoric. Opinion was certainly divided on the subject; acting President Griffith spoke against in the Dáil, for instance, pointing out that the clear implication here was that nationalist Ireland and Ulster were two different countries: 'the resolution was practically a declaration of war on one part of their territory... It would be an admission that Belfast is outside of Ireland.'[9] The Boycott lasted until early 1922, when the pro-treaty Dáil wound it up, and its advertisements ceased. But once again in Irish commercial history a negative consumer choice, urged in contemporary advertisements, had become politically significant.

II

In his preface to a 1918 history of the Irish Volunteers, Eoin MacNeill, Gaelic League luminary, founding editor of *An Claidheamh Soluis*, and first Chief of Staff of the force, commented that the Volunteers were established as a consequence of the fact that 'Ireland was already growing restive in the Parliamentarian harness and disposed towards "self-determination"'.[10] 'SELF-DETERMINATION IS THE QUESTION OF THE HOUR', as an *Irish Independent* banner headline, written by John Fallon of Galway, put it in 1920. 'Ireland demands an *Irish Republic,* and Ireland can only obtain its object by Unity and Strength.' How was this unity and strength to be achieved? All was revealed. 'FALLON', the notice went on, 'is ever foremost in the rank to strengthen the Manhood and Womanhood of Ireland by supplying only the very best of Beef and Mutton. Fallon has already united the housekeepers of Galway, and he will now strengthen them to win their Independence.' 'Build yourself up', the ingenious advertiser declared, 'be on the strong side, and send your orders for Best Home Killed Beef and Mutton [to] JOHN FALLON, VICTUALLER, GALWAY' ('Prompt delivery in City and Suburbs').

Advertisements sometimes reflected the day's tenor, pressing the events of the hour into service in such opportunistic references to current affairs. Fallon's particular method, the puff collateral, we have met before; this man ran a series of disguised advertisements for his meat products during the period of debate about the Anglo-Irish Treaty and the establishment of the Free State, all of which used arresting banners intended to catch the reader's eye. This from April 1921, when Fallon moves from demanding *'an Irish republic'* into Treaty-man mode:

> TO BUILD UP THE IRISH FREE STATE
>
> You must nourish the body well. This can only be done by getting your meat from the best Victualler in the town. JOHN FALLON, Abbeygate Street, holds the laurels for Quality and Cheapness. Whether it be Beef, Mutton, Lamb, Veal, Poultry, Pork or [if] Fish is your choice I can supply you, and remember I only supply my numerous customers with the best that money can buy, and at the cheapest figure prevailing. No Profiteering in my Establishment. Your next order, please, to John Fallon, Abbeygate Street, Galway.[11]

Fallon's drolleries are testimony to the way in which the events of the years between 1918 and 1922 echoed through Irish advertising copy. Collateral advertisements such as his were by no means uncommon in the period. Before the days of radio and television, in times of turmoil people rushed to the press, where advertising banners, masquerading as headline news or editorial polemic, tempted consumers into a sales pitch. 'ECONOMIC RE-BIRTH OF MUNSTER!' yells a banner in the *New Leader* of March 1920: 'Wear O'Gorman's Boots. Made in Cork. 60 Hands Employed. WEAR THEM! WEAR THEM!' Again, in December 1921, readers of the same journal were urged to 'SUPPORT THE FREE STATE!!' This could be achieved, the advertisement maintains, by 'giving employment to Irish Boys and Girls'. 'You can do this', it revealed, 'by buying' the somewhat unfragrant but decidedly Irish 'Mooney's Irish-Made Manure. XXX Superphosphate 35%,' which was 'bagged, stocked and sold only by Eugene McCabe, Kilcogy'.

A similar methodology informs a contemporaneous advertisement for O'Reilly's House for Value in Dublin. What reader of the *Irish Independent* in December 1921 could resist paying attention to the subject of 'HOME RULE OR INDEPENDENCE?' Through the back door arrive the House for Value's clothes, undergarments, corsets and 'warm vests':

> HOME RULE OR INDEPENDENCE
>
> Is mainly a question of finance. It's just the same in the home. There is no independence in any home where the financial strain is excessive. That's where O'Reilly's 'House for Value' Counts. A Great Twelve-Day Bargain Sale is now in progress. Amazing Bargains in Blankets, Quilts and Shirts.
>
> Saturday closing hour is 9pm.
>
> 11 & 12 North Earl St.

Figure C.1 Advertisement for the North Tipperary Maltings Ltd, Nenagh (1921): 'Salute the Free State of Ireland!'.

The eye is caught and the commercial message administered. Again, politics becomes a bait for the canny advertiser.

In like manner to 'Home Rule or Independence', a 1921 puff collateral for the People's Own Tailor's in Eustace Street, Dublin cheekily engaged the eye with a topical banner on the issue which was dividing Ireland, with deadly consequences (not all Irishmen, as per J. J. Murphy and Co.'s witty advertisement of the same year, could agree to differ over a pint of stout):

> TREATY OR NO TREATY
>
> One point we are all agreed on – that THE PEOPLE'S OWN TAILOR'S, at Eustace Street is the best house in Dublin for Ladies' and Gentlemen's Tailoring. CASH or CREDIT. Perfect Fit Guaranteed.[12]

This breezy offering is but one of the many opportunistic advertising responses to the establishment of the Free State, as per 'Two Murphy's Please!' and the aforementioned Fallon's advertisement 'TO BUILD UP THE IRISH FREE STATE' and Mooney's 'SUPPORT THE FREE STATE!!'.

Not all of this commercial material was jocular in tone, however. There were also more straight-faced responses to the establishment of *Saorstát Éireann* in the medium of advertising copy, as per Figure C.1, 'Salute the Free State of Ireland!', an advertisement placed by the North Tipperary Maltings company in the *Nenagh Guardian* in December 1921, which waves off the Irish ship of liberty as it set sail into unknown waters. 'We declare', the copy maintains, 'our Determination to do our part to assist in the Building up of the Fabric of the NEW IRELAND': 'We will give OUR BEST to Ireland.'

This visually striking mixed-media advertisement (in display, in verse and in more orthodox prose copy), which optimistically if mistakenly (at least in the short term) looked forward to 'the blessings that peace will bring to the NEW FREE STATE' sounded many of the key notes in the repertoire of Irish advertising in the period between the 1890s and the 1920s: stirring, if sentimental, nationalist copy, a puff collateral banner, a striking image and, above all, a patriotic appeal to Ireland.

The ingenious North Tipperary Maltings image looked forward to the commercial iconography evident in the Irish Free State and, later, in the Irish Republic, and in its striking use of visual imagery anticipated the extended glory days of Guinness advertising. In previous accounts of Irish cultural history, an advertisement such as this might have been seen as marking the beginning of a tradition of inventive Irish advertising made incarnate in the promotional activities centred on the brewery at St James's Gate. However, 'Salute the Irish Free State' is best understood as the culmination of a body of advertising, much of it ideologically inflected, which resounded noisily through Irish life and culture during the period of the Revival.

Notes

Introduction

1. Declan Kiberd, *Inventing Ireland: The Literature of the Modern Nation* (Cambridge, MA: Harvard University Press, 1996), p. 3.
2. *Gentleman's Magazine*, N. S., vol. 40 (May 1888), p. 195.
3. See p. 9 for bibliographical details.
4. *Pharmaceutical Journal*, vol. 12 (November 1853) p. 209.
5. For the history of Guinness, see S. R. Dennison and Oliver McDonagh, *Guinness 1886–1939. From Incorporation to the Second World War* (Cork: Cork University Press, 1998), Patrick Lynch and John Vaizey, *Guinness's Brewery in the Irish Economy: 1759–1876* (Cambridge: Cambridge University Press, 1960), and David Alan Hughes, *'A Bottle of Guinness Please': The Colourful History of Bottled Guinness* (London: Phimboy, 2006).
6. Hugh Oram, *The Advertising Book: The History of Advertising in Ireland* (Dublin: MO Books, 1986), p. 5. For modern Irish advertising see also Neil O'Boyle, 'Addressing Multiculturalism? Conservatism and Conformity; Access and Authenticity in Irish Advertising', in *Translocations: The Irish Migration, Race and Social Transformation Review*, vol. 1 (2006), pp. 95–120 and the same author's important monograph on the cultural significance of contemporary Irish advertising, *New Vocabularies, Old Ideas: Culture, Irishness and the Advertising Industry* (Oxford, Bern: Peter Lang, 2011).
7. Oram, *The Advertising Book*, p. 3; p. 6.
8. Kiberd, *Inventing Ireland*, p. 3.
9. [Thomas Hood], 'The Advertisement Literature of the Age', *New Monthly Magazine*, vol. 63 (January 1843), p. 111.
10. Jean Baudrillard, *The System of Objects*, tr. James Benedict (London: Verso, 1996), p. 178.
11. James Joyce, *Ulysses*, ed. Hans Walter Gabler (New York, NY: Vintage, 1993), p. 592.
12. Garry M. Leonard, *Advertising and Commodity Culture in Joyce* (Gainesville, FL: University Press of Florida, 1998), p. 1.
13. Jean-Michel Rabaté, 'Modernism and "the Plain Reader's Rights": Duff-Riding-Graves Re-Reading Joyce', *European Joyce Studies*, vol. 14, ed. John Nash (Amsterdam and New York, NY: Rodopi, 2002), p. 32.
14. Testimony to the importance of the subject in Joyce studies is the fact that Wicke contributed an essay on 'Joyce and Consumer Culture' to the second edition of a standard guide to the novelist's work, the *Cambridge Companion to James Joyce* (2004), edited by Derek Attridge.
15. A most welcome recent exception is Stephanie Rains's *Commodity Culture and Social Class in Dublin 1850–1916* (Dublin: Irish Academic Press, 2010). See also Rains's 'Here be Monsters: the Irish Industrial Exhibition of 1853 and the Growth of Dublin Department Stores', *Irish Studies Review*, vol. 16 (November 2008), pp. 487–506, and Joseph McBrinn's fine essay 'The 1904 *Feis na nGleann*: Craftwork, Folk Life and National Identity', *Folk Life*, vol. 45 (2007), pp. 24–39.

16. *Household Words*, no. 157 (26 March 1853), p. 85.
17. Books on these areas are in preparation by our colleagues in the Leverhulme Trust Major Research project 'Consumer Culture, Advertising and Literature in Ireland 1848–1921', Lauren Clark and Alison O'Malley-Younger.
18. John Francis Maguire, *The Industrial Movement in Ireland, as Illustrated by the National Exhibition* (Cork: John O'Brien, 1852), pp. 183–184.
19. Patrick Maume, *D. P. Moran* (Dundalk: Historical Association of Ireland, 1995), p. 13.
20. *The Irish Unionist Pocket Book* (Belfast and Dublin: Unionist Associations of Ireland, 1911), p. 95.
21. Paul L. Fortunato, 'Wildean Philosophy with a Needle and Thread: Consumer Fashion at the Origins of Modernist Aesthetics', *College Literature*, vol. 34 (2007), p. 39.
22. W. B. Yeats, *Essays and Introductions* (London and New York, NY: Macmillan, 1961), p. 526.
23. Gifford Lewis, *The Yeats Sisters and the Cuala* (Dublin: Irish Academic Press, 1994).
24. See p. 277, n.8.3 for bibliographical details. The most sustained examination of the specifically Irish angle of the posters used in Ireland is to be found in Nuala C. Johnson, *Ireland, the Great War and the Geography of Remembrance* (Cambridge: Cambridge University Press, 2003).
25. Maurice O'Connor Morris, *Memini or, Reminiscences of Irish Life* (London: Harrison and Sons, 1892), p. 394.

Prologue – The Irish Advertising Scene from the 1850s to the 1880s

1. *Irish Quarterly Review*, vol. 3 (September 1853), p. 765.
2. Ibid., p. 757.
3. Ibid.
4. 'The Irish Industrial Exhibition', *The Illustrated Magazine of Art*, vol. 2 (1853), p. 135.
5. 'And', the writer comments, 'through the patriotic endeavours of a single individual' (ibid.); that is, the efforts of the railway contractor William Dargan (1799–1867) who funded much of the exhibition.
6. *Irish Quarterly Review*, vol. 3 (September 1853), p. 762.
7. Ibid.
8. Thomas Richards, *The Commodity Culture of Victorian England: Advertising and Spectacle, 1851–1914* (Stanford, CA: Stanford University Press, 1990), p. 53.
9. Maguire, *The Industrial Movement in Ireland*, p. 8.
10. This led advertisers to use a range of untaxed alternatives: handbills, posters, sandwich men and so on. See John Strachan, *Advertising and Satirical Culture in the Romantic Period* (Cambridge: Cambridge University Press, 2007), pp. 18–24.
11. From 1797 onwards, newspaper advertisements were taxed at a flat rate of 3s per insertion regardless of length. The duty was increased in 1815 to 3s 6d and not reduced until 1833, when, after pressure from manufacturers and pressmen alike, it came down to 1s 6d.
12. *Hansard's Political Debates*, third series, vol. 125 (1853), p. 124.
13. Ibid., pp. 1125–1126. Less charitably, Mr Milner also argued that removing the stamp duty, which threatened to stifle the further development of mass market and other newspapers, would also facilitate a measure of social control, most

notably in what he considered to be the most lawless part of the kingdom, Ireland:

> There is one important consideration in this matter with regard to the circulation of newspapers, that in the places where they are freely circulated better order is maintained; and where the deficiency is most apparent, there disorder, outrage, ignorance, and lawless proceedings exist to a proportionate extent. In the country places in England, the deficiency, according to the above estimate, amounts to six and a half times the present supply; in the country places of Scotland, to ten times; and, in the country places in Ireland, to twenty-five times the present supply.
>
> (Ibid.)

14. T. R. Nevett, *Advertising in Britain: A History* (London: Heinemann on Behalf of the History of Advertising Trust, 1982), p. 67.
15. Frank Presbrey, *The History and Development of Advertising* (New York, NY: Doubleday, 1929), p. 90. This is not to say that throughout the whole of the nineteenth century the Irish press was not inextricably linked with advertising. That venerable organ the *Freeman's Journal* began life as the *Freeman's Journal and Daily Commercial Advertiser* in 1806 and the paper was not alone in foregrounding its nature as an advertising medium in its title. The *Dublin Mercantile Advertiser*, founded in 1818, also prospered, and outside of the capital, provincial towns and cities boasted newspapers keen for the advertising shilling, among them the *Belfast Mercantile Journal and Weekly Advertiser* (1807–1852; the paper then became the *Mercantile Journal and Statistical Register* (1852–1893)), the *Clare Journal and Ennis Advertiser* (1776–1917), the *Cork Advertising Gazette* (established 1856, before being incorporated with the *Cork Herald* in 1859), the *Enniscorthy News and County of Wexford Advertiser* (1861–1896), the *Kilkenny Journal and Leinster Commercial and Literary Advertiser* (1830–1922) and the *Western Star and Ballinasloe Advertiser* (1845-1902).
16. *Dublin Advertising Gazette*, 18 August 1858.
17. Ibid.
18. *The Gael*, 1903, p. 222.
19. Published 21 April 1858 to 31 March 1877, after which it merged with the *Commercial Journal*.
20. This publication, originally simply entitled the *Weekly Advertiser*, was, as a front-page banner proudly announced, 'GRATIS!' Its founding editor was John Warren, of Upper Ormond Quay, who was also a general printer as well as a publisher (he advertised this side of his business by promising 'PROMPTITUDE and NEATNESS, with MODERATE CHARGES'). The journal featured advertisements for British as well as Irish goods; Warren employed an English agent, the memorably named Mr W. E. Life, to bring advertising in from Great Britain. Testimony to quite how high the late duty had been were Warren's prices: the first three lines of each advertisement cost one shilling per insertion, with every additional line tuppence (with 'display' – illustrated advertisements – 1s and 6d per column inch). His principal innovation in Dublin advertising freesheets was the *Weekly Advertiser*'s attempt to tempt readers in by featuring a wider range of reading material alongside the paid messages. As well as its many advertisements, the paper also featured poetry, short stories and whimsy, and clippings from both English and American newspapers.
21. Journals such as the *Gazette* promoted their interests in boastful advertisements of their own. In a puff published in the *Literary and Educational Yearbook for 1859*

(1858), the *Dublin Advertising Gazette* ('Proprietors Chamney and Co., 86 Middle Abbey Street, Dublin') described itself as 'the best Irish medium for all kinds of Advertisements', claiming a circulation of some 14,000. In the following year, however, it proclaimed even greater market penetration. On 25 August 1859, an excited banner in small caps for the *Gazette* boasted of its 'GUARANTEED CIRCULATION, TWENTY FOUR THOUSAND, GRATIS!!!' Indeed, because the newspaper was distributed in Dublin before being collected and sent out to the counties (being 'posted to a large number of the Nobility, Gentry and Public Institutions in the Provinces' (25 March 1863), the *Gazette* optimistically claimed a circulation of nigh on 50,000, announcing in 1860 that as it 'was published on Wednesday and recollected on Fridays'; thus 'every copy will have a *double circulation*!' (*Dublin Advertising Gazette*, 22 June). This is not quite *News of the World* levels of circulation (the mass-market paper was selling north of 500,000 copies at this point in time), but, if anywhere near true, was still highly respectable, given that the most notable London newspaper, *The Times*, sold around 60,000 copies per day at the time.

22. This periodical was incorporated into the *Cork Herald* in 1859.
23. *The Literary and Educational Year Book for 1859* (London: Kent and Co., 1858), p. 289.
24. Advertisement in the *Irish Weekly Advertiser*, 10 June 1863.
25. *Irish Weekly Advertiser*, 10 June 1863.
26. In the 1902 *Belfast Directory* for instance.
27. *Irish Weekly Advertiser*, 10 June 1863.
28. Every Dublin Wednesday in the late 1850s saw the production of both the *Gazette* and its principal rival before the establishment of the *Irish Weekly Advertiser*, the *General Advertiser*. A bitter rivalry developed between the long-established paper and the noisy upstart, which the *Gazette* itself described as 'the present war of the Advertisers' (*Irish Advertising Gazette*, 15 September 1858). Certainly the two journals exchanged many antipathetic jibes. An 1859 banner to the *General Advertiser*, for instance, tartly pointed out that it was 'Published Every Wednesday. Delivered Gratis and Left Permanently' ('unlike the *Gazette*' being the unspoken implication). In return, the *Gazette* crowed about its circulation, dismissing its rival as only being capable of distributing a paltry 8000 copies per week and publishing letters from their printers supposedly guaranteeing a circulation more than three times that of the competitor ('the Proprietors of the *General Advertiser* having challenged us to produce the evidence of those respectable gentlemen'): 'We have written to those gentlemen on the subject, and the following is their reply, which is conclusive as to our circulation:

    Steam Printing Office, 23 Bachelor Walk, Dublin, 30th October, 1858.

    Messrs. CHAMNEY & Co., Dear Sirs, – We are in receipt of your note, requesting us to state the number of copies of your ADVERTISING GAZETTE printed at our steam presses. Regarding the statement that the General Advertiser has a larger circulation than your ADVERTISING GAZETTE, in justice to you we must say that is not the fact, as we print a far greater number of your paper than the Local Advertiser [...] We have supplied you with paper for the DUBLIN ADVERTISING GAZETTE since its establishment, and can testify that your average weekly consumption has exceeded 14,000 sheets.

    WM. & EDWARD BYAN. August 21st, 1858'.

The *Gazette* adds 'As 12,000 of these sheets are sent to the country, it is evident that our circulation is fully 26,000, the largest in Ireland' (*The Literary and Educational Year Book for 1859*, p. 289).

29. *Dublin Advertising Gazette*, 18 August 1858.
30. Joyce, *Ulysses*, 1993, p. 93.
31. Ibid.
32. We derive this information principally from the 1852 edition of *Thom's Directory*.
33. However, Johnston's soon found themselves with competition near at hand. The son of one of the original co-owners, Captain Johnston, also called Alexander, when relieved of control of his family's company, promptly established 'Alexander Johnston and Co., Express Newspaper and General Advertising Office, No 34 Bachelor's Walk, Dublin'. In an advertisement cheekily placed on the very next page of the 1852 *Thom's Directory* after the puff for the original Johnston's Newspaper and Advertising Office, he offered 'the same course of zealous exertions in the executing of the Orders of his Patrons, which have been so long pursued by his late father':

    > Alexander Johnston respectfully reminds the Press and the Public of the vast outlay of Capital and Labour which the members of his family expended in bringing to perfection the system of Newspaper and Advertising Agency, which was *founded* in 1819 in this Country by his late father, Captain Johnston, and trusts that the patronage extended over a period of Thirty-two years will still be continued to him as the survivor. He hopes it is unnecessary that he should refer more particularly to any peculiar claims he may have upon the Irish public.

34. Space precludes discussion of these agencies.
35. Successful Dublin vade mecums most notably.
36. For instance James Stevens's *Arthur Griffith, Journalist and Statesman* (1922) and *Dublin and the Sinn Fein Rising* (1916; see p. 205 and p. 280, n. 8.37).
37. The company has a footnote in Irish history as a target for James Larkin's band of union militants in its 1913 quarrel with William Martin Murphy, the proprietor of the *Irish Independent*, which Eason's distributed. See F. S. L. Lyons's *Ireland Since the Famine* for Larkin's quarrel with Murphy, the *Independent* and the Dublin United Tramways: 'Larkin attempted to infiltrate the distribution department of the *Independent*. His men were promptly locked out. He then requested the principal newspaper distributors in the country – Eason's – not to circulate the *Independent*, and when they refused Larkin called a strike there too. Next, his dockers began to refuse to handle "tainted" goods, i.e. goods destined for Eason's' (Lyons, *Ireland Since the Famine* (London: Weidenfeld and Nicolson, 1971), p. 280).
38. Our information is derived from Parker's obituary notice, *Irish Independent*, 23 April 1945.
39. As Hugh Oram has pointed out, Parker and Co.'s first major account was for St Patrick's Hospital, a contract which the company held for over a hundred years (Oram, *The Advertising Book*, p. 13).
40. 'Tell Stannie to go to Eason's in Abbey St where I ordered and paid for a certain quantity of paper, and tell them to forward it to me. They will do this if the carriage is paid. I forgot it in the hurry of going away' (*Selected Letters of James Joyce*, ed. Richard Ellmann (New York, NY: Viking Press, 1975), p. 9). Though Joyce had patronised Eason's in the early twentieth century, it might be pointed out the company did not care to stock his work in their stores in the days of *Saorstát*

Éireann; Eason's son, himself Charles, wrote to George Russell in 1926 that 'As to James Joyce, I need not tell you we have not got his *Ulysses*, nor have we got any other work of his' (Quoted in Donal Ó Drisceoil, 'A Dark Chapter: Censorship and the Irish Writer', in *The Oxford History of the Irish Book, Volume V: The Irish Book in English, 1891–2000*, eds Claire Hutton and Patrick Walsh (Oxford: Oxford University Press, 2011), p. 289).

41. Joyce, *Ulysses*, 1993, p. 148. Hely's address here is as fictional as the copy itself. The company was actually based at 27-30 Dame Street.
42. See Oram, *The Advertising Book*, p. 31.
43. See Chapter 2 for *The Leader*. Professor Colum Kenny, in his fascinating study of his grandfather's career, writes that 'during 1901 Kevin became the advertising manager of a vibrant new nationalist publication called *The Leader*' (Colum Kenny, *Irish Patriot, Publisher and Advertising Agent: Kevin J. Kenny (1881–1954)* (Ox Pictures: Bray, Co. Wicklow, 2011, p. 10).
44. For the Irish Industrial Development Association (IIDA), see pp. 44–46; for Kenny and the IIDA see p. 239.
45. Kenny, *Irish Patriot*, p. 22. Also see p. 27 for the Sinn Féin aonachs. Kenny and Co. were also willing to serve both advanced nationalist and imperial masters; from 1910, the company handled the account for recruitment advertising for the Royal Irish Constabulary (RIC) and, from 1914, Kenny acquired part of the account for the British Army's recruitment drive in Ireland at the beginning of the Great War (see Kenny, *Irish Patriot*, p. 30 for the RIC, and pp. 46–58 for full discussion of the controversies which his work for the Department of Recruiting in Ireland created in nationalist circles).
46. These were James Dignam, Abbey Street; James T. Jameson and Co., Cope Street; Kevin J. Kenny, Middle Abbey Street; Ernest Manico and Co., D'Olier Street; F. B. O'Keeffe, St Andrew Street; Wilson, Hartnell and Co., Commercial Buildings; S. H. Benson, Middle Abbey Street; Eason and Sons, Middle Abbey Street; L. J. Lynch, Nassau Street; J. H. Parker and Co., Dame Street; J. A. Raynor; Mullin and Mullen; Munro and Connolly; and the Reliance Advertising Co.
47. *Dublin Advertising Gazette*, 22 December 1859.
48. *Irish Weekly Advertiser*, 10 June 1863.
49. *Dublin Advertising Gazette*, 25 August 1859.
50. Brian Friel, *The London Vertigo* (Co. Meath: Gallery, 1990), p. 26.
51. *Weekly Advertiser*, 4 March 1863. 'Who can take up a newspaper just now, without being tempted to become an extensive purchaser of real and pure French Colza oil?' asked Dickens's *Household Words* in 1853 (vol. 7 (1853) p. 115).
52. *Irish Quarterly Review*, vol. 3 (September 1853), p. 782.
53. Rains, 'Here be Monsters', p. 493.
54. According to Mairead Dunlevy's *Dress in Ireland* (1989) 'in 1851 [Hyam's] succeeded Moses & Co. at 30 Dame Street, Dublin' (Mairead Dunlevy, *Dress in Ireland* (Cork: Collins Press, 1989), p. 149). The company traded in the same premises until 1923.
55. See Strachan, *Advertising and Satirical Culture*, pp. 125–137.
56. As E. S. Turner once wrote (in *The Shocking History of Advertising!* (London: Michael Joseph, 1952), p. 55).
57. Warren's most famous puff, which dates from the 1810s, shows an illustration (by no less a figure than the great late Georgian satirist George Cruikshank) of a cat spitting at a boot, alarmed at her own reflection in the boot, which is polished to mirror-like lustre by Warren's Matchless Blacking and which she takes for a feline

rival. This image is accompanied by thirty-six lines of jovial verse copy, which begin thus:

> As I one morning shaving sat.
> For dinner-time preparing,
> A dreadful howling from the cat
> Set all the room a staring!
> Suddenly I turn'd – beheld a scene
> I could not but delight in!
> For in my boot, so bright and keen
> The Cat her face was fighting!

See the discussion in Strachan, *Advertising and Satirical Culture*, pp. 1–2.

58. In Hyam's secularising account, the season of Easter is a time to act as a consumer rather than a religious devotee. Given the historical importance of the festival in Ireland, and especially in Catholic Ireland, the references to the season in the context of dressing up one's little darlings in their Hyam's finery might have seemed irreverent, indeed to some even blasphemous.
59. *Irish Weekly Advertiser*, 29 April 1863.
60. Jameson's then Protestant-owned company was sometimes accused of sectarianism by advanced nationalists, and at least once on account of an advert. An announcement in the *Irish Times* for 20 July 1904 reads thus: 'Wanted. A Good energetic Estates Carpenter, Protestant; must be thoroughly acquainted with house, also garden, work, painting, glazing, and so on; to live in bothy, with young gardeners. Apply, with references, stating wages, to J. McKellar, St Marnocks, Portmarnock, Co, Dublin'. This Mr McKellar was an employee of none other than John Jameson, scion of the whiskey family, and on the 30th, that indefatigable nationalist journal *The Leader* pounced, in a leading column:

> Now John does not stipulate that none but 'saved' should drink his whiskey – all are free to drink that. Consider this man who has grown rich on a commodity that has in part been such a curse to Ireland, that has broken up so many homes and ruined so many lives – consider this man stipulating that his estate carpenter must be saved.
>
> (*The Leader*, vol. 8 (30 July 1904), p. 365)

Moran, or a like-minded colleague, adds sarcastically that 'John J. should now address a meeting on the evils of sectarian animosity'.

61. Thomas Hood, 'The Art of Advertizing Made Easy', *London Magazine and Review*, new series, vol. 1 (February 1825), p. 246.
62. This advertisement was published in the *Irish Weekly Advertiser* on 27 April 1863.
63. The methods pioneered by empirics or 'quacks' are hugely important to the development of modern advertising: as Frank Presbrey has written, 'They nursed mediums. They developed copy and mechanics. They tested and determined the value of position in the newspapers.' (Presbrey, *The History and Development of Advertising*, p. 300.)
64. *Weekly Advertiser*, 11 March 1863.
65. See Roy Porter, *Quacks, Fakers and Charlatans in English Medicine* (Stroud: Tempus Publishing, 2000).
66. *Medical Times and Gazette*, 4 October 1862, p. 371.
67. Ibid.

68. A May 1864 insertion of this advertisement has the following similar notice underneath it in the 'Medical' section: 'Dr Smith has just published a FREE EDITION of 20,000 copies of his valuable work THE PRIVATE MEDICAL FRIEND (116 pages) on the Self Cure of Nervous Debility, Loss of Memory, Dimness of Sight, Lassitude, resulting from the secret sins of youth'. 'The Private Medical Friend', predictably, directed readers to cures manufactured by Smith himself.

1 Advertising and the Nation in the Irish Revival

1. *The Shan Van Vocht*, vol. 2 (1897), p. 62.
2. Ibid.
3. D. P. Moran, *The Philosophy of Irish Ireland* (Dublin: James Duffy, 1905), p. 1.
4. James Joyce, *Dubliners*, ed. Terence Brown (London: Penguin, 1992), p. 135.
5. Leonard, *Advertising and Commodity Culture in Joyce* (Gainesville, FL: University Press of Florida, 1998), p. 136.
6. Jason K. Knirck, *Imagining Ireland's Independence* (Lanham, MD: Rowman & Littlefield, 2006), p. 12.
7. *Independent Review*, vol. 7 (1906), p. 309.
8. Whelan and Son of Ormond Quay are the most sustained example discussed in this book (see Chapter 3).
9. *The Leader*, 5 December 1903.
10. Manufactured by Metcalfe's, who also made the splendidly named 'My Pretty Doves' Cigarettes.
11. 'To Gain the Confidence of our Customers', the company declared, 'We send Goods on Approval'.
12. And – presumably not Irish-grown – 'Pure Sugar'.
13. This was made by John Shuley and Co., the 'Irish Colour Printers'. Alongside the 'Gaelic', the company also sold 'Celtic', 'Irish Parchment' and 'Grattan' wrapping paper, all, somewhat conservatively, only available in brown.
14. An advertisement found on the first page of the 23 April issue of *An Claidheamh Soluis*.
15. Joyce, *Ulysses* (1993), p. 93.
16. In W. P. Ryan's *Caoimhghín Ó Cearnaigh* (1913). Cited in Philip O'Leary, *The Prose Literature of the Gaelic Revival, 1881–1921: Ideology and Innovation* (University Park, PA: Pennsylvania State University Press, 1994), p. 438.
17. *The Leader*, 3 October 1903.
18. *The Leader*, 15 October 1904.
19. Douglas Hyde, *Language, Lore, and Lyrics: Essays and Lectures*, ed. Breandán Ó Conaire (Dublin: Irish Academic Press, 1986), p. 157.
20. E. J. Riordan, *Modern Irish Trade and Industry* (London: Methuen and Co., 1920), pp. 312–313.
21. *The Leader*, 20 February 1904.
22. Riordan, *Modern Irish Trade and Industry*, p. 311.
23. Ibid., p. 277.
24. Ibid., p. 315.
25. One is reminded of the oration of Flann O'Brien's indefatigable Irish language purist in that great satire *The Poor Mouth* (1941):

    > Gaels, he said, it delights my Gaelic heart to be here today speaking Gaelic with you at this Gaelic feis in the centre of the Gaeltacht. May I state that

> I am a Gael. I'm Gaelic from the crown of my head to the soles of my feet [...] If we're truly Gaelic, we must constantly discuss the question of the Gaelic revival and the question of Gaelicism. There is no use in having Gaelic, if we converse in it on non-Gaelic topics. He who speaks Gaelic but fails to discuss the language question is not truly Gaelic in his heart; such conduct is of no benefit to Gaelicism because he only jeers at Gaelic and reviles the Gaels. There is nothing in this life so nice and so Gaelic as truly true Gaelic Gaels who speak in true Gaelic Gaelic about the truly Gaelic language.
>
> *The Poor Mouth*, tr. Patrick C. Power (London: Grafton Books, 1973), pp. 54–55.

26. See Joseph McBrinn, 'The *Feis na nGleann*: Craftwork, Folk Life and National Identity', in *Folk Life*, vol. 45 (2007), pp. 24–39.
27. One hundred and eight, according to the *Freeman's Journal* of 26 April 1910.
28. Quoted above with reference to the Irish Exhibition. *Irish Quarterly Review*, vol. 3 (September 1853), p. 767.
29. For Cuffe's subsequent development of the Kilkenny Woollen Mills, see Timothy G. McMahon, *Grand Opportunity: The Gaelic Revival and Irish Society, 1893–1910* (Syracuse, NY: Syracuse University Press, 2008), pp. 147–148.
30. *Freeman's Journal*, 28 October 1910.
31. For Ishbel, Countess of Aberdeen (1847–1939), see Janice Helland, *British and Irish Home Arts and Industries 1880–1914: Marketing Craft, Making Fashion* (Dublin: Irish Academic Press, 2007), pp. 44–61.
32. *The Leader*, 1 September 1905; also quoted in Conor Cruise O'Brien, *The Shaping of Modern Ireland* (London: Routledge and Kegan Paul, 1960), p. 113.
33. *Freeman's Journal*, 22 August 1908.
34. Quoted in McMahon, *Grand Opportunity*, p. 250.
35. This advertisement is also quoted in Dermot Keogh's *Jews in Twentieth-Century Ireland: Refugees, Anti-Semitism and the Holocaust* (Cork: Cork University Press, 1998), p. 54.
36. See p. 233 of this book.
37. Both the Drumcliffe Creamery and the Sligo Manufacturing Society eventually applied for and received the Irish trade mark.
38. Jacqueline Van Voris, *Constance de Markievicz: In the Cause of Ireland* (Amherst, MA: University of Massachusetts Press, 1967), p. 50.
39. *Celtic Review* (1905), p. 349.
40. *Anglo-Celt*, 28 December 1901.
41. *Irish Independent*, 5 April 1939.
42. This exhibition was subsequently also taken to New York. See the *Handbook and Catalogue of Exhibits Compiled and Issued by the Department of Agriculture and Technical Instruction for Ireland* (Dublin: The Department of Agriculture and Technical Instruction for Ireland, 1904).
43. Ibid.
44. Hyde, *Language, Lore, and Lyrics*, p. 189.

2 *The Shan Van Vocht* (1896–1899) and *The Leader* (1900–1936): National Identity in Advertising

1. Maud Gonne, *A Servant of the Queen: Reminiscences*, eds A. Norman Jeffares and Anna MacBride White (Gerrards Cross: Colin Smythe, 1994), p. 176.

2. Tom Clyde, *Irish Literary Magazines* (Dublin: Irish Academic Press, 2003), p. 143.
3. See W. S. Merwin, 'The Old Woman of Beare', *The Hudson Review*, vol. 4, no. 4 (1952), pp. 540–543. Merwin sees the date of that poem as 'uncertain, probably the late tenth or else eleventh century' (p. 540).
4. Richard Harp, 'The *Shan Van Vocht* (Belfast, 1896–1899) and Irish Nationalism', *Eire-Ireland*, vol. 24, no. 3 (1989), pp. 42–52, p. 43.
5. Virginia E. Glandon, 'The Irish Press and Revolutionary Nationalism', *Eire-Ireland*, vol. 16, no. 1 (1981), pp. 21–33, p. 24. Milligan and Johnston's endeavours marked something of a departure from traditional Irish newspaper practices. In Marie Louise Legg's account, 'Newspapers were seemingly founded and run by anonymous people – almost all of them men'. See *Newspapers and Nationalism: The Irish Provincial Press 1850–1892* (Dublin: Four Courts, 1999), p. 13. Another exception to this general rule is Maud Gonne's journal, *L'Irelande Libre* (1897–1898).
6. *The Shan Van Vocht*, March 1899, p. 53.
7. *The Shan Van Vocht*, May 1896, p. 87.
8. *The Shan Van Vocht*, November 1897, p. 211.
9. *The Shan Van Vocht*, June 1898, p. 116.
10. L. Perry Curtis Jr, *Images of Erin in the Age of Parnell* (Dublin: National Library of Ireland, 2000), p. 11.
11. Ibid.
12. Ibid., p. 13.
13. See Susan Cannon Harris, *Gender and Modern Irish Drama* (Bloomington, IN: Indiana University Press, 2002), pp. 47–48 for further discussion of this issue.
14. Anne McClintock, *Imperial Leather: Race, Gender and Sexuality in the Colonial Contest* (New York, NY: Routledge, 1995), p. 354.
15. *The Shan Van Vocht*, October 1897, p. 192.
16. Virginia Crossman, 'The *Shan Van Vocht*: Women, Republicanism, and the Commemoration of the 1798 Rebellion', *Eighteenth-Century Life*, vol. 22 (1998), p. 134.
17. *The Shan Van Vocht*, November 1898, p. 207.
18. Karen Steele, *Women, Press, and Politics During the Irish Revival* (Syracuse, NY: Syracuse University Press, 2007), p. 19.
19. Karen Steele, *Women, Press, and Politics*, p. 32.
20. *The Shan Van Vocht*, July, 1898, p. 131.
21. Declan Kiberd's position is that the question should be 'whose revival? There was certainly no great change in the conditions of the Dublin poor in the early decades of the century'. See 'The Perils of Nostalgia: A Critique of the Revival', *Literature and the Changing Ireland*, ed. Peter Connolly (Gerrards Cross: Colin Smythe, 1982), p. 3.
22. *The Shan Van Vocht*, December 1898, p. 236.
23. *The Shan Van Vocht*, June 1897, back page.
24. Karen Steele, 'Editing Out Factionalism: The Political and Literary Consequences in Ireland's "Shan Van Vocht" ', *Victorian Periodicals Review*, vol. 35, no. 2 (2002), p. 115.
25. Advertisement for Abraham Neill, *The Shan Van Vocht*, February 1896, p. 40; advertisement for Andrew Maguire and J. Shone & Co., *The Shan Van Vocht*, February 1896, p. 39; advertisement for John Magee & Co., *The Shan Van Vocht*, April 1898, p. 75.
26. *The Shan Van Vocht*, December 1898, p. 236.

27. Steele, *Women, Press and Politics*, p. 55.
28. Crossman, '*The Shan Van Vocht*', p. 131.
29. Declan Kiberd, *Irish Classics* (London: Granta, 2000), pp. 225–226.
30. See Crossman, 'The *Shan Van Vocht*', p. 132; Steele, 'Editing out Factionalism', p. 123; Catherine Morris, 'Becoming Irish? Alice Milligan and the Revival', *Irish University Review*, vol. 33, no. 1 (2003), pp. 79–98, p. 93. Richard Kirkland, in 'Dialogues of Despair: Nationalist Cultural Discourse and the Revival in the North of Ireland, 1900–1920' (2003) remarks that the Revival 'developed from a number of more-or-less semi-autonomous coteries and creative intimacies across Ireland and, indeed, the USA and Britain. This heterogeneity has often been overlooked and yet without its recognition it is difficult to decode many of the later tensions implicit to the movement or, of course, the manner in which it would eventually collapse' (*Irish University Review*, vol. 33, no. 1 (2003), p. 70).
31. Steele, *Women, Press and Politics*, p. 33.
32. Crossman, 'The *Shan Van Vocht*', p. 132.
33. Patrick Maume writes [private correspondence] 'Ingram did not expressly disavow "The Memory of the Dead" in later life, though he considered himself an Unionist. He published the following clarification in his *Sonnets and Other Poems* (1900):

    > I have been requested to publish the following note on "The Memory of the Dead": The poem entitled "The Memory of the Dead" was published in the *Nation* newspaper in April 1843 when I was in my twentieth year [...] Some persons have believed, or affected to believe, that I am ashamed of having written it, and would gladly, if I could, disown its authorship. Those who know me do not need to told that this idea is without foundation. I think the Irish race should be grateful to men who, in evil times, however mistaken may have been their policy, gave their lives for their country. But I have no sympathy with those who preach sedition in our own day, when all the circumstances are radically altered. In my opinion no real popular interest can now be furthered by violence.'

34. Timothy J. O'Keefe, 'The 1898 Efforts to Celebrate the United Irishmen: The '98 Centennial', *Eire-Ireland*, vol. 23, no. 2 (1992), p. 54.
35. Ibid., p. 56.
36. Ibid., p. 59.
37. Ibid., p. 60. Patrick Maume points out that Milligan's remark about the 1798 commemorations being used for a Redmondite–Healyite alliance is quite correct; the two smaller parliamentary groups were trying to unite for self-preservation against the larger Dillonite faction and its new organisation the United Irish League, although it was well known that Tim Healy had been a much more vicious opponent of Redmond's mentor Parnell than John Dillon had.
38. *The Shan Van Vocht*, April 1897.
39. *Irish Weekly Independent*, 21 December 1895, cited in Morris, 'Becoming Irish?', p. 91.
40. Crossman, 'The *Shan Van Vocht*', p. 132. See also Steele, 'Editing out Factionalism', p. 123.
41. Timothy J. O'Keefe, '"Who Fears to Speak of '98?": The Rhetoric and Rituals of the United Irishmen Centennial, 1898', *Eire-Ireland*, vol. 27, no. 3 (1992), p. 68.
42. Ibid., p. 73.
43. Of course, this memorialisation is central to many European nationalisms, Benedict Anderson has argued that the tombs of national heroes (even if symbolic, as in the tombs of unknown soldiers), are filled with 'ghostly national

imaginings' which 'transform fatality into continuity, contingency into meaning... If nation-states are widely conceded to be "new" and "historical", the nations to which they give political expression always loom out of an immemorial past.' (Anderson, *Imagined Communities: Reflections on the Origin and Spread of Nationalism* (London: Verso, 1991, rev. ed.), pp. 10–11.)

44. This reiterative impulse was, later, the foundation of Patrick Pearse's famous 1915 speech at the graveside of the Fenian O'Donovan Rossa: 'Life springs from death; and from the graves of patriot men and women spring living nations [...] The English are fools [...] they have left us our Fenian dead, and while Ireland holds these graves, Ireland unfree shall never be at peace.' Indeed, Pearse's Proclamation of the Irish Republic refers to the 'dead generations' who cry out for revolution, and commemorative mourning is seen to be a gesture of national defiance.
45. *The Shan Van Vocht*, June 1898, p. 116.
46. *The Shan Van Vocht*, November 1898, p. 216.
47. *The Shan Van Vocht*, December 1898, p. 236. The adjectival appellation 'chaste', with its specifically sexual and moral judgement, conforms to contemporaneous nationalist notions of legitimate femininity.
48. Joyce, *Dubliners*, p. 187.
49. O'Keefe, 'Who Fears to Speak of '98?', p. 74.
50. *The Shan Van Vocht*, 6 March 1896, p. 49. The Donegal writer MacManus was later to marry Anna Johnston.
51. *The Shan Van Vocht*, November 1897, p. 211.
52. Douglas Hyde, 'The Necessity for De-Anglicising Ireland', in *The Politics of Language in Ireland 1366–1922: A Sourcebook*, ed. Tony Crowley (London: Routledge, 2000), p. 183.
53. *The Shan Van Vocht*, April 1896, p. 68.
54. *The Shan Van Vocht*, December 1898, p. 236.
55. Steele, *Women, Press, and Politics*, p. 32.
56. Ibid.
57. *The Shan Van Vocht*, August 1897, p. 139.
58. Glandon, 'The Irish Press', p. 24.
59. Maume, *D. P. Moran* (Dundalk: Historical Association of Ireland, 1995), p. 13. For Kenny, see p. 27 above.
60. See Chapter 8 of this book.
61. Maume, *D. P. Moran*, p. 39.
62. *The Leader*, 1 September 1900, p. 5.
63. For further discussion of this issue, see Claire Nally, *Envisioning Ireland: Occult Nationalism in the Work of W. B. Yeats* (Oxford: Peter Lang, 2009), pp. 55–62.
64. *The Leader*, May 1906, pp. 174–175.
65. *The Leader* explicitly rejected the notion that it was a 'Catholic paper':

> This is not a Catholic paper, for we are not theologians and have not the training or ability to conduct a Catholic paper. But when we look out on Ireland we see that those who believe, or may be immediately induced to believe, in Ireland as a nation are, as a matter of fact, Catholics [...] We have ample evidence during the last few months for believing that in the main non-Catholic Ireland looks upon itself as British and anti-Irish.

The Leader, July 27, 1901, p. 843. Nonetheless, as Patrick Maume points out, Moran's statement that the *Leader* was not strictly speaking a Catholic paper was probably not prompted by a desire to distance himself from Catholicism; rather it reflected the fact that under Catholic Canon Law as it then stood any paper calling itself a 'Catholic paper' would have to get the diocesan bishop's permission to do so and submit its contents for ecclesiastical approval.

66. *The Leader*, 29 October 1921, p. 272.
67. *The Leader*, 21 February 1920, p. 381, and *The Leader*, 15 May 1920, p. 657.
68. *The Leader*, 21 February 1920, p. 363, 'Maynooth Mission to China' St. Columban's College, Dalgan Park, Galway. Also, 'Convent of the Sacred Heart, Mount Anville, Dundrum, Nr Dublin. A Retreat for Ladies will be given by the Rev. E. Downing S. J., beginning July 19th, ending July 24th. For particulars apply to the Reverend Mother Superior.' *The Leader*, 10 January 1920, p. 235, has a full-page advertisement for 'Candlemas and Altar Wax Candles' which are 'sanctioned by the hierarchy' and manufactured by John G. Rathborne, Ltd, 203 Parnell Street, Dublin. Rathborne carried the Irish trade mark in many of his advertisements.
69. *The Leader*,12 June 1920, p. 68.
70. *The Leader*, 16 October 1920, p. 197.
71. *The New Leader*, 6 December 1919, p. 74.
72. Lisa Godson, 'Catholicism and Material Culture in Ireland 1840–1880', *Circa*, 103 (2003), p, 40. See also Luke Gibbons, *Transformations in Irish Culture* (Cork: Cork University Press, 1996), p. 86 for details of the 'devotional revolution'.
73. *The Leader*, 15 October 1904, p. 125.
74. *The Leader*, 8 October 1904, p. 111.
75. *The Leader*, 2 July 1904, p. 302.
76. *The New Leader*, 6 December 1919, p. 92.
77. D. P. Moran, *The Philosophy of Irish Ireland* (Dublin: James Duffy & Co., 1905), p. 8.
78. Moran, *The Philosophy of Irish Ireland*, p. 40.
79. *The Leader*, 9 February 1901, p. 358.
80. Moran, *The Philosophy of Irish Ireland*, p. 4.
81. Ibid., p. 13.
82. Ibid.
83. Ibid., p. 17.
84. Ibid., p. 111.
85. Maume, *D. P. Moran*, p. 9. See also *The Leader*, 16 July 1904, for a cartoon showing a personified male Ireland wrestling with the snake of anglicisation.
86. *An Claidheamh Soluis*, 8 April 1899, p. 57.
87. *An Claidheamh Soluis*, 19 July 1902, p. 331.
88. In his commentary on *Ulysses*, Declan Kiberd, writing of the *Cyclops* episode and of what he saw as the compromised hypermasculinity therein, maintains that 'The Citizen denounces British violence, but re-enacts it in his Irish nationalist brutality towards Bloom' (p. 1059). The Citizen is, of course, modelled on Michael Cusack, founder of the Gaelic Athletic Association (1884) (see Chapter 3).
89. The west of Ireland, according to Deane, was a 'place that was not yet subject to the effects of administrative, governmental rules and laws, and which therefore preserved among its population the national character in its pristine form, or at least, in such a state of preservation that the pristine form could be inferred from it. It was not only geographically distinct; it was historically precedent to the rest of the country which, especially in Dublin, had been reduced to

a colonized space of imperial administration.' (*Strange Country: Modernity and Nationhood in Irish Writing Since 1790* (Oxford: Oxford University Press, 1997), pp. 52–53.)

90. Interestingly, the pan-Celtic 'Sweet Afton cigarette' (*The Leader*, 20 August 1921, p. 37) shows a poetic vision of Celtic identity common in much tourist advertising today. Featuring a portrait of Robert Burns on each packet, with a rolling vista of hills and countryside, the advertisement explained 'Our Cigarettes are made on the World's latest machinery as installed in our factory at Dundalk'. This is a striking union of the rural and the industrial.
91. Moran, *The Philosophy of Irish Ireland*, p. 18.
92. *The New Leader*, 29 November 1919, p. 50.
93. *The Leader*, 16 July 1904, p. 348.
94. *The Leader*, 7 May 1904, p. 172. Thirty years later the same Belfast company was waving the Union flag. See p. 138.
95. *The Leader*, 21 May 1921, p. 322.
96. *The Leader*, 20 December 1919, p. 160.
97. Moran, *The Philosophy of Irish Ireland*, p. 16.
98. See also *The Leader*, 28 February 1920, p. 392, featuring an advertisement for McCabe's, the 'fish, poultry, game and ice merchants', which also displayed King George V's Royal Warrant.
99. Moran, *The Philosophy of Irish Ireland*, pp. 16–17.
100. Gladiator Soap also employed the recent war for emotive advertising: 'Peace on washing day by using Gladiator Soap. Made in Dublin.' See *The Leader*, 18 December 1920, p. 369.
101. Maume, *D. P. Moran*, p. 13.
102. See pp. 239–240.
103. See pp. 240–241.
104. *The Leader*, 20 August 1921, p. 31.
105. *The Leader*, 12 March 1921, p. 96.
106. George Bornstein, *Material Modernism: The Politics of the Page* (Cambridge: Cambridge University Press, 2001), p. 6.
107. Mathew D. Staunton, 'Types of Irishness: Irish Gaelic Typography and National Identity', in *The Book in Ireland*, p. 138. See also Simon J. Potter, 'Introduction: Empire, Propaganda and Public Opinion' in *Newspapers and Empire in Ireland and Britain: Reporting the British Empire c. 1857–1921* (Dublin: Four Courts, 2004), p. 11.
108. Simon Loxley, *Type: The Secret History of Letters* (London: I. B. Tauris, 2006), pp. 5–6.
109. See Niall Ó Ciosáin, 'Creating an Audience: Innovation and Reception in Irish Language Publishing, 1880–1920', in *The Irish Book in the Twentieth Century*, ed. Clare Hutton (Dublin: Irish Academic Press, 2004).
110. See Seamus Deane, *Strange Country: Modernity and Nationhood in Irish Writing Since 1790* (Oxford: Oxford University Press, 1997), pp. 106–107, on typefaces and national 'authenticity'. See also E. W. Lynam, *The Irish Character in Print: 1671–1923* (Shannon: Irish University Press, 1969).
111. Brian Ó Conchubhair, 'The Gaelic Front Controversy: The Gaelic League's (Post-Colonial) Crux', *Irish University Review*, vol. 33, no. 1 (2003), p. 47.
112. Ó Conchubhair, 'The Gaelic Front Controversy', p. 53.
113. Ibid., p. 58.

114. The Queen also commissioned Christopher Nugent, Lord Delvin, to compose a *Primer of the Irish Language* (c. 1584–1585). See *The Politics of Language in Ireland 1366–1922: A Sourcebook*, ed. Tony Crowley (London: Routledge, 2000), p. 18.
115. See Ó Conchubhair, 'The Gaelic Front Controversy', p. 54, for further discussion.
116. Ibid.
117. Ibid., p. 60.
118. *The Leader*, 29 August 1903, p. viii. Our thanks to Iarfhlaith Watson for his translations of the Irish text here and in subsequent examples in this section.
119. *The Leader*, 12 June 1920, p. 71.
120. *The Leader*, 23 January 1904, p. vii.
121. *The Leader*, 28 January 1905, p. 384.
122. *The Leader*, 26 March 1904, p. 78.
123. *The Leader*, 19 March 1921, p. 111.
124. *The Leader*, 17 December 1921, p. 469.

3 The Sinn Féin Depot and the Selling of Irish Sport

1. The Gaelic Athletic Association was founded in 1884 and – according to Paul Rouse – 'spooked by the arrival of the organisation, existing athletic clubs established the Irish Amateur Athletic Association' in the following year ('Michael Cusack: Sportsman and Journalist', in *The Gaelic Athletic Association 1884–2009*, eds Mike Cronin, William Murphy and Paul Rouse (Dublin and Portland, OR: Irish Academic Press, 2009), p. 54).
2. Some in the GAA, Michael Cusack most notably, considered the IAAA 'West British' and 'Anglomaniac'. Some in the IAAA, on the other hand, such as Dunbar's fellow cyclist Richard James Macredy of Trinity College, editor of the *Irish Cyclist*, had no time for what they saw as the political agenda of the 'Gaelic Union'.
3. Quoted in Rouse, 'Michael Cusack', p. 54, and in Joe Coyle, *Athletics in Drogheda 1861–2001* (Victoria, BC: Trafford Publishing, 2003), p. 190.
4. 9 April, 2 July and 1 October 1881. See Marcus de Búrca, 'The Gaelic Athletic Association and Organised Sport in Ireland', in *Sport in the Making of Celtic Cultures*, ed. Grant Jarvie (London and New York, NY: Leicester University Press, 1999), p. 104.
5. For the quarrel between Cusack and the GAA, see Rouse, 'Michael Cusack', pp. 54–55.
6. For the early history of cycling in Ireland, see Brian Griffin, *Cycling in Victorian Ireland* (Dublin: Nonsuch Publishing, 2006).
7. Both men were graduates of Trinity College and are buried at Glasnevin Cemetery in Dublin. A monument on the younger Dunbar's grave reads 'Erected by the Cyclists and Athletes of Ireland in Memory of a sterling sportsman, athlete and gentleman, John Leopold Dunbar, Official Handicapper, Irish Cyclists' Association and Editor of the *Irish Sportsman*, died 1st April 1891, aet. 34'.
8. Its immediate model was *The Field*, the successful journal established by the novelist and sporting journalist R. S. Surtees in 1853, a journal available in branches of W. H. Smith to this day. As Henry Fazakerley Wilkinson noted in the third edition of his *Modern Athletics* (originally published 1868), 'The *Irish Sportsman* is to Ireland what *The Field* is to England' (*Modern Athletics* (London: The Field, 1877), p. 119).
9. *The Irish Law Times and Solicitors' Journal*, vol. 12 (1878), p. 81.

10. Fazakerley Wilkinson, *Modern Athletics*, p. 119. As late as 1886, the *Sportsman* was advertising itself by virtue of its advertising reach: 'The "Irish Sportsman" circulates most extensively through England, Ireland and the Colonies, and is a valuable medium for all advertising purposes.'
11. Richard Holt, *Sport and the British* (Oxford: Oxford University Press, 1989), p. 240.
12. Quoted in Rouse, 'Michael Cusack', p. 54, and W. F. Mandle, 'The I.R.B. and the Beginnings of the Gaelic Athletic Association', *Irish Historical Studies*, vol. 20, no. 80 (September 1977), p. 426.
13. *Sinn Féin*, 29 September 1906.
14. For the Irish Republican Brotherhood and the GAA, see Mandle, 'The I.R.B. and the Beginnings of the Gaelic Athletic Association', and William Murphy, 'The GAA during the Irish Revolution, 1913–23', in *The Gaelic Athletic Association 1884–2009*, eds Mike Cronin, William Murphy and Paul Rouse (Dublin and Portland, OR: Irish Academic Press, 2009), pp. 62–63.
15. *The Leader*, 13 February 1904, p. 418. Historians concerned with the GAA have frequently agreed with this line. Barrie Houlihan, for instance, has argued that 'The Gaelic Athletic Association . . . played a central role in stimulating cultural . . . resistance to Britain' (*Sport, Policy, and Politics: A Comparative Analysis* (London and New York, NY: Routledge, 1997), p. 41).
16. For the history of the GAA, see Marcus de Búrca, *The GAA: A History*, second edition (Dublin: Gill and Macmillan, 1999), Mike Cronin, *Sport and Nationalism in Ireland: Gaelic Games, Soccer and Irish Identity Since 1884* (Dublin: Four Courts, 1999), Cronin, Murphy and Rouse, eds, *The Gaelic Athletic Association 1884–2009*, Paul Healy, *Gaelic Games and the Gaelic Athletic Association* (Cork: Mercier Press, 1998), and W. F. Mandle, *The Gaelic Athletic Association and Irish Nationalist Politics, 1884–1924* (Dublin: Gill and Macmillan, 1987).
17. Rouse, 'Michael Cusack', p. 53.
18. James Joyce, *A Portrait of the Artist as a Young Man*, ed. Chester G. Anderson (Harmondsworth: Penguin, 1977), p. 202.
19. See pp. 44–45.
20. Joyce, *Ulysses* (1993), p. 251.
21. For examples of publicity material for Sinn Féin, see the database of historical Irish advertising to be found at ccalireland.com, the website of the Leverhulme project 'Consumer Culture, Advertising and Literature in Ireland 1848–1921'.
22. Quoted in Michael Laffan, *The Resurrection of Ireland: The Sinn Féin Party, 1916–1923* (Cambridge: Cambridge University Press, 1999), p. 307.
23. Sinn Féin itself promoted Irish goods at events such as the annual Aonach na Nodlag (Christmas fair), 'Sale-Exhibition[s] of Irish Goods only', which it organised in the Dublin Rotunda from 1908 onwards.
24. For *The Gael* and advertising, see p. 23.
25. See p. 233.
26. *The Gael*, 10 February 1916, p. 16.
27. P. H. Pearse, *The Murder Machine* (Dublin: Whelan and Son, 1916), p. 3. 'The Murder Machine' first appeared in the *Irish Review* in February 1913 and the companion piece 'An Ideal Education' in the same journal in June 1914.
28. Cited in Breandan Mac Giolla Choille, ed., *Intelligence Notes, 1913–1916* (Dublin: State Paper Office, 1966), p. 222. Quoted in Christopher M. Kennedy, *Genesis of the Rising, 1912–1916: A Transformation of Nationalist Opinion* (New York, NY: Peter Lang Publishing Inc., 2010), p. 246.

29. The poem's representative first verse and chorus.
30. Brian na Banban, *The Voice of Banba: Songs and Recitations for Young Ireland* (Dublin: M.H. Gill & Son, 1907), p. 34.
31. Ibid.
32. One example:

> Ceolta na Nollag go raibf it' chroidhe,
> Gaire 'gus aoibhneas 'gus athas flor;
> An dochas nar sgar leis na Gaedheala riamh
> Go mbronnfar go fial ort, a chara dhil.
> ('May the music of Christmas be in your heart,
> Laughter and joy and happiness
> More hope than the Gaels have yet known,
> Let these be granted to you').

We are grateful to Eliza O'Brien for this translation.
33. Brian na Banban, *Signal Fires* (Dublin: M. H. Gill, 1912), p. 26.
34. Sean O'Mahoney, *Frongoch: University of Revolution* (Dublin: FDR Teoranta, 1987), p. 77.
35. Quoted in Uinseann MacEoin, *Survivors: The Story of Ireland's Struggle as Told Through Some of her Outstanding people* (Dublin: Argenta Publications, 1980), p. 167.
36. Ibid. Comerford also scornfully dismissed O'Higgins's efforts in the Uprising: 'I had very little use for him. He was always ready with a graveside speech yet he had barely volunteered himself. He was so opposed to De Valera that he left his wife's funeral when he arrived to attend it' (Ibid.).
37. 'If that advice was more closely followed by business men, editors and Ministers we would be a happy and prosperous country to-day.'
38. A companion volume to Whelan and Son's *Golden Moments with Thomas Davis* (1916), *Golden Moments with John Mitchel* (1916) and *Golden Moments with P. H. Pearse* (c. 1916).
39. *Irish Independent*, 7 April 1923.
40. See p. 238.
41. We derive this information from Séamus de Búrca's *The Soldier's Song: The Story of Peadar O Cearnaigh* (Dublin: P. J. Bourke, 1957), p. 56.
42. And the *Catholic Bulletin*, as Patrick Maume has pointed out (*The Long Gestation*, p. 176).
43. The sub-title of Tom Reilly's study *Joe Stanley: Printer to the Rising* (Dingle, County Kerry: Brandon/Mount Eagle Publications Ltd, 2005).
44. Frank Henderson, *Easter Rising. Recollections of an Irish Volunteer* (Cork: Cork University Press, 1996), p. 31.
45. A 'James Whelan, 17 Upper Ormond Quay, Dublin' being included in the list of prisoners appended to Sean O'Mahoney's *Frongoch: University of Revolution* (p. 195).
46. In the *Irish Independent*, 18 August 1923.
47. 'RUNNING!' An advertisement published in 1930, endorses the 'WIN-AH Running Shoe' made of 'the best Chrome Box Veal Leather' and 'worn by all the leading athletes in Championship and International contests' ('price only 21s, post free').

4 *The Lady of the House* (1890–1921): Gender, Fashion and Domesticity

1. Such was the Findlater profile that Joyce mentions Adam Findlater in *Ulysses*. See James Joyce, *Ulysses: An Annotated Students Edition*, ed. Declan Kiberd (Harmondsworth: Penguin, 1992), p. 69, line 30.
2. Quoted in Alex Findlater, *Findlaters: The Story of a Dublin Merchant Family, 1774–2001* (Dublin: A & A Farmar, 2001), p. 315.
3. *Irish Tatler and Sketch* (October 1969), p. 33.
4. Margaret Beetham, *A Magazine of Their Own? Domesticity and Desire in the Woman's Magazine, 1800–1914* (London: Routledge, 1996), p. 27.
5. See Findlater, *Findlaters*, p. 217 for a reproduction of the 1909 advert.
6. Quoted in Findlater, *Findlaters*, p. 108.
7. This notion of the Irish metropolitan centre is perhaps complicated by what is often seen in Irish studies as Ireland's colonial status in relation to England.
8. Gillian Wagner, *Barnardo* (London: Weidenfeld and Nicholson, 1979), p. 4. John Michaelis Barnardo, a Prussian, and his wife Abigail Matilda O'Brien, an Irishwoman, married in London on 23 June 1837. Their son was to found the children's charity which still bears his name.
9. *The Lady of the House*, December 1920, p. 30.
10. *The Lady of the House*, Winter 1890, p. 34.
11. See Marjorie Ferguson, *Forever Feminine: Women's Magazines and the Cult of the Feminine* (London: Heinemann, 1983).
12. For one example, see *The Lady of the House*, 15 January 1909, p. 25: 'NO BREAKFAST TABLE IS COMPLETE WITHOUT FINDLATER'S NEW SEASON'S MARMALADE'. The jar carries Findlater's brand trademark (AF & Co.), and the date of the company's establishment – 'A.D. 1823'. See also Findlater, *Findlaters*, pp. 128–131 for the company's branding.
13. Erika Diane Rappaport, *Shopping for Pleasure: Women in the Making of London's West End* (Princeton, NJ: Princeton University Press, 2000), p. 176.
14. For example, *The Lady of the House* December 1891, p. 38.
15. *The Lady of the House*, 15 October 1891, p. 14.
16. *The Lady of the House*, 15 April 1920, p. 10.
17. *The Lady of the House*, 14 November 1896, p. 19.
18. Joanna Bourke, *Husbandry to Housewifery: Women, Economic Change, and Housework in Ireland, 1890–1914* (Oxford: Clarendon Press, 1993), p. 1.
19. Ibid., p. 11.
20. Ibid., pp. 216–217.
21. Ibid., p. 12.
22. The Reverend Joseph Guinan, 'Rathmore Revisited', *Irish Monthly* (1915), p. 419; quoted in Bourke, p. 201. Guinan published several novels set in the North Longford area.
23. Le de K. K., 'The Homestead and its In-Dwellers', *Irish Homestead* (29 April 1905), p. 348.
24. 'Nobody has been able to trace a beginning of what we call civilisation, and the more people give you in this respect the more they degenerate' (ibid.).
25. Bourke, *Husbandry to Housewifery*, p. 202.
26. Caitriona Clear, *Women of the House: Women's Household Work in Ireland, 1922–1960* (Dublin: Irish Academic Press, 2000), p. 2.

27. See Bourke, *Husbandry to Housewifery*, p. 204.
28. Ibid., p. 12.
29. Dympna McLoughlin, 'Women and Sexuality in Nineteenth-Century Ireland', *The Irish Journal of Psychology*, vol. 15, no. 2–3 (1994), pp. 266–275, p. 266.
30. See Stephanie Rains, *Commodity Culture and Social Class in Dublin 1850–1916* (Dublin: Irish Academic Press, 2010), p. 67.
31. Theodor Veblen, *The Theory of the Leisure Class* (Oxford: Oxford University Press, 1899/2007), pp. 50–51.
32. Rachel Bowlby, *Carried Away: The Invention of Modern Shopping* (London: Faber and Faber, 2000), pp. 63–64.
33. Diane Barthel, *Putting on Appearances: Gender and Advertising* (Philadelphia, PA: Temple University Press, 1988), p. 40.
34. *The Lady of the House*, Winter 1890, p. 4.
35. Indeed, we have argued in the Prologue to this book that, following the Famine, the 1853 Irish Industrial Exhibition in Dublin was part of contemporary attempts to stimulate economic prosperity in urban areas of Ireland.
36. Lori Anne Loeb, *Consuming Angels: Advertising and Victorian Women* (Oxford: Oxford University Press, 1994), pp. 33–34.
37. *The Lady of the House*, 15 June 1891, p. 32.
38. For 'Scientific Cookery', see *The Lady of the House*, Autumn 1890, p. 17. For the 'prettiest child', see the number for April 1891, p. 9.
39. *The Lady of the House*, 15 January 1910, p. 15.
40. *The Lady of the House*, 15 February 1909, p. 14.
41. *The Lady of the House*, Winter 1890, p. 4.
42. For the latter see Abelson, Elaine S., *When Ladies Go A-Thieving: Middle-Class Shoplifters in the Victorian Department Store* (Oxford: Oxford University Press, 1989).
43. Abelson refers to the introduction of electric light as comprising 'a new reality' (*When Ladies Go A-Thieving*, p. 88).
44. Rains, 'Here be Monsters', p. 492.
45. Bowlby, *Carried Away*, pp. 57–58.
46. The other new feature of modern shopping was illumination as shops were lit by electric light. Notably, the Dublin Electrical Works opened in 1892, and although there were only 650 consumers in 1904, most of these were business and shop premises in Dublin city centre. (Bourke, *Husbandry to Housewifery*, p. 221.)
47. Rachel Bowlby, *Carried Away*, p. 7. Bowlby also notes that women and children are frequently pictured together in advertising (p. 113). For a specifically Irish context, see Rains, 'Here be Monsters', p. 494.
48. Abelson, *When Ladies Go A-Thieving*, pp. 5–6.
49. See Émile Zola's 1883 *The Ladies' Paradise (Au Bonheur des Dames)*, trans. Brian Nelson (Oxford: Oxford University Press, 1995), p. 77.
50. Quoted in Glandon, 'The Irish Press', p. 28.
51. *The Lady of the House*, 15 December 1909, p. 17.
52. *The Lady of the House*, Winter 1890, p. 18.
53. For example, see *The Lady of the House*, 14 November 1891, p. 11 and p. 28.
54. Valerie Steele's phrase in *Paris Fashion: A Cultural History* (Oxford: Berg, 1998, rev. ed.) p. 73.
55. Leigh Summers, *Bound to Please: A History of the Victorian Corset* (Oxford: Berg, 2001), p. 2. Summers declares that she was prompted to write her study by the

fact that 'there has been no sustained feminist criticism of the corset's role in constructing and enforcing the private realm of womanhood' (ibid.).

56. Summers, *Bound to Please*, p. 174.
57. *The Irish Independent*, 1 August 1906, p. 1.
58. See Garry M. Leonard, 'Joyce and Advertising: Advertising and Commodity Culture in Joyce's Fiction', in *James Joyce Quarterly*, vol. 30/31 (summer/fall 1993), p. 586.
59. See *The Lady of the House*, 15 August 1891, p. 18, and 15 September 1891, p. 14.
60. Summers, *Bound to Please*, p. 178.
61. Mairead Dunlevy, *Dress in Ireland: A History* (Cork: The Collins Press, 1999, new ed.), p. 167.
62. See Marie-Louise Legg, *Newspapers and Nationalism: The Irish Provincial Press 1850–1892* (Dublin: Four Courts, 1999), p. 153. If the urban poor wore corsetry, they were probably inherited from their wealthier mistresses, purchased second hand, or made at home from various patterns supplied in women's magazines (although the high-class *The Lady of the House* did not include such samples, other magazines, such as the London-based *Myra's Journal of Dress and Fashion* (1875–1912) carried cut-out patterns for dressmaking).
63. According to Maud Pember Reeves's 1914 *Round About a Pound a Week* (London: Virago, 1979), p. 21.
64. Dunlevy, *Dress in Ireland*, pp. 159–160.
65. See 'Tight-Lacing Becoming Fashionably Again: Ills that Result' in *The Sunday Independent*, 16 August 1906, p. 4.
66. See 'The Modern Corset: A Plea for its Abolition', in *Irish Independent*, 17 October 1907, p. 7.
67. *The Lady of the House*, Winter 1890, p. 14.
68. *The Lady of the House*, 15 August 1891, p. 22.
69. See Strachan, *Advertising and Satirical Culture*, p. 76.
70. *The Lady of the House*, 15 July 1909, p. 25.
71. Ibid.
72. See p. 233 for discussion of the hidden advertisement.
73. *The Lady of the House*, 14 May 1910.
74. Beetham, *A Magazine of Their Own?*, p. 40.
75. Loeb, *Consuming Angels*, p. 34.
76. Tess Marsh, 'Is There More To *Photobits* Than Meets the Eye?', in *James Joyce Quarterly*, vol. 30/31 (summer/fall 1993), p. 882.
77. *The Lady of the House*, January 1891, p. 12.
78. *The Lady of the House*, 12 October 1891, back page.
79. McClintock, *Imperial Leather*, has made a similar observation with regard to soap products and colonial discourses on race. See pp. 31–33 and pp. 207–231.
80. Loeb, *Consuming Angels*, p. 35.
81. *The Lady of the House*, Winter 1890, p. 18.
82. Gillian Dyer, *Advertising as Communication* (London: Routledge, 1988), p. 100.
83. *The Lady of the House*, January 1891, p. 10.
84. Beetham, *A Magazine of Their Own?*, p. 199.
85. Niamh O'Sullivan, 'The Iron Cage of Femininity: Visual Representation of Women in the 1880s and Agitation' in *Ideology and Ireland in the Nineteenth Century*, ed. Tadhg Foley and Seán Ryder (Dublin: Four Courts, 1998), p. 190.
86. Timothy P. Foley, 'Public Sphere and Domestic Circle: Gender and Political Economy in Nineteenth-Century Ireland', in *Gender Perspectives in Nineteenth-Century*

Ireland: Public and Private Spheres, ed. Margaret Kelleher and James H. Murphy (Dublin: Irish Academic Press, 1997), pp. 23–24.
87. Cited in Foley, 'Public Sphere and Domestic Circle', pp. 23–24.
88. Louise Ryan, 'Constructing "Irishwoman": Modern Girls and Comely Maidens', in *Irish Studies Review*, no. 3, (1998), p. 263. Caitriona Clear (in *Women of the House: Women's Household Work in Ireland, 1922–1961* (Dublin: Irish Academic Press, 2000), p. 3), argues that the new state was far from sympathetic to women: 'Women were exempt from jury service, married women barred from public service white collar work, including National teaching, and women's access to factory employment was restricted in 1935. Article 41.2 of Eamon de Valera's Constitution of 1937 identified all women with motherhood and domesticity.' She also maintains that the Catholic Church itself was a frequent agitator for women's involvement in public life and the workforce (pp. 35–36).
89. *The New Woman in Fiction and in Fact: Fin-de-Siècle Feminisms*, ed. Angelique Richardson and Chris Willis (Basingstoke: Palgrave, 2002), p. 8.
90. *The Lady of the House*, 15 January 1919, pp. 7–8.
91. *The Lady of the House*, 15 August 1919, p. 1.
92. See Sarah Wintle, 'Horses, Bikes and Automobiles: New Women on the Move', in *The New Woman in Fiction and in Fact: Fin-de-Siècle Feminisms*, ed. Angelique Richardson and Chris Willis (Basingstoke, Palgrave, 2002), p. 68. See also Rains, *Commodity Culture and Social Class in Dublin*, p. 131: 'What may have been the world's first bicycle factory was established in Dublin in 1888, and the development of the pneumatic tyre, for which Dunlop made its name, was largely conducted in the city.'
93. Ellen Gruber Garvey, *The Adman in the Parlor: Magazines and the Gendering of Consumer Culture, 1880s–1910s* (New York, NY: Oxford University Press, 1996), p. 108.
94. Cited in John B. Cunningham and Joe O'Loughlin, 'O'Loughlin's Bicycle Shop, Belleek, Co. Fermanagh and the Coming of the Bicycle', in *Ulster Folklore*, vol. 44 (1998), p. 95.
95. Ibid.
96. Gruber Garvey, *The Adman in the Parlor*, p. 112. See also *The Lady of the House*, 15 August 1919, pp. 1–2 and p. 8 for 'The Irish Girl: Graceful and Strong', which examines the rise in physical training and sports for women.
97. Clear, *Women of the House*, p. 69.
98. *Ulysses*, ed. Kiberd, p. 213, line 28.
99. *The Lady of the House*, 15 April 1920, p. 17.
100. *The Lady of the House*, 15 July 1919, p. 5.
101. The phrase 'The customer is always right' is commonly credited to either Selfridge or Field himself.
102. See *The Lady of the House*, 15 November 1919, p. 13, and 14 August 1920, p. 14.
103. Rappaport, *Shopping for Pleasure*, p. 74. Writing of London women, Rappaport maintains that 'Depending on the size of her pocketbook, the level of her education, and the nature of her politics and interests, a wealthy woman could find a club that suited her every need' (ibid.). See also Rains, *Commodity Culture and Social Class in Dublin*, p. 130.
104. Rappaport, *Shopping for Pleasure*, p. 75.
105. *The Lady of the House*, 15 April 1909, p. 31.
106. Correspondence to Claire Nally from Alex Findlater, 7 August 2009. See also Findlater, *Findlaters*, p. 390, for a picture postcard of the Tea Room premises and the Civil War damage to the shop premises, July 1922.

107. Rappaport, *Shopping for Pleasure*, p. 101.
108. Claire Nally's thanks to Dorothea Findlater for her recollections of the Tea Rooms on O'Connell Street.
109. Rappaport, *Shopping for Pleasure*, p. 103.
110. Nora Tynan O'Mahony, 'The Mother', *The Irish Monthly*, vol. 91 (1913). Quoted in *Women in Ireland: A Documentary History 1800–1918*, ed. Maria Luddy (Cork: Cork University Press, 1995), p. 17.
111. Diarmaid Ferriter, *Occasions of Sin: Sex and Society in Modern Ireland* (London: Profile, 2009), p. 25.
112. *The Limerick Leader*, 2 May 1928, p. 3.
113. And, indeed, Rome itself. See Louise Ryan, 'Flappers and Shawls: The Female Embodiment of Irish National Identity in the 1920s', in *Women as Sites of Culture: Women's Roles in Cultural Formation from the Renaissance to the Twentieth Century*, ed. Susan Shifrin (Aldershot: Ashgate, 2002), p. 42.
114. Thomas Jay, 'In Lighter Vein', in *The Leitrim Observer*, 1 August 1914, p. 7. The illustration by J. H. Lunn to accompany the text reveals a tall and slender girl in knee-length skirt, towering over her father in an armchair with authoritative gesture, and her brother lurking beside her, being no taller than her hips. The satire on the 'Flapper' betokens rising anxiety regarding the independence of urban women from the Irish family home, in terms of education, fashion and social life.
115. Ryan, 'Flappers and Shawls', pp. 40–41.
116. *The Wicklow People*, 20 October 1928, p. 4, cited in Ryan, p. 41.
117. Ryan, 'Flappers and Shawls', p. 43.
118. Caitríona Beaumont, 'Gender, Citizenship and the State in Ireland: 1922–1990', in *Ireland in Proximity: History, Gender Space*, ed. Scott Brewster, Virginia Crossman, Fiona Beckett and David Alderson (London: Routledge, 1999), p. 98.
119. Ryan, 'Flappers and Shawls', p. 47.
120. Maryann Valiulis, 'Neither Feminist nor Flapper: The Ecclesiastical Construction of the Ideal Irish Woman', in *The Irish Woman's History Reader*, p. 152.

5 Unionism, Advertising and the Third Home Rule Bill 1911–1914

1. Ronald McNeill, *Ulster's Stand for Union* (New York, NY: E. P. Dutton, 1922), p. 3.
2. In his introduction to *Against Home Rule: The Case for the Union*, ed. S. Rosenbaum (London and New York, NY: Frederick Warne, 1912), p. 17, Carson declares that 'Ulster sees in Irish Nationalism a dark conspiracy, buttressed upon crime and incitement to outrage, maintained by ignorance and pandering to superstition' (ibid., p. 27).
3. *The Irish Unionist Pocket Book*, p. 43.
4. Quoted in Riordan, *Modern Irish Trade and Industry*, p. 272. Also quoted in part in McMahon, *Grand Opportunity*, p. 149.
5. In like manner, in the same place, Newell's of Belfast, ladies outfitters 'famed for value, with its frocks, hats, gloves, stockings and undies', featured the banner 'Buy Ulster Goods!' (the implicit subtext here, however, is of course, 'Rather than Free State Goods'.
6. *The Irish Unionist Pocket Book*, p. 95. The Welsh are nowhere to be seen.
7. 'The ABC of Home Rule' (Belfast: The Dublin and Belfast Unionist Associations of Ireland, 1911), pp. 31–32.
8. Ibid., p. 89.

9. Aodh De Blácam, *What Sinn Fein Stands For. The Irish Republican Movement: Its History, Aims and Ideals Examined as to Their Significance for the World* (Dublin: Mellifont Press, 1921), p. 141.
10. Programme, 'The Ulster Unionist Demonstration of 1912', p. 3.
11. 'Six hundred thousand Irish Churchmen are against it. Five hundred thousand Methodists and Presbyterians are against it. Sixty thousand members of smaller denominations are against it. A hundred and seventy-four thousand Protestants in Leinster, and a hundred and six thousand in Munster and Connaught are against it. The educated and loyal Roman Catholic laity are against it. All who care for England and are willing to join in singing "God save the Queen" are against it.' Robert John Buckley, *Ireland as it is and as it Would Be Under Home Rule* (Birmingham and London: Birmingham Daily Gazette Company, 1893), p. 330.
12. 'Are Englishmen willing to be longer fooled by a Government of nincompoops?' asks Buckley (ibid.).
13. Ibid.
14. Maurice Irvine's term for the gatherings in *Northern Ireland: Faith and Faction* (London: Routledge, 1991), p. 81.
15. 'Songsheet: Demonstration, Ulster Hall', 27 September 1912, p. 3. For the 'Orange Tree', a song which dates back to the early nineteenth century, see Donald M. MacRaild, 'The Associationalism of the Orange Diaspora', in *The Orange Order in Canada*, ed. David A. Wilson (Dublin: Four Courts Press, 2007), pp. 25–41. MacRaild has remarked that the 'Orange Tree' 'is a direct arboreal challenge to the "green bough of liberty" '.
16. McNeill, *Ulster's Stand for Union*, p. 3.
17. McNeill claims that 'the women of Ulster were scarcely less active than the men in the matter of organisation. Although, of course, as yet unenfranchised, they took as a rule a keener interest in political matters – meaning thereby the one absorbing question of the Union – than their sex in other parts of the UK. When critical times for the Union arrived there was, therefore, no apathy to be overcome by the Protestant women in Ulster. Early in 1911 the "Ulster Women's Unionist Council" was formed under the presidency of the Duchess of Abercorn, and very quickly became a most effective organisation side by side with that of the men. The leading spirit was the Marchioness of Londonderry, but that it was no aristocratic affair of titled ladies may be inferred from the fact that within twelve months of its formation between forty and fifty thousand members were enrolled. A branch in Mr [Joe] Devlin's constituency of West Belfast, which over four thousand women joined in its first month of existence, of whom over 80 per cent were mill-workers and shop-girls in the district' (*Ulster's Stand for Union*, p. 37).
18. Quoted in Timothy Bowman, *Carson's Army: The Ulster Volunteer Force 1910–1922* (Manchester: Manchester University press, 2007), p. 131. Bowman declares that, unlike the national anthem, UVF songs did not achieve wide currency in the period: 'the songs composed to honour the force were of little artistic merit and were rarely performed, even at the time' (ibid.).
19. Sean O'Casey, *Three Dublin Plays*, ed. Christopher Murray (London: Macmillan, 1998), p. 117.
20. See Roy Douglas, Liam Harte and Jim O'Hara, *Drawing Conclusions: A Cartoon History of Anglo-Irish Relations, 1798–1998* (Belfast: Blackstaff Press, 1998).
21. For the history of mock-advertisements, see Strachan, *Advertising and Satirical Culture*, pp. 73–81.

22. *Townlands in Ulster*, eds W. H. Crawford and R. H. Foy (Belfast: Ulster Historical Foundation in association with the Federation of Ulster Local Studies, 1998), p. 70.
23. The text is slightly altered in the postcard; line three has 'thinned that are thinned' and line 4 'When the names that are twenty ...'.
24. McNeill, *Ulster's Fight for Union*, p. 147.
25. Michael Foy offers a valuable account of the propaganda effort against Home Rule with particular reference to postcards and political cartoons in 'Ulster Unionist Propaganda Against Home Rule', *History Ireland*, vol. 4, no. 1 (1996), pp. 49–53. It might be pointed out that popular ephemera with such ideological sympathies were not absolutely unheard of before 1911. For example, in December 1900, the *Belfast Weekly News* offered a free calendar for 1901 to its readers featuring 'correct portraits of the late Grand Master of the Orangemen of Belfast, Rev Dr Kane LLB and the Present Grand Master Lord Farnham'.
26. *Popular Mechanics* (May 1914), p. 656.
27. Jim Mac Laughlin, *Re-Imagining the Nation State* (London: Pluto Press, 2001), p. 219.
28. *The Fortnightly*, vol. 118 (1922), p. 44.
29. See Chapter 2 of this book, p. 70.
30. See pp. 67–68 of this book.
31. Carson's description of his mood after the signing of the Covenant during his visit to Merseyside in 1912. Quoted in D. M. Jackson and D. M. MacRaild, 'The Conserving Crowd: Mass Unionist Demonstrations in Liverpool and Tyneside, 1912–13', in *The Ulster Crisis 1885–1921*, eds D. George Boyce and Alan O'Day (Houndsmills: Palgrave Macmillan, 2006), p. 232.
32. Geoffrey Lewis, *Carson: The Man Who Divided Ireland* (London: Continuum International Publishing Group, 2005), p. 16.

6 Oscar Wilde as Editor and Writer: Aesthetic Interventions in Fashion and Material Culture

1. In 'The Truth of Masks', Wilde notes, with regard to the theatre, 'that costume could be made at once impressive of a certain effect on the audience and expressive of certain types of character, and is one of the essential factors of the means which a true illusionist has at his disposal' (*Complete Works of Oscar Wilde* (Glasgow: Harper Collins, 1999), *Complete Works*, p. 1161). In 'The Critic as Artist' Wilde states: 'Man is least himself when he talks in his own person. Give him a mask, and he will tell you the truth' (*Complete Works*, p. 1142).
2. Oscar Wilde, 'The Decay of Lying', *Complete Works*, p. 1083.
3. Compare Terry Eagleton's similar taxonomy of 'the Irish Oxfordian socialist proto-deconstructionist' (Terry Eagleton, 'Afterword', *St Oscar* (London: Bookmark, 2004), p. 58).
4. Oscar Wilde, 'The House Beautiful', *Complete Works*, pp. 914 and 915.
5. Oscar Wilde, 'The Decorative Arts', *Complete Works*, p. 936.
6. Wilde, 'The Decay of Lying', *Complete Works*, p. 1075.
7. Declan Kiberd suggests that Wilde's stylised aristocratic posturings were born from his own father's less than careful manners and dress: 'All the norms of his childhood were to be reversed. His father had been laughed at by society, so he would mock society first. His father had been unkempt, so he would be fastidious' (*Inventing Ireland*, p. 35). W. B. Yeats's notes in the *Autobiographies* that 'The Wilde

family were clearly of the sort that fed the imagination of Charles Lever, dirty, untidy, daring', and also refer to an old Dublin riddle circulated at Wilde's father's expense: ' "Why are Sir William Wilde's nails so black?" Answer: "Because he has scratched himself" ' (W. B. Yeats, *Autobiographies*, eds William H. O'Donnell and Douglas N. Archibald (New York, NY: Scribner, 1999), p. 129).

8. Oscar Wilde, 'The Soul of Man Under Socialism', *Complete Works*, p. 1191.
9. Wilde, 'The Critic as Artist', *Complete Works*, p. 1109.
10. In 'The Soul of Man under Socialism', Wilde advocates the further development of modern machinery in order to free man from toil and allow his time to be spent in more artistic pursuits. Though he offers a critique of modern society which has made man 'the slave of machinery [which is] the result of our property system and our system of competition' (*Complete Works*, p. 1183), he also notes that such machinery might be deployed as a force for good: 'so while Humanity will be amusing itself, or enjoying cultivate leisure – which, and not labour, is the aim of man – or making beautiful things, or reading beautiful things, or simply contemplating the world with admiration and delight, machinery will be doing all the necessary and unpleasant work' (Ibid.).
11. Wilde, 'The Decorative Arts', *Complete Works*, p. 930.
12. Wilde, 'The Critic as Artist', *Complete Works*, p. 1115.
13. Walter Pater, *The Renaissance* (Oxford: Oxford University Press, 1998), p. 153.
14. Oscar Wilde, *The Picture of Dorian Gray*, ed. Peter Ackroyd (Harmondsworth: Penguin, 1985), pp. 3–4.
15. Regina Gagnier, *Idylls of the Marketplace: Oscar Wilde and the Victorian Public* (Aldershot: Scolar Press, 1986), p. 5.
16. Pater, 'Winckellmann', in *The Renaissance*, p. 134.
17. Wilde, *Dorian Gray*, p. 4.
18. Rachel Bowlby, *Carried Away*, p. 19.
19. Ibid., p. 61.
20. Theodor Adorno, *Aesthetic Theory*, trans. R. Hullot-Kentor (London: Athlone, 1997), p. 227.
21. Ross Wilson, *Theodor Adorno* (Abingdon: Routledge, 2007), p. 50.
22. Theodor Adorno, 'Culture Industry Reconsidered', in *The Culture Industry: Selected Essays on Mass Culture*, ed. J. M. Bernstein (London: Routledge, 1991), p. 99.
23. Adorno, 'Culture Industry Reconsidered', p. 99.
24. Andy Hamilton, *Aesthetics and Music* (London: Continuum, 2007), p. 167.
25. Gagnier, *Idylls of the Marketplace*, pp. 5–6.
26. In a university notebook from his time at Oxford, Wilde writes that 'Hegelian dialectic is the natural selection produced by a struggle for existence in world of thought' (Michael S. Helfand and Philip E. Smith, eds, *Oscar Wilde's Oxford Notebooks: A Portrait of Mind in the Making* (Oxford: Oxford University Press, 1989), p. 19.
27. Wilde, 'The Truth of Masks', *Complete Works*, p. 1173.
28. See Richard Ellmann, 'Oscar at Oxford', *New York Review of Books*, 29 March 1984, pp. 23–28.
29. Wilde, *Dorian Gray*, p. 3.
30. Ibid., p. 11.
31. Ibid., p. 16.
32. Ibid., p. 28.
33. Ibid., p. 22.
34. Ibid., p. 91.

35. Rachel Bowlby, *Shopping with Freud* (London: Routledge, 1993), pp. 7–8.
36. Wilde, *Dorian Gray*, p. 5.
37. Rachel Teukolsky, *The Literate Eye: Victorian Art Writing and Modernist Aesthetics* (Oxford: Oxford University Press, 2009), p. 135.
38. Flanders, *Consuming Passions*, p. 115.
39. Ibid., p. 117.
40. *The Woman's World*, 'Edited by Oscar Wilde' (London: Cassell & Company Limited, 1888), p. 94. Far from being ubiquitously upmarket in the Liberty manner, the author maintains that by now Japanese imports included many cheap products:

    > Most of the Japanese wares that are sold in England are exceedingly cheap, and there is consequently some danger that they may become vulgarized. But it so falls out that English taste can endure a good deal of such vulgarization; and because a Japanese fan or two may brighten a garret, that is surely no reason why they should cease to beautify a boudoir. A much more imminent danger is that the Japanese may themselves become vulgarized by the absurd imitation of European customs and fashions which is at present the rage in their wonderful island.
    >
    > (Ibid.)

41. Paul Fortunato, *Modernist Aesthetics and Consumer Culture in the Writings of Oscar Wilde* (London and New York, NY: Routledge, 2007), p. 37.
42. See Fortunato, *Modernist Aesthetics and Consumer Culture*, p. 41.
43. See Deborah Chambers, Linda Steiner and Carole Fleming, *Women and Journalism* (London: Routledge, 2004): 'The rise of the New Journalism in the big cities of the United States during the 1880s was undoubtedly a key element in generating openings for women journalists between the 1880s and the outbreak of the First World War' (p. 20).
44. Mary Frances Billington, 'Journalism as a Profession for Women', *Woman's World*, vol. 3, p. 8. Despite her optimism, Billington also comments that 'there are few editors, however, who would trust an important leader into female hands. This may be mere ungallant prejudice, but it is also fact.'
45. Mrs Johnstone, 'December Fashions', *Woman's World*, vol. 1 (1889), p. 74.
46. Declan Kiberd maintains that the 'Englishness' which Wilde sometimes affected 'was really a parody of the very notion. The ease with which Wilde effected the transition from stage Ireland to stage-England was his ultimate comment on the shallowness of such categories' (*Inventing Ireland*, p. 36). James Joyce was less charitable on the matter, identifying Wilde as part of 'that literary tradition of Irish comic playwrights that stretches from the days of Sheridan and Goldsmith to Bernard Shaw. [He], like them, court jester to the English' (Oscar Wilde, 'The Poet of Salomé', in *Occasional, Critical and Political Writings*, ed. Kevin Barry (Oxford: Oxford University Press, 2000), p. 149).
47. Oscar Wilde, 'The Decorative Arts', in *Complete Works*, p. 926. Wilde was also capable of offhand dismissals of England, however, as in 'The Soul of Man Under Socialism' where he maintains that 'No country produces such badly written fiction, such tedious, common work in the novel form, such silly, vulgar plays, as England' (Wilde, 'The Soul of Man Under Socialism', in *Complete Works*, p. 1185).
48. 'Speranza' [Lady Wilde], 'Irish Peasant Tales', in *Woman's World*, vol. 1 (1889), pp. 26–31.
49. 'Some Literary Notes', *Woman's World*, vol. 1, p. 277.

50. See 'Some Literary Notes by the Editor', *Woman's World*, vol. 1, pp. 391–392.
51. Richard Heath, 'Politics in Dress', *Woman's World*, vol. 1, pp. 399–405. Heath also discusses the use of orange ribbons in dress by the Orangemen, and the wearing of green rosettes and green trimmings by the Ribbonmen, while citing 'The Wearing of the Green'. Our thanks to Patrick Maume for advice on the symbolism of the 'square-toed boots'. Maume has suggested that the verses cited are by T. D. Sullivan.
52. H. E. Keane, 'Lace-Making in Ireland', *Woman's World*, vol. 2 (1888), p. 196.
53. Ibid.
54. Mary Jeune, 'Irish Industrial Art', *Woman's World* (1889), vol. 1, pp. 159–160.
55. Janice Helland, *British and Irish Homes Arts and Industries, 1880–1914* (Dublin: Irish Academic Press, 2007), p. 34.
56. Wilde, 'The House Beautiful', *Complete Works*, p. 914.
57. Walter Benjamin, 'The Work of Art in the Age of Mechanical Reproduction', in *Illuminations*, ed. Hannah Arendt (London: Fontana, 1970), p. 215.
58. Oscar Wilde, 'The House Beautiful', *Complete Works*, p. 922.
59. Ibid.
60. Ibid., p. 925.
61. Ibid., p. 926. Wilde developed this notion in 'The Decorative Arts', where he details a visit to the Victoria and Albert Museum (then the South Kensington Museum), 'to see the workmen whom we so much want to reach, and whom it is often so difficult to reach, the weaver, the glass-blower, the woodcarver, the embroiderer, and others with their notebooks open, and I feel certain that the week after such a visit their work is better for their observance' (ibid., p. 931). The development of stores such as Liberty provided a home to these goods from the 1870s onwards. Certainly the artisan model, which pervaded the Arts and Crafts Movement in England did not forgo commercial concerns (see also our discussion of the Yeats sisters' operation in Chapter 7 of this book). In the Adornian manner, 'pure' art and 'pure' commodity are in fact mutually independent, and goods produced by artisans still became part of (albeit high end) commodity culture.
62. Jennifer Wicke, *Advertising Fictions: Literature, Advertisement and Social Reading* (New York, NY: Columbia University Press, 1988), p. 3; p. 14.
63. Ibid., p. 5.
64. Alexis Easley, *Literary Celebrity, Gender and Victorian Authorship 1850–1914* (Newark, DE: University of Delaware Press, 2011), p. 1.
65. Gagnier, *Idylls of the Marketplace*, p. 11.
66. Oscar Wilde, 'Personal Impressions of America', *Complete Works*, p. 939.
67. H. Montgomery Hyde, *The Trials of Oscar Wilde* (New York, NY: Dover, 1962), pp. 42–43.
68. Oscar Wilde, 'Personal Impressions of America' (1882), *Collected Works*, p. 941.
69. Richard Ellmann, *Oscar Wilde* (Harmondsworth: Penguin, 1988), p. 166. Ellmann also notes the fanciful nature of the rumour that Wilde had 'received an offer of $200 a week from P. T. Barnum, who had just bought Jumbo the Elephant from the London Zoo, to lead Jumbo about carrying a lily in one hand and a sunflower in the other'.
70. 'And *The Picture of Dorian Gray* its central text'. Talia Schaffer and Kathy Alexis Psomiades (eds), *Women and British Aestheticism* (Charlottesville: University of Virginia Press, 2000), p. 3.
71. The notion of the 'aesthetic corset' is actually in contradistinction to the realities of the aesthetic dress code, which actively rejected constraints such as stays

and corsets in favour of more fluid and wholesome garments. Wilde himself commented on this issue in his 1884 *Pall Mall Gazette* article 'Woman's Dress', which argues that women should dress 'from the shoulders'. In that case, 'a corset becomes useless':

> Indeed, all the most ungainly and uncomfortable articles of dress that fashion has ever in folly prescribed, not the tight corset merely, but the farthingale, the vertugadin, the hoop, the crinoline, and that modern monstrosity the so-called 'dress improver' also, all of them have owed their origin to the same error, the error of not seeing that it is from the shoulders, and from the shoulders only, that all garments should be hung.
>
> (*Complete Works*, p. 945)

Wilde advocated the combination of the 'Greek principles of beauty with the German principles of health' (ibid., p. 946) which allows great movement of the body, and drapery and folds rather than tight and sturdy garments. Wilde praises Dr Gustav Jaeger's designs as being particularly commendable. Jaeger's principles of dress were, of course, foundational to the upmarket brand of womenswear and menswear Jaeger, founded by Lewis Thomalin in 1884. For Wilde's views on dress reform see also an 1888 'Literary Note' in *Woman's World*: 'And after all, what is a fashion? From the artistic point of view, it is usually a form of ugliness so intolerable that we have to alter it every six months. From the point of view of science, it not unfrequently violates every law of health, every system of hygiene.' Wilde identifies the 'London milkwoman, or the Irish or Scotch fishwife, or the North country factory-girl' as examples of practical, 'hygienic' dress.

72. Cited in Richard Ellmann, *Oscar Wilde*, p. 145.
73. Joseph Bristow, 'Introduction', in *Wilde Writings: Contextual Conditions* (Toronto: University of Toronto Press, 2003), pp. 17–18.
74. Shawn Michelle Smith, *American Archives: Gender, Race, and Class in Visual Culture* (Princeton, NJ: Princeton University Press, 1993), p. 93.
75. This unstable identity, if we accept Kiberd's notion of Wilde parodying Englishness, can be read in postcolonial terms as that mimicry which Homi K. Bhabha sees as 'civil disobedience within the discipline of civility' (Bhabha, *The Location of Culture* (London: Routledge, 1994), p. 121).
76. Wilde, *Dorian Gray*, pp. 143–144.
77. This was the 'Aesthetic teapot' designed by R.W. Binns and modelled by James Hadley, English, Royal Worcester Porcelain Works, marked 1882. One side featured a Bunthorne-type figure with moustache and sunflower, while the other side had a female figure with a lily.
78. Talia Schaffer, 'Fashioning Aestheticism by Aestheticizing Fashion: Wilde, Beerbohm, and the Male Aesthete's Sartorial Codes', in *Victorian Literature and Culture*, vol. 28, no. 1 (2000), pp. 39–54, pp. 39–40. Similarly, Alan Sinfield, in *The Wilde Century* (1994), though maintaining that the modern correlation between homosexuality and femininity was not current in the late nineteenth century, argues that this supposed effeminacy was one of the reasons why, even before his trial in 1895 for gross indecency with another male, Wilde was often intensely vilified by the British Press (*The Wilde Century: Effeminacy, Wilde and the Queer Moment* (London: Cassell, 1994), p. 25. Schaffer further maintains that this unease with the Wildean persona was also related to the author's Irishness, arguing that 'the British public felt hostile to Wilde partly because he was a middle-class Irish subject who appropriated…upper class signs' ('Fashioning Aestheticism', pp. 39–40).

79. Oscar Wilde, *The Picture of Dorian Gray*, p. 6.
80. Joe Moran, *Star Authors: Literary Celebrity in America* (London: Pluto Press, 2000), pp. 16–17.
81. Ibid., p. 17.

7 Consumerism and Anti-Commercialism: The Yeatses, Print Culture and Home Industry

1. W. B. Yeats, 'A General Introduction for My Work' (1937), in *Essays and Introductions* (London: Macmillan, 1961), p. 526.
2. W. B. Yeats, 'The Theatre' (1900), in *Essays and Introductions*, p. 166.
3. The view of the *Daily Express*. Quoted in Marjorie Howes, *Yeats's Nations: Gender, Class and Irishness* (Cambridge: Cambridge University Press, 1996), p. 47.
4. Adrian Frazier, *Behind the Scenes: Yeats, Horniman and the Struggle for the Abbey Theatre* (Berkeley, CA: University of California Press, 1990), p. 2.
5. Frazier, *Behind the Scenes*, p. 7.
6. Quoted in George Cusack, *The Politics of Identity in Irish Drama: W. B. Yeats, Augusta Gregory and J. M. Synge* (New York, NY and London: Routledge, 2009), p. 52.
7. David R. Clark, *W. B. Yeats and the Theatre of Desolate Reality* (Washington, DC: The Catholic University of America Press, 1993, rev. ed.), p. 128.
8. Frazier, *Behind the Scenes*, p. 16.
9. See R. F. Foster, *Modern Ireland 1600–1972* (Harmondsworth: Penguin, 1989), p. 449. See also Douglas Hyde, 'The Necessity for De-Anglicising Ireland' (1892) in Tony Crowley, *The Politics of Language in Ireland 1366–1922: A Sourcebook* (London: Routledge, 2000), p. 184. Hyde identifies England with commercial development but also with an attendant loss of Irish language, tradition and history.
10. W. B. Yeats, 'The Celtic Element in Literature' (1897), in *Essays and Introductions*, p. 178.
11. W. B. Yeats, 'The Theatre' (1900), in *Essays and Introductions*, p. 166. In several of his 'Beggar' poems from *Responsibilities* (1914), such as 'The Three Beggars', 'The Three Hermits' and 'Beggar to Beggar Cried', Yeats advocates the rejection of material goods in favour of visionary experience.
12. Yeats, 'The Celtic Element in Literature', p. 184. Murray Pittock's *Celtic Identity and the British Image* (Manchester: Manchester University Press, 1999) argues that such stereotypical notions of 'Celticism' were employed by the English in the service of colonialism.
13. See Chapter 2 of this book for discussion of Moran's attitudes to these issues.
14. Frazier (*Behind the Scenes*, pp. 16–17). Frazier writes that 'A social contradiction (harmony of aristocracy and peasantry in time of scarcity) is turned into an imaginary unity by means of gathering the potentially opposed classes together against an external enemy: under the leadership of Protestants, Ireland will be saved from England' (ibid.). The underlying implication in this account is that Yeats envisages the peasantry as submissive to the landlord class.
15. Quoted in Richard Ellmann, *James Joyce* (Oxford: Oxford University Press, 1959), p. 765. The young James Joyce refused to add his name to the letter.
16. Lionel Pilkington, *Theatre and the State in Twentieth-Century Ireland: Cultivating the People* (London: Routledge, 2001), pp. 23–24.
17. Ibid., p. 27.

18. See also Pilkington, *Theatre and the State in Twentieth-Century Ireland*, pp. 6ff.
19. W. B. Yeats, *The Countess Cathleen* (1892), in *The Collected Plays of W. B. Yeats* (London: Macmillan, 1952), pp. 6–7.
20. Frazier, *Behind the Scenes*, p. 12.
21. George Moore, *Hail and Farewell*, ed. Richard Allen Cave (Gerrards Cross, Buckinghamshire: Colin Smythe, 1985), p. 540.
22. R. F. Foster, *W. B. Yeats: A Life. The Apprentice Mage, 1865–1914* (Oxford: Oxford University Press, 1998), p. 3.
23. Ibid., p. 4.
24. The poet's father, J. B. Yeats, sold the country estate (560 acres) in Thomastown in 1889, for the sum of £7032, which was all offset against debts on the property, with the exception of £1004 which was used to meet other personal debts. Frazier (*Behind the Scenes*, p. 37) notes that 'even had the estate been kept in the family, and passed entirely to WBY, the eldest son, it would not have freed him from work'.
25. See W. J. McCormack, *Ascendancy and Tradition* (Oxford: Clarendon Press, 1985), pp. 249ff. See also Terry Eagleton, *Criticism and Ideology: A Study in Marxist Literary Theory* (London: Verso, 2006, new ed.), pp. 151–154.
26. Yeats, *Autobiographies*, p. 342.
27. Moore, *Hail and Farewell*, p, 170.
28. W. B. Yeats, 'Ireland and the Arts' (1901), in *Essays and Introductions*, p. 203.
29. Yug Mohit Chaudhry, *Yeats, The Irish Literary Revival and the Politics of Print* (Cork: Cork University Press, 2001), p. 37.
30. W. B. Yeats, Letter to Elizabeth White, 30 January 1889. *The Collected Letters of W. B. Yeats*, gen. ed. John Kelly, 4 vols (Oxford: Clarendon Press, 1986–date), vol. 1, p. 131.
31. W. B. Yeats, Letter to Katherine Tynan [c. 15] June [1888], *The Collected Letters of W. B. Yeats*, vol. 1, pp. 71–72.
32. W. B. Yeats, *Autobiographies*, p. 139.
33. Chaudhry, *Yeats*, p. 17.
34. W. B. Yeats, 'September 1913', from *The Collected Poems*, eds Peter Allt and Russell K. Alspach (New York, NY: Macmillan, 1957), p. 289.
35. Chaudhry, *Yeats*, p. 10.
36. Letter to Stephen Gwynn, 13 June 1906. Quoted in Chaudry, p. 10.
37. Chaudhry, *Yeats*, p. 42.
38. Our thanks to Patrick Maume here. Quoted in Foster, *W. B. Yeats: A Life. The Apprentice Mage*, p. 591. Chaudhry (*Yeats*, p. 41) notes the poet's earnings of £27. 17s. 4d between November 1889 and November 1890 were dependent upon his journalism and related publications in popular newspapers and periodicals.
39. Anthony Bradley, '"Fumbling in a Greasy Till": Nation and Class in Yeats's "Responsibilities"', *Irish University Review*, vol. 30, no. 2 (2000), pp. 289–314; p. 291.
40. Chaudhry, *Yeats*, p. 39. See also Marjorie Howes, 'Postcolonial Yeats: Culture, Enlightenment, and the Public Sphere', in *Field Day Review*, vol. 2 (2006), pp. 54–73, p. 59.
41. W. B. Yeats, *A Vision* (London: Macmillan, 1937), p. 72.
42. W. B. Yeats, *Autobiographies*, p. 170.
43. Troy J. Bassett, 'Fisher Unwin's Pseudonym Library: Literary Marketing and Authorial Identity', in *English Literature in Transition (1880–1920)*, vol. 47, no. 2 (2004), pp. 142–160; pp. 143–145.

44. Ibid., pp. 144–145.
45. Bassett notes that 'The common series name and format imply to the public an internal similarity in terms of narrative type, narrative style, or length, even though most of the entries are written by different authors' (Ibid., p. 147).
46. Ford Madox Ford, *Ancient Lights and Certain New Reflections: Being the Memories of a Young Man* (London: Chapman and Hall, 1911), p. 227. Some of the Pseudonym Library volumes sold in huge numbers. Ford maintains that 'Lanoe Falconer's' [Mary Elizabeth Hawker's] '*Mademoiselle Ixe* [published in the Library in 1890] must have found millions of readers' (Ibid.).
47. W. B. Yeats, *Memoirs*, ed. Denis Donoghue (London: Macmillan, 1972), p. 64.
48. W. B. Yeats, *Autobiographies*, p. 188.
49. Ibid., p. 189.
50. Foster, *Yeats: A Life*, vol. 1, p. 121.
51. W. B. Yeats, *Autobiographies*, p. 187.
52. *The Collected Letters of W. B. Yeats*, vol.1, p. 311.
53. Foster, *Yeats: A Life*, vol. 1, p. 121.
54. W. B. Yeats, *Memoirs*, p. 64.
55. Ibid.
56. *The Collected Letters of W. B. Yeats*, vol.1, p. 303.
57. Gifford Lewis, *The Yeats Sisters and the Cuala* (Dublin: Irish Academic Press, 1994), p. 5. Some critics have persisted in foregrounding Yeats at the expense of his sisters. Jacqueline Genet, for instance, refers to 'The Dun Emer – Cuala Press' as 'Yeats's press'. See 'The Dun Emer and the Cuala Press' in *The Book in Ireland*, eds Jacqueline Genet, Sylvie Mikowski and Fabienne Mercer (Newcastle: Cambridge Scholars Press, 2006), p. 48.
58. Joyce, *Ulysses* (1993), p. 11.
59. See the discussion in Chapter 1, pp. 49–50.
60. Elaine Cheasley Paterson, 'The Dun Emer Guild, 1902–1908' in *The Irish Revival Reappraised*, ed. Betsey Taylor Fitzsimon and James H. Murphy (Dublin: Four Courts, 2004), p. 110.
61. William Morris, 'The Lesser Arts', in *News from Nowhere and Other Writings*, ed. Clive Wilmer (Harmondsworth: Penguin, 2004, rev. ed.), p. 235.
62. The Evelyn Gleeson Papers, Trinity College, Dublin, 10676/1/5, 'The Dun Emer Prospectus' (Winter 1903), p. 2. A similar sentiment is echoed in the following: 'The machine must give place to the hand. The industrial eminence of a nation finally depends on the standard attained by its hand-workers. Among people of cultivated taste the appreciation of it is growing daily, partly because the study of old examples adds to our delight in skill. This delight lies at the root of all art.' See the Evelyn Gleeson Papers, Trinity College, Dublin, 'Lecture', 10676/5/12.
63. Elaine Cheasley Paterson's words in 'The Dun Emer Guild, 1902–1908' p. 111. See Chapter 1 of this book for full discussion of this notion.
64. This is nothing new in Ireland, however; in his economic work, *The Querist* (1735–1737), the philosopher George Berkeley, Bishop of Cloyne, had proposed an 'academy of design' in Ireland 'to help perfect the manufacture of lace, carpets and tapestry'. According to Andy Hamilton's 'The Aesthetics of Design' (2011), the *Oxford English Dictionary* cites this as 'the first use of "design"' as 'the ability to improve the economic competitiveness of commercial goods through their visual appearance' (in *Fashion – Philosophy for Everyone: Thinking with Style*, eds Jessica Wolfendale and Jeanette Kennett (Oxford: Blackwell Publishing, 2011), p. 62).

65. Cheasley Paterson, 'The Dun Emer Guild', p. 114.
66. Nicola Gordon Bowe, 'The Irish Arts and Crafts Movement (1886–1925)', in *Irish Arts Review Yearbook* (1990–1991), pp. 172–185, p. 172.
67. See Elizabeth Wilson, *Adorned in Dreams: Fashion and Modernity* (London: I.B. Tauris, 2003, new ed.), p. 3. Wilson argues that through the consumption and showcasing of particular goods, the body itself operates in symbolic and politically communicative terms.
68. W. B. Yeats, *Autobiographies*, p. 133. See also Gifford Lewis, 'Rediscovered Embroideries by Lily Yeats', in *Irish Arts Review Yearbook*, vol. 14 (1998), pp. 147–150.
69. Joan Hardwick, *The Yeats Sisters: A Biography of Susan and Elizabeth Yeats* (London: Pandora, 1996), p. 118.
70. Ibid.
71. See p. 162.
72. See Elaine Cheasley Paterson, 'The Dun Emer Guild, 1902–1908', p. 109.
73. The Evelyn Gleeson Papers, Trinity College, Dublin, 10676/1/5, The Dun Emer Prospectus (Winter 1903), p. 6.
74. See Simon Loxley, *Type: The Secret History of Letters* (London: I.B. Tauris, 2004), p. 83. The artistic thrift employed in their artistic practice extended to embroidery designs being transferred by pricking through tracings on butter paper, which were offcuts from the printer who supplied Merrion Dairies (Lewis, *The Yeats Sisters*, p. 70).
75. Cited in Lewis, *The Yeats Sisters*, p. 117. 'It is manifest', says Blaikie Murdoch, 'that Miss Yeats has looked for her models to the great British printers of the eighteenth century'.
76. Wade, ed., *The Letters of W. B. Yeats*, p. 391.
77. Letter from Elizabeth Corbet Yeats to P. S. O'Hegarty, 15 September 1939. Cited in Clare Hutton, ed.,' "Yogibogeybox in Dawson Chambers": The Beginnings of Maunsel and Company', in *The Irish Book in the Twentieth Century*, p. 38.
78. Quoted in *The Collected Letters of W. B. Yeats: 1905–1907*, p. 463.
79. Genet, 'The Dun Emer and the Cuala Press', p. 73.
80. Quoted in *The Collected Letters of W. B. Yeats*, vol. 4, p. 463.
81. Ibid.
82. Dun Emer Journal, 1903–1905, in the Cuala Press Archive, Trinity College, Dublin.
83. For examples of Lily Yeats's work, see Linda Seidel, 'Celtic Revivals and Women's Work', in *Imagining an Irish Past: The Celtic Revival 1840–1940*, ed. T. J. Edelstein (Chicago, IL: University of Chicago, 1992), pp. 22–43.
84. Joan Hardwick, *The Yeats Sisters*, pp. 112.
85. Quoted on p. 50.
86. Alice Hart, 'Art and Technical Teaching of the Donegal Industrial Fund' in *Transactions of the National Association for the Advancement of Art and Its Application to Industry, Edinburgh, 1889* (London, 1890), p. 437. Quoted in Helland, *British and Irish Home Arts and Industries*, p. 58.
87. The Evelyn Gleeson Papers, Trinity College, Dublin, 10676/1/5, 'The Dun Emer Prospectus' (Winter 1903), pp. 1–2.
88. The Evelyn Gleeson Papers, Trinity College, Dublin, 10676/1/5, 'The Dun Emer Prospectus' (Winter 1903), pp. 2–3.
89. Edward Martyn, 'A Plea for a National Theatre in Ireland', *Samhain* (October 1901), p. 14.

90. The banners were about 85 × 55 centimetres, and cost four guineas each. The Guild also made vestments for the Cathedral. See Jeanne Sheehy, *The Rediscovery of Ireland's Past: The Celtic Revival 1830–1930* (London: Thames and Hudson, 1980), p. 157.
91. Helland, British and Irish Home Arts and Industries, p. 3.
92. See the Prologue to this book, pp. 20–21.
93. Elaine Cheaseley Paterson, 'The Dun Emer Guild, 1902–1908', in *The Irish Revival Reappraised*, eds Fitzsimon and Murphy, p. 115.
94. *The Daily News*, 18 June 1925, cited in Lewis, *The Yeats Sisters*, p. 169.
95. Cheasley Paterson, 'The Dun Emer Guild, 1902–1908' in *The Irish Revival Reappraised*, eds Fitzsimon and Murphy, p. 114.
96. Helland, p. 4.
97. Letter from John Butler Yeats to his son, 1 June 1906. Cited in Lewis, *The Yeats Sisters*, p. 69.
98. Judith Flanders, *Consuming Passions*, p. 115.
99. Ibid., p. 117.
100. Joan Hardwick, *The Yeats Sisters*, p. 157. See also Gifford Lewis, *The Yeats Sisters*, p. 69.
101. William Maxwell, *The Dun Emer Press and The Cuala Press: A Complete List* (Edinburgh: privately printed, 1932), p. 44. Maxwell, p. 43, carefully notes 'A Broadside is "a sheet of paper printed on one side only" but Miss Yeats's Broadsides are all of four pages printed on both sides'.
102. Gifford Lewis, *The Yeats Sisters*, p. 119.
103. Maurice Rickards and Michael Twyman, *The Encyclopedia of Ephemera: A Guide to the Fragmentary Documents of Everyday Life for the Collector, Curator, and Historian* (London: British Library, 2000), p. 64.
104. Anita Guerrini, 'Advertising Monstrosity: Broadsides and Human Exhibition in Eighteenth-Century London', in *Ballads and Broadsides in Britain, 1500–1800*, eds Patricia Fulmerton and Anita Guerrin, with Krix McAbee (Farnham: Ashgate, 2010), p. 111.
105. Martin Hopkinson, *Ex Libris: The Art of Bookplates* (London: The British Museum Press, 2011), p. 5,
106. Hopkinson, *Ex Libris*, pp. 6–7.
107. Many of these plates are preserved in the Dun Emer and Cuala Press Archive Material held in the Ephemera Collection at the National Library of Ireland.
108. Lewis, *The Yeats Sisters*, p. 60.
109. Hardwick, *The Yeats Sisters*, p. 230.
110. Quoted in Hamilton, *Aesthetics and Music*, p. 168 (Hamilton is citing Jacques Attali, *Noise: The Political Economy of Music* (Minneapolis, MN: University of Minnesota Press, 1985), p. 47).

8 Advertising, Ireland and the Great War

1. *Irish Freedom*, October 1911, p. 5.
2. See p. 220.
3. See Mark Tierney, Paul Bowen and David Fitzpatrick, 'Recruiting Posters', in *Ireland in the First World War*, ed. David Fitzpatrick (Mullingar: The Lilliput Press, 1988), pp. 47–58; James Aulich and John Hewitt, *Seduction or Instruction?: First World War Posters in Britain and Europe* (Manchester: Manchester University Press, 2007), pp. 38–58, and Nuala C. Johnson, *Ireland, the Great War and the Geography of Remembrance* (Cambridge: Cambridge University Press, 2003), pp. 15–55.

4. Mark Wollaeger, for instance, in *Modernism, Media, and Propaganda: British Narrative from 1900 to 1945* (Princeton, NJ: Princeton University Press, 2008), pp. 166–191, has a chapter on recruitment posters and Joyce's *Ulysses*.
5. Patrick Maume, *The Long Gestation: Irish Nationalist Life, 1891–1918* (New York, NY: St Martin's Press, 1999), p. 186.
6. Today the battle cry 'Faugh a Ballagh' ('Clear the Way') is the motto of the modern Royal Irish Regiment, founded 1992.
7. Quoted above at p. 218. The words are an echo of Jesus's 'He that hath no sword, let him sell his garment, and buy one' (Luke 22:36).
8. Richard English, *Irish Freedom: The History of Nationalism in Ireland* (London: Macmillan, 2006), p. 271.
9. 'For John Redmond one word – Judas' (*Irish Freedom*, September 1914). Also quoted in Thomas Hennessey, *Dividing Ireland: World War One and Partition* (London: Routledge, 1998), p. 65.
10. 'Perhaps the most extreme of all' republican journals, as Benjamin Z. Novick puts it in his study of the nationalist press at the commencement of the War, 'DORA, Suppression, and Nationalist Propaganda in Ireland, 1914–1915', *New Hibernia Review/Iris Éireannach Nua*, vol. 1 (Winter, 1997), p. 8.
11. *Irish Freedom*, no. 41, March 1914.
12. Such as this puff for the drapers and manufacturers of clerical accoutrements Gleeson and Company of Upper O'Connell Street, Dublin, which dismisses the economic naysayers who were supposedly doing down Ireland at the time:

    GLEESON AND CO.

    STAND BACK, you who doubt Ireland's Industrial Possibilities. We have entered the citadel after having torn down the old wells of prejudice against Irish Goods. We have opened an Irish Drapery Store at 11 Up. O'Connell Street for the Sale of IRISH GOODS ONLY.

    This advertisement first appeared in 1911.
13. De Blácam, *What Sinn Fein Stands For*, p. 54.
14. Ibid.
15. Quoted in Joseph V. O'Brien's study of early twentieth-century Dublin, *Dear, Dirty Dublin: A City in Distress, 1899–1916* (Berkeley and Los Angeles CA: University of California Press, 1982), p. 253.
16. This was itself suppressed in March 1915, after which Griffith established *Nationality* (which contrived to stretch its run from June 1915 to March 1916).
17. See above, p. 42.
18. Quoted in Johnson, *Ireland, the Great War and the Geography of Remembrance*, p. 34.
19. Novick, 'DORA, Suppression, and Nationalist Propaganda in Ireland, 1914–1915', p. 54.
20. The 'K.O.S.B. murders' is a reference to the shooting of civilians by the Kings Own Scottish Borderers (the 'King's Own Scottish Murderers' to some) at Bachelor's Walk in August 1914 following the Howth Irish Volunteers gun-running episode.
21. Novick includes 'Irishmen – FOOLS!' in a list of proscribed revolutionary Irish publications in 'DORA, Suppression, and Nationalist Propaganda in Ireland, 1914–1915', p. 54. The text is quoted in 'Ex-Intelligence Officer' [William Le Queux], *The German Spy System from Within* (London: Hodder and Stoughton, 1914), p. 148. Le Queux faux-chivalrously, though doubtless wrongly, ascribes the poster to German *agents provocateur* ('The placard in question has been attributed to the few Fenians still remaining in Ireland; but such an aspersion on the

character of these men is the rankest injustice, for even the most rabid of the anti-English in Ireland have realized that a world-war transcends domestic affairs, and Irishmen of all shades of opinion have shown themselves ready to fight the battles of freedom against Prussian militarism').

22. See p. 233.
23. Quoted in Maume, *The Long Gestation*, p. 162.
24. Quoted in Janet E. Dunleavy and Gareth W. Dunleavy, *Douglas Hyde: A Maker of Modern Ireland* (Berkeley, CA: University of California Press, 1991), p. 349.
25. Margaret Skinnider, *Doing My Bit for Ireland* (New York, NY: The Century Co., 1917), p. 231.
26. Ibid.
27. For an examination of the use of 'Humour in Advanced Nationalist Propaganda', see Ben Novick, *Conceiving Revolution: Irish Nationalist Propaganda During the First World War* (Dublin: Four Courts Press, 2001), pp. 188–221.
28. This also conceivably reminded readers of the efforts of the Irish Transvaal Committee in which Maud Gonne, Arthur Griffith and James Connolly were prominent.
29. Francis P. Jones, *History of the Sinn Fein Movement and the Irish Rebellion of 1916* (New York, NY: Kennedy and Sons, 1981), p. 81.
30. 'Boer shape hats' as Hearne's of Waterford called them in its own list of Volunteer equipment.

'Irish Volunteer Suits'. Advertisement for Thomas Fallon taken from the *Connacht Tribune* (2 May 1914), See n.8.32.

31. The sliding 'frogs' mentioned here hold bayonets and so on and are attached to an equipment belt.
32. Fallon's, like many contemporaneous advertisers, was quick to put current affairs to use in its advertising. In May 1914, for example, it exploited electioneering in Galway to sell its 'Irish Volunteer Suits', offering a 'special discount' to members of the force who bought the Volunteer suits (provided that they produced as evidence for the deal 'a card of membership of the Irish National Volunteers'), which were modelled by the dapper gentleman above. This display advertisement appeared in the *Galway Tribune* on 2 May 1914 (in the month James Cosgrave of the Irish Parliamentary Party won the Galway East by-election caused by the death of John Roche). Prospective 'candidates' and Volunteers alike were assured that Fallon's 'Suits must be the best because they are ordered from all parts of the civilised world'.
33. Ibid.
34. We have heard of Riordan before; see pp. 44–45 and p. 225.
35. 'The Industrial Aspect', a letter by Fallon to the IIDA, which was published in the *Irish Independent* on 18 August 1914.
36. 'The King of Cigarettes' as it was labelled in Great Britain.
37. References to current affairs were, it might be pointed out, by no means restricted to disguised advertisements. An advertisement in *Dublin and the Sinn Fein Rising* (published by the advertising agency and publishers Wilson Hartnell in 1916), for instance, sees the upmarket tobacconists Kapp and Peterson, whose factory was at 113 St Stephen's Green West, inviting customers to gawp at the damage done during the Easter Rising to one of its branches: 'Visit our new premises, 56 Lower Sackville Street (Corner, Bachelor's Walk), and see the effects of shot and shell.' This appeared in a display advertisement featuring a drawing of a pipe (alongside the modest protestation that it 'Always [had] a big selection of Peterson's pipes, cigars, cigarettes and ... tobacco in stock').

    In similar fashion, 'We do not *stock Guns*', the picture framers J. H. Martin and Company maintain in 'With the Gun Runners of Ulster' (1915), a pamphlet which deals with the UVF Larne gun-smuggling episode of April 1914 (this itself published by the advertising agency and publisher Eason's). 'But we do', the copy goes on, 'keep a good stock of Pictures, Frames, etc'. Again, in the week after the third Home Rule Bill had passed through parliament, in 1914, Gleeson, O'Dea and Co. announced that 'The way to comfort in your home UNDER HOME RULE is to use Gleeson, O'Dea and Co. The range is an important item in a home. We guarantee the ranges supplied and set by us give perfect satisfaction.'
38. In the 1808 'Prospectus' to the *Examiner* (*Selected Writings of Leigh Hunt*, gen. eds Robert Morrison and Michael Eberle-Sinatra, 6 vols (London: Pickering and Chatto, 2003), vol. 1, eds Jeffrey N. Cox and Greg Kucich, p. 27). In the early days of his newspaper Hunt did not allow advertisements: 'the public shall neither be tempted to listen to somebody in the shape of a Wit who turns out to be a lottery-keeper, nor seduced to hear a magnificent oration which finishes by retreating into a peruke or rolling off into a blacking ball'. Eventually economic realities made Hunt reconsider his position.
39. Joyce, *Ulysses*, 1993, p. 93.
40. The illustration here is worth explaining, given that it has little to do with the concerns of modern warfare, a mine which Mac Sweeny toiled so well.

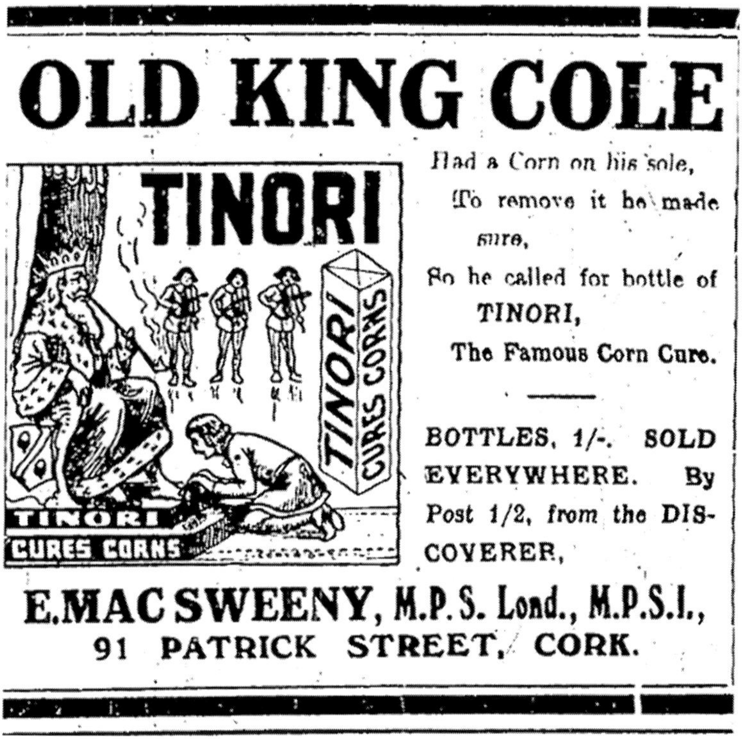

It is borrowed from a previous amusing display advertisement, 'Old King Cole'. Advertisement for E. Mac Sweeny (1917).

Coda – From the Armistice to the Saorstát

1. *The Leader*, 14 May 1921, p. 299.
2. 'Boland's breadvan delivering with trays our daily bread' muses Bloom in 'Calypso' (Joyce, *Ulysses*, 1993, p. 47).
3. Blythe's report went on to state that the Dáil reconsidered its position in late 1920 but because of the recent advent of adverse economic conditions it abandoned a 'scheme for the scheduling of such Irish goods as were produced in sufficient qualities [...] owing to the impossibility in a rapidly falling market of keeping up-to-date a schedule which would have guaranteed the public against being mulcted'.
4. *The Leader*, 10 December 1921.
5. See p. 27.
6. *The Economic Journal*, 1921, p. 246.
7. For the boycott, see Michael Laffan, *The Resurrection of Ireland: The Sinn Féin Party 1916–1923* (Cambridge: Cambridge University Press, 1999), pp. 231–232, and Knirck, *Imagining Ireland's Independence*, p. 54. Knirck argues that 'The policy was popular among many Sinn Féiners and did have some effect on Belfast

businessmen, but it also disastrously constituted a *de facto* recognition of partition. It recognized that Ireland was not the unified entity that Sinn Féin rhetoric proclaimed it to be' (ibid.).

8. A large advertisement on the front page of *The Leader* of 16 April 1921 celebrated what it saw as the embargo's success in caps large and small:

 BELFAST TRADE BOYCOTT

 'They had to TAKE their TRAVELLERS off the ROAD'.

 'The result had been a great DIMINUTION in the DISTRIBUTION TRADE carried on from BELFAST'.

 'This was not a matter which would pass off in a few days'.

 'When their new Parliament was established, the cords which were TIGHTENING them down would be DRAWN TIGHTER and there would be a PERPETUAL BOYCOTT OF BELFAST'.

 'Again THIS WEEK there are SEVERAL LARGE COMMERCIAL FAILURES IN BELFAST AND DISTRICT'.

 The above are extracts from statements made at the Belfast Chamber of Commerce on 7 April 1921.

 PUNISH BIGOTRY.

 KILL PARTITION.

 BOYCOTT ALL BELFAST GOODS.

9. Quoted in Knirck, *Imagining Ireland's Independence*, p. 54.
10. John Bulmer Hobson, *A Short History of the Irish Volunteers* (Dublin: The Candle Press, 1918), p. iii.
11. Another, which dates from September 1920, guys the British Viceroy. Fallon, unlike milord French, has the full support of the Irish people:

 SENSATION IN GALWAY!

 FALLON PROCLAIMED!

 Not by Lord French, but by the General Public, to have the

 Best Meat in Galway City

 This is the unanimous decision of vast numbers of my clients... Place a trial order and you will become a permanent customer. Prices moderate, accounts furnished monthly. Write, call or 'phone to:

 J. FALLON, VICTUALLER, GALWAY.

12. Quoted in Oram, *The Advertising Book*, p. 43.

Bibliography

Anonymous works are listed by title; pseudonymous works by pseudonym.

Primary

The ABC of Home Rule (Belfast: The Dublin and Belfast Unionist Associations of Ireland, 1912).

Buckley, Robert John, *Ireland as It Is and as It Would Be under Home Rule* (Birmingham and London: Birmingham Daily Gazette Company, 1893).

De Blácam, Aodh, *What Sinn Fein Stands For. The Irish Republican Movement: Its History, Aims and Ideals Examined as to Their Significance for the World* (Dublin: Mellifont Press, 1921).

'Ex-Intelligence Officer' [William Le Queux], *The German Spy System from Within* (London: Hodder and Stoughton, 1914).

Golden Moments with Arthur Griffith (Dublin: Whelan and Son, 1917).

Griffith, Arthur, *To Re-Build the Nation* (Dublin: Whelan and Son, 1919).

Handbook and Catalogue of Exhibits Compiled and Issued by the Department of Agriculture and Technical Instruction for Ireland (Dublin: The Department of Agriculture and Technical Instruction for Ireland, 1904).

Henderson, Frank, *Easter Rising. Recollections of an Irish Volunteer* (Cork: Cork University Press, 1996).

Hobson, John Bulmer, *A Short History of the Irish Volunteers* (Dublin: The Candle Press, 1918).

Hood, Thomas, 'The Art of Advertizing made Easy', *London Magazine and Review*, new series, vol. 1 (February 1825), pp. 246–253.

Hood, Thomas, 'The Advertisement Literature of the Age', *New Monthly Magazine*, vol. 67 (January 1843), pp. 111–116.

Huish, Robert, *The Memoirs, Private and Political of Daniel O'Connell* (London: W. Johnston, 1836).

Hunt, Leigh, *Selected Writings of Leigh Hunt*, gen. eds Robert Morrison and Michael Eberle-Sinatra, 6 vols (London: Pickering and Chatto, 2003).

Hyde, Douglas, *Language, Lore, and Lyrics: Essays and Lectures*, ed. Breandán Ó Conaire (Dublin: Irish Academic Press, 1986).

'The Irish Industrial Exhibition', *Illustrated Magazine of Art*, vol. 2 (1853), pp. 135–143.

The Irish Unionist Pocket Book (Belfast and Dublin: Unionist Associations of Ireland, 1911).

Jones, Francis P., *History of the Sinn Fein Movement and the Irish Rebellion of 1916* (New York, NY: Kennedy and Sons, 1981).

Joyce, James, *A Portrait of the Artist as a Young Man*, ed. Chester G. Anderson (Harmondsworth: Penguin, 1977).

Joyce, James, *Dubliners*, ed. Terence Brown (London: Penguin, 1992a).

Joyce, James, *Ulysses*, ed. Declan Kiberd (Penguin: Harmondsworth, 1992b).

Joyce, James, *Ulysses*, ed. Hans Walter Gabler (New York, NY: Vintage, 1993).

Joyce, James, *Occasional, Critical and Political Writings*, ed. Kevin Barry (Oxford: Oxford University Press, 2000).

The Literary and Educational Year Book for 1859 (London: Kent and Co, 1858).
Maguire, John Francis, *The Industrial Movement in Ireland, as Illustrated by the National Exhibition* (Cork: John O'Brien, 1852).
McNeill, Ronald, *Ulster's Stand for Union* (New York, NY: E. P. Dutton, 1922).
Moran, D. P., *The Philosophy of Irish Ireland* (Dublin: James Duffy, 1905).
Morris, Maurice O'Connor, *Memini, or Reminiscences of Irish Life* (London: Harrison and Sons, 1892).
na Banban, Brian [Brian O'Higgins], *The Voice of Banba: Songs and Recitations for Young Ireland* (Dublin: M.H. Gill & Son, 1907).
na Banban, Brian [Brian O'Higgins], *Signal Fires* (Dublin: M. H. Gill, 1912).
O'Brien, Flann, *The Poor Mouth*, trans. Patrick C. Power (London: Grafton Books, 1973).
O'Casey, Sean, *Three Dublin Plays*, ed. Christopher Murray (London: Macmillan, 1998).
Pater, Walter, *The Renaissance* (Oxford: Oxford University Press, 1998).
Pearse, P. H., *The Murder Machine* (Dublin: Whelan and Son, 1916).
Reeves, Maud Pember, *Round About a Pound a Week* (London: Virago, 1979).
Riordan, E. J., 'A Fragment of Irish Industrial History', *Studies: An Irish Quarterly Review*, vol. 7 (1918), pp. 633–642.
Riordan, E. J., *Modern Irish Trade and Industry* (London: Methuen and Co, 1920).
Rosenbaum, S., ed., *Against Home Rule: The Case for the Union* (London and New York, NY: Frederick Warne, 1912).
Skinnider, Margaret, *Doing My Bit for Ireland* (New York, NY: The Century Co, 1917).
Wilde, Oscar, *The Picture of Dorian Gray*, ed. Peter Ackroyd (Harmondsworth: Penguin, 1985).
Wilde, Oscar, *Oscar Wilde's Oxford Notebooks: A Portrait of Mind in the Making*, eds Michael S. Helfand and Philip E. Smith (Oxford: Oxford University Press, 1989).
Wilde, Oscar, *Complete Works* (Glasgow: Harper Collins, 1999).
Wilkinson, Henry Fazakerley, *Modern Athletics*, third edition (London: The Field Office, 1877).
Yeats, W. B., *A Vision* (London: Macmillan, 1937).
Yeats, W. B., *The Collected Plays of W. B. Yeats* (London: Macmillan and Co, 1952).
Yeats, W. B., *The Letters of W. B. Yeats*, ed. Allan Wade (London: Rupert Hart Davis, 1954).
Yeats, W. B., *The Variorum Edition of the Poems of W. B. Yeats*, eds Peter Allt and Russell K. Alspach (New York, NY: Macmillan, 1957).
Yeats, W. B., *Essays and Introductions* (London and New York, NY: Macmillan, 1961).
Yeats, W. B., *Memoirs*, ed. Denis Donoghue (London: Macmillan, 1972).
Yeats, W. B., *The Collected Letters of W. B. Yeats*, gen. ed. John Kelly, 4 vols (Oxford: Clarendon Press, 1986–).
Yeats, W. B., *Autobiographies*, eds William H. O'Donnell and Douglas N. Archibald (New York, NY: Scribner, 1999).
Zola, Émile, *The Ladies' Paradise*, trans. Brian Nelson (Oxford: Oxford University Press, 1995).

Secondary

Abelson, Elaine S., *When Ladies Go A-Thieving: Middle-Class Shoplifters in the Victorian Department Store* (Oxford: Oxford University Press, 1989).
Adorno, Theodor, *Aesthetic Theory*, trans. R. Hullot-Kentor (London: Athlone, 1997).

Adorno, Theodor W., *The Culture Industry: Selected Essays on Mass Culture,* ed. J. M. Bernstein (London: Routledge, 1991).
Anderson, Benedict, *Imagined Communities: Reflections on the Origin and Spread of Nationalism* (London: Verso, 1991, rev. ed.).
Attridge, Derek, ed., *The Cambridge Companion to James Joyce* (Cambridge: Cambridge University Press, 2004).
Aulich, James and Hewitt, John, *Seduction or Instruction?: First World War Posters in Britain and Europe* (Manchester: Manchester University Press, 2007).
Barthel, Diane, *Putting on Appearances: Gender and Advertising* (Philadelphia, PA: Temple University Press, 1988).
Barthes, Roland, *Image, Music, Text,* trans. Stephen Heath (London: Fontana, 1977).
Bassett, Troy J., 'Fisher Unwin's Pseudonym Library: Literary Marketing and Authorial Identity', *English Literature in Transition (1880–1920),* vol. 47, no. 2 (2004), pp. 142–160.
Baudrillard, Jean, *The System of Objects,* trans. James Benedict (London: Verso, 1996).
Beetham, Margaret, *A Magazine of Their Own? Domesticity and Desire in the Woman's Magazine, 1800–1914* (London: Routledge, 1996).
Benjamin, Walter, *Illuminations,* ed. Hannah Arendt (London: Fontana, 1970).
Bhabha, Homi K., *The Location of Culture* (London: Routledge, 1994).
Bornstein, George, *Material Modernism: The Politics of the Page* (Cambridge: Cambridge University Press, 2001).
Bourke, Joanna, *Husbandry to Housewifery: Women, Economic Change, and Housework in Ireland, 1890–1914* (Oxford: Clarendon Press, 1993).
Bowe, Nicola Gordon, 'The Irish Arts and Crafts Movement (1886–1925)', in *Irish Arts Review Yearbook* (*1990–1991*) (Dublin: Irish Arts Review, 1991), pp. 172–185.
Bowlby, Rachel, *Shopping with Freud* (London: Routledge, 1993).
Bowlby, Rachel, *Carried Away: The Invention of Modern Shopping* (London: Faber and Faber, 2000).
Bradley, Anthony, ' "Fumbling in a Greasy Till": Nation and Class in Yeats's "Responsibilities" ', *Irish University Review,* vol. 30, no. 2 (2000), pp. 289–314.
Brake, Laurel, *Subjugated Knowledges: Journalism, Gender and Literature in the Nineteenth Century* (Basingstoke: Macmillan, 1994).
Brewer, John and Porter, Roy, *Consumption and the World of Goods* (London: Routledge, 1993).
Brewster, Scott, Crossman, Virginia, Beckett, Fiona, and Alderson, David, eds, *Ireland in Proximity: History, Gender, Space* (London: Routledge, 1999).
Bristow, Joseph, ed., *Wilde Writings: Contextual Conditions* (Toronto: University of Toronto Press, 2003).
Búrca, Marcus de, *The GAA: A History,* second edition (Dublin: Gill and Macmillan, 1999a).
Búrca, Marcus de, 'The Gaelic Athletic Association and Organised Sport in Ireland', in ed. Grant Jarvie, *Sport in the Making of Celtic Cultures* (London and New York, NY: Leicester University Press, 1999b), pp. 100–111.
Búrca, Séamus de, *The Soldier's Song: The Story of Peadar O Cearnaigh* (Dublin: P. J. Bourke, 1957).
Chaudhry, Yug Mohit, *Yeats, The Irish Literary Revival and the Politics of Print* (Cork: Cork University Press, 2001).
Clark, David R., *W. B. Yeats and the Theatre of Desolate Reality* (Washington, DC: The Catholic University of America Press, 1993, rev. ed.).

Clayworth, Anya, '*The Woman's World*: Oscar Wilde as Editor', *Victorian Periodicals Review*, vol. 30, no. 2 (1997), pp. 84–101.

Clear, Caitríona, *Women of the House: Women's Household Work in Ireland, 1922–1960* (Dublin: Irish Academic Press, 2000).

Clyde, Tom, *Irish Literary Magazines* (Dublin: Irish Academic Press, 2003).

Connolly, Peter, ed., *Literature and the Changing Ireland* (Gerrards Cross: Colin Smythe, 1982).

Cook, Guy, *The Discourse of Advertising*, second edition (London: Routledge, 2001).

Corrigan, Peter, *The Dressed Society: Clothing the Body and Some Meanings of the World* (London: Sage, 2008).

Coyle, Joe, *Athletics in Drogheda 1861–2001* (Victoria, BC: Trafford Publishing, 2003).

Crawford, W. H. and Foy, R. H., eds, *Townlands in Ulster* (Belfast: Ulster Historical Foundation in Association with the Federation of Ulster Local Studies, 1998).

Cronin, Mike, *Sport and Nationalism in Ireland: Gaelic Games, Soccer and Irish Identity Since 1884* (Dublin: Four Courts, 1999).

Cronin, Mike, Murphy, William, and Rouse, Paul, eds, *The Gaelic Athletic Association 1884–2009* (Dublin and Portland, OR: Irish Academic Press, 2009).

Crossman, Virginia, 'The *Shan Van Vocht*: Women, Republicanism, and the Commemoration of the 1798 Rebellion', *Eighteenth-Century Life*, vol. 22 (1998), pp. 128–139.

Crowley, Tony, ed., *The Politics of Language in Ireland 1366–1922: A Sourcebook* (London: Routledge, 2000).

Cunningham, John B. and O'Loughlin, Joe, 'O'Loughlin's Bicycle Shop, Belleek, Co. Fermanagh and the Coming of the Bicycle', *Ulster Folklore*, vol. 44 (1998), pp. 94–99.

Curtis, L. Perry, Jr, *Images of Erin in the Age of Parnell* (Dublin: National Library of Ireland, 2000).

Deane, Seamus, *Strange Country: Modernity and Nationhood in Irish Writing Since 1790* (Oxford: Oxford University Press, 1997).

Dennison, S. D. and McDonagh, Oliver, *Guinness 1886–1939. From Incorporation to the Second World War* (Cork: Cork University Press, 1998).

Douglas, Roy, Harte, Liam, and O'Hara, Jim, *Drawing Conclusions: A Cartoon History of Anglo-Irish Relations, 1798–1998* (Belfast: Blackstaff Press, 1998).

Dowling, Linda, *The Vulgarization of Art: The Victorians and Aesthetic Democracy* (Charlottesville, VA: University Press of Virginia, 1996).

Dunleavy, Janet E. and Dunleavy, Gareth W., *Douglas Hyde: A Maker of Modern Ireland* (Berkeley, CA: University of California Press, 1991).

Dunlevy, Mairead, *Dress in Ireland* (Cork: The Collins Press, 1989).

Dyer, Gillian, *Advertising as Communication* (London: Routledge, 1988).

Eagleton, Terry, *Exiles and Émigrés: Studies in Modern Literature* (London: Chatto & Windus, 1970).

Eagleton, Terry, *St Oscar* (London: Bookmark, 2004).

Eagleton, Terry, *Criticism and Ideology: A Study in Marxist Literary Theory*, new edition (London: Verso, 2006).

Easley, Alexis, *Literary Celebrity, Gender and Victorian Authorship 1850–1914* (Newark, DE: University of Delaware Press, 2011).

Edelstein, T. J., ed., *Imagining an Irish Past: The Celtic Revival 1840–1940* (Chicago, IL: University of Chicago, 1992).

Ellmann, Richard, 'Oscar at Oxford', *New York Review of Books* (29 March 1984), pp. 23–28.

Ellmann, Richard, *Oscar Wilde* (Harmondsworth: Penguin, 1988).

English, Richard, *Irish Freedom: The History of Nationalism in Ireland* (London: Macmillan, 2006).
Farry, Michael, *Sligo 1914–1921. A Chronicle of Conflict* (Trim, Co. Meath: Killoran Press, 1992).
Ferguson, Marjorie, *Forever Feminine: Women's Magazines and the Cult of the Feminine* (London: Heinemann, 1983).
Ferriter, Diamaid, *Occasions of Sin: Sex and Society in Modern Ireland* (London: Profile, 2009).
Findlater, Alex, *Findlaters: The Story of a Dublin Merchant Family, 1774–2001* (Dublin: A. & A. Farmar, 2001).
Fitzpatrick, David, ed., *Ireland in the First World War* (Mullingar: The Lilliput Press, 1988).
Fitzsimon, Betsy Taylor and Murphy, James H., eds, *The Irish Revival Reappraised* (Dublin: Four Courts, 2004).
Flanders, Judith, *Consuming Passions: Leisure and Pleasure in Victorian Britain* (London: HarperPress, 2006).
Foley, Tadhg and Ryder, Seán, eds, *Ideology and Ireland in the Nineteenth Century* (Dublin: Four Courts, 1998).
Fortunato, Paul L., 'Wildean Philosophy with a Needle and Thread: Consumer Fashion at the Origins of Modernist Aesthetics', *College Literature*, vol. 34 (2007a), pp. 37–53.
Fortunato, Paul L., *Modernist Aesthetics and Consumer Culture in the Writings of Oscar Wilde* (London: Routledge, 2007b).
Foster, R. F., *Modern Ireland 1600–1972* (Harmondsworth: Penguin, 1989).
Foster, R. F., *W. B. Yeats: A Life*, 2 vols (Oxford: Oxford University Press, 1998–2003).
Foy, Michael, 'Ulster Unionist Propaganda Against Home Rule', *History Ireland*, vol. 4, no. 1 (1996), pp. 49–53.
Frazier, Adrian, *Behind the Scenes: Yeats, Horniman and the Struggle for the Abbey Theatre* (Berkeley, CA: University of California Press, 1990).
Friel, Brian, *The London Vertigo* (Co Meath: Gallery, 1990).
Fulmerton, Patricia, Guerrin, Antita, and McAbee, K., eds, *Ballads and Broadsides in Britain, 1500–1800* (Farnham: Ashgate, 2010).
Gagnier, Regina, *Idylls of the Marketplace: Oscar Wilde and the Victorian Public* (Aldershot: Scolar Press, 1986).
Garvey, Ellen Gruber, *The Adman in the Parlor: Magazines and the Gendering of Consumer Culture, 1880s–1910s* (New York, NY: Oxford University Press, 1996).
Genet, Jacqueline, Mikowski, Sylvie, and Mercier, Fabienne, eds, *The Book in Ireland* (Newcastle: Cambridge Scholars Press, 2006).
Gere, Charlotte and Hoskins, Lesley, *The House Beautiful: Oscar Wilde and the Aesthetic Interior* (Aldershot: Lund Humphries, 2000).
Gibbons, Luke, *Transformations in Irish Culture* (Cork: Cork University Press, 1996).
Glandon, Virginia E., 'The Irish Press and Revolutionary Nationalism', *Eire-Ireland*, vol. 16, no. 1 (1981), pp. 21–33.
Glandon, Virginia E., *Arthur Griffith and the Advanced-Nationalist Press, 1900–1922* (New York, NY: Peter Lang, 1985).
Godson, Lisa, 'Catholicism and Material Culture in Ireland 1840–1880', *Circa*, vol. 103 (2003), pp. 38–45.
Gonne, Maud, *A Servant of the Queen: Reminiscences*, eds A. Norman Jeffares and Anna MacBride White (Gerrards Cross: Colin Smythe, 1994).
Graham, Colin and Richard Kirkland, eds, *Ireland and Cultural Theory: The Mechanics of Authenticity* (Basingstoke: Macmillan, 1999).

Green, Stephanie, 'Oscar Wilde's *The Woman's World*', *Victorian Periodicals Review*, vol. 30, no. 2 (1997), pp. 102–120.
Greenlaw, Duncan, ' "Preying on Foresaid Remains": Irish Identity, Obituaries and the Limits of Mourning', *Mosaic*, vol. 34, no. 4 (2001), pp. 123–144.
Griffin, Brian, *Cycling in Victorian Ireland* (Dublin: Nonsuch Publishing, 2006).
Guy, Josephine M. and Small, Ian, *Oscar Wilde's Profession: Writing and the Culture Industry in the Late Nineteenth Century* (Oxford: Oxford University Press, 2000).
Hamilton, Andy, *Aesthetics and Music* (London: Continuum, 2007).
Hamilton, Andy, 'The Aesthetics of Design', in *Fashion – Philosophy for Everyone: Thinking with Style*, eds Jessica Wolfendale and Jeanette Kennett (Oxford: Blackwell Publishing, 2011), pp. 53–69.
Hardwick, Joan, *The Yeats Sisters: A Biography of Susan and Elizabeth Yeats* (London: Pandora, 1996).
Harp, Richard, 'The *Shan Van Vocht* (Belfast, 1896–1899) and Irish Nationalism', *Éire-Ireland*, vol. 24, no. 3 (1989), pp. 42–52.
Harris, Susan Cannon, *Gender and Modern Irish Drama* (Bloomington, IN: Indiana University Press, 2002).
Hartley, John, *The Politics of Pictures: The Creation of the Public in the Age of Popular Media* (London: Routledge, 1992).
Hartnett, Michael, *Collected Poems* (Oldcastle: Gallery Books, 2001).
Hayes, Alan and Urquhart, Diane, eds, *The Irish Women's History Reader* (London: Routledge, 2001).
Healy, Paul, *Gaelic Games and the Gaelic Athletic Association* (Cork: Mercier Press, 1998).
Helland, Janice, *British and Irish Home Arts and Industries 1880–1914: Marketing Craft, Making Fashion* (Dublin: Irish Academic Press, 2007).
Hennessey, Thomas, *Dividing Ireland: World War One and Partition* (London: Routledge, 1998).
Holt, Richard, *Sport and the British* (Oxford: Oxford University Press, 1989).
Hone, Joseph, ed., *J. B. Yeats: Letters to his Son W. B. Yeats and Others 1869–1922* (London: Faber and Faber, 1944).
Hopkinson, Martin, *Ex Libris: The Art of Bookplates* (London: The British Museum Press, 2011).
Houlihan, Barrie, *Sport, Policy, and Politics: A Comparative Analysis* (London and New York: Routledge, 1997).
Howes, Marjorie, 'Postcolonial Yeats: Culture, Enlightenment, and the Public Sphere', *Field Day Review*, vol. 2 (2006), pp. 54–73.
Hughes, David Alan, *'A Bottle of Guinness Please': The Colourful History of Bottled Guinness* (London: Phimboy, 2006).
Hurst, Isobel, 'Ancient and Modern Women in the *Woman's World*', *Victorian Studies*, vol. 52, no. 1 (2009), pp. 42–51.
Hutton, Clare, ed., *The Irish Book in the Twentieth Century* (Dublin: Irish Academic Press, 2004).
Hutton, Claire and Walsh, Patrick, *The Oxford History of the Irish Book, Volume V: The Irish Book in English, 1891–2000* (Oxford: Oxford University Press, 2011).
Hyde, H. Montgomery, *The Trials of Oscar Wilde* (New York, NY: Dover, 1962).
Hyland, Paul and Sammells, Neil, eds, *Irish Writing: Exile and Subversion* (Basingstoke: Macmillan, 1991).
Irvine, Maurice, *Northern Ireland: Faith and Faction* (London: Routledge, 1991).
Jackson, D. M. and MacRaild, D. M., 'The Conserving Crowd: Mass Unionist Demonstrations in Liverpool and Tyneside, 1912–13', in eds D. George Boyce and Alan

O'Day, *The Ulster Crisis 1885–1921* (Houndsmills: Palgrave Macmillan, 2006), pp. 229–246.
Jarvie, Grant, ed., *Sport in the Making of Celtic Cultures* (London and New York, NY: Leicester University Press, 1999).
Johnson, Nuala C., *Ireland, the Great War and the Geography of Remembrance* (Cambridge: Cambridge University Press, 2003).
Kearney, Richard, *Transitions: Narratives in Modern Irish Culture* (Manchester: Manchester University Press, 1988).
Kelleher, Margaret and Murphy, James H., eds, *Gender Perspectives in Nineteenth-Century Ireland: Public and Private Spheres* (Dublin: Irish Academic Press, 1997).
Kennedy, Christopher M., *Genesis of the Rising, 1912–1916: A Transformation of Nationalist Opinion* (New York, NY: Peter Lang Publishing Inc, 2010).
Kenny, Colum, *Irish Patriot, Publisher and Advertising Agent: Kevin J. Kenny (1881–1954)* (Bray, Co. Wicklow: Ox Pictures, 2011).
Keogh, Dermot, *Jews in Twentieth-Century Ireland: Refugees, Anti-Semitism and the Holocaust* (Cork: Cork University Press, 1998).
Kiberd, Declan, *Inventing Ireland: The Literature of the Modern Nation* (Cambridge, MA: Harvard University Press, 1996).
Kiberd, Declan, *Irish Classics* (London: Granta, 2000).
Kirkland, Richard, 'Dialogues of Despair: Nationalist Cultural Discourse and the Revival in the North of Ireland, 1900–1920', *Irish University Review*, vol. 33, no. 1 (2003), pp. 64–78.
Knirck, Jason R., *Imagining Ireland's Independence* (Lanham, MD: Rowman & Littlefield, 2006).
Ksinan, Catherine, 'Wilde as Editor of *Woman's World*: Fighting a Dull Slumber in Stale Certitudes', *English Literature in Transition 1880–1920*, vol. 41, no. 4 (1998), pp. 408–426.
Laffan, Michael, *The Resurrection of Ireland: The Sinn Féin Party 1916–1923* (Cambridge: Cambridge University Press, 1999).
Legg, Marie Louise, *Newspapers and Nationalism: The Irish Provincial Press 1850–1892* (Dublin: Four Courts, 1999).
Leonard, Garry M., 'Joyce and Advertising: Advertising and Commodity Culture in Joyce's Fiction', *James Joyce Quarterly*, vol. 30/31 (summer/fall, 1993), pp. 573–592.
Leonard, Garry M., *Advertising and Commodity Culture in Joyce* (Gainesville, FL: University Press of Florida, 1998).
Lewis, Geoffrey, *Carson: The Man who Divided Ireland* (London: Continuum International Publishing Group, 2005).
Lewis, Gifford, *The Yeats Sisters and the Cuala* (Dublin: Irish Academic Press, 1994).
Lewis, Gifford, 'Rediscovered Embroideries by Lily Yeats', *Irish Arts Review Yearbook*, vol. 14 (1998), pp. 147–150.
Loeb, Lori Anne, *Consuming Angels: Advertising and Victorian Women* (New York, NY and Oxford: Oxford University Press, 1994).
Loxley, Simon, *Type: The Secret History of Letters* (London: I. B. Tauris, 2006).
Luddy, Maria, ed., *Women in Ireland: A Documentary History 1800–1918* (Cork: Cork University Press, 1995).
Lynam, E. W., *The Irish Character in Print: 1671–1923* (Shannon: Irish University Press, 1969).
Lynch, Patrick and Vaizey, John, *Guinness's Brewery in the Irish Economy: 1759–1876* (Cambridge: Cambridge University Press, 1960).
Lyons, F. S. L., *Ireland Since the Famine* (London: Weidenfeld and Nicolson, 1971).

MacEoin, Uinseann, ed., *Survivors: The Story of Ireland's Struggle as Told Through Some of Her Outstanding Living People* (Dublin: Argenta Publishers, 1980).
Mac Giolla Choille, Breandan, ed., *Intelligence Notes, 1913–1916* (Dublin: State Paper Office, 1966).
MacRaild, Donald M., 'The Associationalism of the Orange Diaspora', in ed. David A. Wilson, *The Orange Order in Canada* (Dublin: Four Courts Press, 2007), pp. 25–41.
Mandle, W. F., 'The I.R.B. and the Beginnings of the Gaelic Athletic Association', *Irish Historical Studies*, vol. 20, no. 80 (September 1977), pp. 418–438.
Marsh, Tess, 'Is There More To *Photobits* Than Meets the Eye?', *James Joyce Quarterly*, vol. 30/31 (summer/fall 1993), pp. 877–893.
Maume, Patrick, *D. P. Moran* (Dundalk: Historical Association of Ireland, 1995).
Maume, Patrick, *The Long Gestation: Irish Nationalist Life, 1891–1918* (New York, NY: St Martin's Press, 1999).
Maxwell, William, *The Dun Emer Press and The Cuala Press: A Complete List* (Edinburgh: Privately printed, 1932).
McBrinn, Joseph, 'The 1904 *Feis na nGleann*: Craftwork, Folk Life and National Identity', *Folk Life*, vol. 45 (2007), pp. 24–39.
McClintock, Anne, *Imperial Leather: Race, Gender and Sexuality in the Colonial Contest* (New York, NY: Routledge, 1995).
McCormack, Jerusha, ed., *Wilde the Irishman* (New Haven, NJ and London: Yale University Press, 1998).
McCormack, W. J., *Ascendancy and Tradition* (Oxford: Clarendon Press, 1985).
McKendrick, Neil, Brewer, John, and Plumb, J.H., *The Birth of a Consumer Society* (London: Europa Publications, 1982).
McLoughlin, Dympna, 'Women and Sexuality in Nineteenth-Century Ireland', *The Irish Journal of Psychology*, vol. 15 (1994), pp. 266–275.
McMahon, Timothy G., *Grand Opportunity: The Gaelic Revival and Irish Society, 1893–1910* (Syracuse, NY: Syracuse University Press, 2008).
Meaney, Geraldine, 'Race, Sex and Nation', *The Irish Review*, vol. 35, no. 3 (2007), pp. 46–63.
Merwin, W. S., 'The Old Woman of Beare', *The Hudson Review*, vol. 4, no. 4 (1952), pp. 540–543.
Miller, Michael B., *The Bon Marché: Bourgeois Culture and the Department Store, 1869–1920* (Princeton, NJ: Princeton University Press, 1981).
Moore, George, *Hail and Farewell*, ed. Richard Allen Cave (Colin Smythe: Gerrards Cross, 1985).
Moran, Joe, *Star Authors: Literary Celebrity in America* (London: Pluto Press, 2000).
Morris, Catherine, 'Becoming Irish? Alice Milligan and the Revival', *Irish University Review*, vol. 33, no. 1 (2003), pp. 79–98.
Morris, William, *News from Nowhere and Other Writings*, ed. Clive Wilmer (Harmondsworth: Penguin, 2004).
Murphy, William, 'The GAA during the Irish Revolution, 1913–23', in eds Mike Cronin, William Murphy, and Paul Rouse, *The Gaelic Athletic Association 1884–2009* (Dublin and Portland, OR: Irish Academic Press, 2009), pp. 61–76.
Myers, Greg, *Words in Ads* (London: Edward Arnold, 1994).
Nally, Claire, *Envisioning Ireland: Occult Nationalism in the Work of W. B. Yeats* (Oxford: Peter Lang, 2009).
Nevett, T. R., *Advertising in Britain: A History* (London: Heinemann on behalf of the History of Advertising Trust, 1982).

Novick, Ben, *Conceiving Revolution: Irish Nationalist Propaganda During the First World War* (Dublin: Four Courts Press, 2001).
Novick, Benjamin Z., 'DORA, Suppression, and Nationalist Propaganda in Ireland, 1914–1915', *New Hibernia Review/Iris Éireannach Nua*, vol. 1 (winter, 1997), pp. 41–57.
O'Boyle, Neil, 'Addressing Multiculturalism? Conservatism and Conformity; Access and Authenticity in Irish Advertising', *Translocations: The Irish Migration, Race and Social Transformation Review*, vol. 1 (2006), pp. 95–120.
O'Boyle, Neil, *New Vocabularies, Old Ideas: Culture, Irishness and the Advertising Industry* (Oxford and Bern: Peter Lang, 2011).
O'Brien, Conor Cruise, *The Shaping of Modern Ireland* (London: Routledge and Kegan Paul, 1960).
O'Brien, Joseph V., *Dear, Dirty Dublin: A City in Distress, 1899–1916* (Berkeley and Los Angeles, CA: University of California Press, 1982).
Ó Ciosáin, Niall, 'Creating an Audience: Innovation and Reception in Irish Language Publishing, 1880–1920', in ed. Clare Hutton, *The Irish Book in the Twentieth Century* (Dublin: Irish Academic Press, 2004).
Ó Conchubhair, Brian, 'The Gaelic Front Controversy: The Gaelic League's (Post-Colonial) Crux', *Irish University Review*, vol. 33, no. 1 (2003), pp. 46–63.
Ó Drisceoil, Donal, 'A Dark Chapter: Censorship and the Irish Writer', in eds Claire Hutton and Patrick Walsh, *The Oxford History of the Irish Book, Volume V: The Irish Book in English, 1891–2000* (Oxford: Oxford University Press, 2011), pp. 285–303.
O'Keefe, Timothy J., 'The 1898 Efforts to Celebrate the United Irishmen: The '98 Centennial', *Éire Ireland*, vol. 23, no. 2 (1992a), pp. 51–73.
O'Keefe, Timothy J., ' "Who Fears to Speak of '98?": The Rhetoric and Rituals of the United Irishmen Centennial, 1898', *Éire-Ireland*, vol. 27, no. 3 (1992b), pp. 67–91.
O'Leary, Philip, *The Prose Literature of the Gaelic Revival, 1881–1921: Ideology and Innovation* (University Park, PA: Pennsylvania State University Press, 1994).
O'Mahoney, Sean, *Frongoch: University of Revolution* (Dublin: FDR Teoranta, 1987).
Oram, Hugh, *The Advertising Book: The History of Advertising in Ireland* (Dublin: MO Books, 1986).
Pilkington, Lionel, *Theatre and the State in Twentieth-Century Ireland: Cultivating the People* (London: Routledge, 2001).
Pine, Richard, *The Thief of Reason: Oscar Wilde and Modern Ireland* (Dublin: Gill & Macmillan, 1995).
Pittock, Murray, *Celtic Identity and the British Image* (Manchester: Manchester University Press, 1999).
Porter, Roy, *Quacks, Fakers and Charlatans in English Medicine* (Stroud: Tempus Publishing, 2000).
Potter, Simon J., ed., *Newspapers and Empire in Ireland and Britain: Reporting the British Empire c. 1857–1921* (Dublin: Four Courts, 2004).
Presbrey, Frank, *The History and Development of Advertising* (New York, NY: Doubleday, 1929).
Rains, Stephanie, 'Here be Monsters: The Irish Industrial Exhibition of 1853 and the Growth of Dublin Department Stores', *Irish Studies Review*, vol. 16 (November 2008), pp. 487–506.
Rains, Stephanie, *Commodity Culture and Social Class in Dublin 1850–1916* (Dublin: Irish Academic Press, 2010).
Rappaport, Erika Diane, *Shopping for Pleasure: Women in the Making of London's West End* (Princeton, NJ: Princeton University Press, 2000).

Reilly, Tom, *Joe Stanley: Printer to the Rising* (Dingle, County Kerry: Brandon/Mount Eagle Publications Ltd, 2005).
Richards, Thomas, *The Commodity Culture of Victorian England: Advertising and Spectacle, 1851–1914* (Stanford, CA: Stanford University Press, 1990).
Richardson, Angelique and Willis, Chris, eds, *The New Woman in Fiction and in Fact: Fin-de-Siècle Feminisms* (Basingstoke: Palgrave Macmillan, 2002).
Rickards, Maurice and Twyman, Michael, *The Encyclopedia of Ephemera: A Guide to the Fragmentary Documents of Everyday Life for the Collector, Curator, and Historian* (London: British Library, 2000).
Rouse, Paul, 'Michael Cusack: Sportsman and Journalist', in eds Mike Cronin, William Murphy, and Paul Rouse, *The Gaelic Athletic Association 1884–2009* (Dublin and Portland, OR: Irish Academic Press, 2009), pp. 47–60.
Ryan, Louise, 'Constructing "Irishwoman": Modern Girls and Comely Maidens', *Irish Studies Review*, vol. 6, no. 3 (1998), pp. 263–272.
Schaffer, Talia, 'Fashioning Aestheticism by Aestheticizing Fashion: Wilde, Beerbohm, and the Male Aesthete's Sartorial Codes', *Victorian Literature and Culture,* vol. 28, no. 1 (2000), pp. 39–54.
Schaffer, Talia and Psomiades, Kathy Alexis, eds, *Women and British Aestheticism* (Charlottesville, VA: University of Virginia Press, 2000).
Sheehy, Jeanne, *The Rediscovery of Ireland's Past: The Celtic Revival 1830–1930* (London: Thames and Hudson, 1980).
Shifrin, Susan, ed., *Women as Sites of Culture: Women's Roles in Cultural Formation from the Renaissance to the Twentieth Century* (Aldershot: Ashgate, 2002).
Sinfield, Alan, *The Wilde Century: Effeminacy, Wilde and the Queer Moment* (London: Cassell, 1994).
Smith, Anthony D., *Nationalism: Theory, Ideology, History* (Cambridge: Polity Press, 2001).
Smith, Shawn Michelle, *American Archives: Gender, Race, and Class in Visual Culture* (Princeton, NJ: Princeton University Press, 1993).
Steele, Karen, 'Editing Out Factionalism: The Political and Literary Consequences in Ireland's "Shan Van Vocht" ', *Victorian Periodicals Review,* vol. 35, no. 2 (2002), pp. 113–132.
Steele, Karen, *Women, Press, and Politics During the Irish Revival* (Syracuse, NY: Syracuse University Press, 2007).
Steele, Valerie, *Paris Fashion: A Cultural History*, rev. ed. (Oxford: Berg, 1998).
Strachan, John, *Advertising and Satirical Culture in the Romantic Period* (Cambridge: Cambridge University Press, 2007).
Summers, Leigh, *Bound to Please: A History of the Victorian Corset* (Oxford: Berg, 2001).
Sussman, Charlotte, *Consuming Anxieties: Consumer Protest, Gender and British Slavery, 1713–1833* (Stanford, CA: Stanford University Press, 2000).
Tanaka, Keiko, *Advertising Language: A Pragmatic Approach to Advertisements in Britain and Japan* (London: Routledge, 1994).
Teukolsky, Rachel, *The Literate Eye: Victorian Art Writing and Modernist Aesthetics* (Oxford: Oxford University Press, 2009).
Tierney, Mark, Bowen, Paul, and Fitzpatrick, David, 'Recruiting Posters', in ed. David Fitzpatrick, *Ireland in the First World War* (Mullingar: The Lilliput Press, 1988), pp. 47–58.
Turner, E. S., *The Shocking History of Advertising!* (London: Michael Joseph, 1952).

Van Voris, Jacqueline, *Constance de Markievicz: In the Cause of Ireland* (Amherst, MA: University of Massachusetts Press, 1967).
Veblen, Theodor, *The Theory of the Leisure Class* (Oxford: Oxford University Press, 2007).
Wagner, Gillian, *Barnardo* (London: Weidenfeld and Nicholson, 1979).
Warner, Marina, *Monuments and Maidens: The Allegory of the Female Form* (London: Vintage, 1996).
Wicke, Jennifer, *Advertising Fictions: Literature, Advertisement and Social Reading* (New York, NY: Columbia University Press, 1988).
Williamson, Judith, *Decoding Advertisements: Ideology and Meaning in Advertising* (London: Marion Boyars, 2002).
Wilson, David A., ed., *The Orange Order in Canada* (Dublin: Four Courts Press, 2007).
Wilson, Elizabeth, *Adorned in Dreams: Fashion and Modernity*, new edition (London: I. B. Tauris, 2003).
Wilson, Ross, *Theodor Adorno* (Abingdon: Routledge, 2007).
Wolfendale, Jessica and Kennett, Jeanette, eds, *Fashion – Philosophy for Everyone: Thinking with Style* (Oxford: Blackwell Publishing, 2011).
Wollaeger, Mark, *Modernism, Media, and Propaganda: British Narrative from 1900 to 1945* (Princeton, NJ: Princeton University Press, 2008).

Index

Note: locators followed by 'f' and 'n' refer to figures and notes.